Teaching Language Arts to Children

Teaching Language Arts to Children

Karel Rose
Brooklyn College of The City University of New York

HARCOURT BRACE JOVANOVICH, INC.
New York   San Diego   Chicago   San Francisco   Atlanta
London   Sydney   Toronto

Once more for Murray.

Requests for permission to make copies of any part of the work should be
mailed to: Permissions, Harcourt Brace Jovanovich, Publishers, 757 Third Avenue,
New York, N.Y. 10017.

ISBN: 0-15-588808-0
Library of Congress Catalog Card Number: 81-86151
Printed in the United States of America

Cover photo by Marion Bernstein

Illustrations by Marjorie Impell, with the exception of those on pages 12, 106,
226, 244, and 419, which were done by Vantage Art, Inc.

Illustration on p. 131 from Sara W. Lundsteen, *Children
Learn to Communicate: Language Arts Through Creative
Problem Solving*. Prentice-Hall, 1976, p. 81.

Photograph on p. 237 © Ginger Chih/Peter Arnold, Inc.

Copyrights and Acknowledgments appear on pages 487–88, which constitute
a continuation of the copyright page.

Preface

Opportunities for teaching communication skills permeate every aspect of daily life. These instructional moments may be long or short, pre-planned or serendipitous, but they always exist. This introductory text attempts to assist prospective elementary-school teachers to develop the necessary skills for discovering and making the most of these language opportunities.

Though curriculum areas are convenient teaching structures, their walls are invisible to the learning child. Just as instruction in the skills of thinking cannot be organized into neat packages, so is it impossible to relegate the teaching of language arts to only one aspect of the curriculum. Language competence occupies a central and singular place in the creative and cognitive growth of the child. The emphasis of this book, therefore, is on helping the teacher plan language learning activities that are integrated within the total curriculum.

I have attempted in *Teaching Language Arts to Children* to address the personal as well as the professional needs of teachers. Teaching is a highly complex activity, requiring an inspired and knowledgeable human being. The training that this book offers therefore engages prospective teachers in a variety of "hands on" experiences, encouraging them to construct puppets, write poems, read children's books, and practice their storytelling skills. The teacher's judgment is respected, creativity is appreciated, and the reader is always invited to question the theory that directs the practice.

The development of a positive self-concept for teachers and children is a cornerstone of this book. Recognizing the inextricable relationship between language development and self-concept, it includes many activities designed to support this linkage.

Though the roots of *Teaching Language Arts to Children* are the research findings and experiences of experts in the field, I have intended it to be practical. I have tried to write informally, in language that is clear and

v

free of jargon, without reducing complex ideas to simplistic statements. This is a conceptual book designed as a guide for action.

The book is organized developmentally. However, those instructors who prefer a different structure should feel free to reorder the readings, for though the chapters are integrated within a unit framework, they are also separate entities. The text has been written to serve as an introduction to teaching language arts, but many of the activities have proved useful to the more advanced student and practicing teacher.

Part I focuses on what the teacher should know about the professional content of the language arts and its application in the real world of the classroom. Different stages of a child's language development are explored as well as teaching strategies and patterns of classroom organization that meet individual needs. Competence-based education is addressed, but from the perspective of a humanistic framework.

Part II identifies the child as a receiver of language and suggests materials and activities that may assist young students to develop their listening and reading skills. Individual chapters are devoted to listening, reading, and children's literature.

Part III considers how the child expresses language and suggests many instructional strategies for teaching oral and written expression. Learning to write is viewed as a growth process for both students and teachers.

Part IV responds to the problems involved in teaching a child the basic writing skills. The practical aspects of writing are identified and assessed, and suggestions are offered for teaching these essential skills creatively.

Each chapter contains a preview and an afterview to focus the reader's attention on its essentials. Teacher competences are frequently included. In addition to the many activities suggested in each chapter, readers can further their skills by selecting mini-projects from two additional sections entitled "When You Want to Know More" and "In the Classroom." Suggested readings are provided for each chapter. Boxes offer information and practical suggestions that supplement the text.

This is a contemporary book, but material has not been included simply because it is new or fashionable. Much that we know about teaching language arts reinforces the fine work of the past. For example, though the research on listening has been available for some time, it may not have been given adequate attention. Now, in a television age, it takes on new significance.

Throughout the text, attention is directed to some of our deepest concerns: the language-different child, the child with special needs, the importance of non-print communication, and the impact of the media on reading. The activities for children reflect these current subjects, and language arts activities raise issues in ecology, technology, consumerism, and human liberation. A language arts text should be responsive to language change both in content and form. Wherever possible, the language throughout reflects the need for a greater sensitivity to non-sexist expression.

The reader will notice that children's literature appears not only in a separate chapter, but as a resource throughout the book. Similarly, many chapters encourage students and their teachers to use writing as a means of clarifying thinking and finding inner voices. Evaluation is not given a separate chapter, for it is viewed as an essential component of all teaching and is discussed throughout the book.

My sincere appreciation is extended to the editors of Harcourt Brace Jovanovich, whose guidance and support were essential to the completion of this book. Special thanks to William J. Wisneski for his compassion, integrity, and wisdom; to Julia Palmore, whose gentle prodding on copy spurred me on; to Yvonne Gerin for her suggestions with the art work; to Stephen Saxe, who designed the book; and to Nina Indig, the production manager.

I was indeed fortunate to develop this book with the guidance of reviewers whose many helpful suggestions have been incorporated. To Anthony R. Angelo of Central Connecticut State College, Evelyn M. Carswell of the University of Arizona, Sarah Hudelson of Arizona State University, Margaret B. Parke of Brooklyn College of the City University of New York, Sue W. Peterson of the University of Michigan–Flint, and Ruth Stein, educational consultant, I wish to express my thanks.

I am grateful to the many teachers in Great Neck, New York (particularly from the Lakeville School), and in New York City (particularly from P.S. 222) who generously shared not only their materials, but their hopes and dreams for a better education for all children. To my son Andrew's classmates in Great Neck, I express my appreciation for their ideas, their poems, and their enthusiasm.

In untold ways, this book reflects my experience with the many students in my undergraduate and graduate classes who willingly experimented with sections of it and responded with fresh and honest criticism. To my colleagues in the School of Education at Brooklyn College (CUNY) I offer thanks for their support and continuing faith in my endeavors.

The sterling quality of the publications of the National Council of Teachers of English must be acknowledged, for they helped to make this book a contemporary document.

My role as coordinator of the Children's Choices Book Project for two years provided me with the opportunity to learn the responses of thousands of children, thus augmenting my love and knowledge of children's literature and my desire to make it a focus of this book. I am grateful to the Children's Book Council and the International Reading Association for this opportunity.

Finally, may I express my gratitude to my family, who lovingly watched, cajoled, and refreshed me when the going got rough. Without their humor and respect, this might have been a labor, rather than a labor of love.

—Karel Rose

Contents

Part II
Receiving Language   125

Part III

Expressing Language   267

Part IV

The Teaching of Basic Writing Skills   381

PART I

THE TEACHER'S KNOWLEDGE OF LANGUAGE ARTS

CHAPTER 1

The Language Arts and the Elementary-School Child

Preview   This introductory chapter will emphasize the importance of the many conditions that influence a child's language development—conditions that exist within the student, the school setting, and the culture at large. The communication process will be considered from its verbal and nonverbal aspects. The primacy of speaking will be explored along with the importance of self-concept in the development of communication skills. While introducing the basic components of the language arts and their interrelationships, the chapter will also present, in skeletal form, the themes that will be developed in later chapters. Among these are language differences, sex stereotyping, the nature of communication, television and language development, visual literacy, and the relationship between self-concept and language. The final section of the chapter, an overview of the text, will provide a sketch of its general orientation and organization.

"It can't be helped. We are made of layers of language like a Viennese torte."

—William Gass

HUMAN BEINGS need spoken language. Unlike animals whose communication does not require strict verbalization, people throughout the world have had to invent and reinvent precise symbolic language. In so doing, they have unleashed a deceptive power that can either enhance or block real communication. Influenced always by its user's physiology, intelligence, and mood, spoken language may be deliberately employed to disguise, exaggerate, or soften reality. Politicians, advertisers, lawyers, teachers, in fact most literate people, recognize the ability of language to confuse or clarify meaning. Teachers tend to be particularly aware of language as the key that unlocks the mind. Words often are the medium through which children explore their inner and outer spaces. Communicating the joys of language to students and the ways in which words may change lives is a prime responsibility of every teacher.

Every young child is faced with the task of re-creating language. The infant cannot simply begin at the language level of his or her parents. Genetics and environment provide the potential and the head-start, but the skills and principles of language production must be learned anew by each generation. Despite the difficulty of the task, most children embark on the journey with gusto and develop a sense of power as they begin to gain control of the territory.

WHO IS LISTENING?

"Who is listening" is a matter basic to a child's success with language. The child coos, babbles, and finally speaks to the world (those who nurture) and impatiently awaits the response. The quality and frequency of that response will indelibly influence the child's language growth. Consider the case of Max, a five year old and the youngest of eleven siblings.

> "Max," said Aunt Veona. "Are you all right? How do you feel?" Max looked at her. His eyes shifted to the vast crowd of us children who looked at him quietly and expectantly. It was probably the first time he'd ever seen us all silent.

4

Suddenly he removed his thumb from his mouth and shoved his hand into his pocket. A grin split his face.

"Thwell," he said.[1]

Until this moment, Max's means of communication were limited to humming, pushing, pulling, and thumb-sucking. Max sent many nonverbal messages about what he was feeling, but withheld verbal clues. Surprisingly, he did have an adequate vocabulary and facility with language, but apparently no one with whom to share his thoughts.

Fortunately, by the time most children reach five years of age they have found a receptive audience and, as a result, have developed considerable verbal ability. This is the result of a developmental process rather than a singular event, and is preceded by a variety of listening experiences. A child is spoken to, listened to, read to, and responded to, and then, after countless attempts at imitating sounds, bursts forth with coherent speech. The young mind has begun to make connections between objects and sounds, between experiences and words. The cycle of language growth has begun; a lifetime will be spent refining the process.

TALKING: SOUNDS AND SILENCES

For teachers, talking is especially important. It is the activity that we do more than any other as we attempt to educate students; it is the primary tool of the profession. Speech is our paintbrush, our tractor, our calculator. Much of our instruction is and must be verbal, and we rely on the power of language. It is imperative therefore that we know as much as possible about this form of communication.

Learning language is not the exclusive province of the young. We are all continually adding to our knowledge of language. Whether trying to express ideas with greater clarity or eloquence, mastering the new vocabularies of a computerized society, or coaxing mature but more rigid articulatory mechanisms into the positions of a foreign tongue, we are always encountering situations that can give us new language powers. Like our students, we search for the perfect word, the lucid phrase, the simple but sentient sentence. The naming of objects, experiences, and feelings reinforces our personal awareness and helps us decipher an increasingly complex world.

The child attending school for the first time is exposed in a very dramatic way to this process of naming. A seeming obsession with words pervades the school atmosphere. Everything seems to have a label: corners of the room, objects, people, behaviors. Sometimes the profusion of

---

[1] Lael Littke, "The Day We Lost Max," in *Child Development Through Literature*, ed. Elliot D. Landau, Sherrie Landau Epstein, and Ann Platt Stone (Englewood Cliffs, N.J.: Prentice-Hall, 1972), p. 188.

new terms creates anxiety in the child. The skillful teacher keeps this anxiety to a minimum and kindles the young child's curiosity about the many wonderful things in the new surroundings. Properly handled, the process of naming can help the child become comfortable by bringing understanding and order to the vast array of unfamiliar objects and people.

Since listening and speaking are language arts to which the average student has long been exposed, the teacher should capitalize on the youngster's familiarity with the oral/aural mode of learning. Conversation about a cocoon, for instance, cannot help but bring up the words *caterpillar* and *butterfly*. Similarly, discussing an airport, even one built of blocks, will probably generate the use of such words as *Concorde* and *jet stream*. Talking about contemporary events of concern to the children will require other new words. Consider the vocabulary generated by a discussion of Mt. St. Helens *(volcano, lava, eruption)*. The wealth of words nestled in books remains to be unlocked; however, excitement about these words begins long before actual reading starts. Using oral experiences we can help students appreciate that it is through the written word that further knowledge may be discovered.

Teachers should be sensitive to still another dimension of talking, namely, the role of interior dialogue. Outward silence is only the absence of external verbalization; interior dialogue never ceases. Even when we are not listening or talking aloud, we converse with ourselves. This interior conversation is the reaffirmation of our humanness. We stop talking to ourselves only when we die.[2]

But talking aloud is quite threatening for some children. Like Max, who did not speak out for five years, some youngsters are fearful of revealing themselves. Not yet facile with language, they cannot use it without disclosing their innermost feelings; masking is not easy for the unsophisticated language user. Rather then share more of their thoughts than they want to, some children retreat from speech. But of course, the interior dialogue has not stopped. Though the job may be difficult, it is our responsibility as teachers to encourage children to share these inner voices. A supportive teacher who listens with feeling is the best beginning.

THE NATURE OF COMMUNICATION

Communication is the essence of education. We separate teaching into curriculum areas for convenience, but communication remains basic to all content fields. Teachers who "cover the subject" do not necessarily communicate with their students; the transmission of content does not

[2]William Gass, "Learning to Talk," *Washington University Magazine* (Spring 1979), pp. 21–25. (My thinking in this area was influenced by the ideas expressed in this commencement address.)

guarantee the reception of that content. Effective communication is an interchange, a giving and taking, a reciprocal action that permits the presenter and the receiver to exchange roles. These two aspects of communication, reception and expression, are the basis for major sections of this book.

Television, it has been said, communicates. But does it? It is probably more accurate to say that television transmits. Denied the opportunity to be heard in reply, the viewer too often remains inactive, uninvolved, and quiescent. Unable to obtain any immediate clarification of meaning and frustrated by the inability to have an impact on the transmitter, the viewer is lulled into intellectual passivity. True communication does not take place.

The need to communicate is an insistent one. Human survival depends upon the expression and reception of ideas. Researchers have identified a number of corollaries based on this principle. A knowledge of these findings should prove helpful to the teacher planning language experiences for children:

1. The closer a child's language comes to the speech norms of the community, the more effective the child's communication.
2. A child's language ability moves toward the norms of adults.
3. A child needs to be spoken to, listened to, responded to; for the more opportunity a child has to communicate, the more skillful he or she will become at language.
4. The anticipation of a child's needs by a parent or teacher before they are communicated will tend to retard a child's language development.[3]

Humans do not learn to communicate at the same rate. Some need more time than others to pass through the stages involved in clarifying and verbalizing ideas. Too often, adults pressure a child for a pace faster than he or she can handle. The popularity of children's books on this subject attests to the anxiety that many youngsters feel. In *Leo the Late Bloomer*, Leo's father is very worried: Leo cannot read or write, and he never says a word.[4] Leo, unable to tell his father that he is not yet ready for more adult behavior, is always sad. After a time, at the suggestion of Leo's mother, the father stops watching him; he looks at television instead of Leo. One day in his own good time, Leo blooms. He is able to read and write and speak. Leo has acquired these skills late but his joy is no less complete. "I made it," he announces gleefully at the end of this perceptive book. Though Leo is an elephant, he exemplifies a very real frustration in the lives of many boys and girls. Learning, growing, and communicating are not simple matters; some will need more time than others.

---

[3]E. Brooks Smith, Kenneth S. Goodman, Robert Meredith, *Language and Thinking in the Elementary School* (New York: Holt, Rinehart & Winston, 1970), p. 12.

[4]Robert Kraus, *Leo the Late Bloomer* (New York: Windmill Books and E. P. Dutton, 1971).

Another aspect of communication that teachers should consider is the nonverbal aspect. Expression may be through body movements or artistic representations and should be encouraged. Indeed, body language often serves as a springboard to oral and written expression.

Communication in many forms should be supported. For example, in one third-grade class, a student's description of the fight for life waged by the turtles of the Galapagos Islands generated active discussion. Debby pantomimed the movements of a turtle struggling onto the sandy beach. Her body clearly demonstrated the frustrations of the activity. Some children wanted to plan a verbal dramatic presentation; others chose to re-create the experience in writing, and a small group decided to do some research on the lives of turtles.

Whether children use their bodies, speak, or write, the compelling need for expression is clear; and indeed "There is no reception without reaction, no impression without correlative expression."[5] Some young children are more comfortable communicating through body movement or through song than they are speaking or writing. We all respond in our own way to the personal demands for self-expression.

THE "COMFORT QUOTIENT"

The degree to which children share their reactions in class is directly related to what we might call their "comfort quotient." Do they trust in the teacher's fairness and kindness enough to share a less-than-perfect paper? Does the classroom atmosphere allow for differing responses? Are the contributions of all students welcomed? If these questions can be answered positively, the classroom is probably a comfortable place in which to risk active participation. Hence, it is a place where communication thrives. There is a kind of reciprocal relationship between language development and one's "comfort quotient." Language muscles must be flexed in order to grow. And they are most likely to be exercised when the child feels a measure of self-confidence. In turn, as the growth of language skills gains momentum, emotional satisfaction increases. The progress is not always linear, but growth has to be viewed with the long term in perspective.

In recent years, humanistic education has challenged teachers to consider ways of developing environments that foster positive feelings of self. Helping children to recognize how the words they use may affect how they think is a good beginning. Jack Canfield and Harold C. Wells in *100 Ways to Enhance Self-Concept in the Classroom* suggest a number of activities for this purpose.[6] Some of these involve giving more thought-

---

[5]William James, *Talks to Teachers* (New York: Norton, 1958), p. 39.

[6]Jack Canfield and Harold C. Wells, *100 Ways to Enhance Self-Concept in the Classroom* (Englewood Cliffs, N.J.: Prentice-Hall, 1976).

ful attention to words that describe self and recognizing how self-labels can influence actions; one example is the use of "I won't" where children would ordinarily use "I can't." Throughout, the emphasis is on helping young people increase their self-esteem. Obviously, the exercises have limitations. They can be meaningful only if youngsters are prepared to engage in them honestly. The classroom environment can often provide an impetus for those students who are considering doing something about their language and perceptions. The teacher who is concerned about the development of positive self-concept will devise activities that increase children's sensitivity to the relationship between language and feelings.

WHAT ARE THE LANGUAGE ARTS?

The language arts, a series of interrelated thinking processes, include the skills of listening, speaking, reading, and writing. Although these components appear to develop independently, they are, in fact, always functionally interrelated. In the very early stages, children usually follow a developmental sequence and progress from listening to speaking to reading to writing. However, the route does not always remain linear. The work of linguist Carol Chomsky suggests that in the early years, reading and increased knowledge of the language go hand in hand.[7] Once the connections are established, however, each aspect of the language arts reinforces the other, simultaneously and reciprocally. A set of symbiotic relationships is born.

Oral language is a particularly good model to demonstrate this point. Speech not only nourishes itself but simultaneously serves as a springboard to the other language arts.

THE DEVELOPMENT OF LANGUAGE ARTS SKILLS

The development of language arts skills is dependent upon many factors, for experience is reflected in language. Many variables shape vocabulary, syntax, and sentence patterns: intelligence, home environment, cultural heritage, geography, physical attributes, and even popular media heroes. Many recent studies have shown, for example, that differences in the ways the two sexes are generally reared in America contribute to differences in language ability. Girls are spoken to more and encouraged to participate in quiet activities; boys are prodded to be more physical. As a result, many boys enter school with a mental set against reading and

[7]Carol Chomsky, "Stages in Language Development and Reading Exposure," *Harvard Educational Review* 42, no. 1 (February 1972): p. 33.

writing. What is sex-appropriate is internalized by many children by age four. There is even some evidence to suggest that since brighter young-sters understand the subtleties of the societal prescriptions, they con-form to the lock step at an even earlier age. The result is that options are limited. Sally in the old Peanuts joke says it well: "If I'm only going to grow up to be a housewife, why do I have to go to kindergarten?"

It is the teacher's responsibility to recognize and plan for the wide variations that exist in children's language development. The challenge involves knowing what primary materials, experiences, and instructional techniques will suit the particular child at a given time. The areas in which these differences will be most apparent in young children are:

Ability to observe and listen

Ability to deal with abstractions

Ability to understand and speak English

Desire and ability to verbalize experiences

Number and accuracy of concepts acquired

Size and appropriateness of vocabulary

While every child's pattern of language growth is different in some ways, it is helpful to recognize that most children's language abilities progress through the same well-defined stages; these will be discussed in the next chapter. Hence, many school systems identify expected lan-guage outcomes for specific ages and grade levels. If these outcomes are recognized as descriptions and not prescriptions they can be helpful yardsticks.

TEACHING THE LANGUAGE ARTS

Teachers have many and varied opportunities to encourage and develop communication skills. In an atmosphere of warmth and creativity, lan-guage teaching may be carefully planned or arise from the unexpected event. Andrew's mother has brought in applesauce cupcakes to celebrate her son's seventh birthday. The children see them, smell them, touch them, and of course, eat them. Some children want to know how they are made. The teacher, Mrs. Lewis, explains the process and even relates it to a previous class experience, cooking pumpkin pie; she is attempting to build a conceptual network. The children express considerable inter-est, and Andrew's mother is invited to return to assist the children in making cupcakes themselves. What a lot of language power can be ex-tracted from this cooking session. Let us look at how all the language arts might operate during this classroom event:

1. The children observe, listen to directions, and participate in the prepara-tion of the cupcakes.

2. The children watch, smell, touch, and taste the ingredients. Some of their responses are expressed verbally.

3. As the cupcakes are being baked in the oven of the school cafeteria, the children recall and state the steps in the process.

4. The children develop their conceptual abilities as they are encouraged to verbally relate the preparation of the cupcakes to their experience making pumpkin pie.

5. The children become aware of many words related to apples: "What are the names of different kinds of apples?" "Where is the core?" "What is an orchard?" "How can we prepare apples?"

6. With the teacher, the children develop an experience chart—talk written down—about the cooking event.

7. Each child writes an original book on apples, fruits, or recipes.

8. The class listens to a story about Johnny Appleseed; some of the children provide their own oral and written interpretations of the tale.

9. The teacher suggests and makes available books about apples, such books as Nonny Hogrogian's *Apples* and Enzo Mari's *The Apple and the Moth*.

In this situation, teacher and class have participated in a stimulating language adventure. Many additional language activities might be derived from the experience (Figure 1-1).

Among older children, equally rich opportunities for language growth present themselves. A class trip, a visiting poet, a school crafts fair, or a world event can serve to catalyze enthusiastic student participation. What is important is the teacher's sensitivity to the "teachable moment" and knowledge of instructional strategies that will place and keep the language arts at the center of the curriculum.

LANGUAGE PLAY

How do you feel about the following statements?

"After many hours of debate, the senators returned to their digs."

"Fall Status Report: Gloria Vanderbilt switches to plugged-in cords."

"The second act is biodegradable."

As the sentences above suggest, people often have fun with words. They purposely mix metaphors and use clashing connotations for humorous purposes. Word games and word puzzles, which are useful as educational tools, continue to be highly marketable as recreation. Playing with words can be fun and exciting. If teachers can communicate the playfulness inherent in language and the ways in which meanings can be controlled, they are likely to generate great enthusiasm for language among their students.

Children will recognize the playful quality of euphemistic language and its potential for cloaking or clarifying: "He's not a fat kid—let's call

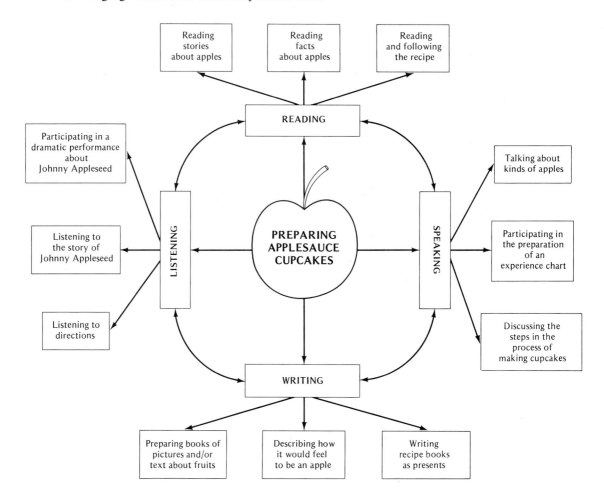

1-1   **The Interrelatedness of the Language Arts**   The preparation of a recipe can lead to many language-related classroom activities.

him a hearty eater." "Is Mr. Jones really a gossip?—I like to think of him as a student of human motivation." "Double Agent Green is not a super spy—she's an information gatherer." A critical approach to language is necessary in helping children become more discriminating in evaluating public and private statements as well as school-related activities.

The exploration of languages within a language can also be exciting. The "slanguage" of a trade or vocation might be analyzed. Many children have been in a cafeteria and have heard the call for "Adam and Eve on a raft"—another way of saying "poached eggs on toast." Do students know what action is involved when a police officer "frisks" a subject? What about the lingo that developed as a result of Watergate? Space exploration? Computer technology? The energy crisis?

"Hi and Lois" © King Features Syndicate, Inc. 1978.

Most children recognize their need for a larger vocabulary, but the fun of acquiring one may not be readily apparent. Why not focus on some of the words that have entered our speech because of cultural changes and scientific advances? A new terminology surrounds our discussions of life-support systems, cable television, humanistic psychology, CB radios, and psychedelic experiences. We are always coining new words to fill gaps in the language. In many cases, both the concept and the term are relatively new. For example, thirty years ago *spacewalk, cablevision, melt-down,* and *parenting* were much rarer terms. Conversely, some words have all but disappeared from the common vocabulary. What ever happened to a trolley car? A dumbwaiter? A crew-cut? Courting? Dunce-caps?

Understanding that language changes is important for children. Correctness is not arbitrary; its purpose is clarity. However, it is important to recognize that background, experience, and appropriateness determine how language is used. Children and teachers become more accepting of expressions that differ from their own when they realize that language reflects change in the world.

When we encourage children to play with puns, explore the origins of their names, or make up metaphors, we are increasing their facility with language. With this greater facility comes heightened pleasure in the identification and expression of their own thoughts. Chapter 14 will suggest ways in which children may blend their natural creativity, sense of play, and language ability.

VISUAL LITERACY

Literacy, the ability to read and write, is essential to modern life. Neither an illiterate person nor an illiterate society can function effectively. But the ability to code and decode thought does not spring full-blown as Athena did from the head of Zeus. Literacy is rooted in the processes of thinking, seeing, and listening. And visual literacy, the ability to decode nonprint messages, bears many similarities to forms of verbal communication. On seeing the bottle, the hungry baby often stops crying. A visual message has been decoded: food is on its way. As we grow older, we become even more aware of nonverbal messages. Each day, we react to modes of dress, body language, billboards, road signs and other environmental signals. We continually read silent, but clear visual messages: "The houses and well-kept lawns are attractive; this must be an affluent neighborhood." "The students and instructors all wear casual clothes to class; it must be a relaxed atmosphere." A well-developed visual sense is a significant asset in verbal communication. The effective reader of visual clues has a head start at becoming a proficient reader of verbal clues, for visual "readings" frequently stimulate oral or written expression. Consider the following progression:

> We look.
> We see.
> We think about what we see.
> We talk about what we see.
> We write about what we see.
> The more we are able to see, the more we may want
>   to talk or write about it.

As in any skill, there are levels of nonverbal decoding. Some people decode nonverbal messages better than others; some grow to adulthood seeing much more than others see. All sighted people can look at the visible world, but many do not (or choose not to) see it. They have developed a kind of functional blindness. Sometimes, they do not see because they are constrained by assumptions about what they should see. Sometimes, they do not see because their abilities to see have not been adequately awakened. They suffer from a kind of visual illiteracy.

Teachers have a splendid opportunity to help students see more perceptively and increase the fund upon which their expressions are based. Although no child is expected to have the deductive powers of Sherlock Holmes, every youngster can be assisted to see more effectively. It is possible that in education we have not given adequate attention to visual literacy. Yet all people continually read the visual clues of society. The more effectively they do so, the more they are able to participate and communicate. The scientist "reads" the findings on a slide; the detective "reads" the body language of a suspect, and the biographer "reads" the artifacts that surrounded a particular person. Effective seeing begins in childhood, and most children are pretty good at it. A teacher can nurture this capability—say, by using wordless picture books, interpreting pictures from many sources, taking walks through the neighborhood noting public places and private spaces, and observing details in natural and people-made environments. Provide a rich fund of visual experiences, and language arts skills will be fostered.

JARGON

Communication depends upon the ability of an individual to express ideas clearly. For educators, achieving this clarity is sometimes a problem. The profession is prone to jargon, as are other areas of specialization. Meanings are sometimes obscured—even from colleagues. Do we all have the same understanding of *individualization? Mainstreaming? Open classroom?* Probably not. Try explaining these terms in very simple language to someone who is not in education. Most complex ideas can be reduced to a few simple sentences by those who clearly understand them. After studying his field with a group of scientists and scholars, one educator declared that "any subject can be taught effectively in some intellectually honest form to any child at virtually any age."[8] What is assumed in this bold hypothesis is that the teacher involved will be able to express the essential nature of the subject—to other teachers and students, we might add.

Why does jargon develop? Frequently, it is a means of protection, a group's way of excluding nonmembers. Have you ever had a physician attempt to explain your symptoms to you? Sometimes, you may find yourself feeling that you lack the intelligence to understand. However, the real problem may very well be the doctor's inability, or unwillingness, to express medical thoughts to a patient in ordinary language. This frequently requires a very clear understanding of basics. The physician may unconsciously feel that explaining medical matters in lay terms compromises a doctor's expertise—or at least the patient's sense of it.

Similarly, educators are often fearful that they are exploring the commonplace and elaborating on the obvious. Sociologist George Homans observes that "we have much anxiety about opening ourselves to the charge that we have discovered at infinite pains what everybody knows."[9] Thus professional jargon may separate teachers and administrators from their adversaries and shield them from such charges.

TELEVISION AND THE SKILLS OF COMMUNICATION

Television should be the visual counterpart of the literary essay; it should arouse our dreams, satisfy our hunger for beauty, take us on journeys, enable us to participate in events, present great drama and music, explore the sea and the sky and the woods and the hills.

—E. B. White

The teacher in America today confronts a generation of children that have been raised on television. In most cases, searching young eyes have

[8]Jerome S. Bruner, *The Process of Educaton* (Cambridge, Mass.: Harvard University Press, 1960), p. 33.
[9]George C. Homans, *The Human Group* (New York: Harcourt Brace Jovanovich, 1950), p. 5.

watched television for forty or more hours a week since age four or five; eager hands have played with disappointing toys, sought and purchased primarily because they looked good on television; hungry mouths have grown accustomed to sweet, artifically-colored products that seductive commercials guarantee to be both good for you and good tasting; and tender ears have been bombarded by authoritative voices advising on how to think, talk, walk, dress, work, and play—and always on what to buy, buy, buy, buy . . . ! Probably the teacher has also spent many hours watching television. What is going on? How did we all get caught? What are the implications for education? What happens to a traditionally print-oriented profession when people spend more than half their lives as receptors of nonprint materials? What happens to their skills of communication?

Most educators continue to ignore the impact of television on children's thinking and learning, despite the fact that the typical child of fifteen has spent more time in front of the television set than in school. This electronic medium has remarkable potential: it can keep the viewer in a mindless, semiconscious state, or it can in E. B. White's now famous words, "restate and clarify the social dilemma and the political pickle."[10] Where is the promise that once was television?

In the fifteenth century, the troubadours threatened to destroy the printing presses; in the early nineteenth century, the Luddites wanted to smash the new industrial machines. Just as better minds prevailed over the Luddites and the troubadours, common sense dictates that we can't throw away television sets or act as if they are not there. But what is an appropriate response? As teachers, we must educate ourselves, and the parents and children with whom we interact, regarding the effects of excessive television viewing on intellectual and emotional growth. We might begin by focusing our concern on the act of watching, rather than on what is being watched. Certainly content is important, but the viewing itself is probably more damaging to the skills of communication.

What *don't* children do because they are watching television? Time is stolen from playing, organized athletic activities, family conversation, walks, bike rides, and other joys of childhood. The constant television watcher is systematically deprived of first hand experiences, and such experiences are the basis for language development.

The act of television watching frequently requires minimal physical, intellectual, and imaginative involvement. Even very young children, for whom movement is as natural as breathing, often sit passively for hours before the television, soothed into a druglike trance. Often, they are watching programs that are boring, inappropriate, even frightening; the medium, with its rapid transmission of images, has them hooked. Its

---

[10]E. B. White, in a letter to the Carnegie Commission on Educational Television, from *Public Television: A Program for Action, the Report and Recommendations of the Carnegie Commission on Educational Television* (New York: Harper & Row, 1967), p. 13.

time constrictions require that life's essence be distilled into twenty-one minute segments (don't forget the advertiser's time)—which provides a "hopped-up" version of reality. For many children, television is "life"—a true representation; but in reality, it educates them to the unreal. Adults come to the medium with an experiential background; children can be victimized by it due to their lack of experience.

Today's teachers, therefore, may inherit students with a special kind of deprivation, one that has little to do with socioeconomic level. This deprivation may produce a malnutrition of the thinking and feeling faculties. Educators, media professionals, and PTA members have noted that "despite discriminate selections, much television viewing has an effect on children's ability to develop cognitively or to develop complex skills."[11] Early childhood teachers have observed that young children play and respond differently than children did in the pretelevision era: play is less imaginative; attention span is shorter; and there is diminished verbal interchange.

Buttressed by what we know about learning and the needs of children, teachers are in a unique position to be child advocates. Just as many of our laws recognize the singular quality of childhood, the media will have to be prodded into providing truly appropriate programming for young people. Children have immature perceptions; many cannot discriminate between commercials and program. They are unaware that the spokespeople for a sponsor do not necessarily believe in the product, but are usually being paid for their endorsement. Other youngsters are further deceived in that they are not yet able to discern that the images in the background are not necessarily smaller or less important; they're just further away. These aspects of cognition will be discussed at greater length in the next chapter.

Educational television and the public broadcasting networks are attempting to improve their offerings. Notwithstanding the superior content of such programs as "Sesame Street" and "Electric Company," children are still mainly consigned to passivity. Effective communication requires both receiving and presenting, and so far there is no effective way to talk back to the set. Addressing itself to this problem, a new series, "Vice Versa Vision," attempts to encourage the child's active participation.[12] Its creator and director, Brooks Jones, tries in a variety of ways to persuade children that television is only a prop. Viewers are encouraged to get off their chairs, to talk, to touch, and respond to the medium's suggestions. There are even times when the screen and audio are blank, so that the children can create by themselves. We need more programming that recognizes that the young viewer, not only the medium, should be active.

[11]Bob Lange, "Television's Role in Education: Is There an Artful Balance?" *Language Arts* 58, no. 1 (January 1981): 94.

[12]"Vice Versa Vision" was developed by Margaret Skutch and Brooks Jones at the Early Learning Center in Stamford, Conn.

All those interested in the welfare of children should be involved in a personal consciousness raising about the harmful effects of excessive television viewing. What can we do? (1) Teachers can assume responsibility for the creative use of television in and out of the classroom. (2) Parents can spend more time watching television with their children and share responses. (3) Children can be trained to be critical and discriminating about what they watch. (4) Educators, parents, and children can meet, form organizations, and generally monitor the offerings of the industry. One such national organization is Action for Children's Television, which has a number of local affiliates.

It is not necessary to throw the baby out with the bath water, however. After analyzing their own television-viewing habits and the messages they receive from the medium, educators and parents have to find ways of dealing with television. The topics considered in a recent conference about television might suggest a direction for such thinking:

> Critical Viewing Skills
>
> Parents' Rights in Broadcasting
>
> The Effects of Adult Viewing Habits on Children
>
> The Schools' Position on Television
>
> The Child as Consumer

Television makes a significant positive contribution to modern life. It has shown us the surface of the moon, the ocean floor, the workings of the brain, and the formation and birth of a human being. Each adult must personally decide when television viewing provides diminishing returns. Children should have the assistance of their parents and teachers in making this decision. While a major scientific achievement, television has no moral sense. It has the potential for good or evil. The decision is ours.

EVALUATION

Since long before "accountability" became a household word, teachers have been concerned with evaluating the work of their students. Their concern has been nurtured by the school system's need to know how students are progressing and how successfully given teaching strategies and instructional patterns are operating. Considerable emphasis has been placed on testing, and teachers have felt additional pressure as a pupil's academic future and even his or her professional success have begun to hinge on the results. Caught in the web of mandated tests, teachers may not always recognize other measurement alternatives, alternatives that answer questions other than "What is Johnny's grade-level equivalent?" At their best, standardized tests provide guidance for the learner and the teacher, identify where the learner is on a continuum, and suggest the need for other means of instruction and evaluation. The teacher is always central to the evaluation process, for he or she

>—makes significant decisions about the means of evaluation and recognizes alternate measurement possibilities that are more closely related to the school curriculum
>
>—looks at the results of a variety of measures and learns about the student's specific inadequacies
>
>—recognizes that progress is individual and uses as a yardstick the child's previous performance rather than an external standard
>
>—scores and evaluates measurement results keeping in mind language differences and other individual factors
>
>—recognizes that each measure is only *one* element in the evaluation process
>
>—places in perspective what is known about how children learn and then interprets measurement findings in terms of this knowledge
>
>—determines if the measures are helpful in diagnosing children's needs as well as in evaluating curriculum

Whether using an established schema for testing language and concept attainment, or informally testing listening abilities in the giving and taking of directions, the teacher must make judgments about appropriateness, individual differences, and relationships to the instructional program. While in no respect a *deus ex machina*, evaluation is an integral component of the total teaching/learning process. (In many subsequent chapters, it will be discussed in relation to specific language arts areas.)

This book is designed to help the elementary-school teacher gain competence in teaching the language arts. Schools are linguistically-centered places, and the elementary-school teacher probably spends the major part of the classroom day dealing directly or indirectly with language development. Whether teaching science, developing an organizational plan that individualizes instruction, or testing a new method of teaching mathematics, you can be sure that success at the endeavor will be directly related to the effectiveness of the communication involved.

Part I will focus on what you as a teacher should know about the professional content of the language arts and its application in the real world of the classroom. What knowledge should you, as a professional, acquire about language, communication, and the role of the teacher? What should you know about the different stages and patterns of a child's language development as you plan for instruction? How do children vary in their use of language? How are language and learning related? What general principles about language are useful in the classroom?

The term *competence-based education* has permeated the educational systems of most states. How might acceptance of this concept influence the teaching/learning act? What is a language arts competence? How is it acquired? How can teacher and student competences be assessed? How can the strengths of competence-based education and humanistic education reinforce each other?

Part II will discuss the child as a receiver of language and will suggest materials and activities that can help children develop the intake skills of listening and reading. Individual chapters will be devoted to listening, reading, and children's literature.

Part III will consider how the child expresses language and will provide instructional strategies for teaching oral language and written expression. Learning to write will not be viewed as a spectator activity, but as a growth process for students and teachers.

Part IV will deal with the problems involved in teaching a child the basic writing skills. The chapters in this section will focus on the practical aspects of writing—handwriting, spelling—and will explore various forms of writing. In its general orientation, the text will recognize that children pass through well-defined stages of growth, but at their own pace. Attention to readiness activities and developmental teaching practices will be present throughout the book.

Afterview Modern science is capable of miraculous feats, but it has yet to discover exactly how the brain produces language. Fortunately, like many motorists, we can become expert at using language without quite understanding what goes on underneath the hood. Language power is intimately related to a child's self-concept which, in turn, evolves from genetic, home, school, and environmental factors. Since these variables can arrange themselves in an infinite number of patterns, it is necessary to analyze each child's language growth separately. It is clear, however, that the environmental factors needed to stimulate language development include an abundance of "hands on" experiences. The passivity of television viewing may be an impediment in this regard.

WHEN YOU WANT TO KNOW MORE

1. Observe and describe the body language used by several children in your class.

2. Tape record the language of some of the girls and boys in your class. What gender differences do you notice with regard to vocabulary (variety and

level), fluency, effectiveness, creativity (choice of words, structures, images, and so on), concepts used.

3. Note individual differences in the ability to observe and listen over an extended period. What strategies do students use to "tune out"?

4. Interview a number of educators and determine whether they share similar definitions of such commonly used educational terms as *open education, back to basics, ungraded curriculum, modular scheduling, differentiated staffing, multimedia emphasis, language-experience approach.*

5. Identify some words that would most likely be familiar to urban children but not to children from a rural area. What vocabularies would be more familiar to the rural student? What are the implications for teaching?

IN THE CLASSROOM

1. Identify a list of regional/geographic words that are probably familiar to the students in your class. Share them with the children, and see if they know them. Develop a lesson that will extend their understanding and vocabulary beyond their geographic limitations.

2. Using some of Norman Rockwell's illustrations, ask a group of children to tell or write a story about what is happening in the picture. Assist them if necessary with the following:
   a. noting details
   b. observing likenesses and differences
   c. identifying shapes
   d. making inferences

3. Take a walk through the neighborhood with your students and suggest that they look for the following:
   a. things that have changed from their original form—a crushed aluminum can, a deteriorated building
   b. evidences of tradition—an old clock, a lighting fixture
   c. things that move that are not humans or machines
   d. sidewalks, sewer covers, roads
   e. shapes and patterns in nature and in people-made objects

4. Using a child's book as springboard, plan a flow chart with a group of children, showing the possible language arts activities.

SUGGESTED READINGS

Cazden, Courtney; John, Vera P.; and Hymes, Dell. *Functions of Language in a Classroom*. New York: Teachers College Press, 1972.

Fast, Julius. *Body Language*. New York: Simon & Schuster, Pocket Books, 1971.

Galloway, Charles M. *Silent Language in the Classroom*. Bloomington, Ind.: Phi Delta Kappa Educational Foundation, 1976.

Hamacheck, Donald E. *Encounter with the Self*. New York: Holt, Rinehart & Winston, 1971.

Lundsteen, Sara W. *Children Learn to Communicate: Language Arts Through Creative Problem-Solving*. Englewood Cliffs, N.J.: Prentice-Hall, 1976.

Purkey, William Watson. *Self-Concept and School Achievement*. Englewood Cliffs, N.J.: Prentice-Hall, 1970.

Rosenthal, Robert, and Jacobson, Lenore. *Pygmalion in the Classroom: Teacher Expectation and Pupils' Intellectual Development*. New York: Holt, Rinehart & Winston, Inc., 1968.

Scheflen, Albert and Alice. *Body Language and Social Order*. Englewood Cliffs, N.J.: Prentice-Hall, 1972.

Thompson, James J. *Beyond Words: Nonverbal Communication in the Classroom*. New York: Scholastic Book Services, Citation Press, 1973.

Van Holt, Jay M. "Visual Literacy: A Valuable Communications Tool," *Instructor* 82, no. 1 (August/September 1972): 130–32.

William, Clarence M., and Debes, John L. *Visual Literacy*. New York: Pitman, 1970.

Winn, Marie. *The Plug-In Drug*. New York: Viking, 1977.

Wood, Barbara S. *Children and Communication: Verbal and Nonverbal Language Development*. Englewood Cliffs, N.J.: Prentice-Hall, 1976.

CHAPTER 2

Language and Concept Development

Preview   This chapter will center on some very difficult but basic questions of concern to the elementary language arts teacher. Are my students really learning? Am I facilitating their thinking? How do I challenge students to grow conceptually? What does learning theory have to do with classroom practice? Thinking, the development of knowledge, and growth in language power are the staples of the teaching/learning diet. To ignore these ingredients is to pass off as trivial the workings of a child's mind.

   The discussion will not assume that educators should be knowledgeable about all aspects of language acquisition. The basic objective of the chapter is to heighten the classroom teacher's knowledge about the activity of thinking and its relationship to language. A second objective is to help teachers develop competence in translating theories about how children learn into everyday classroom practices.

HOW IMPRESSIVE it is that, by the time they enter school, most children have completed the greater part of the language acquisition process. With the wordless years behind them, students have an almost magical control over their environment. But their powers vary widely. Influenced by genetic potential, home environment, sociocultural background, sex differences, and family constellation, some children are better prepared than others for the learning experiences that await them in school. In addition, the quality of a child's nutrition and health strongly influences alertness, readiness for school activities, and mental capacity. Taking these individual differences into consideration, the classroom teacher must structure programs in which all students can learn. "Learn what?" you may ask. The simplest answer is "learn to learn," but its translation into classroom practice is probably the hardest thing you will ever have to do as a teacher.

This chapter will focus on four aspects of language and thought:

1. The nature of language
2. The acquisition of language
3. Concept development
4. Relationships between language and thinking

The assumption is that both the teacher and the students will regard thinking as a priority and foster those activities that value the process of intellectual development over the learning of specific facts. A further assumption is that an awareness of children's thinking and language patterns will help the educator teach more effectively.

THE NATURE OF LANGUAGE

Theory

The nature and power of language were minimally discovered by all of us when we first learned to speak. By the time we entered school many of the concepts noted below were recognized at some level. These concepts have a new relevance for teachers as they try to understand the process of language growth among elementary-school children.

Some Basic Concepts about Language

1. Language is a sound system. One component of language is speech. Speech is an oral system in which separate sounds are put together in patterns to form words and sentences that make sense only to those who understand the language.

2. Words are representational. They are not the thing itself, but symbols for the thing.

3. All languages and dialects of languages have built-in systems, which, though arbitrary, have rules, a prescribed order, and agreed-upon conventions. The system may vary with geographical location, but no language or dialect is superior to any other.

4. Language is basically social. It is acquired from another human being who speaks and to whom we listen. The process is a continuing one.

5. Imitation and repetition play an important role in language acquisition, but most linguists do not believe that language is learned solely through this process.

6. Language is purposive. The acquisition of language is facilitated as children see its power to satisfy needs and accomplish goals. "I want ice cream," "Mommy, come here," "I can't do it."

7. Spoken language is probably the most efficient means for communicating our needs, establishing relationships, and expressing feelings.

8. Language is always changing. Words, like fashions, have their day, and as the world changes so do the expressions of its people.

Classroom Activities on the Nature of Language

Language Is Purposive   As you develop knowledge of the nature of language, it becomes apparent that application of this knowledge should place a high priority on motivational activities. Some suggest that children perceive language as a tool and that their comprehension of the language is clearly related to the comprehension of its uses.[1] This observation has practical translations in the classroom. Teachers would do well to set up situations in which the desire to learn language is sparked by some of the urgency that existed when children were first learning language. That is, they should capitalize on the power of language to satisfy needs, control another's behavior, establish a social relationship, and so on. One researcher, Michael A. K. Halliday, has categorized this purposive language functioning of children (for example, regulatory, imaginative, interactional), and teachers may find his schemata helpful as they go about planning classroom activities to increase language skills.[2] Though the categories or functions were originally developed to analyze the language behavior of very young children, many researchers have used them in observing children's language in school situations.

EXPERIENCES FOR TEACHERS ON THE NATURE OF LANGUAGE

(These experiences are related by number to previously noted concepts.)

1. Listen to a recording in a foreign language (German, Russian, Chinese) and note those sounds or combinations of sounds that do not seem to occur in English.

2. Logos (visual symbols), like words, are representational. Identify some popular commercial logos. What verbal messages do they convey? Develop logos and new words to serve as symbols for such ideas as future shock, human ecology, women's liberation, and so on.

3. With another person, develop twenty nonsense words that include verbs, nouns, and adjectives. Give arbitrary meanings to these words and use them in writing notes to each other.

4 and 5. Observe a child who is about two years old. Note when the child's language is directly imitative of another person. What other factors besides imitation and repetition seem to be operating?

6. Keep a record of the language expressed by a child under three years of age in a fifteen minute period. Note how many of the child's statements or question can be classified as purposive.

7. Spend a half hour in which you try to share your ideas without using spoken language. At the end of the time consider: How efficiently were you able to communicate? What feelings did you have? Were you able to relate with others?

8. Make a list of words that have gone out of style. Identify several words that are newcomers to our vocabulary.

Spoken Language Is Efficient and Functional   The implementation of knowledge about the nature of language is dependent upon the development of activities that spark communication. The social setting of the classroom offers an ideal culture for language growth. Students can explore language through the following classroom experiences:

Participation in social games

Informal conversing and discussing

Planning creative dramatic skits

Working in committees

Performing group tasks and responsibilities

[1]Frank Smith, "The Uses of Language," *Language Arts* 54, no. 6 (September 1977): 638.

[2]Michael A. K. Halliday, *Explorations in the Functions of Language* (London: Edward Arnold, 1973).

Reacting to each other's work

Planning a class project (cake sale, book exhibit, science show, and so on)

Reporting

Informal telephone activities

Language Is a Sound System   With the recognition that language is a sound system, teachers should be aware of the "usual" age at which a child can clearly pronounce specific sounds. In the chart below, these sounds are represented by letters.

3 years	*m, n, ng, p, f, h, w*
3½ years	*y*
4 years	*k, b, d, g, r*
4½ years	*s, sh, ch*
6 years	*t, th, v, l*
7 years	*th* (voiced), *z, zh, j*[3]

If a child is unable to produce the sounds that seem appropriate for his or her age, the teacher might try to discover whether or not the sounds are being heard correctly. (The chapters on reading and listening will provide a variety of suggestions for diagnosing and developing auditory discrimination.) Whatever its cause, poor articulation may be an obstacle to language growth.

In attempting to heighten awareness of the linguistic sound system, Robert B. Ruddell suggests that teachers provide many opportunities for students to informally contrast the English language with another.[4] Consider these activities:

Listening to simple songs in a foreign language

Having bilingual staff or parents recite (and record) simple familiar stories in several languages

Building a class repertoire of oral greetings in various languages

Inviting bilingual staff, students, or parents to the classroom to serve as resource persons by sharing experiences and assisting bilingual students

THE ACQUISITION OF LANGUAGE

Many of you may have wondered why it is so difficult for you to acquire a new language as a mature adult when you performed the task so ably

[3]Mildred A. Templin, *Certain Language Skills in Children: Their Development and Interrelationships* (Minneapolis: University of Minnesota Press, 1957), p. 53; cited in Paul C. Burns and Betty D. Roe, *Teaching Reading in Today's Elementary Schools* (Chicago: Rand McNally, 1976), p. 51.

[4]Robert B. Ruddell, *Reading-Language Instruction: Innovative Practices* (Englewood Cliffs, N.J.: Prentice-Hall, 1974), p. 65.

as a young child. In fact by the time you were five, you had probably mastered most of the rules of your native tongue. You did not consciously apply the rules, but you had internalized them enough to use them in everyday communication. Only in retrospect does learning a language seem easy; at the time, it required a very intense effort on your part. There is, however, some evidence to suggest that language is best learned before puberty, when our language faculties are more flexible.

How language is acquired still remains somewhat a mystery. But the process has been of increasing interest to both researchers and teachers as they continue to recognize that language is the primary source for learning. There are many theories about how language is acquired, and in its own way each contributes something to our understanding. What follows is a brief explanation of some of the most widely accepted theories on how children acquire language and continue to increase their language power.

(1) A basic controversy still exists as to whether language learning is innate, or acquired through an elaborate process. Those who accept the innate, or latent, theory point out that many different languages are learned in similar ways by different children—a strong indication, they say, that the human brain is specially programmed for language acquisition. Noam Chomsky, the noted linguist, observes, "All that is necessary is for the latent structure of that language to be 'triggered' physiologically and for a language model to be available with whom the child may interact."[5]

Many linguists oppose this point of view, though they do agree that experience and social responsiveness are basic for language development. Taking into account the amazing speed with which language is learned, these researchers believe that human beings possess a cluster of cognitive abilities that enable them to symbolize, see relationships, use abstractions, reason by analogy, and so on. It is these abilities, they say, rather than specialized language skills, such as putting sentences together or applying grammatical rules, that control language learning.

(2) As a result of the work of Chomsky, there has been increased exploration by linguists into the relationship between language acquisition and cognitive development. The picture that is emerging reveals that the child is an active language learner continually analyzing what he or she hears and proceeding in a methodical way to put together the jigsaw puzzle of language.[6] What this means is that the child is breaking the system down to its smallest parts and then developing rules for combining the parts. Breyne Arlene Moskowitz uses the example of the child learning negatives. Since the youngster is not able to express a negative in a variety of ways, he or she constructs only a single, very general rule:

[5]Noam Chomsky, "Review of Skinner's Verbal Behavior,"*Language* 35 (1959): 26–58.

[6]Breyne Arlene Moskowitz "The Acquisition of Language," *Scientific American* 239, no. 5 (November 1978): 94.

"Attach 'no' to the beginning of any sentence."[7] The young language learner first expends energy on grasping the main idea and then deals with the details. This process may explain why many children overgeneralize a rule before they are able to apply it correctly. The use of "taked," "goed," and "writed" are common examples of overgeneralization of the "ed" rule for the past tense.

(3) Imitation of the language in the immediate environment is believed by some scholars to play an important role in the acquisition of language. For this reason, they point out, congenitally deaf children are generally limited in their ability to learn normal speech. Many studies show children imitating sounds (others and their own), lip movements, and intonations. Taking this a step further, some psychologists suggest that it is imitation and not thought that motivates the whole process. However, questions might be raised as to whether or not language imitation does not in fact require thought.

The behaviorists are in essential agreement with the imitative theory. They emphasize that imitation is the direct result of reinforcement and that therefore it is a system of rewards that propels children to grow linguistically. Rewards may be verbal ("good girl"), physical (a hug), or facial (a smile). Food or some other present may serve the same purpose. This empiricist explanation of language acquisition reflects a stimulus-response approach to learning as developed in the work of behavioral psychologist B. F. Skinner.

(4) The acquisition of language depends upon the child's knowledge of syntax and consequent ability to apply this knowledge. Syntax refers to the patterns or arrangements of words and phrases. It is concerned with the formation, the order, and the structure of sentences. Obviously, children do not begin their language careers speaking in complete sentences. They use first one-word and then multiple-word structures to communicate their ideas. One word does the work well for a while. When eighteen-month-old Nancy says "No," she means "No, I don't want to go to bed." The child's inflection, body language, and tone of voice all contribute to this one-word message, and the people close to her know just what she means. Telegraphic speech is the term that has been used to describe this early pattern. One or two words are able to communicate the content of longer sentences.

(5) Children acquire semantic knowledge (language meaning) at a slower rate and over a much longer period of time than it takes to acquire information about phonology, morphology, and syntax.[8] As they mature, children begin to recognize that word meanings change and that the "real" meaning of a word is relative to the context, the speaker, and the time.

---

[7]Moskowitz, "The Acquisition of Language," p. 104.

[8]Phonology is the study of how sounds are put together to form words, morphology is the study of word structure itself.

A variety of direct experiences are essential to understanding word meaning. Long after children first use a word, they are still identifying the attributes (cats are furry, and have four legs, whiskers, a tail, and so on) and experiencing the meaning of the word in various settings. They continue in this process until a conventional meaning is absorbed.[9]

Stages in Language Development

Children's language development is viewed by many experts as a series of overlapping stages. These stages and their explanations closely follow the theoretical model of language learning developed by Smith, Goodman, and Meredith.[10] Ages are identified for each stage, but they should be viewed as approximate. Also subject to variation is the rate at which individual children progress through each stage.

The Random Stage (up to 12 months) In the prelinguistic random stage, children babble (combine a consonant and a vowel sound) and play with sounds. The sounds are produced randomly, but by about eight months, the child may be engaging in some intentionally imitative behavior of sounds and lip movements. Though these sounds are not really language, they sometimes serve as communicators, for they attract attention. Often these random sounds are picked up and given meaning by adults in the environment. *Ma-ma* and *Da-da*, easy sounds for the baby to produce, are usually seized upon and repeated by parents as evidence of the child's recognition. By the end of this period, intonation (stress) may enter a child's babbling. What is basically a stream of unintelligible vocalizations may sound something like a sentence because of its cadence and intonation.

The Unitary Stage (up to 24 months) In the unitary stage, the child begins to produce sounds for a purpose—expressing a need or desire. Babbling may stop, and the child begins to speak in units of language. Each unit carries with it a longer message: "Milk" means "I want some milk"; "Car" means "Take me out in the car." Though the child is not yet ready to combine two words syntactically, he or she may nevertheless be developing concepts and thinking about putting words together. This fact was illustrated by Ronald Scollon of the University of Hawaii when he taped the speech of a young child.[11] He discovered that Brenda, his nineteen-month-old subject, was unable to put words together in a

[9]Susanna Pflaum-Connor, *The Development of Language and Reading in Young Children*, 2nd ed. (Columbus, Ohio: Merrill, 1978), p. 40.

[10]E. Brooks Smith, Kenneth S. Goodman, and Robert Meredith, *Language and Thinking in the Elementary School* (New York: Holt, Rinehart & Winston, 1970), pp. 17–26.

[11]Ronald Scollon quoted in Moskowitz, "Acquisition of Language," p. 96.

multiword sentence. However, when he listened to a series of her one-word sentences, it was obvious that Brenda was trying to express a concept for which she would have used a multiword sentence had she advanced linguistically beyond the one-word stage. Evidently, the young child understood more language than she could express.

The unitary stage is also the time when children use what Brown and Bellugi describe as "telegraphic speech": short, simple sentences usually composed of two to four morphemes repeated from the utterances of others.[12] The morphemes selected by the children from another speaker's statement are the content words, not only those that have the most meaning but those that have been given the most stress. Tense endings, contractions, plurals, articles, and the like are disregarded. Thus, in telegraphed speech, "Mommy got all wet" becomes "Mommy wet"; "The duck eats the bread" becomes "Duck eat bread."

The Stage of Expansion and Delimiting (up to 48 months)   At about two years of age, the child's range of spoken language expands from one- or two-syllable utterances to fuller approximations of adult speech. The less important details are filled in. "Out" now becomes "Go out" and then "Jimmy go out" and ultimately "Mommy and Jimmy go out."

With this expansion comes some delimiting. The child shows increased linguistic precision. Since a meaningless utterance does not usually achieve the desired response, children at this stage begin to tailor their utterances more carefully to particular situations. Researchers in language development often focus on the role of parents at this stage. Serving as language caretakers, the adults in the child's immediate environment often unconsciously alter their own speech to meet the needs of the young one and to facilitate his or her language acquisition. By thirty-six months, the child is using a variety of complete, simple English sentences; and by the fourth year, the child's speech resembles that of adults in his or her environment.

The Stage of Structural Awareness (up to 60 months)   During the first years of speech, the child learns much of his or her language in whole units. But this approach becomes increasingly impractical as the child's ideas become more complex; one cannot learn all English utterances as units. Hence, at about age three, the child begins to generalize and acquire control of the rules and patterns of the language. Each youngster does it in a different way. Initially, as indicated previously, children overgeneralize. They assume that all plurals end in "s" (foots, deers), that every past tense is represented by "ed" (I buyed some candy). Once they recognize that different words are spoken with different tones, some chil-

---

[12]Roger Brown and Ursula Bellugi, "Three Processes in the Child's Acquisition of Syntax," in *Language and Learning*, ed. Janet A. Emig, James T. Fleming, and Helen M. Popp (New York: Harcourt Brace Jovanovich, 1966), p. 11.

dren even generalize about intonation. They assume that "dead" is always to be whispered, that "baby" is always to be emphasized.

Overgeneralization should not necessarily be discouraged. Harsh corrections may keep a child from trying out new generalizations. For many youngsters, overgeneralization is a means of testing, a trial-and-error procedure used to flex linguistic muscles.

The Automatic Stage (by 72 months—kindergarten)   By age six, kindergarten age, the child has a large vocabulary of whole utterances that he or she can use accurately. Usually, he or she is also capable of generating new utterances not heard before. The grammar of the language of home and community has been internalized. The child is increasing his or her ability to conceptualize, a fact reflected in the increasing quantity and quality of the child's language.

The Creative Stage   The child who is able to invent his or her own language, despite the pressures that prod one to conform to the language of the community, has reached the creative stage. As the ability to conceptualize, make new connections, and think metaphorically increases, so does the child's need to use language in creative ways. Fortunately, the language mold developed by society has considerable flexibility; there is always room for the language user to push at the doors of convention, to alter the existing language—if only in subtle ways. The young have special powers in this regard, and they should be encouraged to use them. "Creative thoughts require creative language to express them. Emphasis on conformity in language in school or at home stifles not only expression but also thought."[13]

The Role of Adults in Language Acquisition

As has been noted, adults who raise children frequently alter their speech in order to make the language acquisition process easier. Though not all parental strategies are successful, many recent cross-cultural studies suggest that intuitive parental behaviors do facilitate language acquisition. Brian Stross, an anthropologist who relates the findings of his discipline to education, suggests that teachers study these parental behaviors and apply them in the classroom.[14]

The most common parental linguistic technique is "baby talk," which usually includes simplified words (*be-pa* for *grandpa*), special intonations, and a high proportion of questions and shortened sentences. There is lim-

[13]Smith, Goodman, and Meredith, *Language and Thinking*, p. 26.

[14]Brian Stross, "Language Acquisition and Teaching," *Language Arts* 55, no. 6 (September 1978): 751-55.

ited evidence available on the effects of "baby talk" on a child's language development.

A variety of helping strategies are used by parents.[15] "Prompting" is one of them. The parent asks, "Where did Daddy go?" Getting no response, she rephrases the question as "Daddy went where?" Another strategy is "echoing." If the child's sentence is partially unintelligible, the parent may restate as much of it as possible in the form of a question. A child's "with Jenny" may be rephrased by a parent as "Does Jenny want mommy to play with her?" Another helpful tactic is "expanding." The parent takes a simple utterance and expands it to have more meaning. Thus a telegraphed statement like "Kenny play out" becomes "Kenny is playing outside." When a parent repeats and expands a child's utterances in this way, the child is learning not only language but the adult's interpretation of the world.[16]

It would appear that most parents allow their children to grow linguistically at their own pace. The largely intuitive and unconscious language-encouraging techniques used by parents tend to respect children's developmental stages and readiness cues. Parents speak to their children more simply than they do to other adults. This accommodation is indeed fortunate because it is from simpler statements that children learn to construct, analyze, and use language.

The need to communicate propels the child to acquire language. A number of significant corollaries to this need for language acquisition have been identified, and they should be carefully considered by all language arts teachers.

1. The closer the language of the child comes to the speech norms of the adult community, the more effective becomes his communication.

2. There is a continuous tendency, therefore, for the child's language to move toward adult norms.

3. The more opportunity the child has to communicate, the more skill he will develop in use of language and the more acceptable will be his language by adult standards. He needs to be spoken to, listened to, responded to.

4. Anticipation of his needs by a parent or teacher before he communicates them will tend to retard a child's language development.

5. In literate societies, communicative need will play the same prime motivational role in the child's learning to read and write as it does in his learning to speak and listen with understanding.

6. Before change can be achieved in an individual's idiolect, the individual must strongly feel that the change will help him to communicate more effectively.[17]

[15]Roger Brown, *A First Language* (Cambridge, Mass.: Harvard University Press, 1973); cited in Stross, "Language Acquisition," p. 752.

[16]Brown and Bellugi, "Three Processes," p. 15.

[17]Smith, Goodman, and Meredith, *Language and Thinking*, p. 12.

EXPERIENCES FOR TEACHERS ON LANGUAGE ACQUISITION

1. Tape record on at least two occasions the vocalizations of a baby of about six months. Are there sounds that you do not recognize? Does the infant cry in different ways? Can you recognize cooing sounds? Is babbling taking place?

2. Observe a child under three years of age interacting verbally with a parent. Which of the following strategies are being used by the adult to assist the child in acquiring language: (1) simplifying, (2) prompting, (3) echoing, (4) repeating, (5) expanding?

3. Listen to the speech of a child in the unitary stage of language development. What evidence is there of "telegraphic" speech?

4. Listen to the speech of a four- or five-year-old child. What examples of "overgeneralization" can you record? What rule do you think the child is applying in each case?

Classroom Activities to Facilitate Language Acquisition

If the teacher is to facilitate students' acquisition of language then he or she must have a heightened consciousness of those almost mystical "teachable moments" when a child is not only willing but able to learn. This consciousness comes from a blend of knowledge, skills, attitudes, and sensitivity. How can you apply your beginning knowledge of language acquisition to classroom practice? What follows are some suggested strategies, but there is no ultimate translation. Teaching that is student centered and developmental requires that each teacher relate theory and practice in his or her own way.

We have learned that language models in the child's environment are powerful influences on language development. The home serves as the first language laboratory, soon to be followed by the social and cultural setting outside the home. In time, the classroom provides its own unique contribution. In this mini-society, the child is exposed to a variety of language inputs. Exposure, however, is not enough: there must be interaction. It is through this interaction that children will have the opportunity to compare, imitate, practice, and extend their own linguistic repertoire. A language environment that encourages comfortable social patterns and interactions with a variety of models will positively affect children's communication development. The following activities are suggested for the primary grades but would be valuable for all children who require broader experiences with language.

Acquiring Language from Peers:

1. Use a tape recorder so that children may hear their own voices and compare them with those of their classmates for particular patterns of word emphasis.

2. Have children tape-record their original stories. Have the class listen to these stories and then ask questions.

3. Encourage all forms of informal conversation, discussion, and oral reporting.

Acquiring Language from the Teacher:

1. Have children retell stories read by the teacher.

2. Try expanding children's sentences for instructional purposes. Mark, a first grader, said "I happy, today." (By sensitively directing attention to what is missing in the sentence, the teacher may expand the child's linguistic knowledge. Adult expansions of children's imitations may in some way promote language development.)

3. Try to adjust your language to a level that children can understand both in terms of content and structure.

4. Call attention to differences in inflection. Use choral speaking activities, a variety of creative dramatic experiences and the oral reading of literature.

5. Encourage children to play with language intonations in a variety of situations. They will enjoy: raising or lowering their voices (pitch), making their voices loud and soft (stress), and using pauses (juncture).

6. Play recordings of stories read by effective storytellers who may have an accent or speech pattern different from the students'. (Cyril Ritchard's readings of well-known stories serve as models of an English accent.)

The work of Courtney B. Cazden suggests that in language learning children benefit less from adult correction than from conversational interaction. Since communication is after all the purpose of language the elementary-school teacher would be wise to develop as many situations as possible to keep language flowing. In general, the classroom environment should be a place in which language interactions are continually initiated and children are encouraged to question. Dialogue is best kept alive in an informal setting that is rich in conversation.

In one study, Cazden found that the language of individual children was stimulated by reading to them.[18] The physical contact (sitting on the reader's lap, helping to turn pages), as well as the conversation that it stimulated about the pictures, was a more potent language catalyst than the common adult strategy of expanding children's telegraphic utterances.

---

[18]Courtney B. Cazden, "Some Implications of Research on Language Development for Preschool Education" (ERIC ED 011 329), p. 9.

CONCEPT DEVELOPMENT

"Where did I come from?" Laurie asks her mother. At this point, Laurie's mother launches into a detailed explanation of the process of reproduction, failing to notice that her daughter has tuned out. Finally, the confused six-year-old interrupts: "Amy says she comes from Philadelphia; I wanted to know where I come from." This well-worn story has been repeated endless numbers of times because it expresses so graphically the conceptual disparity between children and adults. In order for parents and teachers to respond appropriately to a child's questions they first have to know what is being asked. Sometimes, the best way to find out is for the adult to ask another question and get more clues as to where the child is developmentally. Children who still believe that babies come from a department store, for example, will be unable to appreciate the facts of reproduction. Such children are still too literal, too concrete in their thinking, to deal with what cannot be seen.

Stages in Concept Development

Since what children understand about concepts has much to do with their stage of development, it is important for educators to be aware of children's developmental stages as they attempt to teach language skills. In this area, the work of Jean Piaget, the Swiss scholar, has been most significant. Though there are those who take issue with his findings, most scholars recognize the importance of his contributions.

Underlying Piaget's work is the recognition that children acquire knowledge in a series of stages. This does not mean that every child has the same internal clock controlling concept acquisition. Children's abilities and attitudes reflect both genetic and environmental factors. We are unable to develop a grid that neatly checks off students' progress as they proceed through the various stages. Children show enormous variability in their developmental patterns, for example:

1. Children differ from each other. Eight-year-old Janet shows that she understands the concept of chance or probability (Piaget's term) when, in a game, she opts to predict the location of a desired object from a possible choice of two boxes rather than from a group of five such boxes. Andrea, however, who is also eight, does not yet understand the nature of probability and prefers to choose from the larger group.

2. An individual child is not at the same stage for all tasks. Alex, who has had rich experiences with art materials, demonstrates sophisticated judgment in the use of space on paper but not when it comes to solving spatial problems that relate to his own body movements. He is unable, for example, in a relay race, to place a potato in the center of a circle, for this demands an ability very different from what is required in the act of drawing or painting.

3. An individual child's grasp of a particular concept does not always proceed in an orderly way. On Tuesday, Helene, a seven-year-old, seemed to understand that, though the blue liquid was transferred from a milk bottle to a measuring cup, the quantity remained the same (principle of conservation). On Wednesday, when the process was reversed and the liquid was red, she was not sure. Did personal mood account for her altered perceptions, or was this evidence that her understanding of the Piagetian principle of conservation was unstable? Children move back and forth when they are between stages. "The overall structure that characterizes any given stage is an integration of those that preceded it, and the achievement of that stage is preparation for the next."[19]

Notwithstanding its limitations, Piaget's picture of the stages of cognitive development can be very useful. It provides considerable insight into how the child acquires concepts. Keep in mind, as you read about these stages, individual variability as well as the interdependence of the various stages. One of Piaget's most significant contributions is the theory that the sequence of concept development, though not its rate or depth, remains the same for all children.

Piaget lists four major periods of mental development:[20]

Sensorimotor Period (0–2 years)   The child begins this period as soon as he is born. Living in a highly physical world, the child exercises reflex actions like grasping, sucking, vocalizing, and biting. Some interpretation occurs as the child processes information and slowly begins to construct the beginnings of a cognitive map of his or her world.

The concept of permanence is frequently used as an example to illustrate this stage. The child is unable to realize that an object exists when he or she is not looking at it. Growth is deliberate but slow. Initially, when you cover a colorful ball with a blanket, the child assumes the ball is gone. However, at about a year, the child, if he or she observed you hide the ball, will quickly uncover it. If you then hide the ball in a different location without the child's seeing you do so, and if it were not to be found in the old spot, he or she would give up looking. It is nonexistent as far as the child is concerned. It is not until about the second year that a child realizes that even if the ball is thrown out the window, it still exists.

Preoperational Period (2–7 years)   During the preoperational period, children begin to develop the ability to go beyond the here and now. They develop language, a symbolic process in which abstractions (words) stand for things. The word *milk* represents something satisfying as well as an association with a person. The process of symbolizing continues as

[19]John L. Phillips, Jr. *The Origins of Intellect: Piaget's Theory* (San Francisco: Freeman, 1969), p. 18.

[20]Adapted from Barry J. Wadsworth, *Piaget for the Classroom Teacher* (New York: Longman, 1978), pp. 13–21.

the child grows in language power, there being a reciprocal relationship between language and concept development. During this same period, children learn to count, comprehend simple classifications, and depart even further from their egocentric view of the world. The child begins to realize that people exist for reasons other than to serve his or her needs. Having some knowledge of the physical world from personal experience, children begin to generalize their information: "My television set talks just like I do; it must be alive." The tendency for young children to attribute to inanimate objects the human qualities of will and consciousness is not unlike the behaviors of primitive peoples who tried to explain natural phenomena in terms of human behavior; for example, rain meant that the gods were crying.

Concrete Operations Period (7–11 years)   The conceptual development that occurs between ages seven and eleven permits the child to appreciate general principles that govern the behavior of familiar objects. This may involve classifying things or numbers into groups and recognizing that patterns are based upon specific attributes (size, shape, color, use, and so on).

It is also during this phase that children develop a better grasp of the more elusive concepts of time and space. Time is still viewed mainly as personal and relational, but insight is growing. Before this period, the two weeks before summer vacation seemed like a year. Now the child sees those two weeks in better perspective. There are other slow changes as well. "Before you were born," Glenn's father used to explain, "there was no television, this apartment house wasn't here, and your grandpa lived in a country where no English was spoken." Previously, Glenn was able to repeat all this information, but like most youngsters who enter this period, he was unable to fit this knowledge into his existing frame of reference. He is beginning to appreciate a concept of time that eludes direct experience.

Through experience and maturation, children begin to appreciate the relational aspects of time and internalize the answers to questions like, "How long will it take you to run one mile? Drive one mile? How many hours will it take to get to Disney World by train? By plane?"

The child in this period still has some confusions about space as well. However, there is slowly the recognition, for example, that an object appears smaller than another object of the same size only because it is further away. Abstract geographical concepts of space are somewhat more difficult to appreciate, and for this reason teaching them should be delayed until the child is ready to understand them. Children's concepts are rooted in experience. Vivian may have been told that oranges come from California, but since she sees them bought in plastic bags from the supermarket shelf, it is difficult to reconcile the explanation and her experience. It is not an easy matter for children to understand the functions of places and forces beyond their immediate environment.

Formal Operations Period (11–15 years)   In the formal operations period verbal language begins to be based upon theorizing and hypothesizing. Reasoning is no longer dependent upon the presence of a concrete object; abstractions have equal power. At this stage, the adolescent does not have to see visible evidence of the effects of slavery to understand its relationship to contemporary racism.

The period of formal operations is a dangerous and exciting time. Too much emphasis may be placed on logic; impatience and a "false idealism" may develop; strong group identification also becomes unusually attractive. "This is a 'normal' aspect of the development of formal operations. Further accommodation to the 'real' world may or may not result in an idealism that takes into account reality."[21]

The exciting aspect of this period is the power that it unleashes. As conceptual development grows, the rewards of knowledge become more accessible. Students can read theoretical materials, listen to lectures, and generally appreciate relationships that are based on abstractions. It is also at this time that specialization may occur as children begin not only to understand theory but to create it themselves.

Assimilation and Accommodation

According to Piaget, two processes help the child progress from one period to the next: *assimilation* and *accommodation*. Muriel Beadle uses his biological analogy:

> To live one eats. In order for food to nourish the system, however, it must change its form. Through chewing and digestions, we can incorporate it into the structure of the body. This process, by which various elements in the environment (not just food) are changed and absorbed by the organism, is called *assimilation*. The process by which the body acts on the food (chewing, swallowing, digesting, etc.) is *accommodation*.[22]

In cognition, it is information rather than food that is assimilated. The assimilation of information is a twofold process. As children develop, they take in information and fit it into their existing categories of knowledge. The new knowledge is then recategorized at their own level of understanding and meshed with the existing fund. It is in this way that categories or groupings are enlarged. It is the process of accommodation, however, that provides the real increment. When information that does not fit the old strictures is digested, the brain begins to modify its categories or find new ones. An accommodation, or change in thinking, results.

Let us look at Eric, a fifth grader who has assimilated the information

---

[21]Wadsworth, *Piaget for the Classroom Teacher*, p. 189.

[22]Muriel Beadle, *A Child's Mind* (Garden City, N.Y.: Doubleday, 1970), p. 124.

EXPERIENCES FOR TEACHERS IN CONCEPT DEVELOPMENT

1. Ask some seven year olds the following question: "How do people get babies?" From their answers, what can you deduce about their stage of intellectual development? Ask the same question of eleven year olds.

2. To illustrate the idea that some concepts develop before the language for them, devise activities in which children can nonverbally express concepts (for example, games, constructions, body movements).

3. From your experience, cite classroom situations that revealed that students did not understand the concept of conservation. Relate this to Piaget's theory of intellectual development.

4. Watch several television commercials designed to appeal to children. In what ways to they capitalize on children's confusion about space and size?

5. Give an example of how the teacher's understanding of the periods of mental growth can assist the child in developing positive attitudes about learning. What role does the self-fulfilling prophecy play?

6. To understand the processes of classification and cross-classification important in the development of logical thinking, randomly select several objects in your environment. How many regularities or shared attributes can you discover? Represent your findings graphically. Try a similar activity with students.

that women and men have fixed roles. In his experience, women are mothers, daughters, sisters, teachers, nurses, stewardesses, and so on. And his classifications have never really been challenged. However, in a class study of occupational roles, Eric discovers that women may also be doctors, lawyers, police officers, and pilots, and so begins the process of accommodation.

Another well-worn but helpful illustration of these principles uses the categories of fruits and vegetables. Karen may know that string beans, eggplants, tomatoes, and peas are all called vegetables. However, in the course of working on a science experiment, she discovers that scientists classify any plant that has seeds and flesh as a fruit. Like Eric, Karen must assimilate this information but at the same time expand at least one classifying principle in order to accommodate this new knowledge.

Assimilation and accommodation are lifelong processes. Children and adults are always reworking and altering their perceptions of reality.

Classroom Activities to Facilitate Concept Development

What to teach? How to teach? When to teach? These are the questions asked by teachers every day. The answers must be related in some way to the child's conceptual level, and attention must be given to the sequential order of mental development. Though it does not offer prescriptions, the work of Piaget can provide some answers to these questions.

1. The mode of presentation of the lesson and the materials employed should be suited to the child's conceptual level. There is an emphasis on concrete thought through the use of concrete objects and real materials, particularly for the younger child: "hands on" experiences, trips to a familiar environment (boiler room in the school), body movement games, and the use of real objects as well as representative materials ("This box can be the stove").

2. Strategies are utilized that stress the importance of *many experiences* in learning a concept. The approach is not one of "teacher talk" but "student action." When learning about a ball, for example, a young child experiences many balls: big, small, soft, hard, red, blue, heavy, light. The more diverse and frequent the experiences, the better prepared the child is to identify a ball that is different from the ones that he or she has seen.

Reprinted courtesy of
Bill Hoest and *Saturday Review.*

*". . . and just when I was getting the hang
of the 'Little Hand' and the 'Big Hand'!"*

Let us take the concept of mapping. A teacher's first objective would be to provide students with a variety of map experiences that are personally relevant. The second step would be to provide a number of opportunities for the children to recognize that maps are an abstraction, a symbolic representation in picture form. They might be asked to make a map of their own hands and feet, to view or construct a "block map" of a city street, or to prepare a map of the classroom. Following a trip to the zoo, students might prepare maps showing the location of various animals, the route followed by the bus, or the location of the buildings on the way. The emphasis should be on accumulating as many experiences as possible with a variety of maps. It is through the discovery of as many details as possible that information is accommodated.

3. Students should be provided with experiences that are multisensory. Situations in which only one sense is used may often result in wrong concepts or judgments. We tend to be misled by our senses.

   You might turn to page 227 and read about the story of "The Blind Men and the Elephant" to see how the senses deceive. Consider also the Japanese tale of "Rashomon": the "eyewitness" accounts of a crime with nine "honest" but differing interpretations.

4. Recognizing the importance of experience in conceptual development, the teacher should compensate for gaps in experience by providing students with "near" experiences. These may involve listening to guest speakers (a journalist), exposure to representative materials (a model of the Grand Canyon), dramatic participation in simulated situations (the signing of the Declaration of Independence), viewing films (deep-sea divers at work), reading books (a child's fight against physical disability), and project development (setting up a mini-museum).

5. Use logical thinking games in helping children develop classification systems of increasing difficulty. The one below is from a large number suggested in *Thinking Goes to School: Piaget's Theory in Practice*.

Matching Properties

On the easiest level the children are given objects that differ only in two or more attributes within one obvious dimension, such as objects of different colors or of different texture. In addition, the property by which objects are sorted is also shown by the container. A ready example are two containers, blue and red, into which blue and red objects, respectively, have to be placed.

Similarly, different textures can be sorted: rough styrofoam balls are put into rough styrofoam cups and smooth balls into smooth cups. In another game wooden objects go into wooden boxes and metal objects into metal boxes.[23]

6. Expose students to a variety of concrete problem solving situations that will help them understand the cause-and-effect relationship. Balancing on a board while catching a ball provides practice in both movement and thinking. In the process, many children recognize that if they acknowl-

[23]Hans G. Furth and Harry Wachs, *Thinking Goes to School: Piaget's Theory in Practice* (New York: Oxford University Press, 1975), p. 214.

edge gravity and use it more effectively, they will be in a better position to control their bodies. Social situations may also provide opportunities to see cause and effect operationally. A class that has made a group decision about the acquisition of a guinea pig soon recognizes that the animal is a responsibility and needs care on weekends as well as during school time. They must all share this responsibility and take turns in keeping the pet at their home.

RELATIONSHIPS BETWEEN LANGUAGE AND THINKING

The study of language development in children has undergone many changes in the last fifty years; the current research reflects a concern for the relationship between language and thinking. For a long time, researchers separated these two elements and directed their attention toward the variety in speech patterns and their relationship to culture. Little attention was given to the cognitive processes involved as children made the transition from simple to more complex language. Recently, however, the science of psycholinguistics has shown concern not only for what children *do* linguistically but what they *know* about what they do. Children's efforts to formulate language rules, discussed earlier in the chapter, are being analyzed as examples of how children integrate thought and language. For thinking about language must involve thinking about thinking. Metacognition is the term used by linguists.

Despite the brilliant work of several scholars on the relationship between thought and language, it is still difficult to make definitive statements on this subject. Language arts teachers, nevertheless, should keep abreast of any research that promises to increase our knowledge about the relationship between conceptual and linguistic development.

Some basic questions regarding this relationship are still to be answered:

(1) *Does language serve to catalyze the cognitive process?*

Johanna S. DeStefano in *Language, the Learner and the School* carefully explores the question.[24] The work of L. S. Vygotsky supports the view that words are not merely used to express thoughts; they are the means whereby thought comes into existence.[25] Jerome Bruner and Eric Lennenberg are in essential agreement with Vygotsky on this point. Bruner states that "in children between four and twelve, language comes to play an increasingly powerful role as an instrument of knowing."[26] Lennenberg is even more explicit; he contends that "a word may come to

[24]Johanna S. DeStefano, *Language, the Learner and the School* (New York: Wiley, 1978).

[25]Lev Semenovich Vygotsky, *Thought and Language* (Cambridge, Mass: M.I.T. Press, 1962).

[26]Jerome Bruner, "The Course of Cognitive Growth," in *Language in Education: A Source Book*, ed. A. Cashden and Elizabeth Grugion (London: Routledge & Kegan Paul, 1972), p. 165.

signal or stand for a concept, but the concept itself definitely antedates any linguistic label. In other words, if a child doesn't know the color orange, the word *orange* won't be in the child's vocabulary."[27]

The view that verbal training does not necessarily bring about conceptual understanding was supported in an experiment conducted by Sinclair and Barbel Inhelder.[28] It was found that though children received training and could learn all the verbal formulas about Piaget's principle of conservation, they were still not able to conserve. Teachers will frequently observe this phenomenon. For example, eight-year-old Kenny seems to speak confidently and fluently about dinosaurs using words that place them in a time long past. Yet when confronted with the question of whether or not his great-grandparents had to protect themselves against dinosaurs he is uncertain. His concept of time before he was born is not yet secure. Children know many more words than concepts. Furthermore, the child's concepts are frequently growing and changing while language is relatively speaking less fluid.

(2) *How does learning the language help a child in learning the concept?*

As children engage in a variety of experiences, they learn about their world. A fifth-grade class studying the customs of ancient Egypt is also learning the vocabulary associated with the subject. Such words as *tomb, pharaoh, hieroglyphics,* and *sarcophagus* will become words that the students can think and talk about and later use as tools to express concepts. "Failure to learn the language retards concept formation to a degree that prevents pupils from making progress in their knowledge and understanding of the subject."[29] Teachers often encounter a student who is unable to express clearly a concept that he or she seems to understand. Sometimes, the problem is that the student lacks the language to express the idea.

Language may also influence concept formation in a manner that some call "linguistic precedence."[30] The continuing misuse of language may distort a concept and, in this way, mold thinking. The young child who frequently hears stereotyped language applied to an ethnic group begins to use these words in the same erroneous context. What results is an array of distorted concepts that become very difficult to eradicate even when the logic of the thinking is challenged.

(3) *Can we assume a correlation between conceptual difficulty and linguistic difficulty?*

Many people "mouth" words for which they lack a conceptual understanding. Aware of this phenomenon, scholars like Paul Brandwein in science and Jerome Bruner in social studies have encouraged educators

[27]Quoted in DeStefano, *Language, the Learner and the School,* p. 65.

[28]DeStefano, *Language, the Learner and the School,* p. 66.

[29]Jill Richards, *Classroom Language: What Sort?* (London: George Allen & Unwin, 1978), p. 103.

[30]Smith, Goodman, and Meredith, *Language and Thinking,* p. 87.

EXPERIENCES FOR TEACHERS IN THE RELATIONSHIP BETWEEN LANGUAGE AND THINKING

1. Identify several scientific processes that are relatively easy to demonstrate for the young child but hard to convey to him or her linguistically.

2. List five metaphors—for example, *shoulder the burden, apple of her eye*—and note how the concept of each might be distorted by a child at the concrete stage of language and cognitive development.

3. Present an abstract concept like loneliness to elementary-school children. Ask them to write a story or tell you what the concept means. Note the language used. What judgments can you make about the children's thought level with this concept?

4. Try to get a picture of a child's mental imagery as a clue to his or her cognitive development. Ask the child to describe a dream or an experience. How rich is the language? The imagery?

to teach the fundamental structure of a subject by focusing on thinking and basic concepts rather than on the accumulation of isolated facts.

Though certain concepts may be easier to learn than others, it does not necessarily follow that the language associated with one is easier than the language associated with the other. Some language may be simple in a literal sense but may signify a difficult concept, for instance, proverbs such as "A stitch in time saves nine" or "The early bird gets the worm." In such cases, acquisition of the language is easier than acquisition of the concept.

Language may also be more complex than the concept it describes. A child may find it relatively easy to learn the principles underlying backgammon and still have trouble explaining how the game is played. The vocabulary may be unknown, and the language fluency required may be too great. The game may be more accessible conceptually than linguistically. Another example in which conceptual and linguistic difficulty may differ is illustrated in the case of the advanced reader. I heard a twelve-year-old girl discuss Hannah Green's *I Never Promised You a Rose Garden*. It was obvious that the student grasped the essential story but was really unable to appreciate Deborah's break with reality. The adolescent world was still beyond the reader's conceptual ability though within her reading ability.

Classroom Activities to Relate Language and Thinking

In the context of the relationship between cognition and language, certain additional factors are to be considered. Since it has been shown that different subjects and the great variety of experiences in an ever-shrinking multicultural world make varying linguistic and conceptual demands, it is important that teachers provide for and facilitate experiences in which the child's range, repertoire, and register are nourished. Register here refers to the language changes made by the speaker to fit the situation. A classroom that is rich linguistically fosters and respects individual language variability but at the same time attempts to prepare children for a world that uses concepts and language outside the familiar environment. Toward this end, a teacher should

1. Use records or live storytelling to illustrate the varieties of language styles. Here are some suggestions from different genres:

   Julius Lester, *The Knee-high Man and Other Tales.* Dial, 1972. (Black-American folktale.)
   A. A. Milne, *Winnie the Pooh.* Dell, 1970. (Humorous, literary language.)
   Eve Merriam, *Finding a Poem.* Atheneum, 1970. (A collection of poems that play with language.)

   Encourage children to talk about their reactions to the language and imitate the sound of the varying speech patterns, registers, and dialects.

2. Propose situations in which children can use and see the various purposes and levels of language:

   Your best friend comes to your house and says that he has run away from home. Speak to him about the situation. Discuss it with your mother. Explain the happening to the police when they come to look for him.

   You have lost a very valuable book from the class library. Discuss it with your friend, your teacher, the school librarian.

3. Raise questions about words that are of current interest: words in the political news, words from the arts, teenage language, kid talk. Encourage students to be involved in the clarification of word meanings that are relevant in their lives.

We can also help children make cognitive and linguistic connections by clarifying word meanings. Frequently, children have a different meaning for a word than we do. The greatest disparities usually involve abstract words that do not have a readily observable physical referent. It is important to help children become more precise, handle higher levels of abstraction, and recognize that meaning is very often contextual. Toward these goals, the teacher should

1. Have students create progressive lists of abstract words:

Most concrete	*Concrete*	*Least concrete*
A houseboat on a river	A houseboat	A house
A red flag	Red	A color

| A robin in a nest | A robin | A bird |
| You and me | Men and women | Humanity |

2. Ask students to illustrate abstract words with pictures and/or descriptive sentences. Help your students recognize that definitions and pictures will vary from person to person. The results may be bound together into individual or class books. Some possible beginnings are

   Fairness is . . .   Goodness is . . .

   Patience is . . .   Life is . . .

   Brotherhood is . . .   Love is . . .

3. Help students understand that certain subjects have special vocabularies in which familiar words often carry unusual meanings. Ask the children to provide at least two definitions of each word:

Set	(A mathematician's definition	(Your definition)
Chain reaction	(A scientist's definition)	
Cycle	(A business person's definition	
Ceiling	(An economist's definition	
Signal	(A Boy Scout's definition)	
Field	(A scientist's definition)	
Bank	(A geographer's definition)	
Media	(An artist's definition)	
Records	(An archaeologist's definition	
Shutter	(A photographer's definition)	

4. Expose students to literature that will help them develop a better understanding of abstract concepts. For example:

   Change—Pat Hutchins, *Changes, Changes*. Macmillan, 1973. (A wordless picture book.)

   Security—Julia Cunningham, *Dorp Dead*. Avon, 1980. (A sophisticated work for upper elementary grades.)

   Death—Judith Viorst, *The Tenth Good Thing About Barney*. Atheneum, 1975. (A good introduction to the topic.)

   Emotional problems—Richard Peck, *Father Figure*. Viking, 1978.

   Careers—Gloria and Esther Goldreich, *What Can She Be? A Newscaster*. Lothrop, 1973.

   Good and evil—Walter Wangerin, Jr., *The Book of the Dun Cow*. Harper & Row, 1978.

   Responsibility—Jörg Steiner, *Rabbit Island*. Harcourt Brace Jovanovich, 1978.

The Teacher and Language

A final word should be said about the language used by teachers as they help students develop their cognitive and linguistic skills. It is not always easy to adjust language to the appropriate level, and some teachers are more skillful than others in this regard. The research on this problem suggests the following guidelines:

1. In general, the language of learning needs to be simplified, and teachers should be more aware of their own language behavior.
2. Awareness of personal language behavior may take the form of:
   a. Explanation of the meaning of technical terms (using words that are less difficult and more familiar)
   b. Use of relatively short sentences
   c. Repetition of sentences carrying important basic concepts[31]

Getting to know the way we use language and how language generates knowledge is a major thrust of the Bullock Report.[32] This important British publication investigated literacy problems in England, accepting as a premise the interaction of the child's language behavior and other mental and perceptual powers. What language arts teachers might want to note is that this position led the majority of the Bullock Committee to conclude that all language functions (receptive and expressive) are equally important in conceptual growth, and that the learner's active participation is highly significant in all these functions. Therefore, many of the recommendations focus on assisting the pupils to expand their range of language experiences and uses. This emphasis, while making a greater demand on the teacher's skill, is being recognized on both sides of the Atlantic as not only desirable but crucial for language and concept development.

TEACHER COMPETENCES

In this chapter, four aspects of language and concept development have been considered. These four aspects are expressed as teaching competences in this section. A competence, in this context, is defined as a knowledge, skill, or attitude that the teacher can demonstrate at increasing levels of ability with students. (See Chapter 4 for a detailed discussion of competence-based education.)

1. The elementary language arts teacher demonstrates knowledge of the nature of language itself and the implications of this knowledge for classroom practice.

[31]These guidelines are adapted from Richards, *Classroom Language.*
[32]DES, *A Language for Life* (Bullock Report) (London: Her Majesty's Stationery Office, 1975).

2. The elementary language arts teacher demonstrates knowledge of various theories of language acquisition and development and their implications for classroom practice.

3. The elementary language arts teacher demonstrates knowledge of the process of conceptual development and the implications of this knowledge for classroom practice.

4. The elementary language arts teacher demonstrates knowledge of how language and thinking are related and the implications of this knowledge for classroom practice.

Afterview   Since teachers are always involved in teaching thinking, regardless of the subject, it is particularly important that they have a basic understanding of what happens during the thinking process. A knowledge of language and concept development can provide some significant clues. We begin to understand the connections between language and thinking at the theoretical level, but this relationship takes on a new dimension when teachers relate these theories to their own thinking strategies. As they do, they become more capable of identifying, with only minimal clues, the thinking stages and learning strategies of their students.

The seminal research in the field of learning provides some guideposts for understanding children's language development. However, applying them in the classroom is another matter. Many basic applications have been identified in this chapter. Among the most important is the recognition that language usage is developmental. The majority of children go through identifiable stages, but they do so when they are ready and at their own pace. Chronological age is only a clue, not an answer. As teachers, we should be aware of some of the basic principles in developmental learning; but we must also recognize that the definitive words on language and concept development are yet to be written.

WHEN YOU WANT TO KNOW MORE

1. Language development and concept development are reciprocal processes; however, children usually know more words than concepts. Identify situations in which learning the language can assist a child in learning the concept. Can you cite instances in which concept acquisition seems to precede language acquisition?

2. Observe the language behavior of several parents and their preschool children. Identify the helping strategies the parents use to assist their youngsters' language development.

3. Have the children in class play some games of chance or probability. (*Thinking Goes to School,* by Furth and Wachs, includes many suggestions for such games.) What do you notice about the desires and abilities of different students in this area?

4. Identify a child in what Piaget calls the "preoperational period" (usually ages two to seven). What do you notice about the child's ability to understand classifications? Which ones are understood?

IN THE CLASSROOM

1. Bring in some old etiquette books and readers. Have your students look for examples of how the language has changed. Prepare a chart entitled "Old and New Fashions in Words."

2. To develop children's natural inventiveness with language, encourage the analysis and the personal use of metaphor. Have your students identify films, songs, and sayings that use metaphors. How do the metaphoric and literal statements differ?

3. To help students grow conceptually, develop a series of open-ended questions for your class, questions that do not have right or wrong answers. Indicate to the class that you want to encourage as many ideas or solutions as possible. Use questions like, "What if . . . ?" "What might be done?" "How could you change the situation?"

4. Help children appreciate the variability of language by developing charts of key words in several languages. Such words as *mother, father, love,* and so on, reflect variability as well as similarity.

5. Bring to class several objects useful for expanding conceptual development. See how many concepts may be developed from a single object. For example, an egg may be used to develop many conceptual understandings.

6. Spend some private time with a child in the primary grades. Try to determine from conversations, drawings, and so on, what he or she understands about such subjects as time, space, Piaget's principle of conservation. Repeat the procedure with a child in the middle grades. Summarize and compare the results.

SUGGESTED READINGS

Ausubel, David P. *The Psychology of Meaningful Verbal Learning.* New York: Grune & Stratton, 1963.

Brearley, Molly, ed. *The Teaching of Young Children: Some Applications of Piaget's Learning Theory.* New York: Schocken Books, 1970.

Britton, James. *Language and Learning.* Coral Gables, Fla: University of Miami Press, 1970.

Brown, Roger. *A First Language: The Early Stages.* Cambridge, Mass.: Harvard University Press, 1973.

Dale, Phillip S. *Language Development: Structure and Function,* 2d ed. New York: Holt, Rinehart & Winston, 1976.

Gagne, R. M. *The Conditions of Learning.* New York: Holt, Rinehart & Winston, 1970.

Halliday, M. A. K. *Explorations in the Functions of Language.* New York: Elsevier, 1973.

Labov, William. "The Logic of Nonstandard English" In *Report of the Twentieth Annual Round Table Meeting on Linguistics and Language Studies,* edited by J. E. Alatis. Monograph Series on Language and Linguistics. Washington, D.C.: Georgetown University Press, 1970.

Piaget, Jean. *The Language and Theory of the Child,* 3rd ed., rev. London: Routledge & Kegan Paul, 1959.

Rosen, Connie and Harold. *The Language of Primary School Children.* Baltimore, Md.: Penguin, 1973.

Shefer, Robert E. "The Work of Joan Tough: A Case Study in Applied Linguistics," *Language Arts* 55, no. 3 (March 1978): 308–14, 372. Also see bibliography.

Weeks, Thelma E. *Born to Talk.* Rowley, Mass.: Newbury House Publishers, 1979.

Other Materials

Piaget and Language Arts. Los Angeles: JAB Press. (One cassette tape.)

CHAPTER 3

The Language Arts and the Curriculum

Preview   This chapter will focus on the integrative role of the language arts. The first section will emphasize how we use language to create thinking connections. Though curriculum areas and separate disciplines are convenient organizational structures, language cannot be confined to these arbitrary patterns. Life is not lived in discrete curriculum areas. In the second part of this chapter, activities will be suggested that highlight the ways in which various disciplines use language and the ways in which these disciplines serve as springboards for language growth. A brief section will be devoted to the topic of languages within a language, an important contemporary issue that will be explored in greater depth in subsequent chapters. Throughout, the chapter will emphasize teacher and student awareness of the dynamic role of language in thinking and learning.

AUDREY JONAS, the teacher of a second-grade class, is developing a social studies unit on her school's neighborhood. The children have painted pictures and written stories and poems about how to make the community a better place in which to live. The students are responsible for developing bulletin boards, and a new one is being planned to deal with community problems. "What might be a good title for this bulletin board?" Ms. Jonas asks; an active discussion ensues, and two titles are agreed upon. The children begin the preparation for the display. What curriculum areas are involved? Are the children learning social studies or language arts? What communication skills are being developed?

Ed Jackson is helping his fifth-grade class understand how sound is produced. For the past three weeks, the children have consulted a number of books, constructed their own instruments, and "played" the many instruments available in the classroom. Some of the students have reported their findings. What is being learned, science or language arts?

A sixth-grade class is planning a Japanese garden as a contribution to the school beautification program. Guiding a class discussion of this project, the teacher asks, "How shall we go about it?" Many suggestions are offered, and two children record all the ideas, but no judgments are made. A small committee is selected to review all the possibilities. Its members report back to the larger group and plans are formulated for the garden. The children raise some questions: "What does a Japanese garden look like?" "What weather conditions are necessary?" "How many plants will we need?" "What is a *bonsai?*" From what curriculum area are the answers likely to come? Science? Mathematics? Language arts? Social studies?

COMMUNICATING IDEAS WITHOUT CURRICULAR BOUNDARIES

Obviously, the acquisition of knowledge and the development of communication skills are not confined to one curriculum area. An inescapable interdependence exists among the fields of learning. Whether or not teachers consciously direct attention to the language arts, these skills remain central to the curriculum. The reasons for this are

1. Language is the means for structuring and thinking about existence.
2. The language arts are essential for success in all other curriculum areas.
3. Success at language provides children with a sense of their own power to understand and re-create their world.

4. Linguistic expression offers a necessary release of emotion.

5. Enduring language patterns are developed in the early years of life.

6. The skills of communication are the skills of living.

Words as Concept Hooks

Think of a single word or phrase whose original meaning has been expanded in present-day usage. What comes to mind are words with strong visual images that can be applied in different contexts: words such as *orchestrate, trade-off, double play,* and *beautiful.* These words are so rich that they are able to give form to our concepts and serve as shortcuts in the expression of complicated ideas in many different areas. More important, words such as these can provide us with a structural framework for our concepts. Such words may be referred to as concept hooks. Through these special words, teachers can help children see the connections and classifications that are essential for organizing knowledge; frequently, a single word or phrase of this sort is so complete that it can embody a whole category of ideas.

Edward de Bono, the author of *Wordpower* and an authority in the field of creative thinking, has identified a number of words that might be considered concept hooks.[1] Their meanings usually extend beyond most dictionary definitions, and they have been appropriated by fields as diverse as business, education, and systems management. Consider the terms *strategy, game playing,* and *dialogue.* The usable meanings of these terms are so diverse that they can function as pegs for broad concepts and ideas in many areas.

Youngsters very early in their school careers should be given activities that will enable them to discover how very exciting working with words can be. Identifying words as concept hooks will encourage children to talk about the "real" meanings of the words they use. What does it mean, for example, to be *cool*? With your friends? With your family? With the teacher? As they recognize the many non-dictionary meanings for words, youngsters begin to develop totally new conceptual bundles and thus add to their reservoir of language.

Words that function as concept hooks provide exciting work play activities as children transfer terms from one curriculum area to another. The word *family* usually brings to mind a small group of adults and children. The word takes on a new dimension when we speak of "the family of man." Many scientists refer to all life on earth as "the living family." Mathematicians use the word *family* to group number concepts: "the tens family."

Consider the versatility of the word *mapping* in different curriculum areas. Mapping is most often encountered by young students as they deal

[1]Edward de Bono, *Wordpower* (New York: Harper & Row, 1977).

with the geographical aspects of social studies. Children learn to read maps, identify physical features, and draw maps of their classroom and neighborhood. In an interesting study, Stanley Milgram, a professor of psychology, discovered that people design their own mental maps of the areas in which they live, giving greatest importance to things that are personally meaningful.[2]

Taking a cue from Milgram, you might ask your students to do this sort of cerebral cartography. How do the children see their school in relationship to the neighborhood? Ask them to make a map of the areas most important to them. If the school were destroyed and had to be rebuilt, how would they arrange the new school? What are the boundaries of their neighborhood?

Ask the children to make a map of the human body showing only those parts that are most important to them. What systems in their bodies would they show on the map? Are they just a big head? All heart? A bundle of arms and legs? One big digestive system?

Focus on the sense of the word *map* in the context of *putting on the map:* "President Carter put Plains, Georgia, on the map." Consider the phrase *off the map*, meaning out of existence: "New technological advances have just about taken horse and buggy transportation off the map." Discuss instances in which an individual might need to *map out* a strategy.

Bridge is another word that may challenge the children's thinking and serve as a concept hook. Let your students begin by constructing a physical bridge of wood or paper. They can then go on to discuss the many bridges that exist between different types of animals. What bridges exist from one generation to another? In what team sports are human bridges apparent? How does a football team bridge the distance to the goal? On what occasion might people use their own bodies to construct a human bridge? Children will think of many other possibilities. Not only do we use language in all disciplines but the language of each discipline can be exploited to establish conceptual connections. Metaphors provide one obvious opportunity.

Metaphors as Linguistic Bridges

Many people assume that metaphors are the exclusive property of the poet and the creative writer; however, even a cursory study reveals that metaphors pervade almost everyone's daily communication. The language of the media is highly metaphoric, often filling the need for a shortcut to meaning. We hear and read about "the rat race," "the fever of despair," "the tide of events," and so on.

Simply stated, metaphors are comparisons, very often between unlike

[2]Susana Duncan, "Mental Maps of New York," *New York Magazine*, 19 December 1977, pp. 51–59.

objects or ideas. The book *Happiness Is a Warm Puppy,* by Charles M. Schulz, which has sold millions of copies, is simply a collection of metaphors for children, each metaphor juxtaposing a state of being (happiness) against a variety of seemingly unrelated entities.[3] Happiness is things—"two kinds of ice cream," "pizza with sausage"; happiness is accomplishments—"finding a pencil," "learning to whistle," "telling the time"; and happiness is situations—"walking hand in hand," "keeping a secret," "having a friend." By comparing the abstraction, happiness, to something more concrete, the book focuses on the elusive. Students might be given the opportunity to do this by completing sentences that begin with similar abstractions:

Hope is _____.   Fear is _____.

Beauty is _____.   Death is _____.

Skill with metaphor has little to do with age or maturity. In fact, sometimes youth has an advantage. Youngsters have not yet developed the language restrictions imposed by a lifetime of ponderous clichés. Devising a metaphor is only a matter of allowing imagination to take over. Nancy Larrick's *Green Is Like a Meadow of Grass* is a collection of beautiful metaphors written by children. Its young poets suggest "trees and bushes, putting on nightgowns of snow," "shells that are white wings," "rooftops are chalk boards," and "daffodils are pieces of the sun that have fallen to the ground."[4] Their allusions are fresh, vivid pictures for the reader.

Ordinary classroom activities provide many opportunities for teachers and students to devise and recognize metaphorical expressions. A good place to begin is with the world of advertising, for Madison Avenue is particularly skillful in tying together unlike ideas.

Consider these successful advertisements with your class:

"There is only one Joy." (a perfume)

"You deserve the best." (a diamond)

"Be a beautiful dreamer." (a nightgown)

"Put a tiger in your tank." (gasoline)

"We keep a smile on Mother Nature's Face." (Pacific Gas & Electric Co.)

Ask your students to cut out other printed advertisements that use the metaphoric mode. Explain that the metaphor does not have to be verbal. The ingenuity of the advertising world is that it develops associations pictorially. The visual metaphor is often a beautiful woman with a particular car, washing machine, or brand of cigarettes. Though not directly stated, the subliminal suggestion is that having the commodity brings one closer to her. Beauty . . . but only if you buy the product.

Songwriters, like ad writers, use metaphorical language to link reality

---

[3]Charles M. Schultz, *Happiness Is a Warm Puppy* (New York: Determined Productions, 1962).

[4]Nancy Larrick, ed., *Green Is Like a Meadow of Grass: An Anthology of Children's Pleasure in Poetry* (Champaign, Ill.: Garrard Publishing House, 1966).

and illusion: "Windmills of My Mind," "Time in a Bottle," "Heart of Stone," "The Hungry Years." Children can be encouraged to make up their own song titles in addition to collecting commercial ones. Have them note how an abstraction like time or love is made real by comparison with a concrete object.

Metaphors can also be studied for the insight they offer regarding social values. What do the following metaphors tell about social attitudes?

Sex Roles

"She's only a bird in a gilded cage."
"My heart belongs to Daddy."
"Love is blind."
"Fly me, I'm Janet."

Politics

the Cold War
the domino theory
armchair diplomacy
back-room politics
the "Yellow Peril"
the Iron Curtain countries

Education and Psychology

Head Start
body language
marriage encounter
open education

Metaphors, some say, are celebrations of creative consciousness; they extend the network of possibilities in thinking and feeling.[5] Metaphors free us from the "real meanings" of big words and provide a personalized understanding of language. For example, in an exhibit at the Smithsonian Institution's National Museum of Design in New York, artistic metaphors were used to develop creative thinking about the city. In photographs and drawings, the city was visualized as a series of systems: a sewer system, a subway system, a power system, a school system.[6] You might ask your students to devise their own metaphoric representations of their locality. Machines (a car) or organisms (a human body) that have involved systems could also be metaphorically represented (Figure 3-1). Continue this approach and substitute the word *structure* for *system*. Help the students to design metaphors that relate the word *structure* in different contexts to the human body (bone structure), the city (street structure), a mechanism (frame structure), or an animal (turtle shell).

Ask your students to verbally and artistically devise metaphors involving such words as *blooming* and *protecting*. Show pictures of a flower

[5]Bob Samples, *The Metamorphic Mind: A Celebration of Creative Consciousness* (Reading, Mass.: Addison-Wesley, 1976).

[6]O. M. Ungers, "City Metaphors," in *Man transForms* (Washington, D.C.: Smithsonian Institution, 1976), pp. 112–113.

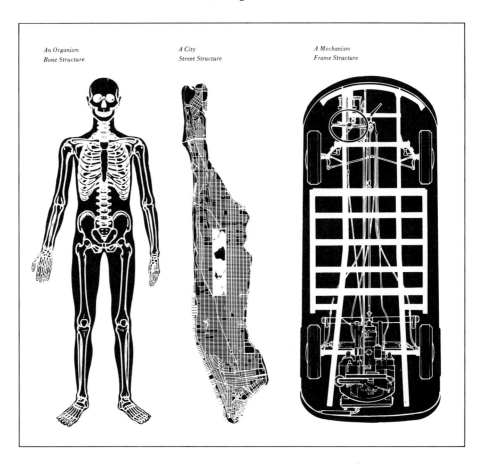

An Organism
Bone Structure

A City
Street Structure

A Mechanism
Frame Structure

3-1   From "City Metaphors" by O. M. Ungers for *MAN transFORMS*, an exhibition sponsored by The Johnson Wax Company at the Cooper-Hewitt Museum, the Smithsonian Institution's National Museum of Design, October 1976.

blooming, a city blooming, a person blooming. How does a city protect itself? A turtle? A person?

In the preceding discussion of metaphors have you stopped to consider the matter of curriculum area? Probably not. For the very nature of metaphorical thinking requires that we jump cognitively wherever imagination takes us.

Life Is Not in Curriculum Areas

Education should be a preparation for life, and life is not lived in separate curriculum areas. Consider this typical morning for many elementary-school children. Andrew, an eight year old, awakens, looks at his clock, and glances out the window to see a snow-covered world. "Where does it all come from?" he wonders. After dressing himself, Andrew goes into the kitchen for breakfast and helps his mother prepare the orange juice. He empties the can of frozen orange concentrate into a pitcher and adds three cans of water to it. While eating breakfast, he reads the offer on the cereal box for a mechanical car. He cuts out and completes the coupon, addresses and stamps the envelope. During this time, the radio has been tuned to the news, and Andrew hears of the president's visit to Asia, a disastrous fire in Las Vegas, and an earthquake in Italy. "Where is Italy?" Andrew wonders. His mother gives him money for lunch, reminding him to bring home the correct change. Before leaving for school, Andrew helps his older sister shovel the driveway. In what curriculum areas has Andrew been functioning? Certainly all the language arts have pervaded his morning. An observable physical phenomenon, snow, has heightened both his scientific and aesthetic sensibilities. Mathematically, he has been challenged by real situations: telling time, counting the cans of water, assessing the car. While shoveling the snow, he has learned about what his body can do as well as the way a simple tool (the shovel) operates to make work easier. Andrew's early morning hours have been highly integrated. What will the rest of the day be like?

The Integrated Day

First adopted by the British infant schools, the concept of the *integrated day* has achieved considerable acceptance in American education as part of the system known as *open education*. As the phrase suggests, the integrated day represents an alternative to teaching arrangements that separate curriculum areas into separate time-restricted packages. Whether designing mobiles, manipulating Cuisinaire rods, or preparing a puppet show, students in open classrooms are expected to be developing skills in more than one curriculum area. Many of these skills are language related, the students' activities requiring that each child submit his or her responses to the group.

As children go through the integrated day they are not made aware of curriculum areas. The teacher does not announce, "We will now do our science lesson." Science is not set apart from the rest of the curriculum. Hence, the following account of classroom activity is more likely:

> Five children are watching the behavior of two hamsters. They write down their observations after much discussion among themselves. A task card has instructed them to weigh and measure the hamsters and mark this information on the chart. They are also recording the hamsters' activity in a five-minute period. They are learning how a scientist works. Sometime later, the children will be encouraged to draw or paint their impressions of the hamsters, factually state the animals' physical characteristics, write about their feelings as they hold them, comment on sex differences, and generally continue to get pleasure out of watching them eat, sleep, and play.

A cornerstone of the open classroom is aesthetic sensibility, which is not necessarily demonstrated through visible artistic accomplishments. Every child cannot be a great artist. "What makes art so important," says Charles E. Silberman, "is that it embodies and unites affective and cognitive experiences and responses. In a sense, art can be defined as the expression of ideas about feeling."[7] In like manner, the experience with the hamsters can heighten a child's sensory awareness and continue to extend perception beyond the concerns of science.

The Newspaper and Its Integrative Function

The newspaper, a major means of communication, illustrates how one aspect of curriculum can be linked to another, both in format and content. Consider these headlines: "Arabs increase price of oil;" "Indians lose suit to regain land on Cape Cod;" "Rain tomorrow;" "Phillies win pennant;" "Farmers ask the President for help." Even for first graders, these issues can be broadly conceived. In a discussion of increased oil costs and the ensuing shortages, students can be asked to consider the effects on their own lives: "Do you remember when we extended the Christmas vacation last year in order to save money on the school heating bill?" "What are some of the ways in which your family can save fuel?" "What can our school do?" They might draw pictures or prepare experience charts about the importance of oil in their lives. Older students might do research on the question of new energy sources. Knowledge from different disciplines will contribute to the child's understanding. Science and social studies may predominate in these activities, but they will all be conducted through the language arts.

Most young schoolchildren are not prepared to read the more sophistiticated newspapers. The text may be too difficult, and much of the information seems remote from their experience. Similar information may be gained from a good children's newspaper, but the number and types of items covered in these publications is often very limited. Thus, it becomes the teacher's responsibility to help children see the relevance of issues removed from their experiences. Recognizing "the difficulty children have in engaging in the abstract, cognitive operations involved in ideological thought," the teacher should try to personalize the knowledge.[8] How, for example, can the continuing problems of the American Indian be made understandable to the elementary-school child? The answer lies in approaching the material at the children's experiential level. The situation may be related to their own ethnic backgrounds, personal experiences with inequality, or the surrounding physical environment.

[7]Charles E. Silberman, "The Role of the Arts," in *The Open Classroom Reader*, ed. Charles E. Silberman (New York: Random House, Vintage Books, 1973), p. 750.

[8]Fred I. Greenstein, *Children and Politics* (New Haven: Yale University Press, 1965), p. 77.

Here are some additional classroom activities in which the newspaper can be used as a springboard to language growth and as a way of highlighting the natural relationships among academic areas:

1. Have children bring old newspapers from home. Help them to identify the many sections in the newspaper. They can then cut and share clippings from different newspapers and begin to set up their own sections. An article on new pollution devices in automobiles may fit into a section on ecology, science, transportation, or leisure activities.

    Rationale: Since many items can be classified in more than one way, practice at classification helps students sharpen their understanding of terms and linguistic relationships. (Hilda Taba's *Thinking in the Elementary School* suggests a helpful strategy for teaching classification.)

2. Bring in or have children find reports of the same story in different publications. In what ways are the reports different? How does one judge the authenticity of the reports? What is the background of the writer? The publication? How do the interests of the writer and the publication influence the content? What evidence is offered? Are the inferences reasonable given the evidence?

    Rationale: Language is a tool for making inferences. As children recognize the logical implications of the information that they receive, their decoding abilities (listening and reading) will improve. They will begin to encode (speak and write) more carefully, becoming more precise in their interpretation of the words.

3. Have children collect newspaper articles about events that occur in other parts of the country or the world. Ask them to discuss the probable effects of these events on their own lives.

    Rationale: The ability to see relationships is an important language skill. As children discover concepts like interdependency, they are preparing themselves to appreciate the universal qualities evidenced in great literature as well as social studies.

In summary, the newspaper can be integrative in several ways: it can be both a curriculum and an approach; and, used in the continuing identification of relationships, it can facilitate the blending of curriculum areas. Effective use of the newspaper in teaching can provide students with relevant, personally meaningful content about which to communicate. A variety of language skills will be utilized in their responses to events of local, national, and international importance.

EXPLORING THE RELATIONSHIPS BETWEEN LANGUAGE ARTS AND OTHER CURRICULUM AREAS

Language proficiency is essential for achievement in all curriculum areas. A number of studies relate language development to total school achievement.[9] This is not surprising, for it is through language that we share our cognitive, aesthetic, and emotional experience. What is surprising is that so few teachers highlight the pervasiveness of our linguistic debt. So far this chapter has focused on the conceptual pathways that students and teachers travel to find meaning. In the pages that follow, the focus will be on curricular activities that highlight the relationships between the language arts and other curriculum areas. Following the Brunerian approach, the activities revolve around selected basic concepts or big ideas that are central to a broad understanding.[10]

Language and Social Studies

Social studies can mean listening to directions for making a Navajo drum, looking at a film about local government, or engaging in role playing to clarify an economic concept. In any case, the skills of communication are involved. Listed below are suggested social studies activities that offer excellent opportunities for the simultaneous development and reinforcement of language skills:

(1) **The Big Idea**   Human experience is continuous and integrated.[11]

   The Activity   *Our Local History*
                          The children prepare a local history of their community. Help them to recognize how they will gather the necessary information:

                          Listening: Interviews with older residents

                          Seeing: Visible structures in the neighborhood (buildings, churches, statues, tombstones)

                          Reading: Tombstone inscriptions, historical markers, legal records

                          Discovery: Artifacts, old photographs, memorabilia

                          The following questions can be used to catalyze thinking:

                          —How does the past history of this community influence our life today?
                          —What would this community be like if it were settled only fifty years ago?

[9]The most comprehensive of these studies, *Language Development: Kindergarten Through Grade Twelve*, was completed by Walter Loban (Urbana, Ill.: National Council of Teachers of English, 1976). See also the work of Roger Brown and Ruth Strickland in this area.

[10]Jerome S. Bruner, *The Process of Education* (Cambridge, Mass.: Harvard University Press, 1960).

[11]The "Big Ideas" in this section are adaptations of basic concepts from Ralph C. Preston and Wayne L. Herman in *Teaching Social Studies in the Elementary School* (New York: Holt, Rinehart & Winston, 1974).

Language Arts Skills	Interviewing, note taking, reading, research and reporting, creative writing

(2) **The Big Idea**   Conflicts result from the unlimited nature of human needs and wants and the limited nature of human and environmental resources.

The Activity   *An Ecological Brainstorm*
Introduce a unit on ecology by surveying what information the children have on the topic. Divide the class into small groups to "brainstorm" the ecology issue. What do they know about the topic? What are the major environmental problems? What are some possible solutions?

Stress that you are seeking as many responses as possible. At the outset, a recorder for each group should list *all* the ideas. After a short period of time, one or two children can select and combine those ideas that seem most worthy of further exploration. They later report back to the larger group for alterations and further suggestion. (See Chapter 9 for further discussion of brainstorming.)

Language Arts Skills   Listening for details, discussion, recording, sorting information

(3) **The Big Idea**   *Human beings are more alike than different.*

The Activity   *A Folktale Fest*
Read to the class a variety of folktales from different cultures. Ask the students to note what values are expressed. What do the people in the folktale believe? Whether the tale is Chinese, Indian, or African, invariably an emphasis on love and the transience of material objects will emerge. Repeat the process with recordings or student storytellers, and encourage the children to uncover those details that focus on the universal qualities of human beings.

Language Arts Skills   Listening for specific details, speaking, storytelling, classifying

Language and Science

Young children approach life like research scientists. They look, touch, taste, smell, and listen; they hypothesize, use trial and error, and verify through repeated experimentation. Characterized by insatiable curiosity, they demand to know "Why," sometimes asking the same questions that perplexed primitive peoples: "Where does the sun go after it sets?" "Why does it rain?" "Will an object always fall down when I throw it up in the air?" In small, successive steps, an attempt is made to impose form on a world that originally seemed formless. The child, like the scientist, seeks out firsthand encounters to feed his or her desire to know. In the school setting, it becomes the responsibility of the teacher to provide the environment, guidance, and materials that will facilitate the child's discovering. In order to unlock scientific mysteries, the child must have within grasp a number of thinking and language skills. He or she must be able to

—formulate questions

—recognize sequence

—make inferences from experience and observation

—classify information

—record information

—identify and find solutions to problems

As the child's intellectual maturity increases, he or she will be expected to go to more difficult sources, questioning and challenging each with vigor.

Listed below are a sampling of science activities, each related to a big scientific idea.[12] For each activity, several related language arts skills are noted.

(1) **The Big Idea**

The organism is a product of its heredity and environment.

The Activity

You Are What You Eat: Food Preservatives
This activity combines science and the skills of classification. Students are asked to bring in labels of contents from cereal boxes, cans, and bread wrappers. Each label is examined to determine if the product contains artificial preservatives. Specific preservatives are identified, and each product is classified according to their presence or absence. Charts can be developed. Children can consult references for experimental evidence that indicates the effects of preservatives on the body.

Language Arts Skills

Reading for specific details, classification skills

(2) **The Big Idea**

Human beings harness energy to perform a wide variety of functions.

The Activity

Toys and Energy
"Structure" an open-ended situation by providing children with many toys. Ask them to bring move-

---

[12]Paul Brandwein's basic structure for science lessons served as the frame of reference for these activities.

able toys from home. Set the scene to discover the facts about motion by supplying some toys that are moved by motors and others that are moved by batteries or wound-up springs. Another group of toys can be moved by a push or pull motion. Prompt the children to raise questions about their experience with the toys. Raise questions about the source of energy and suggest ways of finding answers to these questions.

Language Arts Skills   Identifying and expressing problems, problem solving approaches

(3) **The Big Idea**   *Life and living things change over the years.*

The Activity   *Spinoff to the Space Age*
The purpose of this activity is to encourage children to personalize and write intelligently about the world of the twenty-first-century. In order to respond, they will have to do some research on the topic. While developing a twenty-first-century futuristic vocabulary, they might even prepare a dictionary. They can be asked to respond in writing to one or more of the following questions:

—How will you look in the next century? Will it be necessary to dress differently?
—What will be the effects of pollution on the human body? On animals and plants? On daily life style?
—How will advances in medical science affect you?
—In what ways will new technology change your life?

Language Arts Skills   Vocabulary development, research methods, written expression, making inferences.

Language and Aesthetics

The whole of life enters the elementary-school classroom. In this setting, children can discover an aesthetic world that holds out to them the promise of imaginative, personal growth. Yet early on in many classrooms, something happens that numbs youngsters, forces them into a lock step, and transmits the message that learning is a grim affair. Sometimes this result is due to neglect of the sensory faculties in an attempt to emphasize the "basics." Many children respond to this approach with visible terror. Something natural in them has been tampered with, and they cope by falling into a semi-sleep in which their feelings become dormant.

That our feeling and rational faculties are mutually supportive is not a new idea, but it bears repeating. Human beings function as organic wholes, and the food for feeling is also the food for thinking. The pathways to cognition pass through the territory of the senses, and ideas must first engage the spirit of the learner.

Teaching the whole being means encouraging a child to use the body, the senses, the emotions, and the mind. Children who pretend at balancing their bodies on imaginary surfboards, feeling the waves beneath, are developing new ways of seeing. Youngsters alive to the early morning smells and sounds in their homes are growing new eyes. Every activity that invites children to look more closely, feel more deeply, and think more accurately is simultaneously expanding their vision. Suddenly there will be something to say, a reason to communicate. There has been an impression, expression will follow.

Since the skills of communication depend upon seeing with all our eyes, children should be encouraged to use their senses. Teachers will quickly realize that simultaneously the mind is receiving rich nourishment. Experiences with movement underscore this message. Children have motion built into their bodies. As they use their muscles to jump, climb, and balance, and as they delight in these powers, they are achieving a new understanding of the world aesthetically, physically, and intellectually. The insights emerge from the totality of the experience. Nothing happens alone. How organismic it all is!

An exciting by-product for teachers who encourage sensory awareness in students is that they themselves get a second chance—a chance to go back to that magical time before the long sleep. It is through young eyes that we can reawaken. Jean Henri Fabré, the French naturalist, says it well: "What matters in learning is not to be taught, but to wake up."

Aesthetic experiences are wake-up experiences. In the section that follows, activities will be suggested that strengthen the skills of seeing and sensing. An underlying goal is the education of whole human beings, students who will develop into creative engineers, understanding physicians, sensitive technicians, and cooperative citizens.

(1) **The Big Idea**	*Aesthetic experiences can increase identification and empathy with others.*
The Activity	*Be the Animal* This activity attempts to heighten awareness of things and animals as a way of increasing identification and empathy with people.
	Read *Sylvester and the Magic Pebble,* by William Steig, the story of a loveable donkey who finds a magic pebble and turns himself into a rock. The cartoon-style illustrations offer the child many opportunities to interpret the feelings of Sylvester and his saddened family.

Ask the children to listen for words that provide clues as to how the characters feel. Some questions and activities that might increase empathy include:

—What do you think it feels like to be a donkey? Pretend that you are one.
—What would it feel like to bite off some grass? Pretend to do it.
—Were you concerned about Sylvester? Why?

Other books that might be read and discussed in order to develop the students' empathetic powers include Bernard Waber's *Loveable Lyle* and Marjorie Weinman Sharmat's *Edgemont*.

Language Arts Skills   Listening for details, finding main ideas, following sequence of events

(2) The Big Idea   *Movement, like other aesthetic experiences, serves as a means of expression as well as an emotional release.*

The Activity   *Body Language: Pantomime*
Since experiences in movement should be part of any school curriculum, opportunities should be provided for children to speak with their bodies. The following tasks can provide a beginning:

—"I turn on the television to watch my favorite program and find that the set is broken."
—"I write a letter of complaint."
—"I dry the dishes in a hurry."
—"I wash the car to surprise my father."

Pantomimes should be repeated. Discussion should follow each task to alert students to the ways their bodies might better convey the message.
Questions help:

—Why were you doing the task?
—Where was it taking place?
—How did you feel?

Have children suggest other situations that will demonstrate how movement, the language of the body, communicates as well as words.

Language Arts Skills   Listening, observing details, noting relationships.

Language and Mathematics

A child who does not understand the language of a mathematics problem cannot possibly find the solution. But much more than the ability to read is required. For this reason, practice in solving mathematical problems should begin as soon as the child can decode, or derive meaning from, the spoken word. Mrs. Burton shares a problem with her kindergartners:

"Laurie and Joseph are building in the block corner. Four children can play there. How many more children can we send there? How will we know when we have the four children?" (The children may respond by just looking or counting to find out, but they will react verbally.) Mr. Snyder poses a different problem to his first-grade class: "As I tell you the story of 'Henny Penny,' listen for each new animal that is mentioned. Use your animal cutouts to show each animal. At the end, I will want to know how many animals were in the story. Careful listening will help you to find out." Both teachers are trying to help their students appreciate information, whether it is given or whether they must discover it for themselves. Skillful questioning is required. Students must ultimately learn to ask themselves the questions that a teacher might ask: "What is missing?" "What details are important?" "How can I summarize the problem in my own words?" Teachers are tempted to always provide the answers, and some do, consciously or unconsciously (by pointing or voice emphasis). But if we want children to increase their mathematical and conceptual powers, we must encourage them in problem solving but let them do their own thinking.

The relationship between mathematics and the language arts comes about very naturally. Children listen to number series, they are drilled in multiplication, they read problems, and they write in set notation. All of this is preceded by the physical involvement of the child with a sensory world. Contemporary approaches to mathematics reflect a Piagetian persuasion in their tendency to require that students "do" more and teachers "show" less. The emphasis is on the child's independent discovery of mathematical principles through "hands on" experiences with a variety of concrete objects. In a setting that encourages the manipulation of materials, children observe, measure, sort, classify, solve problems, take notes, discover new vocabulary, and identify logical sequences. Simultaneously, mathematics and language become intertwined.

In any elementary-school class, mathematical and language abilities range across a wide spectrum. Since success in mathematics may or may not be functionally related to level of language development, an accurate assessment of a child's competence in each area is essential. It frequently becomes necessary to individualize instruction by providing settings, materials, and strategies designed to meet specific abilities. An effective setting for diagnosing and meeting individual needs is the learning center. In this environment, which will be discussed at greater length in Chapter 14, the teacher may work with individual children or with small groups.

At the elementary-school level, materials for teaching mathematical principles should fill the classroom. As children handle Cuisinaire rods, measure liquids, construct geodesic domes, arrange discs, use number lines, and manipulate fractional parts, they will be discovering mathematics and the appropriate language for naming objects and communicating findings. The classroom should be a storehouse of things to count, measure, weigh, compare, and contrast. Both real objects (pennies, shells, buttons, marbles, nuts) and representative materials (discs, rods, squared material, multibased blocks) will serve as learning materials.

Children's books (non-texts) can also be a very helpful resource. Unlike a text, an entire trade book may be devoted to the explanation of one or two concepts. By providing graphic examples and a variety of approaches, the trade book can clarify concepts that the test cannot cover in great detail. For example, Robert Froman's *Less Than Nothing Is Really Something*, which has a picture-book format, is successful at explaining negative integers to children. There are a number of good trade books that help children become familiar with different shapes. Among the best is Ethel and Leonard Kessler's *Are You Square?* Some excellent counting books are also available; in *Count and See*, Tana Hoban uses a series of photographs to reinforce the child's concept of number. For the older student, the sense of time is explored in a fascinating book by Seymour Simon, *The Secret Clocks: Time Senses of Living Things*.

The vocabulary of mathematics is often abstract. Symbols abound and concepts may seem remote to the young child. For this reason, it is necessary for the teacher to adapt and relate language and concepts to the child's previous experiences. The word "set" is meaningless until it is related to a specific collection of objects. Things like a set of dishes or a set of blocks are within the child's experience. Classroom activities will uncover such sets as: a *school* of fish, a *flock* of birds, a *herd* of cattle, a *swarm* of bees. You might want to look at *A Gaggle of Geese*, a delightful book by Eve Merriam that identifies unusual words for groups of animals, birds, and fish: "a kindle of kittens," "an exaltation of larks," "a smack of jellyfish."

The concept of the light-year is clarified only by providing examples of the distance that light can travel in a given time, to and from a specific place. Numbers remain arbitrary symbols until they are related to the real world of things. The process of giving meaning to abstract principles is initially a language task. Mathematical terminology may help, but it is through concrete materials and reinforcement throughout the school year that young students are able to appreciate the abstraction.

The following sample activities focus on developing basic mathematical understanding while recognizing the child's ability to conceptualize and use language effectively as the starting point:

(1) **The Big Idea**   *Number names serve to concretely identify the "idea" of number. Every number has many names (2, two, II). There is a difference between an object and a symbol for an object.*[13]

Activity   *Number Names around the School*
After taking a class of children for a walk around

---

[13]The "Big Ideas" in this section are adapted from *Mathematics, Pre-Kindergarten, Kindergarten, Grade One*, Part 1, Curriculum Bulletin No. 6a (New York: Board of Education, City of New York: 1966).

the school, have them write down all the number names they have seen (Exit One, Room 204, class 4-2, Second Floor, P.S. 152, Milk 25¢). Write these numbers on the blackboard, then erase them. Have the children note that only the recorded symbols, the number names, have been erased, not the locations of the places.

Ask the children to make up rhyming oral jingles about the number names:

On the door,   Exit one,
It says 204.   We'll all have fun.

Older children should be able to find less obvious examples of number names around the school (roman numerals showing date of school construction, numbers on machinery). They can also identify other symbols—markings on a musical scale and the notes they represent, names for colors and the colors they represent.

Language Arts Skills   Rhyming, speaking, writing

(2) **The Big Idea**   *A set is a collection of objects, similar or dissimilar, that are being considered a unit. Sets serve to unify mathematics.*

Activity   *Naming Sets*
Have the students select a name for a set whose elements are:

—Mars, Earth, Saturn, Pluto, Neptune, Venus, Jupiter, Uranus, Mercury (planets or heavenly bodies)
—Charlotte, Wilbur, Templeton, Fern (characters in *Charlotte's Web*)
—infielder, shortstop, pitcher, catcher (players on a baseball team)
—president, senator, mayor, governor (government officials or politicians)

This activity can be played as a game, with the students developing their own rules.

Have each of the students list elements and ask the other students to identify the set.

When the concept of well-defined members of sets is established, children can identify sets that contain no elements (empty sets or null sets):

—The set of women who have been president of the United States
—The set of 20¢ pieces
—The set of children who have landed on the moon
—The set of living people who are over 200 years old.

Language Arts Skills	Vocabulary development, identifying relationships, stating and refining rules for games
(3) **The Big Idea**	*Measurement is a mathematical tool used in everyday life. An appropriate unit of measure (gram, milliliter) should be used for the task at hand.*
Activity	*Class Cookbook*

Class Cookbook

Teachers are well aware of the potential for teaching many areas of the curriculum through experiences with food. The class may be divided into groups for this project.

Have a group of children test recipes in preparation for a cookbook that will ultimately belong to the class. In the process of cooking, children will be required to estimate, measure, add, subtract, multiply, and divide. They will learn to "feel" metric measures. The recipes may be an outgrowth of work in social studies.

Another group can review the recipes before writing them into the cookbook. They should check the following:

—Are the measurements accurate?
—Is the sequence logical?
—Does the language clearly state what is to be done?

A third group can prepare a section in the cookbook that will serve as a glossary. Difficult words should be alphabetized, defined, and classified into categories. For example:

Activities: *blending, kneading, freezing*
Amounts: *pinch, half dozen, gram, milliliter*
Substances: *yeast, chicory, dough*
Tools: *thermostat, spatula, skillet*

Language Arts Skills   Reading, writing, classifying, vocabulary development, using the dictionary, identifying and following sequence of events

LANGUAGES WITHIN A LANGUAGE

Language power grows not only horizontally, transcending curriculum boundaries, but vertically as well. As individuals acquire language, they begin to stretch the boundaries of their skills. They develop separate vocabularies for communicating with different groups. Language becomes a flexible tool, one that may reflect identification with a particular background (regional, ethnic, economic) or occupation.

Language growth may emerge through the acquisition of new vocabulary: mathematical words (*isosceles*), legal words (*subpoena*), regional words (*grits*), or "hip" words (*gig*); or through the use of familiar words in a new context ("Adam and Eve on a raft" for poached eggs on toast). Variations on a language always develop and are shown through differences in punctuation, grammar, and accent. Since few people speak only one form, or dialect, of their native language, it is helpful for teachers to appreciate the richness that different dialects and styles can bring to communication. The uniqueness of individuals is nowhere more apparent than in their dialects. No two people speak or write exactly alike.

Each of the statements below reflects a particular dialect and provides evidence of the adaptability of language to individual and group needs:

1. "To grow up decent, our children need new clothing to present themself in school in proper neat!! The sun have to shine for our childrens too. Amen."
2. "He's a real cool guy."
3. "Did you collar the skell?"
4. "Criterion-referenced measures were applied to the performance of mainstreamed children in an open classroom."

Do some of these sentences seem like a secret language or code? Neither language nor people are homogeneous. Groups within the culture develop a kind of linguistic shorthand to communicate with other members. A speech community is founded.

Let's look at each of the examples of dialect. The first one, taken from a sign, is an example of Black English. According to linguist J. L. Dillard, this written form would seem more natural, more grammatical, to some than a form involving "themselves," "neatness," and "has."[14] Dillard contends that Black English is a language with its own coherent structure, and patterns. Fewer problems might arise in classrooms where children speak Black English if teachers appreciated the reasons for the language. Dillard emphasizes that Black English "has a history as any other language has a history."[15]

The question of whether or not Black English should be taught or accepted in public schools has certainly not been resolved. But teachers who appreciate the black child's linguistic heritage can break down barriers, build up trust, and begin to develop the youngster's language power. Black English is more than a collection of words with structural connections; it is a way of communicating about life. Black English will be discussed in different contexts in subsequent chapters.

The second sentence might be spoken by a fourth grader describing a peer. The precise meaning of "cool" is probably understood by both the speaker and the listener. "Did you collar the skell?" is police shorthand

[14]J. L. Dillard, *Black English* (New York: Random House, Vintage Books, 1972), p. 23.
[15]Dillard, *Black English*, p. 34.

meaning "Did you arrest the derelict?" The last sentence is in educational jargon. It assumes that the listener knows the meaning of *criterion-referenced measures, mainstreaming,* and *open classroom.* While relatively familiar to professional educators, these terms are gobbledygook to most people.

Does a Tower of Babel exist within a single language? Are we really communicating with one another? Talking and writing do not guarantee communication. Teachers and students should recognize the existence of languages within a language.

Slang

Slang has always existed. Very often, after years of usage, certain words once considered slang become acceptable and find their way into most dictionaries. Words like "hip" and "square" are not included in *Webster's Third New International Dictionary.*

Children use slang for many reasons. Sometimes, it is a way of identifying with the peer culture, a statement of independence from adult standards. Slang becomes a kind of private language through which peers can communicate. To totally deny children the use of slang in the classroom is to force a creative means of expression underground, with a probable decline in communication. This is not to suggest that offensive slang is to be accepted in school. Even most students make that distinction. Encourage youngsters to analyze their slang and to understand how it functions in their world. The names of songs and musical groups are a good beginning; they tend to communicate a range of feelings about time, love, and nature. The names of rock groups especially, whether ordinary or outlandish, become a part of popular culture. You might have your students identify recent groups whose names include a color (Blues Magoos, New Riders of the Purple Sage, or Yellow Pages), a form of wildlife (The Chipmunks, The Monkees, and The Iron Butterfly), or some type of transportation (Jefferson Starship, Led Zeppelin, Detroit Wheels, Orient Express).[16]

As teachers, our purpose is to encourage communication. We cannot ignore any of the resources in the culture, particularly those that most excite the interest and imagination of many students. Through an intelligent examination of slang, students may recognize that the real purpose of language arts lessons is to develop precise communication skills that will serve them everywhere.

Jargon

Jargon, another category of select language, is language that is the outgrowth of a particular profession or specialty. Often commonplace words

[16]Clair Schulz, "We Shall Know Them by Their Roots," in *Verbatim* 4, no. 2 (September 1977): 1.

are used but given eccentric meaning. A piano in the language of jazz is a "box"; "two bull's-eyes" is the short-order cook's call for two fried eggs. Sometimes a whole new terminology develops.

Charlton Laird in *Language in America* refers to "novae" in the language; words or groups of words that undergo a sort of meaning explosion.[17] Initially, the vocabulary may be limited to a particular group; but, not infrequently, it soon becomes available to the larger society. Consider the case of "space language." Now that leaving the planet and returning has been accomplished, such terms as *countdown, blastoff, catwalk,* and *life support systems* have become part of the elementary-school child's everyday vocabulary.

Sports provide another source of colorful jargon. Sometimes, the terms evolve from usage and are confined to the sport; the "fly pattern" of football is an example. At other times, words are transferred directly from ordinary language because of their descriptive quality: the "helicopter turn" in skiing. In still other situations, a word takes on a different meaning; use of the word "ace" for a nonreturnable serve in tennis illustrates this phenomenon. Conversely, terms from sports may become part of everyday language. Hence "ball game," once applied only to an athletic contest between two teams, is today often used in references to situations far removed from the field of sports: "The teacher who transfers from a large urban school system to a small rural one finds herself in a new ball game."

Since many children have considerable familiarity with the words of sports, your students might enjoy developing their own lists of such words. Some of them—like "buttonhook" in football, "daffy" in skiing, and "lob" in tennis—might even be described through pictures.

Jargon is frequently disallowed, on the grounds that it obscures meaning. This can be true, but it does not have to be. The initial purpose of jargon is usually greater precision. However, after a while the meanings of certain words become muddled through their overuse; and thus it becomes more likely that a speaker and a listener will have different definitions of the same word. When a psychologist speaks of "a really meaningful relationship," what is he or she actually trying to say? Unfortunately, non-communication may be a by-product of jargon.

Afterview   This chapter has attempted to demonstrate that a heightened awareness of the way words work will lead to greater language power. Concept hooks, metaphors, and integrated activities all provide evidence that sound cognitive functioning has a language base. The language arts remain the center of the curriculum because they reinforce and are reinforced by most other learnings; there is a continuing reciprocity. Language growth may result from doing a science experiment,

[17]Charlton Laird, *Language in America* (New York: World Publishing, 1970), p. 433.

squeezing a ball of clay, or measuring a rectangle. In turn, language power enables the scientist, the artist, and the mathematician to go beyond the constraints of culture and to new creations.

Teachers should think about language as a conceptual and contextual bridge. Whatever your teaching style, your recognition of relationships between the language arts and other curriculum areas will provide advantages. The mass of material that today's teacher is expected to "cover" can best be handled through the recognition of such relationships, the implementation of "big ideas" that transcend curriculum areas, and the understanding that language, like life, cannot be neatly packaged into discrete compartments.

WHEN YOU WANT TO KNOW MORE

1. To recognize languages within a language, record several job-related words and phrases used by the following people: short-order cooks, teachers, construction workers, and physicians.

2. Dialects are very often regional. Interview people who grew up in different parts of the country. What differences do you note in vocabulary, the naming of objects, and colloquial expressions?

3. Develop your understanding of the adaptability of language by identifying words that are obsolete, words that have taken on new meaning, and words that are newly created. For example:

   Obsolete words: *davenport, victrola*
   Words with new meanings: *chauvinist, modular, jogging*
   New words: *disco, sexist, gasohol*

4. Examine several "how to" books for children in the creative and practical arts. Explain how these books may be used as catalysts for language skills.

IN THE CLASSROOM

1. Ask your students to translate the multiple meanings of the word *spinoff* into construction projects, art activities, and original stories. How do the experiences of a character within a story lead to a spinoff of other events? What were spinoffs from specific international events? A flow chart may help the children see how one change gives rise to another.

2. Using a contemporary issue, plan several lessons that spring from the exploration of a "big idea" (Technology has changed our lives; Energy needs create interdependence). Identify the activities and language skills to which you will direct attention.

3. Have your students examine the names of rock music groups. Which groups use color, animal, or transportation names in their titles? Find other means of organizing the names of these groups.

4. Ask your students to identify and explain new words and new meanings for old words that have developed because of advances in technology. Help them prepare an illustrated chart. Some starters: *video, stereo, digital, handhelds, feedback, databanks*.

SUGGESTED READINGS

Carlson, Ruth Kearney. *Enrichment Ideas: Sparkling Fireflies*. Dubuque, Iowa: Wm. C. Brown, 1970.

Cole, Natalie Robinson. *The Arts in the Classroom*. New York: John Day, 1940.

Hansen-Krening, Nancy. *Competency and Creativity in Language Arts: A Multiethnic Focus*. Reading, Mass.: Addison-Wesley, 1979.

Lakoff, George, and Johnson, Mark. *Metaphors We Live By*. Chicago: University of Chicago Press, 1980.

Linderman, Earl W., and Herberholz, Donald W. *Developing Artistic and Perceptual Awareness*. Dubuque, Iowa: Wm. C. Brown, 1964.

Montebello, Mary. *Children's Literature in the Curriculum*. Dubuque, Iowa: Wm. C. Brown, 1972.

Neuenschwander, John. *Oral History as a Teaching Approach*. Washington, D.C.: National Education Association, 1976.

Tiedt, Pamela L., and Tiedt, Iris M. *Multicultural Teaching: A Handbook of Activities, Information, and Resources*. Boston: Allyn & Bacon, 1979.

Tooze, Ruth, and Krone, Beatrice Perham, eds. *Literature and Music as Resources for Social Studies*. Englewood Cliffs, N.J.: Prentice-Hall, 1955.

Robertson, Jean. "Using Social Studies Content to Develop Reading Skills." In *The Quest for Competency in Teaching Reading*, edited by Howard A. Klein. Newark, Del.: International Reading Association, 1972.

Other Materials

Layton, James. *Reading in the Content Areas*. Los Angeles: JAB Press. (Two cassette tapes.)

The Read-Along Science Series: 1) Dinosaurs, 2) Mammals of Long Ago, 3) Fossils. New York: Guidance Associates. (Filmstrip, cassette or record.)

The Read-Along Social Studies Series: 1) Airplanes, 2) Ships and Boats, 3) Trains, 4) Trucks and Buses. New York: Guidance Associates. (Filmstrip, cassette, or record.)

CHAPTER 4

Competence-Based Education and the Language Arts

Preview   This chapter will identify the essential components of competence-based programs and suggest how the most positive features of these programs might be utilized by language arts teachers. The trend toward competence-based education results from the concern for accountability and the new advances in educational technology. Competence programs are constructed around precise statements of teaching behavior. Each competence may be considered a kind of behavioral objective. The analysis of competence-based education will provide the occasion for a discussion of evaluation, measurement, and behavioral objectives.

Competence-based education has caused considerable controversy and has been accused of reducing teaching to a mechanical act. This chapter will describe the ways in which certain principles of the competence movement may blend with the philosophy and practices of humanistic education. Teachers of language arts concerned with development in the cognitive and affective domains can gather the best from both perspectives as they explore those competences that are essential for performing teaching tasks. A variety of activities will be suggested for the teacher who wishes to become more proficient in general language arts competences.

IN RECENT YEARS, the competence-based education movement has polarized professional educators. At one extreme, there are the "systems people," who see education in terms of behavioral objectives, instructional packages, and specific assessment criteria. They are opposed by the "humanists," who focus on the personal discovery of meaning and are uncomfortable with the notion that teaching and learning behaviors can be fractioned into accurately measurable parts. Politicians, parents, physcians, the schools, and the courts have all gotten into the act. Hundreds of millions of tax dollars have been spent investigating the relationship between teacher performance and pupil achievement.

The term itself, competence-based education, is an unfortunate expression: it seems to imply that the search for competence in education is a new venture. Yet what have we been doing all along, if not refining the art and craft of teaching in order to increase pupil performance? The competence-based movement was not intended as an attack on teachers; it resulted from concern about declining pupil performance throughout the country. Studies indicate, however, that there is no single cause for the decline. Television, changing values, more permissive teaching approaches, less homework, and a host of other phenomena have been cited as contributory factors. As teachers, we are concerned. In what ways have we exacerbated the problem? How can we help to stem the tide?

WHAT'S IN A NAME?

Competence-based education might best be defined as a plan of action that requires teacher and/or pupils to demonstrate an identified set of behaviors at a given level of performance. There are strengths in the structure of the program. Its methodology and the focus on the identification of performance objectives, enabling activities, and evaluative procedures can assist teachers to increase their effectiveness with students.

First, let us clearly define the term competence. In some programs, competence means potential: what the child or teacher is capable of doing. In others, competence carries the notion of mastery. In this text, the word *competence* will refer to a *demonstrable* behavior, knowledge, skill, or attitude that can be observed and measured in performance. It may exist at varying levels of proficiency. An example of a teacher competence in language arts would be "The teacher demonstrates knowledge of correct punctuation, form, grammar, and word usage." The means of measuring this competence might be an examination, a written essay, or observation in a classroom. An example of a student competence in language arts would be "The student checks the accuracy of spelling through the use of the dictionary." The competence might be measured through observation of the student's performance or through a written test.

Certain features identify most competence-based programs. Almost all are predicated on the assumption that a teacher will attain and be able to demonstrate competence in the essential tasks of teaching. Performance goals are specified and agreed to in advance of instruction; students and/or teachers are held accountable, not for passing grades, but for the satisfactory demonstration of certain competences. The competences are clarified through the identification of specific behavioral indicators or assessment criteria. Thus teachers who have in their repertoire a competence that involves the individualization of instruction will demonstrate certain behaviors: they will encourage children to make choices, utilize a variety of instructional materials, vary time allocations for different children, and so on. As may be apparent to you, there are some inherent difficulties with this procedure, many of them revolving around the question "How can we measure the complex behaviors involved in the teaching/learning connection?"

THE PROBLEMS OF MEASUREMENT

Although many significant teaching behaviors can be fitted into a competence-performance-assessment pattern, accurate measurement of competences can be difficult. Some competences are not directly translated into overt behaviors that can be reliably and consistently evaluated. How does one measure, for example, a teacher's sensitivity to the language styles of children from different ethnic groups? This is not to suggest that there are not certain clues for evaluating behavior in this area; the difficulty lies in placing these clues on a grid and quantifying them. Rating behavior on an objective scale, within a particular time frame, is not always possible.

Thus a significant number of teaching behaviors evade objective measurement. The reasons vary. Some behaviors are not always present; others can be masked by the teacher or the situation. In a large number of cases, the behavior can only be inferred from the teaching circumstances. Is the behavior, therefore, less important? In the art of teaching, it may very well be that those competences that are the most elusive are the most significant. Teachers' attitudes fall into this category, as do techniques that encourage communication, approaches that develop positive self-images, and responses that reflect understanding of different cultural backgrounds.

Which are more significant: the teaching skills that can be judged with considerable reliability, or teachers' attitudes that are difficult to measure? Could it be that those competences that rely heavily on personality are the most important for pupil learning? Or, do you agree with the mother who said to her son's teacher, "Teach, you learn him, I'll love him."

Obviously, when we are dealing with a complex human activity like the teaching/learning process, we must recognize certain limitations. We should appreciate the many contributions the competence approach can make to teaching, but we should not capitulate to a business model of productivity, storage, and retrieval.

THE LARGER QUESTION: EVALUATION

Whether or not the competence-based approach prevails, the evaluating of teaching will always be of deep concern. Knowing whether objectives are being accomplished is critical to an effective education program. It is also of deep and continuing concern to the dedicated teacher. Though we have some knowledge of the complexities of the teaching/learning process, we are considerably less sophisticated about how to record and measure the dimensions of this process. For example, we can see the behavior of a motivated child; we can recognize emotional reactions to a meaningful literary experience; we can observe how an effective teacher individualizes instruction; but we are only hypothesizing when we attempt to quantify these complex phenomena. How can we measure the degree to which interest in Africa was sparked by a filmstrip? How do we know (in an objective way) that exposure to literature makes a difference? On what evidence can we determine whether it is the poem, the teacher, or the reader's mood that makes a particular literary work personally meaningful?

When we look at human behavior, we are faced with a multifaceted picture. What aspects of that picture do we select for observation? Since teaching is an art, it cannot be reduced to a set of skills that are readily programmed. The effective observation of one human being interacting with another requires a battery of cognitive and affective skills. No instrument has yet been designed to measure, in an ever-changing setting, the different and highly specialized tasks of teaching. A computer will not do; it has to separate cognitive and affective functioning and, in so doing, fragments the teaching act. The only instrument adequate to the complexity of the task is another human being.

Educators have naturally been wary of attempts to reduce the teaching/learning process to a set of measurable behaviors; they know the complexity of educating even one child. However, in a general way, competence-based programs may make an important contribution by prodding the profession to further define significant competences and direct more attention to how these competences can be measured in the classroom. The whole question of evaluation is getting some valuable rethinking.

What is evaluation? Many definitions are similar to J. D. Finn's, referred to in *Measures for Research and Evaluation in the English Language:* "Evaluation is much broader in scope than measurement and may be considered the judgment of value or worth of an object, event or idea according to one or more criteria."[1] Evaluation therefore will involve a variety of assessment procedures, probably over a long period of time. It may include testing but frequently requires a range of other procedures: observation, oral and written statements, interviews, and so on. Many student and teacher competences cannot be assessed with test-type procedures, making it necessary to use a variety of quantitative and qualitative approaches.

What assessments and criteria can be used to evaluate teaching performance? In a competence program as in any assessment of teaching performance, a series of specific behaviors are looked at; this scrutiny often involves a variety of instruments: written works, videotapes, in-person observation. In many cases some kind of rating instrument is applied.

The difficulty lies in the large number of behaviors to be rated under each competence. For example, in assessing a teacher's competence with creative dramatics, many facets of behavior would have to be considered. Are appropriate situations selected for dramatization? Is the teacher supportive of creative responses? Does the teacher capitalize on the "teachable moment" for developing children's language abilities? As a guide, these behavioral criteria are a beginning, but they are not the total picture. Interaction between teachers and students is more than the sum of individual behaviors. Information that can be catalogued on a rating instrument is useful; however, given the many variables in human interactions, professional judgment must be combined with the results obtained through any rating instrument.

One popular instrument that has been used by teachers to look at the classroom verbal behavior of teachers and pupils is the verbal interaction category system developed by Edmund Amidon and Elizabeth Hunter; it is based upon a system of interaction analysis developed by Ned Flanders. Specific categories of classroom talk are identified and verbal behaviors can be recorded and tallied.

BEHAVIORAL OBJECTIVES

A statement of objectives in behavioral terms is a main feature of competence-based programs. Behavioral objectives are not new; they have just become more visible with advances in technology. Educators have always valued and utilized some kind of objectives in their work; objectives are essential in teaching and in the evaluation of what is taught. A

---

[1]J. D. Finn, in *Measures for Research and Evaluation in the English Language Arts* (Urbana, Ill.: National Council of Teachers of English, 1975), p. ix.

behavioral objective is a determination concerning what an individual will be able to do or demonstrate as a result of the (learning) experience. Statements of behavioral objectives describe visible and sometimes measurable behavior. The more precise the statement of the objective, the easier it is to evaluate the learning experience.

Many teachers have utilized Robert F. Magen's *Preparing Instructional Objectives* as a guide in first identifying and then developing behavioral objectives.[2] The text, a type of programmed instruction, helps the teacher prepare objectives in language that describes what the learner will be doing. See if you can change the wording of the objectives listed below so that they are behaviorally stated:

> The teacher knows how to teach creative writing.
>
> The teacher understands the theories of Piaget.
>
> The student appreciates poetry.
>
> The student grasps the significance of *Alice in Wonderland*.
>
> The teacher has faith in the democratic process.

Cognitive versus Affective Objectives

As noted previously, certain objectives are more difficult to evaluate than others because they cannot be accurately measured. Cognitive objectives deal with specific thinking skills and are easier to evaluate than affective objectives, which involve feelings, attitudes, and values. In their very important study *The Taxonomy of Educational Objectives*, Benjamin S. Bloom and others noted that considerably more work has been devoted to cognitive objectives than to affective ones; in many ways the situation with respect to affective objectives is almost primitive.[3]

The Cognitive Domain

The area of cognition, which focuses on the development of intellectual abilities, has always been considered appropriate turf for the school. The Bloom study organizes cognitive phenomena into six categories: knowledge, comprehension, application, analysis, synthesis, evaluation.[4] In or-

---

[2] A competence may not always meet the criteria for instructional or behavioral objectives established by Mager. Terminal behavior is a component of Mager's definition and includes the naming of the act that will be considered evidence that the learning has been achieved. In competence programs, this evidence is often stated as an aspect of evaluation in the form of assessment criteria.

[3] David R. Krathwohl, Benjamin S. Bloom, and Bertram B. Masia, *Taxonomy of Educational Objectives: The Classification of Educational Goals; Handbook II: The Affective Domain* (New York: McKay, 1964). p. 21.

der to clarify the components of each of these categories, a teaching competence is suggested for each one:

1. *Knowledge*
   The teacher demonstrates knowledge of the content and basic structure of the language arts.
2. *Comprehension*
   The teacher is able to prepare a sociogram of his or her class and discuss the sociograms's implications.
3. *Application*
   The teacher utilizes problem solving techniques to encourage the students' development of logical processes.
4. *Analysis*
   Recognizing the strategies that children use to gain attention, the teacher develops instructional patterns that will involve each child fairly.
5. *Synthesis*
   The teacher integrates into the teaching situation the results of research on listening.
6. *Evaluation*
   The teacher diagnoses and evaluates students' growth in spelling using teacher-made materials.

You will notice that in each of these objectives, observable behavior is being described.

The Affective Domain

Though the importance of the affective domain in learning has long been recognized, this area has not been well classified. The evaluation of the affective domain presents problems because feelings are not always externally visible. *The Taxonomy of Educational Objectives*, attempts to address some of these measurement difficulties by identifying the components of affective objectives on a continuum. The suggestion is that individuals will pass through five general levels—and a number of sublevels—as they deal with affective phenomena. The major categories are: receiving, responding, valuing, organization, characterization by a value or value complex.[5] This progression may be clarified if we give an example of a teaching competence in the affective domain at each of these levels. The teacher's sensitivity to children's use of imaginative language is the primary focus:

[4]Benjamin S. Bloom and David R. Krathwohl, *Taxonomy of Educational Objectives: The Classification of Educational Goals; Handbook I: The Cognitive Domain* (New York: McKay, 1956), p. 18.

[5]Krathwohl, Bloom, and Masia, *Taxonomy of Educational Objectives; Handbook II: The Affective Domain*, pp. 176–85.

1. *Receiving*
   The teacher listens for and identifies examples of imaginative language in children and recognizes how this contributes to a child's language growth.

2. *Responding*
   The teacher develops many activities with the students to highlight their awareness of imaginative language.

3. *Valuing*
   The teacher plans a school program in which experts discuss the importance of children's imaginative development with the faculty and parents.

4. *Organization*
   The teacher practices techniques for incorporating imaginative language experiences into many aspects of the curriculum.

5. *Characterization by a Value or Value Complex*
   The teacher develops research projects, teaching strategies, and units of study that give major emphasis to the development of imaginative language.

Notice that, like the objectives in the cognitive domain, these statements are in terms of overt behavior.

It is not assumed, nor is it necessarily desirable, that all objectives are realized at the final level. The preceding illustrations are used only to demonstrate that the statement of affective objectives in behavioral terms is possible and can help suggest evaluative strategies.

THE QUESTION OF ACCOUNTABILITY

Can we use pupil performance as a criterion for judging teacher success? Is learning always immediately evidenced in performance? Many teachers have had students return several years later to express thanks for insights that were not realized or demonstrated at the time that the teaching occurred.

Accountability assumes responsibility. Teachers should certainly be held responsible for many aspects of classroom life. What occurs within a classroom does contribute to achievement in basic skills, good attendance, and desired student behaviors.[6] The key word, however, is *contribute*. The totality represented by a pupil's learning performance frequently involves a number of variables over which the teacher has no control. Teachers cannot be held accountable for the world outside the classroom. If the school were a scientific laboratory and students were culture-free, we might be able to discover which factors have the most impact on the learning process and ultimately be able to control them. However, in the real world the discovery remains incomplete and the controls impossible.

---

[6]Jane A. Stallings, "How Instructional Processes Relate to Child Outcomes in a National Study of Follow Through," *Journal of Teacher Education*, 27, no. 1 (Spring 1976):47.

Some research even suggests that "non-school" factors may be more important as determinants of educational outcomes than "school" factors are.[7] Given the effects of many variables, it follows that teachers should not be certified on the basis of their students' learning performance. We do not license dentists on the basis of their ability to relieve pain in a percentage of their patients, nor do lawyers pass the Bar because they have proved that they can win the cases of their clients.

Considering the available data, an "accountable" teacher might best be described as one who identifies each student's level in the hierarchy of learning tasks and plans appropriate instruction to facilitate learning. Teachers who systematically and continuously organize and reevaluate the teaching/learning process, and its concomitant strategies, utilizing professional judgments for their decisions, may be considered accountable.

HOW CAN THE COMPETENCE MOVEMENT ASSIST LANGUAGE ARTS TEACHERS?

Dedicated teachers are always seeking to improve their effectiveness. Like Jonathan Livingston Seagull, they want to fly higher and higher. New movements in education may provide some ideas on how to improve teaching, but the principles and systems that undergird any program should be fully understood. Competence-based programs can assist the language arts teacher. Working with an identified set of competences (for teachers and students) and being aware of procedures for developing and monitoring proficiency can be helpful. Consider the following excerpts from the handbook of one teacher education institution:

1. A teaching competence is one which has been deemed essential in order to perform the tasks one must do.

2. In order to enable the teacher to become proficient in a competence, it will usually be necessary for him/her to engage in a variety of activities. These *enabling activities* might include: the study of references, site visits, observational reports, review of instructional resources, preparation and execution of lessons in simulated and real situations.

3. Teacher performance will be assessed, utilizing one or more *instruments* (for example, examinations, logs, research papers, observation, conferences, videotapes).

4. Assessment criteria should specify the behaviors that the student should exhibit when the competence is in his/her repertoire.[8]

---

[7]Robert W. Heath and Mark A. Nielson, "The Research Basis for Performance-Based Teacher Education," *Review of Educational Research*, 44, no. 4 (fall 1974):463–84.

[8]Maureen Murphy and Karel Rose, *Student Handbook* (Brooklyn, New York: Brooklyn College, 1976), p. 2.

What can aspects of this program or similar programs tell those who teach language arts?

(1) *Language arts objectives can be defined in competence terms.*

Remember, a competence-based objective is stated in performance terms. It focuses on those knowledges, skills, and attitudes that can be satisfactorily demonstrated.

> *Example of a competence-based objective:*
> The teacher demonstrates critical knowledge of the breadth and scope of children's prose literature and uses established criteria in evaluating literature for children.

> *A similar objective not written in competence terms:*
> The teacher understands the breadth and scope of children's prose literature and knows the importance of criteria for evaluating literature for children.

What language differences exist between these two objectives? What are the implications for evaluation? The answer to the first question is easy. In the non-competence-based objective, the words "understands" and "knows" replace "demonstrates" and "uses." The second question calls for a more complex response. "Demonstrate" and "use" are explicit enough to be observed. I cannot see, or check off as readily, the teacher's ability to "understand" and to "know." The competence approach, through specific language, provides direction for assessment. However, it is not always possible to express objectives in "measurable" language.

(2) *Enabling activities can be used to increase proficiency in a specific competence.*

The following sample of enabling activities goes from less complex to more sophisticated ways of assisting the teacher to become increasingly effective in the children's literature competence described above:

—Read extensively in children's literature.

—Study and discuss appropriate references in the field.

—Observe and record the ways in which children's literature may serve as a resource for language development activities.

—Plan for, and read or tell to children, a story using a visual aid.

—Share with children and colleagues a variety of literary selections using other than print materials (filmstrips, tapes, puppets).

—Prepare, demonstrate, and make available to colleagues protocol materials (models) of teaching behaviors designed to stimulate children's enthusiasm for literary experiences.

Can you suggest another activity for developing a teacher's competence in children's literature?

(3) *Assessment criteria for each competence can be identified.*

Assessment criteria must be broad-based, however. Teaching is an art and cannot be reduced to a single set of skills; it is a combination of skills, knowledges, and attitudes. The following is a competence that would not be difficult to assess: "The teacher demonstrates the ability to make functional use of the basic communication skills." Criteria could include a specified grade on a written examination, an assessment of handwriting measured against a scale, and a rating of oral speech using an appropriate standard. However, in evaluating a competence in which the teacher "demonstrates the ability to heighten children's awareness of poetry," the criteria would encourage a variety of less objective measures.

Using professional judgment, the observer would look for teaching behaviors that: *encourage* pupils to think about the poem, *praise* imaginative responses to poetry, and *sensitize* children to the poetic experience. Can you suggest several other teaching behaviors that would encourage pupils to think about a specific poem?

You can see that the specificity of the criteria must vary with the nature of the competence. Nevertheless, the judicious and flexible use of assessment criteria can be invaluable to the professional growth of the language arts teacher.

(4) *Attention can be directed toward recognizing and evaluating the causal relationship between teacher performance and pupil behavior.*

For reasons noted in the previous section, evaluation cannot always be accompanied by objective instruments. The teaching/learning act cannot be measured with trivial criteria. Reliance frequently must be placed upon professional judgment.

Competence-Based Education in a Humanistic Learning Environment

What children learn has a lot to do with both what teachers teach and how they go about teaching it. The *what* is the content, and it is directly related to the teacher's knowledge of subject matter. The *how* concerns the skills necessary for the teaching of that content. A skillful teacher utilizes strategies that take into account what is known about how children learn. However, knowledge and skill are not all; the teacher's attitude represents another variable. These three—knowledge, skills, and attitude—are interdependent. If we separate them too discretely for measurement purposes, the forest is lost for the trees. How then, do we achieve the combination that will help professionals analyze and improve their performance?

Both humanistic education and competence-based education attempt to address this problem. Each movement has its own emphasis and philosophical touchstone.

Humanistic education focuses on the teacher's attitude and the student's self-concept. The emphasis is on building the learner's capacity for self-instruction and personal development. A positive self-concept is viewed as essential to high scholastic achievement.[9] The manner in which the teacher responds to the student and the resulting interpersonal quality of the learning environment are thus very important. The teacher's knowledge and skill must be implemented in a setting that is supportive of the individual student. Teacher effectiveness or competence is conditioned, therefore, by many personality variables.

Competence-based education, while recognizing the importance of attitude and environment, concentrates on explicitly defined competences and assessment criteria. Taking advantage of new developments in the social and behavioral sciences, supporters of competence-based education sometimes apply systems analysis to teaching. Thus they often speak of delivery systems for learning and management systems for accountability.

How can we reconcile a systems-management approach with a nurturing classroom environment? How might accountability be interpreted to include objective measures and professional judgment? How can the best thinking from each of these movements be blended to reflect a more dynamic approach to teacher education?[10]

Frame of Reference   Humanistic education, with its emphasis on historical, philosophical, and psychological backgrounds, can serve as a frame of reference for the competence movement. Consider this language arts competence: "The teacher is able to utilize techniques that develop children's discussion skills." The usefulness of a philosophy course to such a teacher is not readily apparent. However, teachers exposed to philosophy may be better prepared to consider alternate ways of thinking. Having personally experienced the process of philosophical discussion, they might begin to value the lessons of logic and the importance of prodding pupils into seeing points for themselves. Similarly, a teacher who is familiar with psychological principles of motivation might be more effective as a discussion leader. Can you think of a specific teaching behavior that might be influenced by the teacher's familiarity with historical content?

Improving Teaching Skills   Competence-based education can contribute to attempts to improve the skills of teaching. Competences that deal with specific skills can be judged with considerable reliability. In the competence "The teacher demonstrates knowledge of specific techniques for teaching and evaluating the use of grammar," there is a definite behavioral product that can be observed. The rules of grammar can be programmed and quantified. They can be placed on a checklist and scored

[9]Gerald Weinstein and Mario D. Fantini, eds., *Toward Humanistic Education: A Curriculum of Affect* (New York: Praeger, 1970), p. 32.

[10]It should be noted that most competence-based programs are highly individualized. Teachers are expected to proceed at their own rates; comparisons, rather than involving a colleague, relate only to the individual's personal progress.

with objective accuracy. Teachers can be made aware of their weaknesses and work to improve their performance. At the same time, they must recognize that only a segment of teaching behavior is being extrapolated for purposes of measurement. Can you suggest specific teaching behaviors that can be sufficiently quantified to be placed on a check list?

Teacher Behavior as Evaluative Criteria   Competence-based education focuses on those teaching behaviors that can be precisely measured. Often excluded from consideration are important behaviors that are difficult to observe and evaluate, for example, thinking, appreciating, valuing. Though difficult, it is necessary to carefully identify these behaviors with the appropriate criteria. We may never choose to subdivide them to the satisfaction of a statistician; however, taking a cue from competence-based education, we can ground our judgments, whenever possible, in the behavioral evidence from specific teaching practices. Can you identify specific teaching behaviors that are successful in encouraging children to appreciate poetry?

The Utilization of Broad-Based Criteria   Statements of competence can be valuable in directing attention, but the criteria must be broad-based enough that assessment does not become compartmentalized. As an illustration, consider the important language arts competence, "The teacher demonstrates an ability to select and tell stories that will help children develop a variety of listening and literary skills." Since the teaching/learning act cannot be segmented for purposes of measurement, we must observe all of its aspects simultaneously: the choice of story, the physical placement of the children and the furniture, the story-reading technique, the responses of the children, and the manner in which discussion develops. You can probably think of other variables, for various assessment models would be appropriate. What criteria would you establish for evaluating the following competence: "The teacher demonstrates knowledge of a variety of approaches for teaching creative writing?"

The convenience of an all-out systems method for teaching cannot be denied, but, as yet, there is not adequate evidence to justify this approach. We do not even know that one set of teaching competences is more productive of learning than another. Serious consideration must be given to the view that teaching is an art and cannot be reduced to a set of skills.

Using Competences to Develop Language Arts Proficiency: A Sample Competence

The teacher demonstrates the ability to translate knowledge about the breadth, scope, and artistic qualities of poetry for children into appropriate techniques and strategies.

How the insights of competence-based education and humanistic education may be blended to increase teacher effectiveness may be summarized as follows:

Competence-Based Education	Humanistic, Competence-Based Education
1. Identifies and catalogues the aspects of behavior (competences) that teachers should be required to demonstrate.	1. Identifies and clusters the aspects of behavior into larger segments, using fewer competences.
2. Defines competences in performance terms, using language that is directed toward precise measurement.	2. Defines skills competences in performance terms that suggest precise measurement, but recognizes that all teaching behaviors cannot be expressed in language that permits quantification.
3. Identifies enabling activities that help teachers develop competence.	3. Recognizes and identifies many varieties of theoretical and practical activities that help teachers develop competence.
4. Identifies behaviors that *should* be exhibited by students and teachers.	4. Identifies a sampling of behaviors that *could* be exhibited by students and teachers over a period of time.
5. Identifies assessment criteria, often using a scaled measure for each competence.	5. Improves conditions for analyzing cause and effect in the learning/teaching relationship, but identifies only broad-based criteria that lean heavily on professional judgment.
6. Suggests competences that focus on the individualization of instruction.	6. Adapts many competences to fit in with an individualized learning environment.

Developing a competence usually requires that a teacher engage in a variety of activities, in and out of the classroom setting. These activities might include the study of references, (research studies, curriculum bulletins, teacher's manuals), site visits, observational reports, review of instructional resources, and the preparation and execution of lessons in simulated and real situations. Listed below are sample activities that a teacher might undertake in order to develop the competence above. Also identified are sample evaluation instruments for use in a teacher education course or a teacher center.

Sample Activities for the Teacher	*Sample Evaluation Instruments*
1. Study and discuss references in the field of poetry and oral interaction for children and adults; focus on poetry's contributions to enjoyment, insight, self-exploration, appreciation of imagery and beauty. Develop a file of poems grouped according to themes, style, or some other feature.	Card file
2. Read poems that focus on chosen themes and evaluate each poem according to the criteria established for readers in various age groups.	Individual record, written product (log, paper, lesson plan, examination)
3. Introduce peers to selected poems and demonstrate a knowledge of poetry as well as the art of oral interpretation.	Written product, self/peer evaluation
4. After consulting appropriate references, observe and record ways in which poetry may become an integral part of the reading program, a springboard to other curriculum areas, and a source of language development activities.	Written product
5. Experience a poetry reading with another teacher and/or students.	Group discussion
6. Study and discuss references that might help children write their own poetry and increase their understanding of how an imaginative writing style develops.	Group discussion, demonstration
7. Plan activities with students that translate their studies into practice. (Share poetry, elicit poetry from students, and so on.)	Lesson plan, self/peer/supervisor observation, videotape, conference
8. Recognize and explain ways in which poetry experiences can contribute to the humanities curriculum.	Group discussion, written product
9. Through readings and recollections of personal experiences, become aware of the misuse of poetry in the classroom.	Conference, group discussion
10. Record (on videotape, audiotape) segments of teaching/learning behavior that use poetry for understanding.	Videotape, audiotape, records
11. Taking into account the diversity of interests, abilities, and ways of knowing, use media other than print (filmstrips, tapes, films, records) to expose children to poetry selections.	Self/peer/supervisor observation, conference

Sample Activities for the Teacher	*Sample Evaluation Instruments*
12. Prepare and make available to colleagues protocol materials (models) of teaching behaviors that focus on "poetry for enjoyment" and individualized methods of stimulating enthusiasm for the poetic experience.	Written product
13. In a descriptive document, identify the work of the teacher as a classroom manager and coordinator of the services of other adults and show how this additional adult assistance can be utilized in a poetry program.	Written product

Further Language Arts Competences

Any catalogue of teaching competences can be challenged: Are they the most appropriate ones for the field in question? Should their number be expanded or reduced? In any effective competence program, it is frequently necessary for teachers to rethink and perhaps redefine the competences. Listed below are some general language arts competences that are typical of those compiled for teachers; later in the text, more specific teacher and student competences will be suggested.

1. The teacher demonstrates the ability to make functional use of the basic communication skills.

2. The teacher demonstrates knowledge of various theories of language acquisition and development, and their implications for language arts curricula.

3. The teacher demonstrates knowledge of the content and basic structure of curricular foundations in language arts.

4. The teacher demonstrates the ability to differentiate the various levels, purposes, and types of listening.

5. The teacher demonstrates the ability to produce handwriting, manuscript and cursive, in accordance with standard models.

6. The teacher demonstrates a knowledge of correct punctuation, form, grammar, and word usage.

7. The teacher demonstrates critical knowledge of the breadth and scope of children's prose literature.

8. The teacher demonstrates the ability to identify the breadth and scope of poetry for children.

9. The teacher demonstrates knowledge of the various approaches to vocabulary selection and to the teaching of spelling.

10. The teacher uses appropriate evaluative procedures as an integral part of the total learning context.

11. The teacher utilizes resources and learning strategies from the other areas of the curriculum in teaching language arts.

12. The teacher demonstrates sensitivity to the impact of a teacher's verbal and nonverbal communication on students.

Afterview   There are those who view teaching as an art that cannot be reduced to a set of skills. Others subscribe eagerly to some well-defined system of accountability. In theory, the convenience of an all-out systems method for teaching cannot be denied; however, there is not yet enough research to proclaim such a method. Before we allow the mythology about these two attitudes to divide the profession, let us consider some points of agreement:

1. Teacher competence is the meshing of cognitive learning and affective experience.
2. The ability to demonstrate competence is essential to teaching.
3. The identification of objectives linked to appropriate evaluation criteria is a prime concern.

The challenge in education today evolves from political pressures, from economic laws of supply and demand, and from the cry for accountability in all occupations. Teachers and administrators are being forced to rethink and be more precise about role and job definitions. The most promising response seems to be a blend of humanistic education with the valid principles of competence-based education.

Clearly education is and should be changing. However, ruled by a desire to create an orderly system, some educators are perhaps being seduced by technology. Undoubtedly computer-assisted instruction will continue to transform aspects of teacher education, but computers do have limitations. As George Leonard notes, "What we are learning is not that our computers are any less wonderful than we had imagined but that human abilities are far more wonderful than we had dreamed."[11]

WHEN YOU WANT TO KNOW MORE

1. Identify several language arts teaching competences in which overt behaviors can be judged with considerable reliability. Which competences are difficult to measure? Why is this so?

[11]George Leonard, "In God's Image," *Saturday Review*, 22 February 1975, p. 13.

2. What are some of the qualities of superior teachers? Try to list as many of their behaviors as you can in performance terms.

3. Suggest several teaching/learning situations in which cognitive and affective processes are interdependent.

IN THE CLASSROOM

1. Teach a lesson in which you hope to demonstrate your sensitivity to the strategies for developing positive self-images in children. What teaching behaviors do you plan to demonstrate? (These could be used as assessment criteria.)

2. Identify specific behaviors of individual children that provide evidence of competence in particular spelling tasks.

3. Plan and execute a lesson on choral speaking. Ask a colleague to observe the classroom session and to identify how your teaching behaviors contributed both positively and negatively to the teaching/learning situation.

SUGGESTED READINGS

Amidon, Edmund, and Hunter, Elizabeth. *Improving Teaching: The Analysis of Classroom Verbal Interaction.* New York: Holt, Rinehart & Winston, 1967.

Burns, Paul C. *Diagnostic Teaching of the Language Arts.* Itasca, Ill.: F. E. Peacock, 1974.

Combs, Arthur W. *Educational Accountability: Beyond Behavioral Objectives.* Washington, D.C.: Association for Supervision and Curriculum Development, 1972.

Fagan, William T.; Cooper, Charles R.; and Jensen, Julie M. *Measures for Research and Evaluation in the English Language Arts.* Urbana, Ill.: National Council of Teachers of English, 1975.

Flanders, Ned A. *Teacher Influence, Pupil Attitudes and Achievement.* Cooperative Research Monograph 12, U.S. Department of Health, Education and Welfare, Office of Education. Washington, D.C.: U.S. Government Printing Office, 1965.

Kean, John M., and Personke, Carl. *The Language Arts: Teaching and Learning in the Elementary School.* New York: St. Martin's Press, 1976.

Kibler, Robert J., et al. *Objectives for Instruction and Evaluation.* Boston: Allyn & Bacon, 1974.

Mager, Robert F. *Preparing Instructional Objectives.* Palo Alto, Calif.: Fearon Publishers, 1962.

Peter, Lawrence J. *Competencies for Teaching: Teacher Education.* Belmont, Calif.: Wadsworth Publishing, 1975.

Robinson, H. Alan, and Burrows, Alvina Treut. *Teacher Effectiveness in Elementary Language Arts: A Progress Report.* Urbana, Ill.: National Council of Teachers of English, 1974.

Tyler, Ralph W. and Wolf, Richard. *Crucial Issues in Testing.* Berkeley, Calif.: McCutchan Publishing, 1974.

Vander Werf, Lester S. *How to Evaluate Teachers and Teaching.* New York: Rinehart and Company, 1958.

Other Materials

Hefter, Richard, and Moskof, Martin. *A Shuffle Book.* New York: Western Publishing, 1970. (Cards that enable children to make up a variety of phrases, sentences, and stories.)

Lee, W. R. *Language Teaching Games and Contests,* 2d ed. Oxford, England: Oxford University Press, 1979.

Littell, Joseph Fletcher, ed. *The Language of Man.* Evanston, Ill.: McDougal, Littell and Company, 1971. (A series of six books.)

Tiedt, Sidney W., and Tiedt, Iris M. *Language Arts Activities for the Classroom.* Boston: Allyn & Bacon, 1978.

CHAPTER 5

Managing the Individualized Language Learning Environment

Preview Of all the grand aims that teachers have, probably the one most difficult to realize in the classroom is instruction that meets the individual learning needs of each child. Dedicated educators, nevertheless, continue to explore and discover new strategies for reaching this objective. After briefly discussing some of the recent advances in education that have brought about an increased interest in individualization, this chapter will focus on a new conception of the teaching role: the teacher as manager. Since the term *individualization* has various interpretations, it will be approached here from many vantage points. Principles of individualization will be identified along with the effects of this philosophy on teaching functions. The learning center will be discussed as one instrument for individualizing instruction, and the meaning of individualization will be considered with respect to both traditional and open classrooms. For the teacher who wishes to develop an individualized language arts program or who has mainstreamed students, a variety of practical strategies will be offered and specific teaching competences will be identified. There will also be suggestions regarding the keeping of records, organizing, scheduling, the evaluating of individualized learning programs, and mainstreaming, both in traditional settings and in open classrooms.

I T IS SEPTEMBER again. Students and teachers have returned from their summer vacations. It is an anxious time for all. The children wonder: "Will the teacher like me?" "Will I be smart?" The teacher wonders: "Will the children like me?" "Will I be able to manage the class?" "How can I plan instruction that meets their individual needs?" What difficult questions to answer! As the world has grown more complex, so has the classroom. The information explosion doubles human knowledge every ten years. New electronic resources are available, computers already assist in the learning process, and additional personnel with a variety of technological skills stand ready to be recruited. On the basis of what we now understand about children and how they learn, long, formal lessons are giving way to shortened, integrated experiences in which discovery by the child is encouraged. In this "brave new world," teachers are questioning practices that have not been questioned before. As a result, the role of the teacher is undergoing radical changes.

WHAT EVER HAPPENED TO . . . ?

Life in classrooms was less complex years ago, when there was fixed furniture, one textbook for each subject, and one teacher in each room. What ever happened to fifteen minutes of penmanship, fifteen minutes of spelling, and fifteen minutes of composition? What ever happened to children who sat quietly and listened and listened and listened? Well, we hoped that they listened, and we hoped that they learned. Today's classrooms are very different from those of the past. Changes in educational philosophy have caused many American schools to make radical changes in both the scene and the scenario of learning. In most institutions, things even look different. Fixed furniture has been replaced by moveable desks and chairs. Learning centers are in evidence. There are fewer "sets" of books, and a variety of reading materials are available. The first teaching machine, the textbook, has been augmented by a whole variety of instructional devices, many of which are used outside the classroom, in the corridors, libraries, or resource laboratories. Silence is no longer golden. Children are encouraged to talk to each other as well as to the teacher. In many classrooms, you see a teacher assisted by one or more "helpers," who may range in age from six to sixty-six. These "helpers" or teaching assistants may be other children, student teachers, paraprofessionals, curriculum specialists, community representatives, parents, or administrators.

Within this rearranged context, the teacher's role has been altered.

There is traffic to manage. A flexible time schedule is required, and a wide variety of materials, media, and human resources are available. In relinquishing the exclusive right to deal directly with each child in every classroom situation, the teacher has become freer to plan, manage, delegate, counsel, and facilitate the individualization of instruction. Most importantly, the new multidimensional role of the teacher is a recognition that no one person or teaching material should have a franchise on the education of the learner. R. M. Hare, the English philosopher, says it another way: "There is a limit in practice to the amount that can be taught to someone by someone else."[1] Carl Rogers, the educational psychologist and teacher, suggests that teachers should see themselves pri-

---

The following is a list of rules for teachers posted by a principal in 1872 in the City of New York:

1. Teachers each day will fill lamps, clean chimneys and trim wicks.

2. Each teacher will bring a bucket of water and a scuttle of coal for the day's session.

3. Make your pens carefully. You may whittle nibs to the individual tastes of the pupils.

4. Each teacher may take one evening each week for courting purposes, or two evenings a week if they go to church regularly.

5. After ten hours in school, the teachers should spend the remaining time reading the Bible or other good books.

6. Women teachers who marry or engage in unseemly conduct will be dismissed.

7. Every teacher should lay aside from each pay a goodly sum of his earnings for his benefit during his declining years so that he will not become a burden on society.

8. Any teacher who smokes, uses liquor in any form, frequents pool or public halls, or gets shaved in a barber shop will give good reason to suspect his worth, intentions, integrity, and honesty.

9. The teacher who performs his labors faithfully and without fault for five years will be given an increase of twenty-five cents per week in his pay providing the Board of Education approves.

This material was selected by Seneca Furman, Board of Education of the City of New York.

---

[1] R. M. Hare, *The Language of Morals* (New York: Oxford University Press, 1964), p. 61.

marily as facilitators of learning who structure an environment in which children actively participate in solving problems. The school in which teachers and learners assume responsibility for initiating, structuring, and questioning is one in which teachers can heave a sigh of relief. No longer must they pretend to be argus-eyed and omniscient. But this view of the teacher is a distinctly modern phenomenon. Note the rules for teachers just over a hundred years ago shown on the preceding page.

WHY THE CHANGE?

Organizational patterns that alter the traditional subject-by-subject, rigidly scheduled "teacher talk" approach to curriculum do not necessarily reflect a change in objectives. Our goals in the language arts continue to revolve around the development of effective communication skills for all students. Experience and current research suggest that we can best develop communicative power in children by giving them many, many opportunities to exercise their language muscles; that is, they must continually *use* language in a great variety of situations. Modern educational thought has also helped us to recognize that effective communication is dependent not only on skills but on activities that increase one's joy and relatedness to the language experience. "Significant learning takes place when the subject matter is perceived by the student as having relevance for his own purposes."[2] A writing experience, for example, becomes relevant only when it goes beyond rote recording and serves the practical or creative needs of the writer.

The mini-revolution in educational thought has been reflected most obviously in new teaching strategies and organizational plans. What are these changes and how are they reflected in the classroom?

(1) There is a growing awareness of how children learn. In this area, the influence of Jean Piaget, the Swiss psychologist, has been most significant. Piaget's theories emphasize that the "learning of facts depends in part on the child's general capacity to relate these specific facts to other facts in a meaningful manner.[3] The compartmentalized learning of isolated facts and skills that typified schools of fifty years ago involved little attempt to relate a child's thinking and intelligent comprehension. The contextual framework was missing. We cannot, for example, expect a youngster to learn the spelling of the word *kangaroo* without having heard or read the word, or without having had some visual experience that identified what a kangaroo is.

(2) There is a new knowledge from psychology and linguistics, knowledge that was simply unavailable a few decades ago. Today, we can more

[2]Carl R. Rogers, *Freedom to Learn* (Columbus, Ohio: Merrill, 1969), p. 158.

[3]Hans G. Furth and Harry Wachs, *Thinking Goes to School: Piaget's Theory in Practice* (New York: Oxford University Press, 1975), p. 13.

clearly identify the stages of a child's development, the significance of the self-concept, and the impact of personal participation and independence in the learning process. These findings suggest that, if we want to develop a child's sense of purpose and control over language and learning, classroom experiences should be directed toward increasing the child's interaction with the environment. The research is new, but not the idea. John Dewey's *Democracy and Education* (1916) suggested that "the inclination to learn from life itself and to make the conditions of life such that all will learn in the process of living is the finest product of schooling."[4]

(3) The technological revolution has emptied into the classrooms of America an array of multimedia instruments. This equipment may prove to be supportive of the teaching effort, providing an opportunity for greater individualization of instruction. Or as some suggest, the machines may take over the teacher's responsibilities and dehumanize education. B. F. Skinner, a pioneer in programmed instruction, argues for a powerful educational technology with reinforcement carefully controlled, contingent upon specific responses. Does this mean turning all classrooms into laboratories and elaborate media centers? An ultramechanized approach would certainly be cause for concern. Many educators ask, "Is any hardware, no matter how sophisticated, capable of serving the needs and goals of a human enterprise like education?" It is easy to be seduced by the economics of automation, by the appeal of individualization, and by the new freedom for the teacher, but the question is "Can the 'new' industry adapt its offerings to the needs of education?"[5] Educators at all levels will have to provide input through much research and practical experience. One thing is certain—educational technology and electronic communication are upon us. We must be equally certain that teachers are making wise decisions about how and when to use these new electronic assistants.

(4) Running parallel with interest in technology has been the trend toward humanizing life in classrooms. Schools have become more comfortable places in which to live and learn. Open education, the American version of the British infant schools, has prospered in some areas, and a variety of nongraded, team-taught organizational plans have also been successful. As the "back-to-basics" movement has gained momentum, these programs have often been severely criticized. But as Charles E. Silberman states in *Crisis in the Classroom*, "schools can be humane and still educate well."[6] It is not necessary to sacrifice knowledge or intellectual rigor when we emphasize the affective aspects of personal develop-

[4]John Dewey, *Democracy and Education: An Introduction to the Philosophy* of Education (New York: Macmillan, 1916) p. 60.

[5]Frances Keppel, "The Business Interest in Education," *Phi Delta Kappa*, (January 1967): 190.

[6]Charles E. Silberman, *Crisis in the Classroom* (New York: Random House, 1970), p. 208.

ment. It is not necessary for reading scores and language fluency to plummet as we encourage youngsters to develop healthy self-concepts. The fundamentals should include penmanship, mathematics, and reading skills, but also creative writing, athletic appreciation, and the development of positive human relationships.

(5) There has been concern about the efficiency of the group instruction attempted in many American classrooms. Some observers note that grouping "is likely to be very effective for some learners and relatively ineffective for other learners."[7] The harms of this "error-full" system, they suggest, can be minimized by making early instruction individualized, by reducing the number of errors in teaching and learning in the important, early years.

INDIVIDUALIZING INSTRUCTION

People unquestioningly do what is expected of them more often than not. Popular songs notwithstanding, too few youngsters grow up "free to be you and me." All of us recognize that no two people, apple trees, or kittens are exactly alike. Most of us believe that society needs individuals who cannot be manipulated. But the distance between belief and behavior can be immense. Individualization as a classroom practice challenges us to act out our beliefs. As teachers we have to ask, "Do I believe in the technique's basic principles?" Sometimes words become slogans. Individualization sounds like something positive, but over the years it has become a term that means many different things.

Teachers of language arts should be particularly sensitive to the ways in which words can become what Edward de Bono, an authority on creative thinking, calls "convenience packages." Such terms may be honestly or purposely misinterpreted. For this reason, the meaning and intent of *individualization* here should perhaps be made clear:

Individualization encourages

Self-understanding

Respect for the unique qualities in one's self and others

Being real

Originality and creativity

Independent thinking and action

Individualization discourages

Self-development at the expense of others

"Looking out for Number One"

Competitiveness

[7]Benjamin S. Bloom, *Human Characteristics and School Learning* (New York: McGraw-Hill,

Human separation

Always doing your own thing

Finding one's own individuality is a lifelong process. In the early stages, children need the assistance of sensitive adults. Without an awareness and respect for one's own identity, there can be no link to other people.

THE PRINCIPLES OF INDIVIDUALIZATION

Individualization is a way of working with children that can be part of any organizational plan. It is not a fad; it has endured because teachers know from experience that learning to learn is an individual matter. The degree to which a program is individualized in any given classroom depends upon the teacher's skill and commitment to the approach. In general, the major principles upon which individualization is based are the following:

1. All children are special. They have different needs, and they learn at different rates and in different ways.
2. It is the responsibility of the school to meet any needs of children that are educational in nature.
3. The learner is to be trusted. Positive teacher perceptions can increase effective intellectual functioning.
4. Every child is entitled to an education suited to his or her learning style.
5. Instructing large groups, though outwardly efficient, has many liabilities. It is effective for some learners, ineffective for others.
6. All children do not have to be taught everything. Some children learn without school instruction; some children must be taught the same thing in many ways.

INDIVIDUALIZATION AND THE TEACHER-MANAGER

It is not difficult to see how additional personnel and a greater variety of self-instructing materials may free the classroom teacher to meet individual learning needs more effectively. But what are the logistics? What new roles does a teacher-manager assume? As an individual or a team leader, the teacher's responsibilities flow from the diagnosis of individual learning needs and styles. This analysis enables the teacher, in consultation with the learners and available personnel, to plan learning activities and teaching strategies. In addition, the teacher-manager, along with teaching assistants, does the following:

Assumes and delegates instructional responsibilities
"Mr. Scott, the paraprofessional, will continue to work with John and Susan

on the *st* consonant blend, while I am working on reading abilities with the group that is reading *Ramona and Her Father*."

Orders and prepares materials and supervises their use
"We will need to use a variety of print and nonprint materials in teaching the mechanics of expression."

Makes available new instructional devices when appropriate
"Ms. Lang, our student teacher, will show a group of children studying poetry how to use a tape recorder in writing their own poetry."

Arranges the use of teaching machines and appropriate packaged learning programs
"Jimmy, you can work in the Language Arts Lab on the module for increasing reading rate. At the next session, you may want to take the test."

Devises a flexible physical setting that maximizes effective individual and group functioning
"The writing tables should be placed near the window and away from the woodworking corner."

Allocates time slots but allows individual needs to alter time patterns
"The next period will be ninety minutes instead of the usual hour, in response to requests for more time to complete projects."

5-1   Functions of the Teacher-Manager

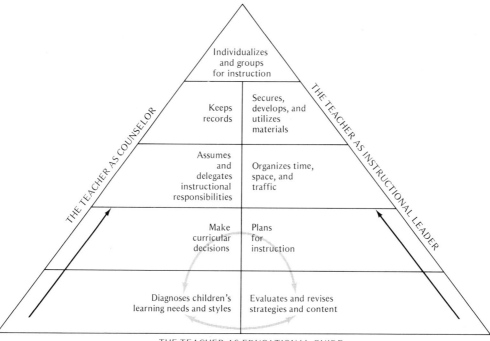

Manages the traffic so that the atmosphere is conducive to work and contemplation

"Jean, I know that you have been looking forward to working with Mr. O'Hara today, but I've arranged for him to spend an extra half-hour with you tomorrow."

Records individual progress

"It appears that Michael is more comfortable and shows a higher achievement level when material is presented visually rather than merely described.

Evaluates the effects of programs and materials

"The individualized reading program is more effective when it is preceded by a long period of preparation for self-directed learning. It will, therefore, be necessary to evaluate individualization in various ways."

The teacher-manager described above is free to function in a number of roles: resource person, counselor, group leader, organizer, instructor, mentor. Being a manager does not mean being a foreman; a factory concept of productivity cannot be applied to education. Teachers who wish to individualize instruction will indeed have to be skillful managers of the many facets of classroom life, but they must recognize that the system exists only to serve the learning needs of the children. (Figure 5-1 uses a pyramidal structure to illustrate how all managing functions are based upon and flow from the teacher's diagnosing, planning, and evaluation.)

LANGUAGE LEARNING CENTERS AND INDIVIDUALIZATION

One type of language learning environment that facilitates individualized instruction is the *learning center*. Learning centers provide a laboratory setting in which children have the opportunity to confront new concepts and test their language skills; in these centers, individualization and independence can flourish. There may be a center devoted to spelling skills or one that focuses attention on abbreviations. There may also be centers formed around students' special interests—the school newspaper, for example. There may be a number of centers in a classroom or they may operate in a classroom corner (Figure 5-2).

Language learning centers have evolved from the recognition that children learn at different rates and in different ways. Learning centers are an attempt to meet these individual differences by allowing children to move at their own pace in a setting in which there are no public signals regarding the child's progress. Because the students are involved in independent work, the teacher is freed to help those who require more direction. Basic to the operation of a learning center is the assumption that children can and should exercise considerable self-direction in their learning.

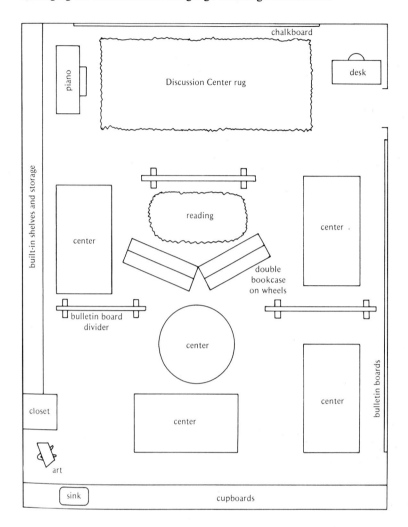

5-2   **Suggested Floor Plan Utilizing Learning Centers**

From LANGUAGE EXPERIENCE ACTIVITIES, by Roach Van Allen
and Claryce Allen, p. 37. Copyright © 1976 Houghton Mifflin Company. Used by permission.

Whether the learning center uses materials developed by the teacher
and/or a commercial publisher, the materials are usually sequentially
arranged and designed to be used independently by the child. Most kits
or learning center materials contain instructions, practice sheets, answer
keys, and individual record files. However, since language learning centers are probably new to the child's environment, unfamiliar language
concepts and skills are introduced and periodically reinforced by the
teacher. It is usually not until after this initial personal contact that chil-

dren are ready for the independent work that a learning center requires.

Individual language concepts can be identified and coded in relation to specific learning center activities. A child may learn that description is essential for language elaboration by doing activities in a language center that asks for riddles or in one that directs attention to description through the construction of a game. The same skill might also be taught in a center that focuses on similes and metaphors in poetry. A helpful resource for teachers interested in developing learning centers in the classroom is *Language Experience Activities,* by Roach Van Allen and Claryce Allen.

Language learning centers help children sense their language power by ignoring the pressures of time and trusting the child's ability to self-discover. The pacing of the learning is the concern of the learner alone. Each child is allowed to experience the joys of invention and accomplishment.

INDIVIDUALIZATION AND THE LANGUAGE ARTS

There comes a day in the lives of most teachers when they recognize that whole-class teaching is not as efficient as it may appear. Yet, since it also has certain advantages, teachers should realize that individualization does not always require teaching on a one-to-one basis. The two approaches can be blended.

On the whole, it is best to individualize those language arts activities for which it is difficult to find a common denominator. Particularly suited to an individual approach are experiences in language that have a strong personal component, such activities as writing and reading. Talk sessions, on the other hand, can be valuable group experiences in which the interests and abilities of many students converge. Creative

---

FACTORS TO BE CONSIDERED WHEN PLANNING INSTRUCTION

The child's cognitive style: Logical? Intuitive?

The child's emotional makeup: Excessive need for recognition? Self-confident?

The child's learning preference: Independent activities? Teacher-dominated activities? Self-selected activities? Assigned activities?

The child's tempo: Slow starter? Dives in? Fast learner? Slow learner?

The child's best approach: Visually? Orally? Combined Approach? Print materials? Nonprint materials?

The child's conceptual level: Concrete? Abstract? Where on the continuum?

The nature of the content: Too difficult? Too simple? Level of interest?

dramatics is another activity in which the needs of individual students may be met within the larger group.

Before you individualize even one area of the curriculum, you may want to ask yourself some questions:

1. How do I diagnose individual abilities and needs?
2. What will be the sources for instruction?
3. What changes in classroom organization and scheduling are necessary?
4. What records should I keep?
5. How will I evaluate the effectiveness of individualization?

Let us attempt to answer some of these questions by exploring how one fifth-grade teacher individualized a creative writing program.

Diagnosis of Individual Abilities and Needs

Richard Tarr chose an informal teacher/student assessment technique. After looking through the student's writing folders, teacher and student, together, identified the student's writing strengths and weaknesses; and the student left the conference with a brief written informal evaluation. Mr. Tarr kept duplicates of these evaluations for his records. Figure 5-3 shows such forms.

5-3   An Informal Evaluation

Name:	Danny Kavanaugh
Class:	5–2
Date of conference:	December 4
Writing strengths:	Imaginative ideas, clear organization
Areas that need work:	Use of descriptive words, topic sentences, proofreading skills
Plan of action:	Do pages 8, 14, and 18 in *Making It Strange,* Book 4. Select two creative writing assignments from the writing center. Proofread three pieces of someone else's writing. Arrange for conference when work is completed.

Sources of Instruction

1. *Teacher-Made Materials:* Mr. Tarr made available a number of writing springboards: pictures, objects, ads, anecdotes, poems, stories, and so on. These were kept in the writing center in large, attractive boxes.

2. *Commercial Materials:* Mr. Tarr did not use commercial materials, but for some students, the selective use of commercial materials or programs may be very helpful. Since many of the materials are quite expensive and often may not meet individual needs, the teacher cannot always rely upon them. The many commercial materials for creative writing include *How to Make Old Time Radio Plays* (Dead Pan Productions) and *Creative Approaches to Non-verbal Filmstrips* (Weston, Conn.: Weston Woods).

3. *Children's Books:* Many trade books were available in Mr. Tarr's classroom. Clipped to the back cover of each book were suggestions for writing to be attempted on completion of the book. Children were asked to write a different ending, tell about a character who made them laugh, or describe what the hero looked like.

4. *The Writing Center:* Mr. Tarr set up a writing center similar to the one described earlier. His students went there to find writing ideas, use materials, deposit their completed work, proofread other students' work, and actually do their writing. The writing center contained bulletin boards, a typewriter, paper of varying surfaces and sizes, and an assortment of writing tools. Workbooks, language arts series, assorted dictionaries, and word games of all kinds were also in evidence.

5. *Peers:* Other students were a source of instruction in the classroom. Peer assistance was valued by teacher and students. Mutual support was provided through the discussion of ideas, proofreading, and evaluative comments. Mr. Tarr devoted class time to developing criteria for evaluating creative writing. The emphasis was on inventiveness, sincerity, and original use of language.

6. *Teacher and Assisting Personnel:* In Mr. Tarr's classroom, there was a student teacher who was included in the teacher's planning. Provisions were made for this person to assume selected teaching responsibilities:

    Monitoring (helping some children find a suitable activity, getting the slow starter on his or her way, generally noting what is going on)

    Conferencing ("What have you been doing?" "How can I help?")

    Individual tutoring (getting thoughts down, talking out ideas)

    Small group instruction (explaining topic sentences, writing haiku poetry)

    Whole class instruction (teaching proofreading techniques, selecting main ideas)

Classroom Organization

Mr. Tarr's room was generally organized in a manner that encouraged individual and group interactions. The writing center was in a quiet corner with cushions and table space for writing. There were open spaces in the classroom where children could place their chairs for small group sessions. To facilitate the flow of work, a variety of containers were available in the center which Mr. Tarr labeled Completed Work, New Writing Ideas, To Be Proofread, and so on.

   Mr. Tarr also developed systems for the storage and return of materials, systems involving orange crates, old bookcases, and cartons. Appropriately labeled folders contained separate worksheets, and old milk containers bearing the students' names served as places to put writing. Sign-up sheets for teacher conferences were in a prominent place so that the children could schedule them themselves.

Schedules

When Mr. Tarr initiated this approach, all the students worked simultaneously for a prescribed period. This was a comfortable way to begin. However, as the program developed both the children and the teacher felt more confident and allowed the individualized writing period to spill over to other times of the day. Students began asking: "Can I finish the story now?" "I have nothing to do; can I go to the writing center?" "Is it all right if Johnny and I do our proofreading now?" A different type of

5-4   Student's Record of Writing Activities

My Writing Record		
Date	*What I Did*	*Approximate Time Spent*
2/18	Wrote poem	Half-hour
2/20	Wrote poem	20 minutes
2/21	Proofread stories in folder	20 minutes
2/26	Started story about inflation	Half-hour

scheduling began to evolve in response to student needs. With the help of certain youngsters, a weekly schedule was developed. Sometimes, everyone was to be writing; but more frequently, some children were to be writing while others were doing other activities. Individualization began to catch on and grow. A few children were allowed to work on their own in other areas. The time originally spent by the whole class doing individual writing assignments now was used to individualize spelling. The children were still writing, but at other times during the day.

Records

Managing an individualized program can be a difficult chore. But record keeping, even if it involves only brief notations, can provide the teacher with a secure sense of what is going on and what needs to be done. In Mr. Tarr's classroom, both students and teachers assumed record-keeping responsibilities. The students had their writing folders and also recorded writing activities in their notebooks (Figure 5-4). The teacher kept

5-5   Individual Profile

Name:	Janet Spier
Conferences:	1/11, 1/29, 2/6, 2/8
Small group work:	Proofreading, finding a title, humor in writing
Sample work completed:	Diary, A Humorous Incident, What the 1980s Will Bring, Animals in My Life
Preferences:	Writing about self, animals
Strengths:	Logical thinker, diligent worker, enjoys writing
Weaknesses:	Getting to the point, often too literal, run-on sentences
Comments:	Her writing expresses loneliness. Should be encouraged to read and write fantasy. Encourage proofreading and shared writing experiences with others. Start on writing longer pieces.

an index card for each student on which he recorded a variety of information about the child's writing (Figure 5-5).

Mr. Tarr also kept a class record so that an overview would be available (Figure 5-6). At a glance, he could tell that a large number of students needed assistance with the mechanics of expression. He also became aware that it had been some time since he had had a conference with Ellen, and that proofreading skills were generally in need of attention; a class lesson would be appropriate.

Teacher Time

The way in which teachers choose to divide their time during individualized sessions will vary. Mr. Tarr spent his time during a forty-five minute individualized period in the following manner: he responded to children's questions and assisted where necessary for fifteen minutes, he taught the use of a thesaurus in a learning center for twenty minutes, and he recorded his observations for the remaining ten minutes. During the same time, the student teacher read poetry to a small group of stu-

5-6   Class Profile

		Skill Needs			
Name	Vocabulary	Mechanics	Proofreading	Spelling	Conference
Ellen Abelson		√	√		9/20
Rick Antor		√		√	9/21, 10/5
Bonnie Brown		√			9/24, 10/2
Steve Cione			√		9/23, 10/9
Diana Herman		√			9/22, 10/3
Ped Lundy		√	√		9/22, 10/5
Ken Morris			√		10/3, 10/9
Lisa Queen				√	9/24, 10/8
Paul Raab	√				9/23, 10/4
Reneé Rourke			√		9/22, 9/29
Donna Siken		√			10/4
Peter Smith	√				9/21, 9/27, 10/2
Lin Yao	√		√	√	9/18, 10/3, 10/8

dents who needed to heighten their sensitivity to words. She also spent a few minutes speaking with one boy who had difficulty verbalizing ideas. On other days, Mr. Tarr divided his time differently. The needs of the group dictated the time arrangements.

These happenings in Mr. Tarr's class represent the first stage in a program of individualized instruction. Many teachers have had considerable success at individualizing aspects of the curriculum, but it is important to start slowly. Classroom management techniques, traffic flow, physical arrangements, and individual goal setting by students must be part of a gradual process. Both the students and the teacher have to recognize the support systems that are necessary in order for an individualized program to function effectively. What appears to be a free-flowing arrangement has in fact been carefully worked out. Individualization requires considerable prethinking, organization, structuring, and management.

Evaluation

Mr. Tarr considers evaluation an ongoing responsibility to be shared by student and teacher. Positively oriented, evaluation in his class emphasizes what the students have done well and how they may continue to be successful. Writing is scrutinized with particular care since the child is frequently sharing his or her innermost thoughts. Lack of success may be more of a blow to the self-concept of the student than to his or her writing skill. Mr. Tarr helps his students establish success-oriented criteria and the conviction that performance can be improved. Here are some of those criteria:

1. Uses descriptive words
2. Tells about feelings
3. Creates good topic sentences
4. Tries to write on a variety of topics

The success-oriented approach offered in Benjamin Bloom's *Human Characteristics and School Learning* assumes that ninety percent of students can reach "mastery level" if the expectations of their teachers are success oriented. Bloom suggests a number of "mastery learning" strategies; he recognizes that children learn at different rates and require different types of instructional assistance to achieve mastery.

In Mr. Tarr's class, evaluation results from casual observation, conferences, work with groups, and the reading of finished works in the children's folders. Evaluation always results in feedback to the children if they have not been directly involved in the process. Feedback is an important concept in evaluation for it alerts the student to behavior that should be reinforced or altered.

A variety of criteria are used by the teacher in evaluating the success

of the individualized writing program. Some have to do with a general-
ized approach to individualization:

1. Is the student able to self-select activities?
2. Is the student able to complete activities?
3. Is the student able to work independently in evaluating and checking his
   or her performance?

Other criteria focus on the writing process itself:

1. Is the response imaginative?
2. Is the use of language improving?
3. Is the student writing longer works?
4. Does the student seem to enjoy the writing process?
5. Does the student seem anxious to share the writing?

Determinations based on these criteria are noted on the records kept
for each student.

INDIVIDUALIZATION AND OPEN EDUCATION

Though the model for open education is derived from a program developed in the British infant schools during the 1960s, there have always
been educators in the United States who have supported its basic tenets.
"Open education is characterized by a classroom environment in which
there is a minimum of teaching to the class as a whole, in which provi-
sion is made for children to pursue individual interests and to be actively
involved with materials, and in which children are trusted to direct
many aspects of their learning."[8]

Many educators in the United States and Great Britain have been at-
tracted to the philosophy and practice of open education because of its
emphasis on individualization. As a result, a number of school systems
have encouraged teachers to "open" their classrooms. However, teachers
who wish to develop open classrooms should recognize that they will
have to make some basic changes in their thinking about how children
learn. Open education is somewhat different from individualizing in a
structured classroom. In the open classroom, the students not only work
at their own pace, using a variety of modes and materials, but also assume the responsibility for determining their educational goals.

In the traditional classroom, students are usually required to learn a
prescribed curriculum. The open classroom, by comparison, seems un-
structured, noisy, and generally overwhelming. It takes some time to appreciate that the arrangement of the room, the profusion of materials,
and the activity of the children are the overt manifestations of a definite,

[8]Lillian S. Stephens *The Teacher's Guide to Open Education* (New York: Holt, Rinehart &
Winston, 1974), p. 27.

well-ordered philosophy. You will soon note that in the open classroom the teacher and the student spend much time together developing individual goals. Not infrequently, teacher and student choose what should be learned; but in some areas, teachers prescribe goals. However, the use of materials, the modes of learning, and the time arrangements are most frequently the responsibility of the learner.

Some teachers express concern over the lack of specific curricular goals in certain open education programs. However, if we recognize that the knowledge explosion has made it almost impossible to cover all the "essentials," and that it has even become increasingly difficult to determine beyond a certain point what is essential, the setting of content goals takes on a new light. This is not to suggest that students should not be taught reading and basic mathematical skills, but only to point out that there are a number of questions about how such teaching can best be accomplished. Perhaps the school time of most students is better spent learning how to solve problems, how to use reference materials, and how to improve their thinking skills, rather than in rote learning of specific content.

As knowledge proliferates, experts in various fields have had to consider what learnings are most important. Some have suggested that learning the application of principles is more important than learning specific content. Chapter 3 provided several examples of activities that revolve around selected basic concepts that are central to a broad understanding.

INDIVIDUALIZATION AND MAINSTREAMING

Mainstreaming is the term given to a policy and procedure in which exceptional children (handicapped or gifted) are integrated into the regular classroom. Recent federal legislation has been particularly concerned with the handicapped. Public Law 94–142, the Education for All Handicapped Children Act of 1975, requires that educators prepare programs that will enable all handicapped students to participate in the "least restrictive environment." Though the word *mainstreaming* is not mentioned, priority is given to placing youngsters with special needs in regular classes to the maximum extent possible.

The word *mainstreaming* may be relatively recent but the notion itself is rooted in individualized instruction that dates back to the one room schoolhouse. Both mainstreaming and individualization assume that all children benefit from environments and programs that respect the uniqueness of the learner. Effective teachers have always mainstreamed; that is, they have always recognized that even in the regular classroom there is a broad range of abilities, potential, and learning styles. In the mainstreamed classroom, the range of individual differences is just greater.

Classroom teachers need assistance in coping with their anxieties about relating to the mainstreamed child. Not only are they concerned with adapting curriculum to a variety of handicapping conditions, such as physical disabilities, behavioral disorders, learning problems, or speech and hearing disorders, but they also wonder how the mainstreamed child will adapt to the new environment. Teachers need assurance that they are not expected to be some kind of super-specialist who understands the intricacies of each handicapping condition.

What then can the regular classroom teacher do to assist the mainstreamed child in the area of language arts? All that is discussed in this text about readiness and language development is applicable to the mainstreamed child. The difference is in degree and emphasis. Finding the optimal situation and materials and matching them to the child's level of development is important so that the child is not presented with what he or she already knows, or with materials or situations far beyond his or her present abilities. It is extremely helpful for the teacher to be able to consult with specially trained personnel and agencies and to have access to appropriate materials and literature. When available, the standard written evaluation of special education students, the Individual Education Program (IEP), can provide valuable information about levels of academic performance, recommended degree of mainstream participation, and short-term instructional goals.

As groups of teachers and schools prepare themselves to assist the mainstreamed child, they might wanted to consider these suggestions:

Gather a resource file of lesson plans, teaching materials, audio-visual materials, games, puzzles, and techniques used in special education classes that might be useful to personnel in the mainstream.

Observe special education programs that are located in the school or district.

Plan special mini-units for joint participation of handicapped and nonhandicapped students in such areas as Manual Communication, How Glasses Alter Vision, Tools for the Physically Handicapped, and so on.

Develop special instructional units for mainstreamed children.

Identify stories about handicapped people in reading lists.[9]

Many suggestions for creating different kinds of learning opportunities can be found in *Mainstreaming Language Arts and Social Studies: Special Ideas and Activities for the Whole Class*, by Anne Adams, Charles Coble, and Paul Hounshell.

One further way in which teachers can prepare themselves for working in mainstreamed classrooms is through an exploration of personal feelings about people with special needs. Understanding and sensitivity may grow from

---

[9]Adapted from *Special Education and Mainstreaming Handbook* (New York: Community School District 22, 2626 Haring Street, Brooklyn, New York, 1979), pp. 23–24.

Reading about the experiences of exceptional people

Interviewing people with special needs

Speaking with parents of exceptional children

Engaging in role playing experiences in which they are handicapped

The recognition that each child is unique brings with it a commitment to adapt existing programs and strategies. With the mainstreamed child, the demands upon the teacher are greater. More of the same good teaching is necessary. In summary, this may mean

—more time
—more drill
—more repetition
—more personal assistance
—more adaptation of existing programs
—more organization
—more teacher support
—more individualization
—more language experiences
—more teacher planning

DISCIPLINE IN THE INDIVIDUALIZED CLASSROOM

Certain rules in the individualized classroom may differ from those found in a more traditional setting. In an individualized setting, there is considerable movement as children go to different areas in the room, change seats, gather or return materials. Since the children's activities are not strictly monitored and the teacher is not necessarily aware of the purpose of each movement, the child senses a greater freedom. Feeling fewer restrictions, students may be less in need of "breaking out." Furthermore, the opportunity to discover interesting work increases in an individualized setting. The child who is involved is much less likely to present problems.

One other aspect of the individualized classroom that may minimize discipline difficulties is the fact that class rules are developed by the group. Apparently, greater participation in the formation of rules leads to greater personal interest in observing these rules. Since the presence of disruptive children in the classroom frequently causes other students stress and reduces teacher effectiveness, strategies that prevent disruption should be given careful consideration.

TEACHER COMPETENCES

The teacher who individualizes instruction should be able to demonstrate the following competences:

1. The teacher is able to diagnose individual abilities and needs.

2. The teacher provides and suggests sources of instruction in the form of teacher-made materials, children's trade books, and other commercial materials.

3. The teacher establishes learning centers for individualized instruction.

4. The teacher plans the use of auxiliary teaching personnel.

5. The teacher organizes a physical environment conducive to individual activities.

6. The teacher schedules time for individual and group activities.

7. The teacher records valid information about each student.

8. The teacher evaluates individual growth and class adaptability to an individualized program.

9. The teacher is able to budget time efficiently.

10. The teacher understands the assets and liabilities of individualization.

11. The teacher should demonstrate sensitivity in dealing with mainstreamed students.

12. The teacher should demonstrate rudimentary knowledge about exceptional children and request the assistance of specialists when necessary.

Afterview   Individualized instruction, which provides many opportunities to develop language and to identify and correct errors, may be one way for teachers to meet the needs of all learners in a classroom situation. The teacher-manager concept and the sensitive and intelligent use of additional human and technological resources is one way of translating some of the more recent educational research. Individualization is not a new idea, but it is a costly one. The price for educating all children is very high. The price a society pays for not educating them is even higher.

WHEN YOU WANT TO KNOW MORE

1. Which aspects of language are best learned in a group situation? In an individualized setting? Question several children at different grade levels regarding how they prefer to learn: in groups, with another child, individually. Try to determine which activities are preferred in each setting.

2. Contracts were originally developed during the era of progressive education and used in the Winnetka and Dalton schools. Find out how contracts might be used in individualized programs today. What is their purpose? Under what circumstances are they most efficient? Write out a contract form that a fifth-grade child might use for an independent project. (A good discussion of contracts appears in Lillian S. Stephens, *The Teacher's Guide to Open Education.*)

3. What criteria would you use to evaluate the success of an individualized program?

4. Study the list of competences on page 120. Which one do you feel prepared to demonstrate? What activities might prepare you to demonstrate the remaining competences?

5. Do the following exercise with a small group: Have each member select one major handicap with which he or she could possibly cope (deafness, blindness, mental retardation, paralysis from the neck down). Have each person explain the reasons for the choice and ask each to consider the following questions: How would the handicap affect your present job or life style? How would family and social relationships be affected?

IN THE CLASSROOM

1. With a small group of children (not more than five), develop an individualized writing program. In conferences with each child, establish personal objectives and plans of action for them. List the advantages and disadvantages of the program from the point of view of the teacher and the student.

2. Observe a teacher in a traditional classroom on two mornings and note his or her roles and functions. Arrange a similar observation of a teacher in an open classroom. Talk with each teacher to discover which of their roles they view as most important. What conclusions can you draw about each teacher's philosophy of education?

3. In order to heighten awareness of some of the problems that face blind people, lead a small group of nonhandicapped children in the following activity: A blindfolded child is guided by another youngster on a short walk outside the classroom; the partners reverse roles for the return walk. When the walks are finished, have the students discuss their feelings as guide and as "blind" person.

4. Read the Individual Educational Program (IEP) for a mainstreamed child in your class and then consult with special education personnel. Taking into consideration the short-term instructional goals, plan a series of appropriate language arts lessons.

SUGGESTED READINGS

Baruch, Dorothy Walter. *New Ways in Discipline: You and Your Child Today*. New York: McGraw-Hill, 1949.

Charles, C. M. *Individualizing Instruction*. Saint Louis, Mo.: C. V. Mosby, 1976.

Featherstone, Joseph. *Schools Where Children Learn*. New York: Liveright, 1971.

Flanigan, Michael C., and Boone, Robert S. *Using Media in the Language Arts: A Source Book*. Itasca, Ill.: F. E. Peacock, 1977.

Lee, Dorris M., and Rubin, Joseph B., *Children and Language: Reading and Writing, Talking and Listening*. Belmont, Calif.: Wadsworth, 1979.

Moffett, James, and Wagner, Betty Jane. *Student-centered Language Arts and Reading K-13*, 2d ed. Boston: Houghton Mifflin, 1976.

Petreshene, Susan S. *Complete Guide to Learning Centers*. Palo Alto, Calif.: Pendragon House, 1978.

Sheviakov, George V., and Redl, Fritz. *Discipline For Today's Children and Youth*. Washington, D.C.: Association for Supervision and Curriculum Development, 1956.

Silberman, Charles E., ed. *The Open Classroom Reader*. New York: Random House, 1973.

Smith, James A. *Classroom Organization for the Language Arts*. Itasca, Ill.: F. E. Peacock, 1977.

Other Materials

Dunn, Kenneth, and Dunn, Rita. "60 Activities that Develop Student Independence." *Learning* 2 (1974): 73–77.

Greff, Kasper N., and Askov, Eunice N. *Learning Centers: An Ideabook for Reading and Language Arts*. Dubuque, Iowa: Kendall/Hunt, 1974.

Lorton, Mary Baratta. *Workjobs: Activity-Centered Learning for Early Childhood Education*. Menlo Park, Calif.: Addison-Wesley, 1972.

Norton, Donna E. *Language Arts Activities for Children*. Columbus, Ohio: Merrill, 1980.

Allen, Roach Van, and Allen, Claryce. *Language Experience Activities*. Boston: Houghton Mifflin, 1976.

PART II

RECEIVING LANGUAGE

CHAPTER **6**

Listening

Preview   Although the primacy of listening has been established, this first and most pervasive language skill has been relatively neglected in the classroom. There is growing recognition, however, that changing communication patterns make the skills of listening more important than ever. After a discussion of listening in relation to the other language arts, levels of listening, and strategies for "tuning out," this chapter will consider practical ways to motivate listening in the classroom. The listening problems of nonstandard-English-speaking children will then be addressed. The remainder of the chapter will deal with a variety of listening activities designed to develop specific listening skills, such as following directions, recognizing sequence, remembering details. Many of these activities may be adapted to whole-class teaching situations, groups, or individual children working in learning centers. Sample lesson plans in listening will be offered and specific teacher competences identified.

"Good boys and girls never talk,
but they should listen.
We should listen and listen and listen!"

To you, *teacher,*
And your words, your words, your words.
Your words, your words, your words,
your words!

—Albert Cullum

Mommy! Mommy! You're not listening.
Teacher! Teacher! Why don't you listen to what I am saying?
Therapist! Therapist! No one ever listened to me.

IT IS ALMOST an epidemic. Many children grow to adulthood feeling that no one has listened to them, and too often their perceptions are painfully accurate. American society places such high priority on verbalization that the listening/speaking transaction has been distorted. Once we have learned to speak, and as we become increasingly fluent, listening grows more difficult. Drunk on the sound of our own voices, we too often listen only as a temporary courtesy extended while we await an opportunity to speak. True listening demands maturity, judgment, and control, and it is a primary catalyst in the learning process. The caring teacher who listens to students encourages further communication. At its best, the process is one of mutual respect and signals a departure from the traditional teacher role of "giver of the fire." The listening teacher makes use of silence as well as the ability to articulate. Active listening helps a teacher hear a student's interior voices.

THE TEACHER WHO LISTENS

How many of the teachers who have taught you were good examples of the teacher as listener? Despite the awareness of the last twenty years that the helping professions must also be the listening professions, minimal attention has been given to training or even predisposing teachers to listen. Since teachers serve as role models for their students, simply advocating the development of listening skills is unconvincing if teachers are themselves unwilling to listen. Listening is a neglected competence in the education of teachers and students. Certain experiences and behaviors seem to characterize "listening teachers":

1. They are listened to. In the job situation, they come in contact with supervisors and colleagues who listen.

2. They are sensitive to the many ways in which stress may distort their ability to listen.

3. They are aware of how threatening situations and people's criticism of the teaching role may pressure them to talk more and listen less.

4. They are able to step back and evaluate their own listening skills and strategies for "tuning out."

5. They are dedicated to structuring positive and responsive classroom environments.

6. They seek opportunities to create informal classroom situations that encourage students to talk more freely.[1]

SELECTIVE LISTENING: A SURVIVAL SKILL

As television and other electronic communications proliferate in a world forever broadcasting, the skills of listening assume new importance. The sounds of progress are an incessant intrusion on our inner space, a major contributor to a new and booming ecological monster: noise pollution. For some the cacophony of city streets is as much a sensual assault as the exhaust fumes from cars and smokestacks or the stench given off by chemical wastes. Even in many homes, "tuning out" has become a basic survival skill, silence a luxury for the few. As streets, public buildings, even homes grow noisier than ever, selective listening becomes a necessity—a skill that many children perfect with ever-increasing proficiency as they continue through school.

Classrooms and schools, by necessity, have also become noisier places. In the attempt to create more responsive, individualized environments for all children, every inch of available physical space is being utilized. Halls, lunchrooms, and auditoriums are almost always in use, and passing through a quiet area has become a rare experience. Programs are modularized, children go to and from learning centers, specialists come to the school, and public address systems and bells clang out their messages.

Classrooms are laboratories with teacher-managers coordinating the efforts of adjunct personnel. The open classroom, the learning centers approach, the use of programmed materials, and the accessibility of technological equipment, though valuable additions to the learning/teaching process, bring with them increased noise levels. The following in a

[1]Adapted from Sidney Trubowitz, "The Listening Teacher," *Childhood Education* 51, no. 6 (April/May 1975): 319–22.

Drawing by Ed Fisher; © 1979 The New Yorker Magazine, Inc.

"At least it's better than those awful radios."

fourth-grade class is not atypical: a small group in the corner is preparing a creative dramatics presentation; John is in the writing center typing his poem; Sharon and Laurie are building a bookcase; the student teacher is showing a filmstrip to a small group while the rest of the class is studying letter-writing skills with the teacher. In such a situation, teachers and children have to learn to disregard certain noises or be distracted from the task at hand. Effective listening must of necessity be selective listening.

The teaching of listening has been neglected for many years. This probably came about because

1. Listening skills are initially acquired quite naturally in response to the spoken word. Many teachers felt that their time would be better spent emphasizing those skills that require more systematic instruction.
2. It is difficult to assess a student's listening competence.
3. Research on the relationship between listening and language acquisition has not been conclusive.

However, ever since the word went out several years ago that listening was the most ignored yet simultaneously the most pervasive language activity (children may spend up to 75 percent of their school day listening), teachers have begun to focus on listening instruction. Recognizing that it is neither necessary nor practical to wait for all the research pieces to fit into place, educators are developing a variety of approaches for teaching listening.

The experience of many teachers with children clearly demonstrates that listening is the foundation for literacy: the listening vocabulary is the child's first vocabulary. Without the aural (listening)/oral (speaking) component, there would be no language. Without people who are skilled listeners, we could not run our government, meet the basic needs of our people, explore old and new worlds, or enjoy the fruits of our labors. Aural literacy, the ability to listen effectively, is the spark plug of human communication.

Listening occupies large blocks of a student's time, both in and out of school. Some educators indeed contend that the teaching of listening skills is one of the teacher's most important functions, for these skills are the base from which all other communication skills develop (Figure 6-2).[2]

The storytellers of yesteryear knew the power of the spoken word, and for many centuries people learned about their ancestors and distant places mainly by listening to lively narrations. Reputations and sagas traveled from country to country by word-of-mouth long before the printing of books. The recent reappearance of the oral history (now usually taped and transcribed for publication) may in some ways represent a return of the spoken word to its exalted position.

One could make a case for the teaching of listening skills based only on the need to assist children to become more critical consumers of television and advertising. New kinds of storytellers have entered young-

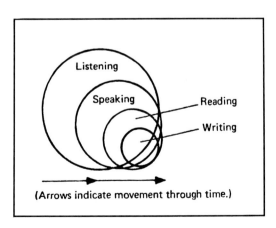

(Arrows indicate movement through time.)

6-2

Four Overlapping Vocabularies

From Sara W. Lundsteen, *Children Learn to Communicate: Language Arts Through Creative Problem Solving*, Prentice-Hall, 1976, p. 81.

[2]Sara W. Lundsteen, *Children Learn to Communicate: Language Arts Through Creative Problem Solving* (Englewood Cliffs, N.J.: Prentice-Hall, 1976).

sters' lives in the form of talk-show hosts, news commentators, and favorite characters. All frantically compete for the listener's attention. Children need guidelines for listening to and evaluating the contemporary gurus.

LISTENING AND THE OTHER LANGUAGE ARTS

Listening and Speaking

Listening is a decoding skill; it involves the taking in and transformation of language. Chiefly an internal encounter, it becomes discernible only through the encoding processes of speaking or writing. Some very attentive listeners do not necessarily express their understanding verbally. Sometimes this lack of verbalization is more a reflection of emotional style than intellectual ability.

Without a human model with whom to interact linguistically, that is, listen to and speak to, a child does not develop human speech as we know it. Observe the difficulties that deaf children experience in learning to speak. The lack of access to a verbal model as a source of feedback places severe constraints on the ability of the hearing impaired to reproduce sounds. Deaf children acquire language fluency, if at all, at a much later age than children with normal hearing.

Listening and Reading

The relationship between listening and reading is somewhat different. Both are decoding skills, but they depend upon different stimuli. Sound symbols (phonemes) are the basis of aural literacy, while reading is dependent upon visual symbols (graphemes).

However, listening provides the foundation for reading. Auditory discrimination is the first step in the reading process. Children learn to read by associating sounds with printed symbols; the sounding out of words is a technique often used by beginning readers. A frequent phenomenon used to demonstrate how listening may improve reading is voice variation. Pauses, inflections, or tone when speaking can later provide clues to meaning when reading. As Figure 6-2 illustrates, teachers need to help young children increase their listening vocabularies, for these words most frequently form the basis of reading and writing vocabularies. A limited listening and speaking vocabulary usually ensures an equally if not greater deficiency in reading and writing.

Several studies have affirmed that listening instruction improves reading.[3] Most recent research focuses on common elements in the two de-

---

[3]Sam Duker, *Listening Bibliography*, 2nd ed. (Metuchen, New Jersey: Scarecrow Press, 1968).

coding processes that relate to the development of comprehension skills. One researcher exploring the relationship between listening and reading skills has had considerable success at developing questions that go beyond the simple recall of information and reflect the kinds of skills important for later advanced reading.[4] The emphasis was on questions that required the recognition of main ideas, interpretation of emotions, and applications to real-life situations—questions that asked "how" and "why" rather than "what," "when," or "where."

Some researchers have attempted to develop listening comprehension scales based on developmental factors. Questions were ordered through various levels, ranging from no comprehension to the highest levels of inferential comprehension. The development of listening comprehension skills was seen as a building block for similar skills that are used in reading.[5]

Another link between listening and reading is provided when there are opportunities for the development of cognitive skills important to the listening and reading processes. The ability to select, classify, and see relationships becomes part of the individual's repertoire of thinking strategies. As a developmental process it should be related to what we know about the stages of children's learning. To this end, it has been suggested that listening comprehension skills be taught in an orderly way: literal comprehension (factual recall), then interpretation (finding relationships), then critical listening (evaluation). It may also be wise to give students extensive practice in literal comprehension and interpretation before requiring them to make critical judgments.[6]

Listening and Writing

The kind of listening that involves attending to our inner voices forges a link between listening and speaking. One of the principles of this book is that writing, a vital means of self-expression, is nourished by all other language experiences. Listening, more than any of the other language skills, may be the route through which we touch our inner being, our inside awakeness.

LEVELS OF LISTENING

At a very crowded and elegant British cocktail party, the host reportedly walked from one person to another and said, with a smile on his face, "I

---

[4]Carol Vukelick, "The Development of Listening Comprehension through Storytime," *Language Arts*, 53, 8 (November/December 1976): 889.

[5]Doric C. Crowell and Kathryn H. Au, "Using a Scale of Questions to Improve Listening," *Language Arts* 56, no. l (January 1979): 40.

[6]Daniel J. Tutola, "A Cognitive Approach to Teaching Listening," *Language Arts* 54, no. 3 (March 1977): 264.

hope you choke to death tomorrow morning." Not one person seemed to "hear" what was said, for the most frequent response was, "Thank you very much and you too." With due respect for English courtesy, we still have to assume that the recipients of the host's remark were operating at a very low level of listening efficiency. They were *hearing* sound waves, *listening* to some of the words but certainly not *auding*, a process that involves discrimination, evaluation, and processing of the message. An emotional factor may also have been operative in this situation. Relying heavily on other clues, the social setting, the smile on the speaker's face, his stance, and their own expectations, the recipients of the remark were perhaps unable to accept what they heard and quickly reinterpreted it. Obviously, many of the activities we classify as "listening" are merely its barest components.

Various texts offer different labels for each of these listening levels. The nomenclature is unimportant. What is significant is that teachers recognize that there is a listening hierarchy used and abused selectively by all of us. The first two stages, hearing and listening (sometimes called auditory discrimination) are prerequisites for the highest level, which involves comprehension. Hearing is simply the ability to receive and process sound waves. Listening is the recognition of the sounds of words or word-parts and the identification of variations in the components of sound, for example, hearing rhymes, consonant blends, endings, and so on. The auding or comprehension level is what most teachers refer to when they speak of listening. They are concerned with those skills that translate the spoken word into meaningful understanding through the discovery of main ideas, the perception of relationships, and the ability to draw inferences from a listening experience.

Once it has been determined that the child has no physical problem in the reception of sound waves, and that there has been no unusual interference by external circumstances, attention can be directed to the second stage, which involves activities for developing auditory discrimination. (Later sections of the book will discuss strategies for helping youngsters identify sound similarities and differences.)

Auding, in addition to being a high-level skill, is one that is continually undergoing refinement. Therefore, any practice at interpreting and judging linguistic variations contributes to a child's auding competence. One other significant component in developing a high level of listening is the recipient's willingness to attend to the listening material and be engaged by it.

"Tuning Out"

It is particularly easy for the student to "tune out" selectively because of the nature of listening itself. There may be an almost complete shut-out of sounds, or it may be a partial process. Auding can still be taking place, though at a very low level. The differential between the rate of speaking and listening makes it possible to grasp what is being said by the relatively inattentive listener. It has been shown that though we could listen at an average rate of four to five hundred words per minute, most people speak at about one hundred and twenty-five words per minute; there is considerable time left over for musing, daydreaming, and general mental meandering. Wandering away because of the time gap is only one of the means listeners use to "tune out." Its popularity among schoolchildren must be due in part to the privacy it provides. The following strategies for not listening, adapted from Ralph Nichols, are practiced by listeners of all ages.

1. Putting down the subject or the speaker
   "What makes him an authority on marital counseling?"
   "Some people can talk about anything."

2. Seeking distractions
   "I wonder where she bought her dress."
   "That man in the first row can't seem to settle down."

3. Refusing to accept the speaker and be even temporarily engaged by his perspective
   "I never would agree with his viewpoint. Look at his voting record."

4. Opting only for what is easy
   "How does she expect me to remember what I learned about the American Revolution?"

5. Reacting overemotionally to individual words, the topic, the setting, or the speaker's background
   "There he goes again with all that Communist jargon. Next he'll suggest that we overthrow the government."

6. Listening only for facts
   "What did he say was Rousseau's first name? That would be a good question on an exam."

7. Jumping to conclusions before hearing the speaker out
   "I bet that he suggests competence-based tests for all school systems."

8. Allowing personal reactions of prejudice, resentment, or boredom to take over
   "I never heard a philosopher who understood the practical realities of urban education."[7]

Motivated Listening

In teaching, the problem of actively engaging the listener is a large one. Much depends upon the child's willingness to participate in the process. It's the old question of motivation. Phrased from the child's perspective, it says, "Why do I have to listen?"

[7]Ralph G. Nichols and Leonard A. Stevens, *Are You Listening?* (New York: McGraw-Hill, 1957), pp. 104–12.

A fourth-grade teacher asked his students to tell under what circumstances they recall listening most carefully in or out of school. The children's responses provide us with some clues about motivation for listening:

"When you were telling us how to bind our stories into a book."

"When our counselor gave us directions on how to get to the campsite."

"When my father told me why he was so angry."

"When my grandmother described her experiences as a little girl in Europe."

"When my brother told a ghost story."

"When Mr. Gold explained the rules for the scavenger hunt."

"When you told me how much you liked my report."

When children have to act on the knowledge gathered from the listening experience, they tend to listen better. The best listening is purposive. Opening instructions like those below present a real reason for listening:

Project: "This is the way to construct a papier-mâché puppet."

Task: "Deliver this message [orally] to all of the fifth-grade classes."

Responsibility: "When Sara comes back, tell her about the plans for the party."

Evaluation: "I am going to ask five questions. Write down your answers."

Certain situations require careful listening. It is likely that if you found yourself on a sinking ship you would certainly attend to the last-minute directions on how to use the lifeboats. Urgency and utility contribute to attentive listening. Though a call for action cannot pervade every situation, it is an important initial ingredient for promoting good listening. Rapt attention is not always necessary, however. Different activities require different levels of listening.

A LISTENING ENVIRONMENT

Though poor listening is frequently related to inattention on the part of the listener, environmental factors can make or mar the listening mood. The sensitive teacher can in relatively subtle ways structure a mood that invites attentive listening. Some teachers have moveable furniture arranged in a circular fashion for listening activities, maximizing the possibility of eye contact. And aware of how a room that is too warm or too cold may cause even the most dedicated listeners to be restless, many teachers make a special effort to maintain a comfortable room temperature.

Speakers as well as listeners have responsibilities for the auding process. First, they must always speak loudly and clearly enough. Their material should be unified and not develop many ideas simultaneously. The tone of voice should not be scolding or intimidating. After the listener's initial shock, a voice louder than necessary does not generate greater attentiveness. Another important asset is the ability to make frequent eye contact with the audience. While not all teachers will develop the dynamic qualities that allowed storytellers of old to mesmerize their audiences, it is still possible for teachers to set the stage, create a mood, and improve their speaking styles.

READINESS FOR LISTENING

Assessing a child's readiness for listening requires a consideration of the general skills used in perceiving. Listening is not a discrete function. Rarely do we just listen. Most frequently, listening is combined with looking and sometimes with reading. If a visual image is not available, our imaginations may go to work, creating in our minds pictures to further fix what is being heard. If one mode of intake is functioning inefficiently, we compensate and bring others into play. Thus, if the listener has been distracted and lost the trend of what has been said, he or she may look around and search for peripheral clues: the reactions of other students, the chart on the blackboard, the printed material that has been distributed.

Many experts recognize the important role of sight in listening. The authors of a remarkable book, *The View from the Oak*, speak of the human "umwelt", our sensory composite for perception, and note how one sense takes over for another when necessary.[8] Examples in nature abound where this occurs, for the natural world provides special compensations: near sightless bats have remarkable sensors that pick up objects in their path, while aquatic animals develop their other senses because of limited underwater vision. Children can become aware of their own "umwelt" temporarily when they play games in which one sense is eliminated and they have to rely on another. Some popular ones include pin the tail on the donkey, blindman's buff, and marco polo, all of which involve locating things or people while blindfolded by listening to voices. Marco polo is played in the water.

Important factors to be taken into account in determining a child's readiness for attentive listening are physical development and emotional maturity. In order to listen, the child must be prepared to concentrate for a short but sustained period of time. Most students have had the opportunity to listen since they were born, but doing more of what comes

[8]Ann and Herbert Kohl, *The View from the Oak: The Private Worlds of Other Creatures* (San Francisco: Sierra Club Books, 1977), p. 36.

SOME READINESS ACTIVITIES IN LISTENING

Once a teacher notices behavioral indications of a student's listening immaturity, certain readiness activities can be employed to increase the child's listening skills. In many cases these activities are suitable for anyone wanting to improve his or her concentration and verbal responsiveness. For example:

Behavior: The child is unable to concentrate even for brief periods on what a speaker is saying.

What can the teacher do?
1. Encourage the child to sit close to the speaker.
2. Provide an informal and relaxed physical setting.
3. Set up a system in which children alternately read to each other. Gradually increase the time from three to five minutes.

Behavior: The child is unable to control responses and frequently interrupts the speaker.

What can the teacher do?
1. Provide additional attention in other situations.
2. Encourage and offer positive feedback for courteous behavior.

Behavior: The child overreacts to an effective speaker.

What can the teacher do?
1. Provide situations in which the importance of not responding until the speaker is finished is practiced.
2. Set up opportunities that encourage taking turns (games, looking at materials, doing jobs).

Behavior: The child is unable to listen without the use of concrete materials.

What can the teacher do?
1. Provide many listening activities in all curriculum areas.
2. Increase visualization through music. Play musical recordings. Child draws what he or she hears. (Emphasize that no drawing can be wrong.)

Behavior: The child resists listening activities.

What can the teacher do?
1. Be a listener. Model effective listening behaviors.
2. Point out the many activities in which listening is required.
3. Provide opportunities to play listening games (telephone, recall order of things given orally).

Behavior: The child appears unresponsive.

What can the teacher do?
1. Provide many listening situations that are practical and require immediate action (instructions for a game, directions for a class project).
2. Be certain the material is interesting to the child and at the appropriate level.
3. Trust the child with important oral messages.

naturally is not enough in the case of listening improvement. Systematic practice is necessary if children are to progress to the highest listening level.

The listening child usually exhibits some of the following characteristics:

Looks at the speaker

Seems desirous of eye contact with the speaker

Appears involved in the topic and ready to respond

Does not react to every distraction

Is relatively quiet physically

In most cases, the classroom teacher is not trained to assist children who demonstrate any organic or physical dysfunctioning in hearing. Children having listening difficulties that seem to be physiological or perceptual in nature should be referred to and provided with the appropriate medical or psychological assistance.

LISTENING AND NONSTANDARD ENGLISH

The child's first vocabulary, the listening vocabulary, develops from early experiences in the home. It is through this first vocabulary that children begin to learn who they are, who cares for them, and how they are perceived. By the time the child enters kindergarten, this listening vocabulary has been used to build a speaking vocabulary. The language of the home has become an integral part of the youngster's presentation of himself or herself to the world.

In the United States, children who come from a linguistic environment in which the adults speak Standard American English (SAE) usually have an advantage in school. When the home environment provides a language experience that differs from the school language experience, either in *kind* or *quality,* the child often has difficulty achieving in school. This difficulty can be partially described as linguistic, but a share of the problem arises from the way in which the child perceives his or her opportunities in the school and in society.

The teacher, as an official of an important societal institution, can assist youngsters whose language varies from the standard to recognize certain realities while providing support and opportunity. What are these realities? Standard American English is the language of government, industry, and the learned professions in the United States.

It is an asset in our society to speak Standard American English in most vocational and educational situations. Power in American society is for the most part in the hands of those who speak the standard form.

It is deceptive for teachers to give students the impression that it is easy to succeed in the United States without a fluent command of Standard American English. All of this does not suggest that one language or dialect is superior to another. Teachers must be extremely cautious not to imply even subtly that the language the child brings to school is undesirable. The suggestion that home vocabulary and language style has no place is a criticism of the child and, by implication, the child's family, traditions, and values. However, children can be helped to appreciate that there are levels of language used in different situations. Rather than a question of a right or wrong language, the issue is one of appropriateness.

Though bilingual children and those with nonstandard language patterns may present different teaching challenges, all language learners require environments that are rich in firsthand listening experiences. The class trips, discussions, telephone activities, sound games, and story hours suggested throughout the chapter increase fluency and are equally valuable for children whose language patterns differ from SAE. In addition, a variety of experiences to develop auditory discrimination in the form of games and exercises are important for developing listening vocabulary. (Consult the section on identifying similarities and differences in sounds in our language later in this chapter.)

The school-age child who is given instruction in standard English learns initially by listening. In many ways this is difficult for the youngster who already has command of a language. The need to acquire the language has lessened. Once again the key is motivation. Part of the problem lies in teacher guidance and student perception of the opportunities that will be available through increased language fluency. Will the acquisition of Standard American English make any difference in the child's life? Will academic success unlock any doors? These are questions that we would like youngsters to answer in the affirmative. In those beginning stages, when the child is acquiring a new listening vocabulary, and with it a heightened perception, the teacher transmits more than words. He or she communicates faith and support, and helps the child recognize that school achievement and language power are one means for realizing individual potential in the personal and job-related aspects of life.

A CLASS LEARNS TO LISTEN

Audrey Gerson, a fourth-grade teacher, was convinced that listening was a very important skill and that it could be taught. Her problem was to persuade her students that their listening skills could in fact be improved. She decided to speak with the children as she would to her colleagues. She had them engage in a little experiment. "We'll try to discover how important listening is in our lives," she said one morning, "and identify some of our personal listening styles. Let's start by writing down some of the situations in which you are required to listen." The children were rather surprised that the list soon covered three chalkboards and that so many occasions in any given day required listening. Watching television headed the list, followed by a great variety of school-based activities and the use of stereos, radios, tape recorders, and telephones. The students began to focus on some of the subtler forms of listening. Robert mentioned "eavesdropping" on his parents as they talked about his Christmas present. Katy told how she heard the sound of her grandfather's heartbeat "monitored" in the hospital. Some children wondered whether "wiretapping" or "bugging" could be considered another form of listening. Angela was sensitive to a different kind of listening experience, the nonverbal sounds in the environment. Picking this up, Ms. Gerson asked the children to focus on the sounds that heralded spring. Their dialogue was rich with examples of nonverbal communicators: the birds outside the window, the lawn mowers, the wind. "I can almost hear the crocus turning toward the sun," said poetic Lillie.

The animal world served as a natural springboard for sensitizing children to the role of nonverbal sounds in communication. The teacher helped them to discover that

1. Owls catch their prey not because of their large eyes but because they hear them.
2. Whales send messages that can carry over fifty miles and then swim toward each other's sounds.
3. Dolphins can locate floating objects from their sounds and reflections.
4. Dogs can hear sounds that humans can't.
5. Bird calls are extremely varied and the slightest changes differentiate a species.
6. Moles are blind but have unusually acute hearing.

Another form of motivation used by Ms. Gerson was to help children recognize their own communication styles. With their help the following list was placed on the chalkboard:

1. Are you primarily a listener or a talker?
2. In what situations do you do an about face?
3. Are there some people to whom you listen more attentively?
4. What kinds of situations improve your listening?
5. Do you learn best by listening? Seeing? Reading? Or any combination of modes?

This personal and private evaluation of their listening styles helped the children to recognize and respect their own differences. They began to make a list of strategies that can be used to tune out, one similar to the list on page 000. From this the students identified their own tactics. The openness of the discussion and the recognition that all people use some of these strategies made free interchange possible.

"What interrupts your listening in school?" Ms. Gerson wanted to know. A number of factors were identified:

—the garbage truck outside

—monitors coming in and out of the classroom

—the public address system

—other children playing around

—their own desire to be interrupted

—their mood that day

—things that worried them

Suggestions were provided by the class for overcoming some of the distractions. The group agreed that a comfortable setting, an understanding of what you are listening for, and a concern about the listening material are among the most important factors that motivate listening.

You might want to have your students prepare personal listening books highlighting the role of listening in their lives. Topics such as the following could be considered:

A Listening Profile

How I Tune Out and In

If I Couldn't Hear

Instead of Listening I _____

A Cartoon about Courteous Listening

Wiretapping as a Listening Skill

Listening in Nature

Me as Listener

How I Learn Best

How Much Peripheral Listening Is Possible?

The Sounds of Silence

Preparation of Lesson Plans

A lesson plan for developing listening skills is a helpful device for teachers and students. Of course, the teacher will not always adhere to this written prescription but will alter and innovate as necessary. That the lesson plan is more common in the other language arts may be one reflection of the general neglect of education in listening. A useful lesson plan is one that focuses the teacher's attention on what is known about children's learning and that accommodates the styles of the learners and the teacher (see the sample lesson plan on p. 143).

A LESSON PLAN FOR CRITICAL LISTENING

Grade: Fifth

Specific lesson: Critical listening—propaganda techniques

Rationale: Advertisers bombard the public with persuasive messages. Survival requires being able to analyze how these messages relate to individual needs.

Evidence of readiness: Children have indicated that they have often been the victims of false advertising: buying toys advertised on television, sending for tokens on cereal boxes, and so on.

Motivation: Cite examples of products that have had misleading advertising.

Instructional objective: After listening to several tape-recorded commercials, the children will be able to identify specific language that might be confusing.

Materials: Taped recordings of commercials

Teacher reference: Charles Winick et al., *Children's Television Commercials: A Contest Analysis* (Praeger, 1973)

Procedure:
1. Class discusses advertising and its purposes.
2. Small "buzz" groups listen to and evaluate recorded commercials.
3. Commercials are written on the chalkboard for purposes of language analysis.
4. Students focus on language that tends to mislead in a different group of taped commercials.

Evaluation:
1. Have children identify persuasive language on tape-recorded commercials.
2. Have children write persuasive commercials utilizing a variety of propaganda techniques, and discuss them with the rest of the class.
3. Have children write more "honest" commercials and discuss them with the class.

Provisions for future learning: The use of propaganda techniques in the speeches of political candidates

Listening in Learning Centers

The integration of listening with experiences in all curriculum areas is apparent in classrooms with learning centers or other individualized arrangements. For example, in one science center, Jody has picked up a task card that directs her to a cassette on which underwater sounds are recorded. She will write down her responses to this "soundscape." In the social studies center, Emily is reading the text of John F. Kennedy's inaugural address while listening to a recording of it. Nearby, Ira and a small group are listening to the student teacher explain how to conduct interviews. Adam is in the music center reading Mary O'Neill's *Hailstones and Halibut Bones*, a book about colors, as he listens to a recording of *Till Eulenspiegel*, the musically colorful tone poem by Richard Strauss. Lee is in the language arts center listening to a recorded folktale. Obviously, a number of these activities require hardware and technological equipment. Very often this equipment is available only in special rooms in the school, such as the library or media center. Listening activities do not necessarily require the use of electronic equipment, however. Activity cards can be very effectively used in the learning center. *Doing Things with Language: Informing*, by Carole Urza, is one of the many commercial kits that include cards suggesting oral language activities for children. The teacher, students, and auxiliary teaching personnel can also devise many listening opportunities. A variety of activities can thus be made available in learning centers each day, as specific assignments or for self-selection. Many of such activities are catalogued in the book *Language Experience Activities*, by Roach Van Allen and Claryce Allen.[9]

A SELECTION OF LISTENING ACTIVITIES

Learning to listen requires a battery of skills. And, like all learning, it is a developmental process with regressions and progressions; students and even teachers need refresher courses. What appear to be the most elementary exercises to increase an aspect of listening sensitivity may be of value even to a mature person. For this reason, the activities listed below are not targeted for particular grades; individual differences should determine the appropriate placement of specific listening activities. The listening skills toward which these activities are directed are

   Following directions and listening closely

   Recognizing nonverbal sounds

   Identifying similarities and differences in sounds

   Using contextual clues

   Identifying main ideas

   Remembering and noting details

   Recognizing sequence of events

---

[9]Roach Van Allen and Claryce Allen, *Language Experience Activities* (Atlanta: Houghton Mifflin, 1976).

Encouraging sensory images from oral description

Listening critically

Listening appreciatively

Following Directions and Listening Closely

1. Play games that depend on following directions accurately (Simple Simon, relay races).

2. Provide opportunities for following oral directions in performing specific tasks, for example, how to do a Virginia reel, how to get to the school library, how to prepare a writing folder.

3. Give an oral message to be delivered verbally. Gradually increase the complexity by adding another step, stop, or piece of information.

4. Have children listen to a telephone number or any series of numbers or words, and then ask them to recall all or part of the series. Highlight the importance of relationships for memory.
   Number series: 852 063 10 7 4
   Word series: ball, bat, base, bunt, baseball

5. Utilize mental arithmetic problems of increasing difficulty.

6. Give oral assignments that are equally as important as written assignments.

7. Provide a series of directions that relate to classroom activities: heading papers, care of painting corner, making a paperbag puppet.

8. Have children prepare sound effects for a popular story. (*Three Billy Goats Gruff* is a good one.)

9. Read stories that have extended repetitive word patterns and encourage children's responses. Some appealing stories for this purpose are *The Little Red Hen,* Jack Kent's *The Fat Cat,* and Wanda Gag's *Millions of Cats.*

10. Update games: In my grandmother's trunk might become in my space station. Each child adds an item that he or she would put into the space station, after repeating in correct order all the items previously mentioned.

   Lloyd Harnishfeger's *Basic Practice in Listening* suggests a variety of games and activities for providing practice in following oral directions.[10]

Recognizing Nonverbal Sounds

1. Note the use of school bells, gongs, and musical instruments to transmit messages during the school day.

[10]Lloyd Harnishfeger, *Basic Practice in Listening: Games and Activities* (Denver: Love Publishing, 1977).

2. Provide opportunities to listen to rhythm instruments and help children discover the different sounds and rhythms.

3. Encourage children to use instruments very softly as accompaniments to poems and rhymes.

4. Highlight situations in which children have to discover the source of sounds in and out of the classrooms: in a closet, outside the door, down the block, and so on.

5. Prepare a class sound story: using a familiar or original story, ask children to add appropriate sounds as background as the story is told.

6. Have children prepare a "soundscape," a presentation in which a place is identified by its sounds. Some areas with distinctive soundscapes are undersea, a forest, an airport, a space station, an animal pound.

7. Have children clap and act out different rhythms to recognize how patterns and rate suggest varying movements: running, swaying, hopping, walking.

8. Play musical selections and ask the class to identify their diverse moods.

9. Heighten awareness of pace by reading a story at different speeds.

10. Note street sounds on a walk with the children. A good reference is *The City Noisy Book,* by Margaret Wise Brown.

11. Ask about or provide firsthand experiences involving amusement park sounds: crashing of cars, whir of machinery, musical backdrops.

12. Have children observe birds and animals and note how they make sounds.

13. Prepare a tape recording of sounds to be used for different purposes: a storm, a haunted house, an experience in outer space, a jungle safari, and so on.

14. Ask children to note both the obvious and subtle sounds that indicate weather conditions: What noisy items do we wear when it is about to rain? What is the sound of hailstones? How does a gentle breeze sound?

15. Have the class listen to sound effects on records and identify them.

16. Prepare a "you are there" experience with sounds: an airport, a noisy restaurant, a fireworks display, a hospital nursery.

17. Ask children to add sound effects to a silent filmstrip.

18. Play games interpreting and acting out what music conveys: galloping, skating, marching, putting the baby to sleep, swinging.

19. Have children develop their own effects for the sounds around us: in the playground, on the bus, in a quiet house, in an airplane, in the kitchen.

20. Make up a game using a bag of sounds. Have children place a variety of items that make noise in a bag. Others guess the item from the sound.

Identifying Similarities and Differences in Sounds

1. Play rhyming games (clap when you hear a word that does not rhyme).
2. Read out loud both poetry that rhymes and poetry that does not rhyme.
3. Read poetry that relates sounds to words. David McCord's "Tick-Tock Talk" is very good for this purpose.
4. Read the nonsense words of a Dr. Seuss book and note how, what, and why they communicate.

6-3

From *Take Sky*, by David McCord. Little, Brown and Company, 1961. Copyright © 1961 by David McCord.

Goose, Moose & Spruce

Three gooses: geese.
Three mooses: meese?
Three spruces: spreece?

Little goose: gosling.
Little moose: mosling?
Little spruce: sprosling?

89

5. Have children raise their hands when they hear a word read that begins with a particular sound, has a long vowel, or ends in a plural.

6. Highlight words that have their own sounds: boom, shriek, whir.

7. Read these stanzas from a poem by Emily Dickinson that describe a train. Note how the sounds of the words contribute as much as the meaning of the words.

> I like to see it lap the miles,
> And lick the valleys up,
> And stop to feed itself at tanks;
> And then, prodigious, step
>
> Around a pile of mountains,
> And, supercilious, peer
> In shanties by the sides of roads;
> And then a quarry pare
>
> To fit its sides, and crawl between,
> Complaining all the while
> In horrid, hooting stanza;
> Then chase itself down hill.

8. Have a jingle marathon. Divide the class into teams or groups, with one team supplying a product while the second team supplies a two-line rhyming jingle; then reverse the procedure. Assuming soap is the product, the jingle might be:

> I use my soap both night and day,
> If not my friends will keep away.

9. Find selections in which words were chosen partially on the basis of sound. Highlight the musical qualities. Note, for example, alliterative phrases (Smiling Sally sipped a syrupy soda) and onomatopoeic words (buzz, bellow, gobble, chirp, shrill, clatter, bleat, squish).

Using Contextual Clues

1. Have children identify pauses and changes in tone in a spoken or recorded passage.

2. Ask children to guess each other's mood from the tone of voice. Ask children to explain how the voice provides a clue to mood.

3. Help children recognize how the relationship between parts of a sentence is a clue to meaning. Have someone read part of a sentence and ask different students to provide suitable endings or beginnings:

The Bionic Woman can ⎯⎯⎯⎯⎯⎯⎯⎯⎯
Pockets are good for ⎯⎯⎯⎯⎯⎯⎯⎯⎯
One day I came upon ⎯⎯⎯⎯⎯⎯⎯⎯⎯

⎯⎯⎯⎯⎯⎯⎯⎯⎯ on Halloween.
⎯⎯⎯⎯⎯⎯⎯⎯⎯ as he dropped to the floor.
⎯⎯⎯⎯⎯⎯⎯⎯⎯ and the turtle won the race.

4. Eliminating the key word or words, read a selection aloud. Have students suggest substitute words:
    Anne ran screaming down the street after she saw the ⎯⎯⎯⎯⎯
    I don't know why my ⎯⎯⎯⎯⎯ fell into the hole.

5. After reading aloud a series of questions, have children discuss what happens to the voice at the end of a sentence.

6. Write a list of words or statements on the chalkboard that can be given different meanings through voice intonation. Have the statements read by different children and ask the others to guess the speaker's intent. Some examples are "Me," "Okay," "I came in first," "But it costs too much," and "Who's afraid?"

7. Have the same passage read by different children with variations in mood and intent. The opening paragraph of fairy tales, nursery rhymes, or selections from the Bill of Rights are good material for this exercise.

Identifying Main Ideas

1. Ask students to develop a title for an orally presented or recorded version of a story, discussion, or poem.

2. Have children listen to a story and identify its main points, recognizing that there is often more than one.

3. Have children suggest a headline for a brief news story heard on radio or television.

Remembering and Noting Details

1. Ask children to analyze elements of a story and to support their analysis by citing details: Hansel and Gretel's stepmother was an unpleasant person because . . . Santa Fe is a lonely place to live because . . .

2. Ask children to listen to a radio newscast at home. What were some of the important details that helped to give a picture of the situation?

3. Before reading *Sylvester and the Magic Pebble,* by William Steig, ask the children to listen for some of the events that made Sylvester feel hopeless.

Recognizing Sequence of Events

1. As you read a passage, have children raise their hands when they hear words that suggest sequence *(before, while, following)*. Many of the paragraphs from the opening chapters of fairy tales can be used for this purpose.

2. Tell a familiar story in which the order of events is altered. Ask the children to set the events in order. (Start *Snow White and the Seven Dwarfs* with the arrival of the prince. Tell the story of Lynd Ward's *The Biggest Bear*, but begin when he is fully grown and no longer a cub.)

3. Ask children to listen for the order in which things happened to the cap seller in *Caps for Sale*, by Esphyr Slobodkina.

4. Give a set of oral directions. Have one child carry them out as the group checks for correct sequence.

Encouraging Sensory Images from Oral Description

1. Have someone describe a picture that only he or she can see. Encourage listeners to paint the picture in their own minds. Show the picture afterwards and have listeners check whether their images in any way matched the picture.

2. Read selections that are rich in "color" and "sound" words and set a mood. Have children describe or draw their impressions of them. For example: "My sister's voice is little and sharp and high like needles flying in the air."[11] Also see Mary L. O'Neill's poem "Sound of Fire" in her collection of sound poems, *What Is That Sound?*

3. Help children visualize the pictures behind words by asking questions like "What does the place look like in the story?" "Can you see that character?" "Can you picture yourself in that story?"

4. Provide music as a background for poetry reading. (A lyre or guitar is particularly effective.)

Listening Critically

1. Read aloud a purposely vague description of an exciting event. Leave out important details. As the children discuss the selection, note the misunderstandings that arise when communication is imprecise.

2. List on the board some words that are overused in conversation. Write down all the definitions suggested by the children. Discuss the confu-

---

[11]Florence Parry Heide, *Sound of Sunshine, Sound of Rain*, (New York: Parents, 1970).

sion of meaning. Some good words for this purpose are *gross,* and *cool.*

3. Have the class listen to a radio commercial. Identify the ways in which language is being used to persuade. (Specify words, tone of voice, pauses, and intonation.)

4. Have children tape-record their readings of the same selection at various times during the year. What changes in volume, rate, inflection, and emphasis do they note as they compare the different recordings?

5. Read a list of emotionally laden words without showing any reaction *(beggar, cheap, killer, prince, slob, goddess, liar).* Have students determine whether the words have an unpleasant or pleasant connotation. Explain that some words carry a high emotional content because of their association.

6. Ask the children to listen to a newscast and try to determine the newscaster's point of view. Establish guidelines for determining the reliability of commentators: Do they use language that is sensational? Do they present ideas in a straightforward manner? Do they provide evidence for their point of view?

7. Have someone read a political speech to the class, or have the class listen to a political speech on radio or television. Ask students to look for the following: bias, exaggeration, name-calling, insufficient evidence, conflicting statements, glittering generalities, favorable association, testimonials. A good source for information on propaganda techniques is *Language Arts: A Curriculum Guide, Levels K–12,* Las Vegas: Clark County School District.

Listening Appreciatively

1. Expose students to a variety of expert readings of dramatic and expository literature. Compare and contrast performances. Two of the companies that offer excellent selections are Folkways/Scholastic Records and Listening Library, Inc.

2. Read descriptions of sounds to students and encourage them to think about the sounds around them. What sound is made by a star falling? What sounds come from a meadow? What are some night sounds? Books of poetry such as *Sound of Sunshine, Sound of Rain,* by Florence Parry Heide, capture sounds in imaginative language.

3. Help children have fun with their own voices. Tape-record a selection and then amplify it. Encourage them to do a recording in a whisper, altering pitch, volume, and rate. The following sentences lend themselves to being read in a variety of ways: "I am lonely, tired, and forgotten. I have been in this lifeboat for three days. Will I ever be saved?"

4. Heighten awareness of some of the common and pleasant sounds made by musical insects. Ask children to listen for the sounds made in summer by the cicada, the katydid, the grasshopper, and the cricket.

5. Provide recordings or have children prepare tapes of bird calls of their region.

6. Read a variety of nursery rhymes to children in all grades. Guide students in recognizing how the rhythmical qualities contribute to the enjoyment. They can clap out rhythm as the rhyme is read.

7. Play records that require participation on the part of the child. Ella Jenkins has recorded two excellent participation records for Folkways: "Play Your Instruments and Make a Pretty Sound" and "You Sing a Song and I'll Sing a Song."

8. Provide many opportunities for children to listen to music and sing songs.

CHILDREN'S LITERATURE: A LISTENING SOURCE

Many writers for children are particularly sensitive to sounds and silences. They are able to express for young people what Thoreau wrote for more mature readers, "Silence is audible to all men, at all times, and in all places. She is when we hear inwardly, sounds when we hear outwardly.[12]

Poetry is very helpful in guiding children's awareness of sounds. Tape-record or read some poems to highlight the ways in which listening experiences may enrich thinking and feeling. Listening to poetry will help children appreciate facts about sound in language, such as:

1. Long vowels require a slower-paced rhythm.
2. Short, clipped words may be used for humor or excitement.
3. Rhythm can add to the meaning of words.
4. Certain combinations of sounds enhance meaning, as in Eve Merriam's "Gaggle of Geese," Laura E. Richards' "Skinny Mrs. Snipkin," or John Graham's "A Crowd of Cows."
5. Alliteration, the repetition of the same or similar sounds, serves to focus attention on sound relationships. Many nursery rhymes like "Peter, Peter, Pumpkin Eater" employ this device.

The following poetry collections have many sound poems that will captivate youngsters:

Shel Silverstein, *Where the Sidewalk Ends.* Harper & Row, 1974.
Eve Merriam, *A Gaggle of Geese.* Knopf, 1960.

[12]Henry David Thoreau, *Henry David Thoreau's Classic Writings: Reflections At Walden,* ed. Peter Seymour and James Morgan (Kansas City: Hallmark Cards, 1971), p. 44.

David McCord, *All Day Long*. Little, Brown, 1966.
Nancy Larrick, *On City Streets: An Anthology of Poetry*. M. Evans, 1968.
Mary L. O'Neill, *What Is That Sound?* Atheneum, 1966.
Myra Livingston, *Listen Children Listen*. Harcourt Brace Jovanovich, 1972.
Aileen Fisher, *Sing, Little Mouse*. T. Y. Crowell, 1969.
Jane Yolen, *How Beastly! A Menagerie of Nonsense Poems*. Collins, 1980.

Some individual poems that provide sound experiences are

John Updike, "Sonic Boom"
Edward Lear, "There Was an Old Man in a Tree"
Anna Grifalcon, "City Rhythms"
Charlotte Zolotow, "Things That Sing"
David McCord, "Scat. Scitten."
A. A. Milne, "The Three Foxes"
William Jay Smith, "Laughing Time"

The dimensions of sound are not apparent only in poetry. To further facilitate the child's awareness of the repertoire of sounds, read from and set out books that explore sounds from many vantage points. Beginning experiences with a foreign language will heighten sensitivity to sound, and students will develop a new sound vocabulary as they explore the thumping, clanging, tweeting noises in the world. Some good references are

Margaret Wise Brown, *The City Noisy Book*. Harper & Row, 1976.
Carl Sandburg, *The Wedding Procession of the Rag Doll and Who Was In It*. Harcourt Brace Jovanovich, 1978.
Polly Cameron, *I Can't Said the Ant*. Coward, 1961.
Esther Hautzig, *At Home: A Visit in Four Languages*. Macmillan, 1968.
Bette J. Davis, *Musical Insects*. Lothrop, 1971.
Francine Jacobs, *Sounds in the Sea*. Morrow, 1977.
———*A Secret Language of Animals*. Morrow, 1976.
Charlette Zolotow, *If You Listen*. Harper & Row, 1980.

A child's joy and sensitivity to sound patterns can also be enhanced by the oral reading of stories and songs with repetitive aspects or refrains. Children can tape their own readings or simply listen to a story being read to the class.

TEACHER COMPETENCES

The competences noted below are by no means an exhaustive list nor does the order of presentation indicate that one competence has priority over another. It is only through a variety of activities, the study of references, review of instructional resources, and the preparation and execution of lessons that teachers will grow and refine the multifaceted demands of the teaching/learning relationship in the quest for competence.

1. The teacher values listening as a learning skill by serving as a role model.

2. The teacher assists children to increase their listening and speaking vocabularies.

3. The teacher is able to evaluate the children's interest, motivation, and skill in listening.

4. The teacher demonstrates his or her knowledge of the relationship between listening and the other language arts by developing listening activities which reinforce speaking, reading, writing, and thinking.

5. The teacher is able to identify the three listening levels.

6. The teacher is able to personally recognize and help students identify the various strategies they use for "tuning out" environments with a minimum of distractions.

7. The teacher is able to plan activities which enable students to identify why listening is an important survival skill in today's world.

8. The teacher and the students arrange an optimal listening environment, one that is climactically and physically comfortable with a minimum of distractions.

9. The teacher is able to identify signs of listening difficulties and can provide readiness activities at an appropriate level.

10. In order to sensitize children to sounds in the world, the teacher is able to cite examples from nature and plan appropriate activities.

11. The teacher provides children who do not speak Standard American English with appropriate listening/speaking activities in an emotionally supportive environment.

12. The teacher provides children with opportunities for hearing and using different language patterns.

13. The teacher is able to prepare, execute and individualize lessons which develop listening skills in the following areas: following directions, recognizing nonverbal sounds, identifying similarities and differences in sounds in our language, using contextual clues, identifying main ideas, remembering and noting details, recognizing sequence, encouraging sensory images from oral description, listening critically, and listening appreciatively.

14. The teacher is able to cite and use examples from children's literature to enhance children's listening levels.

Afterview   For many years, listening was a neglected area of the curriculum in the elementary schools. Recently, however, researchers and experienced teachers have recognized the importance of developing sophisticated listening skills. The demands to listen have increased as well as our knowledge about how listening should be taught. Ideally, the teacher serves as a listening role model respecting her own silence as well as her ability to articulate. As they work with children on developing the art of listening, teachers recognize the ways in which listening provides a foundation for the other language arts. Current research seems to indicate that many of the skills necessary for effective listening are important for success in reading as well.

There are basically three listening levels: hearing, listening, and auding. Since motivation plays a major role in a child's listening skills, it is helpful for youngsters to analyze not only their listening styles but the environmental factors that may cause them to "tune out" or "zero in" on what is being said.

WHEN YOU WANT TO KNOW MORE

1. Try to identify your learning style. How do you prefer to receive information? Is it through listening or reading? A combination of the two? Does the preferred mode change with the kind of information?

2. What might be some of the implications for not listening in social relationships? To what extent do you hear what you want to hear? Give some examples.

3. Using the questions on page 141, evaluate your personal listening style. Compare your findings with someone else's. What differences and similarities do you note?

4. To discover how effectively people listen try this experiment: Give a brief discussion (about 10 minutes) on an interesting topic to a small group of adults. Then ask what they heard. Ask them again in 48 hours. About what percentage of the information was retained in each situation? Were your findings in agreement with studies that have shown about 50 percent retention immediately after hearing a discussion, 25 percent retention 48 hours later? What are the implications for the classroom?

IN THE CLASSROOM

1. Observe a large group of children listening to a speaker—during an assembly program, for example. What strategies do some children use to "tune out"? How do they compare with the strategies mentioned in the chapter?

2. Suggest listening activities for primary-grade children that could be used in a learning center. A good reference is *Competency and Creativity in Language Arts: A Multi-Ethnic Focus,* by Nancy Hansen Krening.

3. Develop a self-evaluation form that a student or teacher might use to determine listening efficiency.

4. Prepare a lesson plan for third graders that has the following behavioral objective: After oral experiences with literature, the students will be able to recognize how sounds contribute to enjoyment.

5. Find several children's books that have an appealing repetitive pattern. Read them to a group of children and note their reactions.

6. Use "compressed listening" materials with a small group of children. These materials are records and tapes in which about four to five hundred words are spoken in a minute. Story records played at a faster speed will serve the same purpose. Ask children to recapitulate the story and to discuss how they had to alter their listening style.

SUGGESTED READINGS

Chenfeld, Mimi Brodsky. *Teaching Language Arts Creatively.* New York: Harcourt Brace Jovanovich, 1978. (See Chapter 4: "Listening: a Forgotten Art?")

Duker, Sam. *Teaching Listening in the Elementary School: Readings.* Metuchen, N.J.: Scarecrow Press, 1971.

Hansen-Krening, Nancy. *Competency and Creativity in Language Arts: A Multiethnic Focus.* Reading, Mass.: Addison-Wesley, 1979. (See Chapter 3: "Music and Listening.")

Meers, Hilda J. *Helping Our Children Talk: A Guide for Teachers of Young or Handicapped Children.* New York: Longman, 1976.

Nichols, R. G., and Steven, Leonard. *Are You Listening?* New York: McGraw-Hill, 1957.

Pilon, A. Barbara. *Teaching Language Arts Creatively in the Elementary Grades.* New York: Wiley, 1978. (See Chapter 3: "Listen, My Children.")

Sund, Robert B., and Carin, Arthur. *Creative Questioning and Sensitive Listening Techniques: A Self-Concept Approach,* 2d ed. Columbus, Ohio: Merrill, 1978.

Other Materials

Carlson, Bernice Wells. *Listen! And Help Tell the Story.* Nashville, Tenn.: Abingdon Press, 1965.

Harnishfeger, Lloyd. *Basic Practice in Listening: Games and Activities.* Denver, Colo.: Love Publishing, 1977.

Palmer, Hap. *Feel of Music.* Freeport, N.Y.: Educational Activities, 1974. (One cassette tape.)

Russell, D. H., and Russell, E. F. *Listening Aids Through the Grades.* New York: Teachers College, Columbia University, Bureau of Publications, 1959.

Scholastic Listening Skills, Units I and II. Englewood, N.J.: Scholastic Book Service, 1977. (Ten cassette tapes.)

Wagner, Guy; Hosier, Max; and Blackman, Mildred. *Listening Games: Building Listening Skills with Instructional Games.* Darien, Conn.: Teachers Publishing, 1962.

CHAPTER 7

Reading and the Language Arts

Preview   The relationship between reading and the other language arts has been documented in many research studies, and the success of a reading program often depends upon a concern for general language growth. Success in reading, furthermore, should not be defined by the ability to unlock words but by active participation in the reading process. Children learn to read by reading, and a reader is someone who reads.

Reading readiness and prereading activities will be discussed in this chapter as a springboard to all aspects of language growth. Two reading approaches that do not make a sharp distinction between learning to read and the development of general language abilities, *language-experience* and *individualized reading,* will be described in detail. Since many teachers of language arts will encounter children who speak Black English as well as those for whom English is a second language, this chapter will discuss teachers' attitudes and strategies for teaching reading to these youngsters. The language-delayed child will also be discussed, as will the implications of mainstreaming. Evaluation and its relation to reading progress will be considered, as well as the development of test-taking abilities as a survival skill in many school systems.

Reprinted with permission of Clem Scalzitti
and the International Reading Association.

"It's a book, dear. It's what they use to make movies for TV."

A GENERATION AGO, the idea of reading a book would not have been viewed as having any comic potential. But the truth is that interest in reading has declined in the past twenty years as the electronic media have started to replace print as a source of information. Teachers note that they find it more difficult to turn their students on to books, and about 1.4 million Americans over fourteen years of age cannot read and write a simple message.[1] Though a number in this group are foreign-speaking newcomers, many were born in America and spoke English as a first language. There is yet another dimension to the reading problem which goes beyond literacy (the ability to read and write). Among those who have functional reading skills, the desire and need to read seems to be on the downswing.

[1]Wanda Danksza Cook, *Adult Literacy Education in the United States* (Newark, Del.: International Reading Association, 1977), p. 103.

LITERACY IS NOT ENOUGH

Judging by the pounds of paper that are devoted to a consideration of which method works best in the teaching of reading, one would think that this is our major problem. The irony of the situation is that the real dilemma is not a methodological one. Over the years, many different approaches have served to teach reading effectively. It is not a question of *which* program or *what* approach but rather *how* children can be encouraged to develop an interest in reading. At a time when our knowledge about the reading process is increasing and when funding for research is available, it is more important than ever to identify priorities. Today, maybe even as we stand at the threshold of new knowledge about reading, our most basic problem is translating that information into programs that develop reading interest. We must focus not only on how to teach reading but on how to teach children to want to read. Until we recognize that literacy is not enough, we will be trapped by an overemphasis on technology, trivial competences, and empty slogans like "back to basics." Teaching children to read is not the answer if it becomes a trite, mechanical activity: "Schools are ordered to teach all children to read quickly and well, but they are then cut off from new knowledge and the possibility of using it in creative innovations."[2]

As many forces compete for children's time, and television continues to cast its magic spell, the major question is: Of what good is reading beyond functional literacy; what need does it serve in our lives? It seems strange for print-oriented professionals like teachers to have to justify reading. But clearly, there is a need to do so. The success of a reading program is dependent upon the teacher's belief and continuing communication to students that reading is a worthwhile and satisfying activity.

Books may help children find out how to build a rabbit hutch, understand why countries declare war, or appreciate what their ancestors knew about medicine. Even more important, books may make youngsters laugh, cry, or look at themselves more perceptively. Children read when they can personally relate to the material. Whether the child is reading imaginative literature or the latest scientific data, the most important ingredient is personal involvement. For this reason, if we want children who can and do read, much thought and effort must be expended in developing programs which focus on fostering favorable attitudes toward reading. In this regard, the joyful sharing of books can be of great assistance. It has been said that literature is the best reading program ever invented. It develops interest as well as language skill. The

---

[2]Kenneth S. Goodman, "Breakthrough and Lock-outs," *Language Arts* 55 (November/December 1978): 19.

research of Carol Chomsky indicates that exposure to literature through personal reading or being read to has the added advantage of increasing children's linguistic skills.[3]

Teachers of language arts should recognize that the success of a reading program often depends upon a comprehensive foundation in listening and that speaking well is often a crucial cornerstone in reading success. Reading is a language process that builds on and revitalizes all other aspects of communication.

Many people act as if the difficulties in teaching children to read occur from not finding the right program. Actually the solution lies not in hooking into any particular method but in getting children to read by any means. Children learn to read only by reading. But you may say, "In order to read, certain skills are necessary." Obviously, if they do not know the sounds of letters and the meanings of words, children will not become inspired readers. But we don't want to raise a generation of "word-decoders." Reading is so much more than unlocking words; it is a vital link in the whole communication process.

UNANSWERED QUESTIONS ABOUT READING

There is much about reading that we do not yet know. Though the research evidence is growing, there is considerable disagreement among the experts. Skilled teachers as well see no easy answers as they apply research findings in the real world of their classrooms. Which method is better for Richard, who has difficulties with comprehension? When is the best time to begin to teach Lisa to read? Teachers have many questions about the reading process itself. Is reading a set of discrete skills to be practiced and learned separately or an experience-oriented process involving the whole child? Is the phonics approach superior to a whole-word strategy? Is context critical in reading comprehension, or is comprehension only a matter of sound/symbol generalizations? Since "the great debate" (as one popular reading text was subtitled) will continue for many years, it is important that teachers recognize that whether they emphasize code (rote skill) or meaning (understanding) in reading instruction, neither approach can exclude the other.

The next section will review some current research findings and teaching practices that help to bring into focus the dimensions of the reading process. At first glance, to the layperson, reading may not appear to be quite so complex as it has been made to seem. You hear people say, "In my day, most kids learned how to read. What's the problem today?" Others comment, "The old methods worked on us. Why change them?" Of

---

[3]Carol Chomsky, "Stages in Language Development and Reading Exposure," *Harvard Educational Review* 42 (February 1972): 1–33.

course, many well-meaning critics of contemporary practices may not give full consideration to forces that have had a significant impact on reading: different child-rearing practices, new cultural values, altered attitudes about the purposes of education, the omnipresence of television, emerging knowledge about reading, and a redirection of energies on the part of children themselves.

WHAT WE DO KNOW ABOUT READING

Recognizing that there is still controversy about many aspects of reading, let's begin with a list of some of the points on which reading experts generally agree:

1. Children learn to read by reading.
2. Language development contributes to reading success.
3. Experience plays an important role in learning to read.
4. A positive environment assists the reader.
5. Family background affects reading achievement.
6. The teacher matters in reading achievement.
7. There is no one magic method for teaching reading.
8. Learning to read is a cumulative and lifelong process building on previous skills.
9. It is important that children acquire independent skills for unlocking words.

Before we can understand how children learn to read, it is necessary to have some understanding of what the reading process involves. Here is what some authorities and critics have said:

> The process of reading is extremely complex. . . . A child must be able to perceive and interpret the symbols set before him; follow the linear, logical and grammatical patterns of the written words; recognize the connections between symbols, sounds and what they represent; relate words to experiences; remember and incorporate new ideas; make inferences and evaluate the material read and deal with personal interests and attitudes.[4]

> Reading is a communication process; it is the processing of written language symbols so as to arrive at a meaningful interpretation of an author's intentions, attitudes, beliefs and/or feelings. How meaningful the interpretation is depends on the reader's intentions, attitudes, beliefs, and/or feelings as well as the reader's skill, experience and intellectual purpose.[5]

[4]Paul C. Burns and Betty D. Roe, *Teaching Reading in Today's Elementary Schools* (Chicago: Rand McNally, 1976), p. 3.

[5]Mary Anne Hall, Jerilyn K. Ribovich, and Christopher J. Ramig, *Reading and the Elementary School Child*, 2nd ed. (New York: Van Nostrand, 1979), p. 8.

Reading is a psycholinguistic guessing game. It involves an interaction between thought and language.[6]

Reading is more than merely recognizing the words for which certain combinations of letters bring about a correct recall. It includes the whole gamut of thinking responses: feeling and defining some need, identifying a solution for meeting the need, selecting from alternative means, experimenting with choices, rejecting or retaining the chosen route and devising some means of evaluating the results.[7]

Reading means getting meaning from certain combinations of letters. Teach the child what each letter stands for and he can read.[8]

The letters in a piece of English writing do not represent things, or even words, but sounds. The task of the reader is to get the sounds from the written or printed page.[9]

As teachers and researchers look for the ways children learn to read naturally, they become aware that children use their full competence with language. They use their syntactic, semantic and phonological systems as they learn to read.[10]

The contradictions implied by these definitions explain why so many different systems for teaching reading have evolved. An analogy may help: If swimming is defined as an innate human behavior, then I might not hesitate to throw an infant into a swimming pool. On the other hand, if I believe that swimming requires a certain muscular development, learned skills, and emotional willingness, then I am more likely to postpone a child's swimming until sometime after the infant stage. Similarly, the way in which one defines the reading process directly affects the methods used in teaching. Even a casual survey of the manuals that accompany different reading series will show variations in vocabulary, format for reading lessons, and specific teaching strategies. The general orientation may also vary. In some manuals, the emphasis is on meaning; in others the deciphering of the code is paramount. One guidebook may stress visual and aural word identification, while another develops an experience-oriented approach in which children personally discover the common elements of language. Ideally, the approach you use flows naturally from your definition and understanding of the nature of the read-

[6]Kenneth S. Goodman, "Reading: A Psycholinguistic Guessing Game," in Harry Singer and Robert B. Ruddell, eds., *Theoretical Models and Processes of Reading*, 2nd ed. (Newark, Del.: International Reading Association, 1976), p. 498.

[7]Dewy Woods Chambers and Heath Ward Lowry, *The Language Arts: A Pragmatic Approach* (Dubuque, Iowa: William C. Brown, 1975), p. 114.

[8]Rudolph Flesch, *Why Johnny Can't Read* (New York: Harper, 1955), p. 121.

[9]Leonard Bloomfield and Clarence Barnhart, *Let's Read—A Linguistic Approach* (Detroit: Wayne State University Press, 1961), pp. 31–32.

[10]Kenneth Hoskisson, "Learning to Read Naturally," *Language Arts* 56 (May 1979): 495.

ing process. However, amazing as it may seem, despite all these variations in technique children have learned to read with almost every method!

THE TEACHER IS PARAMOUNT

You may wonder at this point why the classroom teacher should be concerned with a definition of reading when the reading experts themselves cannot agree. If you accept the premise that the teacher is central in the development of the child's skills and attitudes toward reading, then the greater the ambiguity and conflict among the experts, the more important it becomes for the teacher to appreciate the source of these differences, if for no other reason than to be wary of simple solutions, panaceas, or "foolproof formulas." The teacher cannot magically produce good readers; but through his or her expertise, the reading process of students can be facilitated. The teacher, not a manual, is pivotal in preparing a youngster for the reading experience. The teacher serves as a kind of nerve center through which the child passes on the road to becoming a reader. Scientific knowledge about how a child learns to read is growing, making it more important than ever for teachers to be tuned into new streams of thinking. It is both the teacher's right and obligation to hold this new information up in the light of his or her personal and professional experience. It is this understanding that earns for the teacher the title of professional. A well-intentioned adult who lacks this knowledge is not a qualified teacher.

Despite the growing body of knowledge in reading and the proliferation of programs, the problem still lands in the lap of the classroom teacher. To use an old truism; "the buck stops here." Teaching is a practical activity and judgments have to be made "on the spot." Certainly dedicated teachers are always expanding their own knowledge through courses, staff development conferences, and a general spirit of inquiry about the field, but in the last analysis, it is the teacher not the method that determines the outcome. Furthermore, research suggests that a combination of approaches will yield better results than a single instructional method.[11] Whichever instructional approach a teacher selects, the following considerations should have priority in the deliberations:

1. Learning to read is a complex operation.
2. Reading methods will be eclectic and adapted to individual needs.
3. The teacher's attitude is pivotal in reading success.
4. Reading manuals have many limitations and can only tell "what" to do, not "when" or "if."

[11]Robert Karlin, *Teaching Elementary Reading*, 3d ed. (New York: Harcourt Brace Jovanovich, 1980), p. 15.

HOW A CHILD LEARNS TO READ

Carol   Carol was listening to Mrs. Abrams read the Russian folktale "My Mother Is the Most Beautiful Woman in the World," the story of a little girl, Varya, who becomes separated from her "beautiful" mother. The townspeople who join in the search are surprised to discover when the mother and child are reunited that their perceptions of beauty are very different from those of the little girl. They see the mother as an ugly, toothless hag, whereas the child sees only a beautiful woman.

As Carol listened to the story she was able to identify with little Varya's plight, thinking simultaneously about her own relationships and experiences. As she considered whether or not the townspeople would find the girl's mother, how the story would end, and generally wondered how the problem would be solved, she was learning to read. Though not even looking at the printed page, Carol was indeed performing reading functions: she followed the sequence of events, made inferences, and used contextual clues. In making sense out of written language materials orally presented, she was learning to read.

John   John approaches the reading process somewhat differently. Sitting on his mother's lap as she reads *The Runaway Bunny*, he holds the book with her, helps turn the pages, and is generally aware of the physical properties of the printed material. It is obvious that he is listening, for occasionally he asks a question. From time to time, he touches the book and casually sweeps his eyes across the page following his mother's eye movement. He appears to fill in the contextual gaps by looking at the illustrations, building a bridge between the abstract words and his conception of reality. For example, when the mother bunny becomes a gardener to catch her runaway son who is hiding as a crocus in the garden, John uses the picture to provide some necessary clues about the location of the baby bunny.

In the beginning, the physical closeness and the association of pleasure with the experience is a decided asset for the new reader. The pictures too serve an important function. They provide an accessible contextual clue and a head start in image making. Soon the child will be able to supply his own pictures for new stories. His mind's eye will be ready to relate what he already knows to the printed word. On some occasions, he may even relate pictures and words so closely that he memorizes whole parts of the text and chastises his mother when she skips a section. There is some research that indicates that this memory aided by pictures may be an important phase in the reading process.

Linda   Linda is "reading along" with a record that tells the story of *The Little Engine that Could.* She begins to recognize in the text some familiar words that she has met looking through other books. This occurs only after many experiences with the same story. In the case of Linda, we know that she has also heard *The Little Red Hen* a number of times and chanted along with the words. Her "sudden" recognition of words used in both stories is not at all surprising.

Scott   Scott is rereading *The Snowy Day*. Because he relates the pictures and the sounds of the words to his own experiences, he is able to understand the story. However, if he were to meet the word "snow" in another context, he might have some difficulty. Scott's teacher has suggested that he read another book about snow, *Katie and the Big Snow*, so that he can develop an additional frame of reference. This variation is important so that the child can expand his concepts and build out from what is already known. The process of learning to read must involve adding, deleting, and generally reinforcing or altering previous conceptions if fluency is to develop.

Sondra   Sondra is reading *Georgie*. Though able to recognize and decode the words, she does not really understand the story. This becomes obvious when she is asked to make inferences about what will happen, draw conclusions, or compare some of Georgie's experiences to her own. Sondra needs assistance in understanding the writer's message for her experiential background is limited. The gaps in what she brings to the reading situation are even more apparent when she picks up *Changes, Changes*, a wordless picture book. She cannot fully enjoy the story, for her conceptual frame of reference is too limited. It is beyond her experience to anticipate the various quick changes that the pictures suggest. Though the direct reading of words is not involved, the same thinking processes are operative in the interpretation of pictures. Sondra needs exposure to a variety of new sensory experiences and the opportunity to expand her thinking beyond the word-by-word or even page-by-page analysis of reading material. In addition to experiences, the use of a variety of open-ended questions may be helpful.

Annie   Annie is reading a simple story about whales. Though her vocabulary is limited, she is very interested in sea animals and uses contextual clues and her own background to decode difficult words like *mammal*, *blubber*, and *ocean*. However, if the word *giraffe* had suddenly appeared in the story, her system of association would certainly have become confused. Annie is also assisted in reading by her knowledge of syntax. Thus, "the whale felt the waves washing over him" meets her expectations. She could not accept or understand "felt the waves washing over him the whale." Her experiences with language have led her to expect a certain pattern. The research of P. D. Pearson suggests that this expectation and cueing system assists the child in the process of reading.[12] By being able to predict not only appropriate vocabulary but language order as well,

[12]P. D. Pearson, "Some Practical Applications of a Psycholinguistic Model of Reading," in *What Research Has to Say About Reading Instruction*, ed. by S. Jay Samuels, (Newark, Del.: International Reading Association, 1978).

Annie builds on what she already knows, increasing her chances for a successful reading experience.

David   Children do not always learn to read using a book. David has drawn a picture of his baby brother. He has talked to his teacher about the picture, and she has written his words underneath the drawing: "This is my fat brother Mark. He cries a lot." David is able to read back the transcribed words. His own "talk written down" has provided the transition between speaking and reading. At a later time, he will be assisted to dictate longer "experience stories," rearrange the words in the sentences and read his sentences to other children.

In summary, children may learn to read by each of these methods:

1. Bringing meaning to the printed page
2. Hearing written language spoken
3. Becoming aware of the physical properties of books and the way talk is written down
4. Interpreting pictures in books
5. Associating a pleasurable experience with reading
6. Recognizing words in new contexts
7. Being exposed to quality reading materials with contextual variety
8. Thinking and interpreting beyond what is actually stated
9. Utilizing a cueing system that relates vocabulary to what they know about the subject and the conventional arrangement of words in sentences
10. Seeing their spoken language transcribed into writing

READING AND A CHILD'S LANGUAGE DEVELOPMENT

Reading does not take place in a vacuum. It has a social context and is reciprocally intertwined with listening, speaking, and writing. Reading skills are enhanced when there are activities that stretch thinking skills and foster opportunities for translating reading experiences into thinking. Reading and the other language arts act in concert. It is difficult to separate the contributions of each area since tests of reading ability are still not adequately designed to measure much more than the ability to read for information. However, we do know that students with superior language skills are usually better readers. Walter Loban's landmark study looked at elementary children from kindergarten through sixth grade and found that those youngsters who scored high in language also scored high in reading achievement.[13] Activities that result in listening,

[13]Walter Loban, *Language Development: Kindergarten Through Grade Twelve* (Urbana, Ill.: National Council of Teachers of English, 1976).

speaking, writing, dramatizing, and so on, have a strong potential for increasing reading abilities as well as catalyzing interest in language itself. The nature of the interaction, the which-comes-first dilemma, cannot be answered since the background, abilities, and interests of the learner are the most significant factors.

Reading is related to language knowledge, and language knowledge grows with reading. Though knowledge depends upon cognitive abilities (understanding of syntax, word meanings, sound/symbol relationships, and so on), cognitive abilities, in turn, are affected by such motivational forces as the awareness that reading increases our communication with others. Once children know that written and oral language is made up of words that convey meanings, they develop consistent expectations for meaningfulness in reading.[14]

The acquisition of reading skill seems to have the potential for expanding children's language power. Referring to a study by Ragnhild Soderbergh with deaf children, Thelma E. Weeks has concluded that oral language is not intrinsically primary, though it is usually acquired first.[15] When the two modes of language are acquired at the same time, each will enrich the other. Weeks further notes that reading increases the child's vocabulary, provides more encounters with different sentence structures than speech, and assists spelling. Though the positive effects of early reading on language are said to be retained, we might question whether this qualitative increase in language skills is due to early reading or to the same abilities that enabled this early reading to happen. The work of Strickland, Brittain, Durkin, and Clark, among others, suggests that reading and language achievement correlate. The exact nature of the impact of one upon the other needs further clarification.

READING READINESS

There is almost as much controversy about when to teach a child to read as there is about how. Studies indicate that an early start in reading is an asset in school, but poor timing or the wrong approach may boomerang and even retard reading progress. The term *reading readiness* refers to the optimum time to begin the learning of reading, the moment at which the child is magically able to attack and begin to comprehend the symbolic scribbles known as words. Here are some questions to ask yourself about reading readiness:

---

[14]Susanna Pflaum-Connor, *The Development of Language and Reading in Young Children* (Columbus, Ohio: Merrill, 1978), p. 124.

[15]Thelma E. Weeks, "Early Reading Acquisition and Language Development," *Language Arts* 50 (May 1979): 520.

1. *Which of the following activities prepare the child for reading?*

> Walking on a balance beam
>
> Listening for rhyming words
>
> Arranging letters on a flannel board
>
> Doing picture puzzles
>
> Inserting pegs in holes
>
> Listening to a story
>
> Expanding experiential background
>
> Providing conversational opportunities
>
> Planning trips
>
> Establishing an emotionally supportive environment

The answer is all of the above. For readiness activities are designed to assist the child prepare for the physical, psychological, and intellectual demands of reading.

2. *Which of the following characterize the child who is ready to read?*

> Follows simple directions
>
> Recognizes details in pictures and stories
>
> Interprets pictures
>
> Shows interest in words
>
> Asks to take books from the library
>
> Demonstrates awareness of print in the environment
>
> Follows a story sequence
>
> Waits his or her turn
>
> Chooses to look through books

Once again, any or all of these behaviors may signal readiness to begin formal reading instruction. Many of these behaviors involve physical, psychological, and intellectual responses. Readiness for reading is not a discrete set of skills; it involves the whole child.

Some Readiness Activities

Reading readiness activities are based on the assumption that what happens to a child before he or she ever picks up a book makes a difference in the childs' success at reading. Ideally, these activities are not offered as isolated experiences but are woven into larger units of work. Furthermore, not every child needs to be taught every skill; some children will already have good left-to-right eye coordination or the ability to recognize sound similarities. What follows therefore are suggested guidelines which it is hoped the teacher will creatively modify to meet the situation. Reading readiness activities are usually aimed at developing

—physical readiness

—auditory perception skills

—social and emotional readiness

—left-to-right eye coordination

—visual literacy

—language abilities

—concepts and vocabulary

Physical Readiness   Beginning reading instruction may be facilitated if children have some control over their large and small muscles. However, maturation varies widely; and some children will develop the necessary muscle control later than others. Provide practice for large motor skills by providing time for running, jumping, skipping, bouncing a ball, passing objects quickly, balancing, and dancing. Provide opportunities to develop small muscle skills through writing, cutting, drawing, pasting, tearing, lacing, buttoning, sewing, manipulating puppets, gardening, building, stacking, arranging books on shelves, making paper chains, and so on. Note any obvious physical disabilities or health problems.

Auditory Perception Skills   The ability to discriminate among different sounds is essential to a reader. It will be difficult for the child to read the word if he does not hear it accurately and cannot distinguish between similar sounds. Not infrequently, the child who does not hear the sound correctly, will say, read, and write it inaccurately.

Before reading this section turn to page 147 in Chapter 6 for a variety of suggestions on developing auditory perception skills.

After children have had many opportunities to listen to the sounds in the environment as well as a variety of instrumental sounds, the focus should be on noting likenesses and differences among the sounds of words. Experiences with rhyming words, word families, and words with similar beginnings and endings are all valuable, for they help the youngster with discriminations crucial to reading.

What the Children Can Do

1. Listen to music.
2. Play games.
   Take turns saying
   Family words
   Rhyming words
   Words that start or end with the same sound

"Can you guess?" Think of something that lives on a farm and starts with a *p*. Develop variations.

"What sound is it?" Children cover their eyes and try to guess the sound (chalk on the blackboard, window opening, dropping an eraser, flag blowing, and so on).

3. Make sound collections of pictures or objects that make loud, soft, scary, squeaky, deep, or sad sounds.

4. Prepare dictionaries by collecting and pasting in a book pictures of items that begin with the same sound.

How the Teacher Can Help

1. Read Mother Goose rhymes, nonsense poems, and stories to children.

2. Provide time for singing.

3. Encourage jingles, jump-rope rhymes.

4. Show sets of pictures (or prepare a chart of objects) that begin with the same sound.

5. Highlight similarities: Is this a "cat" or a "can"? A "sled" or a "bed"?

6. Show a sound collection: for instance, "a bag filled with *s*" (sand, soap, stone). Help children focus on initial sounds of objects.

7. Encourage children to imitate a variety of sounds (wind wailing, lion roaring, door squeaking, car starting).

8. Read pairs of words and ask children to raise their hands when they hear two the same:

jam	Jim	hand	handy
got	hot	list	last
bay	bay	all	all

9. Use some of the fine books for children that are sound sensitizers:

Margaret Wise Brown, *The City Noisy Book.* Harper & Row, 1976.
——— *The Country Noisy Book.* Harper & Row, 1976.
Lee Bennett Hopkins, *City Talk.* Knopf, 1970. (Children's cinquain poetry.)
Karla Kuskin, *Roar and More.* Harper & Row, 1977.
David McCord, *Away and Ago.* Little, Brown, and Co., 1975.
Mary O'Neill, *What Is That Sound?*
Peter Spier, *Crash, Bang, Boom.* Doubleday, 1972.

10. *Commercial Materials*
All manuals in basal readers have suggestions for auditory discrimination activities (Figure 7-2).

Social and Emotional Readiness   Children who do not pay attention or follow simple directions will have additional difficulty with reading. There are some helpful procedures that the teacher may utilize with these children before they are confronted with printed material. Most important is that the situation be emotionally comfortable so that there is less chance for the child to associate negative feelings with reading.

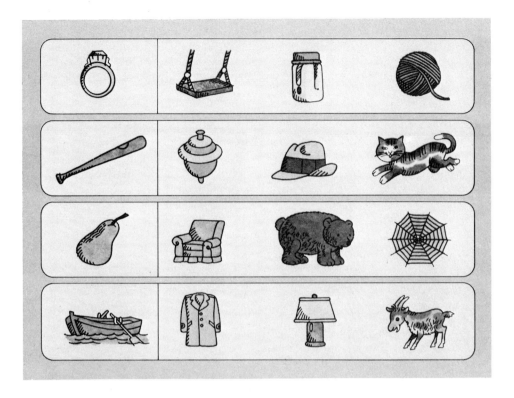

7-2   **Auditory Discrimination of Rhyming Words**   The student is asked to mark all the pictures representing words that rhyme with the word for the object depicted at the beginning of the row.

Reproduced by permission of Harcourt Brace Jovanovich, Inc. from *Look, Listen and Learn* by Margaret Early, © 1979 by Harcourt Brace Jovanovich, Inc.

The teacher who wants to equip children for behaviors necessary in the reading situation should provide opportunities for them to

1. Follow simple directions.

   (Give simple directions for games or activities—folding papers, delivering messages, arranging books—gradually increasing in complexity.)

2. Work independently.

   (Encourage children to "try it" themselves, to select something to do when a task is completed, to go on to the next step without the teacher, to value their own efforts.)

3. Cooperate with a group.

   (Encourage children to share materials and work in small committees; explain why everyone has to wait his or her turn.)

4. Listen attentively.

(Plan activities that coincide with the rhythms of younger children: alternate quiet and active experiences, don't make activities too long, choose appropriate times of the school day. Be sure that children see the need for the activity and have some level of interest.)

Left-to-right Eye Coordination   Since the English language is read from left to right, it is important that English-speaking children become accustomed to this progression. It is obviously not possible to plan for all the opportunities to teach this skill, but capitalize on the many incidental occurrences that can build awareness of right and left.

What the Children Can Do

1. Arrange numbered cards in a left-to-right sequence.
2. Arrange story pictures in a left-to-right sequence.

How the Teacher Can Help

1. Organize games that use right and left. (loopy loo, Simon says, and so on)
2. Give directions using right and left.
3. Call attention to left and right hands, eyes, sides of the room, and so on.
4. Place pictures on flannel board in a left-to-right sequence.
5. Encourage children to read objects in a picture from left to right.
6. Note that we write from left to right.
7. Read stories to children and on occasion place finger under the words as you read.
8. Point out left-to-right direction when writing and reading experience charts.

Visual Discrimination and Visual Literacy   Sometimes incorrectly referred to as visual discrimination, visual literacy (a broader term) goes beyond seeing to imagining. In a sense, a visually literate person makes the invisible visible. He or she perceives, discriminates, and makes judgments about the visual world at a high level of competency.

Visualizing and reading are related, for both acts require the participant to bring meaning to the page. Children preparing to read therefore must develop visual as well as verbal vocabularies. As Renee Queen has noted, "A richness of visual vocabulary facilitates the development of verbal vocabulary and verbal skills."[16]

There is a need for teachers to help children develop visual literacy skills as well as a variety of discrimination abilities. However, many children do come to school with a solid background in visual discrimination.

[16]Renee Queen, "Photography: How It Makes Learning the Three R's Easier," in *Photography as a 4th R* (New York: Popular Photography, Ziff-Davis Publishing, 1977), p. 8.

We must be cautious not to teach what they already know. It has been reported that "certain traditional readiness activities may be designed to teach skills that large numbers of pupils already possess."[17] This is not to suggest that some children still do not need practice recognizing shapes and letters. However, becoming visually literate is equally important and more difficult. It heightens the youngster's awareness not only of print in the environment but of many other factors that contribute to communication. Visual literacy activities do not preclude or have to follow visual discrimination exercises. A child learning to read depends as much upon perceptual and critical abilities as upon facility to identify similarities and differences among letters.

Visual Discrimination Activities

What the Children Can Do

1. Play with picture puzzles, match shapes, trace sandpaper letters.
2. Note differences and likenesses in shapes and sizes of objects: real, representative (pictures), and symbolic (letters).
3. Match words in lists of words of increasing difficulty.

Which word is like the first one?

Spot	Tom Jill Spot Bud

Spot	Speed Spot Sue Sandy

4. Play "the tray game." (This game builds visual memory. Place five objects on a tray. Allow a small group to view the objects briefly then remove the tray. Children name as many objects as they can remember. Variations include removing one object and having children tell what has been taken. The number of objects may be increased or decreased.)

How the Teacher Can Help

1. Ask children to interpret pictures—to name objects and observe details within them, and to explain their meaning: "What is Andrea doing?" "What is she wearing?" "Where is she?"
2. Show that words stand for things: use signs, posters.
3. Plan community walks to alert children to the role print plays in their environment. Children can reproduce print messages in school (street signs, traffic signs, billboards, store signs, skywriting, graffiti, addresses, advertisements in store windows, bus stop signs, names on trucks, license plates).

[17]Edward Paradis and Joseph Peterson, "Readiness Training Implications from Research," *The Reading Teacher* 28 (February 1975): 445.

4. Prepare envelopes with assorted objects of different sizes, shapes, and colors. Children sort them into visually similar categories.

5. Prepare a chart or work sheet of letter forms that starts with gross differences then moves to more difficult discriminations.

6. Farr and Roser suggest the following activity: Cut out several geometric forms and hold them up in front of the children for three to five seconds. Then ask the children to reproduce the forms on paper.[18]

7. Develop a task card that raises questions about one of the following:
   —Sequence of events
   —Details (shapes, colors, numbers, letters)
   —Classifications (animals, things that go, babies)

The task card may be read to the children (Figure 7-3).

7-3

Task Card

1. Look at the picture.
2. How are these coins different?
3. How are they the same?
4. Can you read the dates on any of these coins?
5. Write down your answers and place them in the task card box.

---

[18]Roger Farr and Nancy Roser, *Teaching a Child to Read* (New York: Harcourt Brace Jovanonvich, 1979), p. 141.

Visual Literacy Activities

What the Children Can Do

1. Look at the pictures in Tana Hoban's *Look Again.* This wordless picture book is full of visual surprises—things that are not what they seem to be. Initially, the child is shown only a small portion of a photograph. The surprise comes when the page is turned and the total object emerges. This book also provides the opportunity for teaching the concept that seeing is a matter of perspective.

2. Look at Joan Walsh Anglund's *Cowboy's Secret Life* in which the cowboy's fantasies are depicted in red while his real life story is in black. Two stories are being told simultaneously. *Jane Wishing*, by Tobi Tobias, is another good book for this purpose.

3. Look at sequential pictures of people and try to imagine what the subjects are thinking in each situation.

4. Look at pictures in which the object is only partially shown and draw what is missing.

elephant   rabbit   house

How the Teacher Can Help

1. Develop task cards that encourage the child to make inferences based on a picture. "What do you think will happen?" "What caused the problem?"

2. Keep a file available of rich, challenging pictures that you have collected from magazines, travels, instructional materials.

3. Focus on mood by providing pictures in different media: photographs, line drawings, collages, water colors, and so on. For example, children may look at several snow scenes, city views, or forest settings. How do they differ? *Sylvester and the Magic Pebble*, by William Steig, shows the same hill through the seasons. Ask the children to identify similarities and differences.

4. Take children on a walk in the neighborhood. Ask them to share what they see in the environment. Focus attention on buildings, roads, street lights, signs without letters, and so on.

5. Identify specific pictures in children's books that raise questions and encourage creative thinking. Books containing appropriate pictures include

Lynd Ward, *The Biggest Bear*. Houghton Mifflin, 1952.
Margaret Wise Brown, *Goodnight Moon*. Harper & Row, 1947.
Pat Hutchins, *Rosie's Walk*. Macmillan, 1968.
Louise Dickerson, *Good Wife, Good Wife*. McGraw-Hill, 1977.
Evaline Ness, *Sam, Bangs and Moonshine*. Holt, Rinehart & Winston, 1965.
Kit Williams, *Masquerade*. Schocken, 1980.

Word Awareness   While children's language abilities show wide variation, all children can increase their linguistic skills. As stated earlier, language proficiency and reading achievement are positively correlated. Time spent developing linguistic fluency has a payoff when the child is ready to learn specific reading skills. For example, the youngster who has heard many stories has a head start in developing abilities that lead to listening, speaking, and reading fluency (see Chapters 6 and 9). Experiences with drama, storytelling, dictation of stories, and poetry provide understanding of sequence, new vocabulary, and so on. Though not directly teaching reading skills, these nonreading experiences with communication usually translate into tangible reading benefits.

The building of word awareness comes from experiences with both oral and written language. Children need many opportunities to experience words as symbolic representations, concept hooks, and carriers of meaning. Word awareness involves exploring how context can help to explain meaning as well as how language is related to the situation. What follows are some selected activities for helping children to explore words in their world:

What the Children Can Do

1. Match words and pictures.

2. Cut pictures out of magazines or draw their own to illustrate commonly used words.

3. Dictate all the words they associate with a particular concept or word. Listed below is one first grade's list for the word *apple;* though most children in the class were unable to read the list, the words on it were part of their speaking vocabulary:

   Apple

Apple pie	tree
Apple sauce	fruit
Johnny Appleseed	dumpling

   Try the same technique with words like *monster, television, baby*.

4. Match popular advertising logos and objects with the appropriate words, for example, dinosaur (BP gasoline), golden arches (McDonald's).

How the Teacher Can Help

1. Using large clear manuscript letters, label many of the items and centers in the classroom.

2. Prepare labels for children to wear while assuming certain roles in classroom work or games (leader, Simon, teacher, mother).

3. Label directions in the room (left, right, up, down) as well as colors and ordinal units (first, second, and so on.)

4. With the help of the class, prepare an experience chart on a relevant activity. Have the children illustrate the chart with pictures and three-dimensional objects. (See Figure 7-4 and the directions below.)

7-4   **Experience Chart**

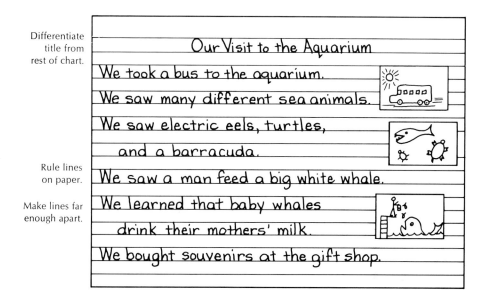

Differentiate title from rest of chart.

Rule lines on paper.

Make lines far enough apart.

Our Visit to the Aquarium

We took a bus to the aquarium.

We saw many different sea animals.

We saw electric eels, turtles, and a barracuda.

We saw a man feed a big white whale.

We learned that baby whales drink their mothers' milk.

We bought souvenirs at the gift shop.

HOW TO PREPARE AN EXPERIENCE CHART

1. Select an experience in which the students have participated.
2. Write the students' reactions to this experience on the chalkboard.
3. Help the students determine the sequence of the sentences.
4. Use manuscript writing in most situations.
5. Have the students title the chart.
6. Transcribe the chart onto oak tag or some other large paper; write large enough so that the chart can be easily read from a distance.
7. Ask the students to illustrate the chart with their own drawings, three-dimensional objects, or photographs.

5. Make signs for classroom use:

We are one big, happy family.

Class 1-4 is in the gym.   This is the Reading Roost.

6. Write a short common word on the chalkboard and have children suggest
   longer terms that include it. Encourage and accept all variations:

   cat   cats, catnip, cattail
   mash   mashes, mashing, mashed potatoes, smash
   barn   barns, barnyard, barn raising, barn dance
   peach   peaches, peachy, peaches and cream, peach pie

Concepts and Vocabulary   Reading is a cognitive act that requires conceptual as well as language facility (see Chapter 2). As has been noted,
many concepts develop in a child's mind before the language for them.
Indeed, all of us have experienced knowledge that we cannot express.

Since language develops from the concrete to the abstract, it is important that children be given many and varied opportunities to travel on
this continuum. Concepts are abstractions and words are abstractions;
but words can clarify concepts. Concepts are best learned in experiential
situations in which children make perceptual contact with an idea.
Words that do not represent tangible things have no meaning to children
until they are given a concrete frame of reference. A child cannot touch
"love" or "yesterday" or "death." Experiences give meaning to concepts.
Many of the word awareness activities in the previous section are concept builders. The experiences suggested below also expand the child's
conceptual framework by providing a frame of reference:

What the Children Can Do

1. Play "categories," a game in which a category is given (animals, jobs, vegetables, kitchen objects) and the players have to guess the object.
2. Act out abstractions: one child acts out a word that is not an object and
   the other children guess the idea (happy, dream, the family, friendship).
3. Cut out pictures or create objects that have the same shape but different
   purposes.

How the Teacher Can Help

1. Stress relational concepts:

   The book is under _____.
   The chalk is next to_____.
   The chair is near_____.

   The concept of opposites may also be taught at this time.

2. Do classification projects.

3. Show films that provide vicarious experiences with unfamiliar ideas.

4. Provide practice with concepts and vocabulary of size, time, and space (small–large, upper–middle–lower, top–bottom, now–later, before–after); for example, ask children to draw a picture with large and small circles.

5. Take the class on a food-maker tour. If possible go behind the scenes at food plants so children can see the various people, processes, and machinery used in manufacturing food. The concept that food does not "grow" on supermarket shelves will be better understood. Many local factories offer such tours.

6. Provide many activities for sensory experiences:

   A tasting test.
   A bag of sounds. Place unusual sound makers in a bag.
   A touching board. Paste a variety of textures on a board
     for children to feel. Have them add to the board items
     that have a similar texture.
   A favorite smell. Have children bring to class an item that
     they like to smell.
   A sight sensation. Show a filmstrip that includes unusual scenes
     of space or underwater life.

7. Have available some of the many fine children's books that help
   to clarify the essentials of an abstract concept. Some particularly good
   descriptions can be found in the following books:

   George Ancona, *Faces*. Dutton, 1972.
   Judi Barrett and Ron Barrett, *Animals Should Definitely Not Act like People*. Atheneum, 1980.
   Ed Emberly, *The Wing on a Flea*. Little, Brown, 1961. (Shapes.)
   Nonny Hogrogian, *Apples*. Macmillan, 1972.
   Ruth Krauss, *A Hole Is to Dig*. Harper & Row, 1952. (Children's definitions.)
   Alice and Martin Provensen, *What Is a Color?* Golden Press, 1967.
   Seymour Simon, *The Secret Clocks*. Viking Press, 1979. (Time senses of living things.)
   Peter Spier, *Fast-Slow-High-Low*. Doubleday, 1972. (Opposites.)

   Alphabet and counting books are also helpful for teaching the concept that symbols represent a variety of ideas.

Determining Reading Readiness

Teachers who have been preparing and selecting readiness materials and experiences for their pupils may not need a formal reading readiness inventory. However, since many factors have to be considered, a check list like the one in Figure 7–5 may be helpful. In fact, who is ready to read sometimes becomes apparent early in the term. This does not mean that additional readiness skills are not necessary, but it does suggest that

Check List for Reading Readiness

Physical Readiness

1. Eyes

    a. Do the child's eyes seem comfortable (does not squint, rub eyes, hold materials too close or too far from eyes)?

    b. Are the results of clinical tests or an oculist's examination favorable?

2. Ears

    a. Is it apparent through his response to questions or directions that he is able to hear what is said to the class?

    b. Does he respond to a low-voice test of 20 feet, a whisper test of 15 inches?

    c. Do the results of his audiometer test indicate normal hearing ability?

3. Speech

    a. Does he articulate clearly?

    b. Does he speak in a group with some confidence?

    c. Does he speak without gross errors in pronunciation?

    d. Does he respond to suggestions for speech improvement?

4. Hand-Eye Co-ordination

    Is he able to make his hands work together in cutting, using tools, or bouncing a ball?

5. General Health

    a. Does he give an impression of good health?

    b. Does he seem well nourished?

    c. Does the school physical examination reveal good health?

Social Readiness

1. Co-operation

    a. Does he work well with a group, taking his share of the responsibility?

    b. Does he co-operate in playing games with other children?

    c. Can he direct his attention to a specific learning situation?

    d. Does he listen rather than interrupt?

2. Sharing

    a. Does he share materials, without monopolizing their use?

    b. Does he offer help when another child needs it?

    c. Does he await his turn in playing or in games?

    d. Does he await his turn for help from the teacher?

3. Self-reliance

    a. Does he work things through for himself without asking the teacher about the next step?

    b. Does he take care of his clothing and materials?

    c. Does he find something to do when he finishes an assigned task?

    d. Does he take good care of materials assigned to him?

Emotional Readiness

1. Adjustment to Task

    a. Does the child see a task, such as drawing, preparing for an activity, or cleaning up, through to completion?

    b. Does he accept changes in school routine calmly?

    c. Does he appear to be happy and well adjusted in schoolwork, as evidenced by relaxed attitude, pride in work, and eagerness for a new task?

    d. Does he follow adult leadership without showing resentment?

YES NO

1. ☐ ☐
2. ☐ ☐
3. ☐ ☐
4. ☐ ☐
5. ☐ ☐
6. ☐ ☐
7. ☐ ☐
8. ☐ ☐
9. ☐ ☐
10. ☐ ☐
11. ☐ ☐
12. ☐ ☐
13. ☐ ☐
14. ☐ ☐
15. ☐ ☐
16. ☐ ☐
17. ☐ ☐
18. ☐ ☐
19. ☐ ☐
20. ☐ ☐
21. ☐ ☐
22. ☐ ☐
23. ☐ ☐
24. ☐ ☐
25. ☐ ☐
26. ☐ ☐
27. ☐ ☐
28. ☐ ☐
29. ☐ ☐

2. *Poise*

   a. Does he accept a certain amount of opposition or defeat without crying   30. ☐ ☐
   or sulking?

   b. Does he meet strangers without displaying unusual shyness?   31. ☐ ☐

Psychological Readiness

1. *Mind-Set for Reading*

   a. Does the child appear interested in books and reading?   32. ☐ ☐

   b. Does he ask the meanings of words or signs?   33. ☐ ☐

   c. Is he interested in the shapes of unusual words?   34. ☐ ☐

2. *Mental Maturity*

   a. Do the results of the child's mental test predict probable success in   35. ☐ ☐
   learning to read?

   b. Can he give reasons for his opinions about his own work or the work of   36. ☐ ☐
   others?

   c. Can he make or draw something to illustrate an idea as well as most   37. ☐ ☐
   children of his age?

   d. Is his memory span sufficient to allow memorization of a short poem or   38. ☐ ☐
   song?

   e. Can he tell a story without confusing the order of events?   39. ☐ ☐

   f. Can he listen or work for five or ten minutes without restlessness?   40. ☐ ☐

3. *Mental Habits*

   a. Has the child established the habit of looking at a succession of items   41. ☐ ☐
   from left to right?

   b. Does his interpretation of pictures extend beyond mere enumeration of   42. ☐ ☐
   details?

   c. Does he grasp the fact that symbols may be associated with spoken   43. ☐ ☐
   language?

   d. Can he predict possible outcomes for a story?   44. ☐ ☐

   e. Can he remember the central thought of a story as well as the important   45. ☐ ☐
   details?

   f. Does he alter his own method to profit by another child's example?   46. ☐ ☐

4. *Language Patterns*

   a. Does he take part in class discussions and conversations?   47. ☐ ☐

   b. Is he effective in expressing his needs in classroom situations?   48. ☐ ☐

   c. Are the words used in the pre-primers and the primer part of his listen-   49. ☐ ☐
   ing and speaking vocabulary?

   d. Does he understand the relationships inherent in such words as *up* and   50. ☐ ☐
   down, *top* and *bottom*, *big* and *little?*

   e. Does he listen to a story with evidence of enjoyment and the ability to   51. ☐ ☐
   recall parts of it?

   f. Is he able to interpret an experience through dramatic play?   52. ☐ ☐

7-5   **Reading Readiness Check List**

From *Manual for Teaching the Reading-Readiness Program*, Revised Edition, of
The Ginn Basic Readers by David H. Russell and others, © Copyright, 1964,
1957, 1948, by Ginn and Company (Xerox Corporation). Used with permission.

reading instruction should begin. Children who are ready will give us the signal; they will read. Remember some children learn to read without formal instruction. This does not mean that they had no preparation to do so. It is simply that the process was a less formal one than has been described. Some children accomplish many readiness tasks before beginning school. In many of these cases, the learnings were incidental rather than consciously planned by adults.

You may wish to determine your students' reading readiness through formal measures. Most basal reading series provide some form of readiness test but they usually measure achievement only (criterion referenced). On this type of test, scores are not interpreted by comparison with other children. Standardized readiness tests, however, are norm referenced and do attempt to relate results to a sample population. Some popular commercial readiness tests are

> Clymer-Barrett Prereading Battery. Princeton, N. J.: Personal Press, 1969.
>
> Metropolitan Readiness Test, rev. ed. New York: Harcourt Brace Jovanovich, 1976.
>
> Murphy-Durrell: Reading Readiness Analysis. New York: Harcourt Brace Jovanovich, 1965.

THE READING SKILLS: WHAT ARE THEY?

For the purposes of this text, reading skills may be divided into four categories:

> Word Recognition Skills
> Comprehension Skills
> Work Study Skills
> Appreciative and Critical Reading Skills

Word Recognition Skills

Though different reading approaches may stress one word-attack method over another, they do not totally exclude other means of analyzing words. It is usually a matter of emphasis. Whatever method is used should develop the child's storehouse of words as soon as possible. Teachers should not be overly concerned with which words are selected. Basal reading systems differ on which words should be learned first. For this reason, teachers should trust their professional judgment and not adhere slavishly to the instructions in any particular reading program. Experts themselves are divided over which approach works best. It is only the teacher in a day-to-day confrontation who can make the match between teaching strategy and the child.

Whole Word Analysis   With this approach, children memorize how the whole word looks and, in doing so, develop a sight vocabulary. (words that are immediately recognized without analysis). Though a child who uses whole word analysis may make errors that seem to indicate a lack of reading skills, as advocates of whole word analysis point out, the errors usually reflect an understanding of context. For example, a youngster using whole word analysis may read "The girl is wearing a red blouse" as "The girl is wearing a red shirt."

One of the means used by some children to develop a sight vocabulary involves the recognition of words by their shape. This is known as configuration. In this "gestalt" approach to word analysis, the child sees the word *foot* not as individual letters but as a composit shape:

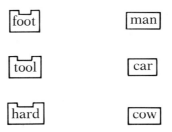

Obviously, the problem with this means of word recognition is that many words have the same shape:

foot	man
tool	car
hard	cow

Nevertheless, for some children this method serves as a useful beginning strategy.

Recognizing the shapes of words is not the only means used to develop sight vocabulary. Teachers may increase their students' sight vocabularies by providing experiences in general language awareness:

> Pair familiar words and pictures.
>
> Print children's names on cards placed at their desks, on bulletin boards, on work charts or folders.
>
> Present new words in contextual frameworks that provide a clue to meaning.

The connection between the child's previous experience with the word and its retention as a sight word is crucial. Children are able to acquire some very difficult sight words quite easily. This is because these words are laden with meaning for the youngster. Sylvia Ashton-Warner's *Teacher* describes how the Maori children quickly learned to read "organic" or "one look" words, such as *frightened* and *ghost* because these words had intense meaning in their lives. The length of a word is not a major obstacle in this sort of learning.[19]

Contextual Clues   Adult readers frequently rely on contextual clues to get meaning from printed material. Closely allied with comprehension, the use of contextual clues assists the reader in understanding general content when word meaning is not immediately apparent. There are two kinds of contextual clues: picture clues and sentence clues.

There are youngsters who use contextual clues without being taught to do so; others have to be encouraged through such comments as "Read to the end of the sentence" or "What is Bill playing with in the picture?" For children who do not recognize the advantages of using context, materials are available in most reading series. Some reading specialists recommend that these children also be exposed to more spoken language as a way of heightening their awareness of the value of context.

When children begin learning to read, they usually rely heavily on picture clues. Pictures accompany most materials that young children read. Workbooks also provide considerable practice in using picture clues. For some children, pictures provide a necessary psychological support and encourage staying with the reading process without becoming discouraged. However, a number of texts caution against reliance on picture clues, suggesting that a continuing dependency may result.

Wordless picture books and photographs are used by many teachers to show youngsters how pictures may increase understanding. Questions may be asked by the teacher that involve the naming of objects ("What does the boy have in his hand?") or seeing relationships ("Why is the girl crying?"). Some wordless picture books are listed on page 230. You also might want to refer back to the section on visual literacy earlier in this chapter for information on how to use pictures.

Phonic Analysis   Though phonic analysis is probably the most common strategy for unlocking words, it should not be the only one taught. The objective of phonics instruction is to make youngsters aware of the relationships between sounds and letters. Very often in a phonics lesson you will hear the teacher say something like, "In the word *late* the letter *a* says its own name. Can you think of other words in which *a* says its own name?" Since the letters in English do not always conform to a single sound—the *a* in *late* does not sound like the a in *car* or *bat*, for instance—children have to develop a variety of understandings about sound/letter correspondences.

Most reading programs have a prescribed phonics content. The following list, taken from one popular reading text, is typical:

[19]Sylvia Ashton-Warner, *Teacher* (New York: Bantam, 1963), p. 36.

Phonics Content

Auditory discrimination ⎫ Prereading
Visual discrimination ⎬ Content
Letter names ⎭

Single consonant sound-letter (phoneme-grapheme) correspondences, initial, final medial positions
Consonant digraphs
Consonant clusters
Silent consonants
Consonants representing more than one phoneme
Consonant substitution and phonogram patterning
Vowel sound-letter (phoneme-grapheme) correspondences
     Long or glided
     Sort or unglided
     R-controlled
     Digraphs
     Dipthongs
Vowel generalizations
Vowel substitution and phonogram patterning
Syllabication ⎫ May be of questionable value in a reading program[20]
Accent ⎭

Since facility with phonic analysis gives children the power to decode any word, the strategy has great value. However, it is important that children not be allowed to concentrate on this kind of word analysis to the exclusion of a word's contextual framework. An inappropriate emphasis on phonics may lead to disaffected, inefficient readers.

Structural Analysis   Sometimes called morphemic analysis or combining forms, structural analysis is the decoding of a word by identifying and combining the units of meaning within it. These units include

Prefixes and suffixes

Word endings (*ed, ing, s*)

Smaller words in larger words

Compound words

Syllabication and accent

The use of structural clues as a means of decoding words should be developed along with other word-attack strategies.

The language arts teacher who is sensitive to word building activities will find many opportunities to give children practice in combining words and parts of words. Starting with known sight words, students

---

[20]Hall, Ribovich, and Ramig, *Reading and the Elementary School Child*, p. 129.

can begin to build their own words. As children say the words, the teacher may write them down on the chalkboard or on charts. Here is a chart dictated by second graders:

foot {
Big Foot
footprint
football
footstool
hotfoot
}

day {
today
daytime
daybreak
Sunday
daylight
daydream
}

Comprehension Skills

The objective of all reading strategies is obviously to improve comprehension. Those techniques referred to as comprehension skills focus on developing the young reader's abilities in such areas as word and sentence meaning, sequence of events, identification of main ideas, recognition of relationships, awareness of details, and drawing inferences.

A variety of materials are available for teaching these skills; and whereas some children begin school with adequate word recognition skills, all children can profit from direct instruction in comprehension, for its boundaries are unlimited. The teacher should begin by determining each child's present level of reading comprehension. An informal textbook test may be used, such as the one described on page 212, in which those children who can answer the questions in their selection with about 75 percent accuracy are considered to be at that reading level or higher. Further testing at the next level may be necessary. The results from standardized reading tests may also be analyzed.

Here are some suggestions for focusing children's attention on selected comprehension skills:

1. *Learning main ideas*

   Ask children to provide new titles for a story.

   Have children look at a picture and express its main idea.

   Have children watch a television broadcast, and report its main idea for a classroom television guide.

2. *Learning sequence of events*

   Have children look at a newspaper article and underline words that denote time (after, before, during, and so on).

   Identify a crisis point in a story told to the class and ask students to tell what happened just before or just after.

Have children arrange several historical or fictional events in chronological order.

3. *Seeing relationships*

Cut a number of brief articles from a children's newspaper *(Junior Scholastic, Weekly Reader)* and have the children classify them under general headings, for example, sports, animal life, or space. These articles can then be mounted on a classroom chart for reinforcement.

Have children prepare a series of items for a "which doesn't belong?" game. The categories chosen should be compatible with the students' age level:

Toys—doll, truck, egg, game
Sesame Street characters—Big Bird, Ernie, Abe Lincoln, Burt
Cities—New York City, Portland, Italy, Boston

Encourage children to develop their own classifications:

Objects that move
Imaginary characters
Tools
Words of action
Words about government
House words

A word of caution: Too much emphasis on skills may detract from the basic objective—getting a child to read. The minute fragmentation of the reading process can cause a child to think that reading is merely an empty exercise that provides little or no pleasure.

Work Study Skills

Work study skills allow students to cope with greater independence and responsibility in the development of their own comprehension abilities. Some of these skills are

Using reference materials (dictionaries, encyclopedias, and so on)
Interpreting graphic aids (charts, graphs, maps, cartoons, tables, records, and so on)
Summarizing
Taking notes
Outlining

Also sometimes considered work study skills are such library skills as:

Alphabetizing
Using the card catalogue
Using tables of contents and indices

Appreciative and Critical Reading Skills

For some experts, the development of appreciative and critical reading skills is most important. A critical reader evaluates, interprets, and searches for implied meanings in the reading material.

The development of appreciative and critical reading skills should start in the primary grades because these skills are necessary in all language activities. The child who watches television, listens to a classmate's talk, or plans a presentation needs these skills. Teachers can begin to focus the younger child's attention on these matters by means of some well-directed questions. One teacher encouraged a group of first graders to think critically about Margaret Wise Brown's *The Runaway Bunny* by asking them the following questions:

1. How do you think the mother bunny felt about the baby? How do you know?
2. Can you understand why the bunny ran away?
3. Did the bunny go any place that you would have wanted to go?
4. Is there anything true about this story?
5. Do the pictures really show what is going on in the story? How could they be made better?
6. Do you think that the author told the story well? Why do you think so?

Asking even young children to read critically and appreciatively is showing them that you value their responses. When students question what they read, they have the opportunity for intellectual growth. This understanding combined with emotional readiness is the beginning of appreciation. It is through critical reading that children grow conceptually, and this growth is a lifelong process. A Harvard University report on reading recommends that definite programs be initiated in which all children are taught critical and creative reading skills at levels appropriate to their development, and that teachers find ways to stimulate thinking beyond the literal meaning of passages read.[21]

APPROACHES TO TEACHING READING

Which reading program has the answer? Which one spells success? The proliferation of reading programs on the market would suggest that no one system or approach is right for every child. Each has its limitations and advantages. If we turn to research findings, it becomes obvious that

---

[21]Mary C. Austin and Coleman Morrison, *The First R: The Harvard Report on Reading in Elementary Schools* (New York: Macmillan, 1963), p. 222.

we are often comparing apples and oranges. Not only are there many uncontrolled variables but the philosophic bases of the programs are at variance. It is difficult to compare a linguistic approach with a language-experience approach.

It is not within the province of a book devoted to language arts to analyze the various reading programs. It is assumed that teachers responsible for teaching reading will want to use a text designed specifically for that purpose. The emphasis here is on programs that view reading as an aspect of the total communications framework, one that does not separate the language arts but seeks as many points of integration as possible. Two reading approaches that do not make a sharp distinction between learning to read and the development of general language abilities are the language-experience approach and individualized reading.

The Language-Experience Approach

The language-experience approach is based on the assumption that children should learn to read utilizing their natural language patterns and vocabulary. Roach Van Allen, who has developed a number of materials for this approach, states its essence in this way:

> What I can think about, I can talk about.
>
> What I can say, I can write—or someone can write for me.
>
> What I can write, I can read.
>
> I can read what I write, and what other people can write for me to read.[22]

What does this mean? Just imagine that you and a young child are marooned on a desert island. The child speaks fluently but has not yet learned to read. There are no books or printed matter, but you do have a few writing materials and decide to use them to record your experiences on the island. The child frequently expresses curiosity about the strange characters you place on the paper and at one point asks to be taught how to read them. How would you go about teaching the child to read? Is it possible without the usual armamentarium that accompanies beginning reading programs?

Firstly, recognize that your materials are not quite so limited as you had first suspected. The basic ingredients for learning to read are available: two people who can speak with one another using words with agreed upon meanings (the child's natural language), a desire to decode letters and words, and the objects and experiences that the island pro-

---

[22]Address delivered at the International Association Conference, Seattle, Washington, May 1967; reprinted in *Reading and the Elementary School Child; Selected Readings on Programs and Practices*, ed. Virgil M. Howes and Helen Fisher Darrow (New York: Macmillan, 1968), p. 263.

vides. Here are some suggestions for beginning the teaching of reading on your desert island:

1. Ask the child to bring some favorite objects to you. Does the child know their names? Talk about them.

2. Place the objects on the floor of your shelter and label them.

3. Encourage the child to read the words that you have just written down.

4. Ask the child to tell the story of one of these objects. If necessary, ask such questions as "Where were they found?" "How did they get there?" "What do they mean to you?"

5. After writing down some of the child's comments in brief sentences, encourage the child to read back his or her own words.

6. Continue your conversations and the sharing of stories about life on the island.

7. Write down some of the child's stories and encourage him or her to read back what has been written.

8. Collect these stories and place them between two large fronds so that the child may have them available for rereading.

Though it is hardly likely that you will ever have to teach reading on a desert island, it may be helpful to have isolated and placed in bold relief an essential factor in teaching a child to read: the use of the child's spontaneous spoken language. The text for the language-experience approach is "talk written down," a continuing experience chart that bridges the gap between the two stages of language development, speaking and reading.

Beginning Reading   If you were going to use the language-experience approach in your classroom, you would set up a highly individualized reading program. You might begin by labeling pictures, objects, or places in the room and encouraging those students who were able to read these labels. Gradually, you might replace individual words with single-sentence descriptions. As the program progressed, one child or a small group could dictate observations that you would then transcribe onto charts. These comments would evolve from the children's interests, experiences, feelings, and concerns, in or out of school. They might be single-sentence statements about their hobbies, their pets, or their families, or questions that they would like answered. These experience charts ("talk written down") help children recognize the relationship between speaking and reading (see Figure 7-4). Students should be given many opportunities to read back these charts. However, in the early grades, the teacher may have to do the reading with the students following along.

Though language patterns found in experience stories are often more complex than those in basal reading series, "children seem to find their own language patterns much easier to read than those in the basal reader."[23] This is probably because of the personal association and the natural use of context. In fact, basal readers have been criticized for a formalized sentence structure that, though keyed to grade, is unlike normal conversation patterns.

Illustrations can be valuable aids in the development of experience charts. They may be provided by the teacher or the children. Original work, cut-out pictures, or small three-dimensional objects may be used. In one first-grade class in Lenox, Massachusetts, youngsters brought in photographs from home and attached them to their papers. The teacher, assisted by a paraprofessional, spoke to each child about his or her picture, and then wrote down a sentence or two for each youngster, being careful to use the child's words. Gradually, the children developed small collections of these mini-stories and kept them in attractively decorated folders. These personal stories were reread by the children, who thus had a continuing opportunity to connect the spoken and the written word.

The "Key" Vocabulary   The language-experience approach is not limited to the development of charts. In *Teacher,* Sylvia Ashton-Warner describes how she encouraged Maori children to share with her what she called their "key vocabulary." She then wrote down these very meaningful and usually highly emotional words and gave them to each child. Interestingly, the children did not need accompanying pictures to recognize their words. It was as if they had already advanced a stage and created word pictures in their minds. With this "key vocabulary," the children began to dictate and write their own stories.

The concept of a "key vocabulary" has been adopted in many classrooms. The words may come from an experience chart or a personal book of writing. Children can identify this personal file of words by underlining them in a story. (Some teachers prepare multiple copies of experience stories.) Once the child's known words are identified, the teacher or classroom assistant writes them on small cards and gives them to the child. This is the beginning of a word bank that continues to grow as the child's reading vocabulary increases. These words may be kept in a small box and then used in a variety of ways. Experience charts and children's writing are not the only sources of vocabulary words. Reading matter or materials brought from home may provide new words. One first grader brought in a new game that he had received for his birthday. He had no difficulty in reading its name, "Uncle Wiggly," and so these words were placed in his word bank. The names of advertised products are frequently additions to word banks. Many children include the name of their favorite breakfast cereal, television program, or fast food chain.

---

[23]Burns and Roe, *Teaching Reading,* p. 263.

Word Banks   Even a very small group of known words can constitute a word bank. Two words selected by the child may be put together (big rock, sad pet, baby eats, Randy runs), then a sentence/story may be developed by the child with the teacher transcribing it. As word banks grow, so do the number of possible activities: acting out words, finding the words in books, making picture dictionaries, and writing new stories with the words. Children can suggest words that have similar meanings, or similar sounds, and build new words from those that they already know.

Word banks have been popular in open education programs. Some have suggested that children be given a choice of attractive blank books so that they can make their own reading books. Encouraged by the teacher, a youngster gives each book a title incorporating his or her own name—for example, "Andrew's Dog." The child then draws his first picture in the book and most likely tells the teacher something about his drawing. The teacher then transcribes one of these first sentences into the book and the child reads the sentence back. Next the teacher places each of the words in the sentence on a separate small card. These cards are then used for a variety of exercises: matching the words on the cards with words in the sentences, playing a game in which one or more words are left out, rearranging the words in the sentence, and so on. The word cards are then placed in a large pocket fastened to the back cover of the book and become the first words in the child's word bank. A new page is done almost every day, and the word bank grows. When about five pages have been finished, the first reading book is considered complete. The process begins anew with the second book.[24] Since the books and the words express the child's own language, oral and written, the child begins to see the relationships between language forms.

Obviously, a classroom in which this approach is being used is one in which much talking goes on. It is also one in which there should be many rich and wonderful things to talk about: interesting objects (a turtle, a magic box, a cactus, a plastic model of a dinosaur, a pasta collage) and unusual corners (the clay center, the listening center, a place to relax). Attractive books and book advertisements are probably also in evidence. The teacher who uses this program will have to be well-organized and provide time for youngsters to read their own stories as well as those of their classmates. Children's stories can be duplicated, then simply bound or put in folders. Many teachers use the language-experience approach without knowing it. Whenever children keep writing folders, read what they have dictated or written, or use their own word cards, the language-experience approach is in operation.

---

[24]Ellen Blance, Ann Cook, and Herb Mack, *Reading in the Open Classroom: An Individual Approach* (New York: Community Resources Institute of the City University of New York, 1971), pp. 8–12.

Structuring the Program   The ultimate aim of the language-experience approach is the same as that of most other reading programs: to develop children who can, do, and choose to read. "Once a child has visited a bakery, baked cookies, made up a story about the experience, and read the story, he or she may be interested in reading other stories about baking."[25] The mechanics of the program are usually a variation of the following:

1. The child dictates a story from his or her experience.
2. The story is transcribed.
3. The child reads back the transcribed story on a number of occasions.
4. Word banks are developed.
5. The child has further experiences that may relate to the subject of the story and discusses them.
6. Further transcriptions are made.
7. The child begins to read material related to the information on the charts.
8. The child reads material that is not necessarily related to the topic.
9. The child is slated for skills instruction according to need.

Teachers disturbed by the lack of structure in this approach can make use of the prepared materials that are available for guidance. But the strengths of the program lie in the use of the child's experience. In addition, principles of learning lacking in many other approaches to reading are utilized: "The language experience is individualized; related to individual self-concept; significant to the real needs of each child, unitary, or whole-learning, rather than fragmented bit-by-bit increments of vocabulary artificially strung together.[26]

Individualized Reading

Individualized reading, a program of seeking, personal pacing, and self-selection of reading matter has tremendous appeal among students and teachers. Students experience the joy of reading, and teachers accomplish a basic reading goal—having children learn to enjoy reading. Many teachers have discovered that an individualized reading program realistically meets the problem of individual differences. The enthusiasm of many teachers for the program is based to a large measure on positive experiences with it. It is a special happening to observe children in a variety of comfortable, contorted positions deeply engrossed in their reading. There is a chuckle here, a pout there, a groan from the back, but in general total immersion in books. The atmosphere catches even the

---

[25]Farr and Roser, *Teaching a Child to Read*, p. 452.
[26]Robert C. Aukerman, *Approaches to Beginning Reading* (New York: Wiley, 1971), p. 301

reluctant reader. Reading looks like fun. For this reason, many advocates of individualized reading have hailed it as the "Reading Renaissance."

Individualized reading is more than a reading approach or method. It is a way of thinking about reading that focuses not only on classroom organization, techniques, and materials, but on children's developmental needs as well. When children select and read books at their own rate, they are not bound by goals set for a group, goals that are of necessity compromises. An important aspect of this program is the anonymity, the lack of public knowledge about each child's reading progress. It is a private matter and an individual responsibility.

Classroom Practices in Individualized Reading   Individualized reading involves individual, group, and whole-class instruction in reading and does away with groups based upon "total" reading ability. When groups are organized, they are only temporary, each usually having one specific purpose. A small group may be organized to teach the consonant blend *br;* as children accomplish this task, they leave the group. The assumption is that every child does not have to be taught every skill. Some children will already know how to use contextual clues or the short sound of "u." Why waste their time teaching them what they already know and running the risk of tarnishing their interest in reading?

The many children's trade books used in this program cover every imaginable subject from poetry to science. Though some teachers of reading may use this program three days a week and a basal series the other two days, there are those who employ an individualized approach exclusively.

Individualized reading bears some similarity to the language-experience approach. Teachers using individualized reading in the primary grades generally begin by reading many attractive books to their students and by building experience charts using the vocabulary from these books. The books are always available to the children, and many do pick them up and try to read them. Though some may not really be reading, they are experiencing the books on some level. And even at this level, the principle of individual choice of books and personal control of rate operates. Teachers also receive many clues about readiness.

The reading period may last about one hour (though time will vary with age level) and can be organized in this way:

Part I Preparation (about 10 minutes)
  Teach an advanced skill to the whole class.
  (Note children who need more help and individual attention.)
  Give the pooling assignment (an activity that the class shares at the end of the reading period).

Part II Reading by the children (about 45 minutes)
  Listen to individual children read and note difficulties.
  Do individual or group teaching.
  Briefly sit with each child and hear or discuss what is being read.

Part III Pooling time (about 10 minutes)
> Have children share reactions to their reading experiences.

Basic to the success of the program is the teacher-student conference. Through discussions and oral reading, the teacher is able to diagnose individual difficulties, assign each child to a particular group, and provide appropriate learning materials. For this latter purpose, many teachers utilize selected workbook pages and selected teaching materials.

The following is one possible distribution of a teacher's time for a week:

Monday	Whole class, 5 individual conferences
Tuesday	Whole class, 2 skill groups
Wednesday	Whole class, 10 short conferences, 1 skill group
Thursday	Whole class, 25 short conferences
Friday	Whole class, 1 small group, 2 individual conferences

The teacher finds out about the child's reading progress in a variety of ways:

Conference

Small group session

Class session

Sharing activities

Follow-up activities

Experiences in other curriculum areas

The pooling period serves an important role in this program. It is during this time that children catch from each other the excitement of reading. And there is much to talk about. As one youngster put it, "If we all read the same book, what is there to say?" Pooling may take many different forms depending upon the needs of the group. It may immediately follow the reading period and be of rather brief duration, or it may be considerably more extensive both in time and preparation. Here is a selected list of pooling activities that many teachers have found successful:

Pooling about language
Write words, phrases, or sentences that make you hear, feel, taste, smell, or
> touch things.
Find action words, picture words, descriptive words, words of emotion.
Find words that were made longer by endings.
Note adjectives that are used to describe a character or setting.
Copy an interesting conversation.

Pooling about characters
Describe a character that you liked.
Tell about a character whose personality and behavior changed.
Draw or tell in words what you would have done if you were one of the
> characters.

Tell about a character who reminds you of yourself.
Write a thumbnail sketch of one of the characters. (Make a large paper thumbnail.)
Prepare a monologue as one of the characters.

Pooling that develops special skills
Cartoon a story.
Make a map showing where the story took place.
Write a movie script for a section of the book.
Make a time line showing the sequence of events in the story.
Prepare a questionnaire for those who have already read the book.
Discuss the point of view of the author. What was his or her "big idea"?

Cartoon by Rick Detorie. Used with permission.

"Read it again, only this time with more emphasis on character development and less on plot mechanics."

Pooling as a springboard to creative activities
Create a series of original illustrations for the story.
Retell the story in a dramatization or puppet show.
Advertise your book to another class by means of posters, dioramas, newspapers.
Prepare a choral reading selection.
Read a part of your book or poem with a musical background
Create a filmstrip based on the story.
Write a new adventure or experience for your character.
Recreate a biography or autobiography as a "This Is Your Life" show.

Figure 7–7 shows the type of information that might be generated in a pooling session on a biography or autobiography.

7-7

POOLING ACTIVITY FOR BIOGRAPHY OR AUTOBIOGRAPHY

(Sample categories: change to fit personality.)

Name of book _____

Author _____

Birth _____

Death _____

Nationality _____

Schooling _____

Special talents as a child _____

Personality traits as a child _____

Profession _____

Hobbies _____

Accomplishments and awards _____

Influences on life _____

Quotation _____

Picture, symbol, or

artistic representation

of this individual

The Teacher and Individualized Reading   Some teachers' comments about individualized reading follow:

"Individualized Reading is a way of life in the classroom."

"I can do Individualized Reading all day. It is easy to teach all curriculum areas with this approach."

"The idea for a class science fair was developed because so many children were reading science materials. After one particularly exciting pooling session, a group decided that they knew a lot and had something to offer."

"*Eloise* ran through the class like a brush fire. After a visit from Kay Thompson, the author, and Hilary Knight, the illustrator, the class did a musical adaptation of the book. It seems to me that this reading program is more than a method; it is a philosophy, a general approach to teaching."

Children have had this to say:

"Mrs. Kraus, you owe me ten minutes of reading."

"I'm finally reading about children like me."

"The program makes me feel grown up. I now can read books published for older children."

"The new program isn't like the others, just sitting in your desk reading a reader with the same characters for years and years."

"For once I'm reading about children who live in apartment houses."[27]

This is not to suggest that individualized reading presents no difficulties. The program requires dedication, organizational skills, and considerable work on the part of the teacher. But many of the objections to individualized reading may be the result of misconceptions about the basal reading system itself. "Basic reader systems are not methods. They are applications of methods. If the teacher knows her methodology, she can apply it to any material.[28] The acceptance of individualized reading may also be undermined by the assumption that learning happens only when there is teacher involvement and the failure to recognize that individualized reading does not exclude directed periods of instruction.

READING AND THE LANGUAGE-DIFFERENT CHILD

The language-different child can be classified into two categories: speakers who use a nonstandard dialect and those whose first or home language is not English. As an example of nonstandard dialect, let us look at Black English.

---

[27]Karel Rose (Newman), "Individualized Reading in Action," in *Individualizing Your Reading Program*, ed. Jeanette Veatch (New York; G. P. Putnam's Sons, 1959), p. 216.

[28]May Lazar, Speech delivered at Fordham University, July 1956.

Many articles in newspapers and magazines have focused on the often divisive question of whether Black English is a language or a dialect. Most linguists, however, have clear definitions of these terms: a *dialect* is defined as a variety of language distinguished from other varieties of the same language because of geographical or social factors; a *language* is a body of words and the systems for their use common to a people of the same community, nation, or cultural tradition. But to dwell on the language/dialect issue is to beg the educational question. Black English *is* the means of verbal communication that many children bring to school.

A variety of textbooks and trade books written in Black English are now available. (You might want to look at the picture books of Lucille Clifton.) The attempt to codify and use Black English in a written form does raise some questions, particularly if books in Black English are used as basic reading texts. Recognizing that learning to read Standard English is a survival skill in the United States, many educators and Black parents take issue with the use of readers written in Black English. Bernard R. Gifford, a research scholar at the Russell Sage Foundation and a former deputy chancellor of the New York City school system says, "I have met no one who advocates teaching Black English. I have a strange feeling in my belly that any one who does so is just indulging in another expression of racism."[29] Furthermore, there is no research evidence to support the use of dialect readers for any group. This is not to suggest, however, that the classroom of selected trade books in Black English is not a constructive way to help youngsters bridge the gap between home and school.

The challenge for teachers and textbook writers is to scrutinize, utilize, and develop materials that build on the cultural experiences of Black children. Many problems arise when home experiences and language differ from school experiences and language. Researchers refer to the problems as "dialect interference." If the experiences of children are urban, then the language of some of their reading materials should include "city" words: curb, apartment house, subway, and so on. The content should also reinforce the emotional attachments and the shared heritage of Black people. These children should be reading some stories with content about Africa, about the South, about jazz. A good example of a book that builds on the Black cultural experience is *Ben's Trumpet*, by Rachel Isadora, a story that rhythmically describes a young Black child's yearning to be a jazz musician.

The teaching of reading to children who speak Black English requires that the teacher understand the root causes of certain dialect differences and be able to distinguish dialect interference from reading error. "If

---

[29]Quoted in Robert Blair Kaiser, "Wrestling With Meaning of 'Black English,'" The New York Times, 27 November, 1979, p. C4.

children read 'he walks to school' as 'he walk to school,' they are not making a reading mistake but are performing a remarkable linguistic translation from standard to nonstandard English. . . . In other words, this is not a reading error but an example of dialect interference."[30] The child obviously understands the meaning of the sentence and is accomplishing the primary reading objective.

Teachers are often uncertain how to write down the stories that children tell using their home language. Some authors suggest that the teacher write *exactly* what the child says without the inclusion of nonstandard usage. Here is one suggestion: "The child dictates: 'Harry said he's not gonna go!' Teacher writes: 'Harry said he's not going to go!' " The child will then read back what the teacher has written and will probably say 'gonna.' "[31] To correct the spoken word would go counter to the advantage of this technique: the child's awareness that reading is "talk written down." The research of Pat Rigg also suggests that children's dictated stories should be transcribed using standard spelling. "Den day went to de store," is written "Then they went to the store."[32]

There is still another aspect to consider in teaching the speaker of Black English to read. If a child is unable to read back correctly in the standard dialect, can we correctly assume that the child has not understood what he or she has read? Not necessarily, for we are finding out that "children may understand many aspects of language before they are able to produce language themselves."[33] This thinking has led some authorities to suggest that emphasis not be placed on oral reading at the expense of meaning.

The chances are very good that in your teaching career you will encounter many students for whom English is a second language. Though most of these students are Hispanic in origin, significant numbers of them speak Russian, Italian, Greek, or one of the Oriental languages. Since these children are of school age, they have certain fixed language patterns. You may recall from the chapter on language and concept development how our abilities to learn a new language decrease with age. Even the necessary physical abilities (use of tongue, lips, and so on) become rooted in certain patterns. This is a problem since some languages form sounds differently than others. For those children who start school without a solid language base in their native tongue, the difficulty is further compounded. For learning to read in any language is built on a foundation in listening and speaking.

[30]Jean Malmstrom, *Understanding Language: A Primer for the Language Arts Teacher* (New York: St. Martin's Press, 1977), p. 72.

[31]Example taken from Farr and Roser, *Teaching a Child to Read*, p. 455.

[32]Pat Rigg, "Dialect and/in/for Reading," Language Arts 55 (March 1978): 289.

[33]Yetta M Goodman and Rudine M. Sims, "Whose Dialect for Beginning Readers," in *What's New in Reading?* ed. Iris M. Tiedt (Urbana, Ill.: National Council of Teachers of English, 1974), p. 29.

You may not be able to speak the language of such students, but as a trained language arts teacher you can still make a significant contribution to their reading development. The same basic principles apply in developing the language fluency of all children:

The child should feel comfortable in the classroom.

The child should experience some success with language.

The child should have considerable exposure to listening and other oral work.

The child should have opportunities for verbal expression on a one-to-one basis.

This is not to suggest that a teacher who speaks only English is the teacher who can best teach reading to the bilingual youngster. However, since bilingual personnel are not always available, other teachers must be prepared to tackle the task. Providing multifaceted, plentiful oral experiences in a supportive classroom environment is an important beginning.

The Teacher's Attitude toward Different Cultures

One of the ways in which a teacher may assist bilingual youngsters to feel more comfortable in the classroom is by showing a sincere respect for their cultural heritage. A child's language is one of the most visible features of this heritage. If you have Mexican children in your classroom, for example, it would be important to acquaint yourself with some aspects of Mexican culture not only in Mexico but here in our own country. Find out how Mexican-Americans live. Become familiar with some children's books about Mexico, but watch out for stereotypes and a bland "sameness." Most important, recognize that not all members of the same group are alike. America is a multicultural environment and, as The National Commission on the Reform of Secondary Education stated, one educational goal is to provide "experiences in harmony while maintaining individuality."[34] A teacher should accept, learn about, but not judge the culture of his or her students.

It is a good idea to initially seat the language-different child near other students who speak the child's language. The feeling of security will offset the disadvantage of overdependence on peers for assistance. In the near future, seats may be changed so that the child is near students with whom he or she must make use of English in order to communicate. These contacts will allow the student to stretch his or her new language skills.

[34]Quoted in Raymond J. Rodriguez, "Toward Pluralism: Multicultural Learners," *Language Arts* 55 (September 1978): 731.

Special Programs

Children whose first language is not English and who have not become fluent in English by the time they enter school need help in the language from personnel other than the classroom teacher. As a result, ESL (English as a second language) and bilingual programs have been established in many schools. Both types of programs provide instruction in two (or more) languages. However, bilingual programs place considerably more emphasis on maintaining the native language than do most ESL programs. Children in bilingual programs are usually grouped according to grade or need and given instruction outside their regular classroom. If there are a number of children on the same grade level who have English as a second language, a permanent class may be formed.

A number of points of view have emerged as to how these children should receive instruction. An important question that has not been resolved is whether or not instruction in reading should be given in the first language or the new one. Some research has concluded that there is no clear advantage in learning reading in the first language. On the other hand, research has not shown any harm resulting from learning reading in the first language.[35]

How Can Non-Bilingual Teachers Help?

Most bilingual programs take an audiolingual approach and attempt to provide non-English speakers with a large variety of sound experiences. It is helpful for such students to hear the rhythms of the language. Mother Goose rhymes and other poetry presented by the teacher or on records make an excellent beginning.

Similarly, the regular use of simple oral greetings and farewells can heighten auditory awareness: phrases like "Hello! I am Jose. I come from Puerto Rico," or "Hello! I am Olga. I come from Denmark." Every child may have a chance, if he or she wishes, and this can then be made into a game: "Can you now tell us the names of any of the children and where they come from?"

Other games might involve the hiding of objects. One child hides an object. The others ask, "Is it under the desk? Near the chair? On top of the closet?"

Children who have not yet mastered English may only be ready to mention the object by name, but the desire to play will propel them to develop the necessary vocabulary. Use of the tape recorder, records, pantomime, and role playing are also valuable instructional aids. For further

---

[35]Pflaum-Connor, *Development of Language and Reading*, p. 64.

suggestions, you might want to look at Joan Kaye's article, "Help! Pedro Can't Speak English."[36]

Mary Finocchiaro, a bilingual advisor with the New York City Board of Education, suggests that teachers of Puerto Rican children learn a few key Spanish words: "Look," "Listen," "Repeat," "Say," "Ask," "Answer," and use them along with their English equivalents.[37] If a large number of students in your class speak the same language, but not English, you might want to learn to speak the language.

Attention should be given to a variety of language experiences, not only the audiolingual. In all youngsters the development of reading abilities is inextricably tied to general language competence. Therefore, bilingual children should be provided with many of the opportunities identified in the readiness section of this chapter. There should be available many "hands on" materials that encourage communication, including picture books and visual materials that relate to the child's life outside the classroom.

If you are unable to provide adequate instruction for a non-English speaking child, you will have to make other arrangements. Are there people in the school or community who speak the child's language? Here is where your role as a teacher-manager comes into play. Whether the adjunct personnel are parents, aides, student teachers, the child's peers, or community volunteers, the teacher should plan the class day with their services in mind. How might their skills be used most effectively? Will they tell stories to the children? Prepare tapes? Provide readiness activities? Work on projects? Special events may be planned.

One second-grade class with five Spanish-speaking children planned a luncheon assisted by their mothers. The luncheon gave these youngsters the opportunity to share their heritage in a pleasurable way, while enriching the knowledge of the other children; there were linguistic as well as emotional benefits. Foods and utensils were labeled in two languages. Simple recipes were printed by the teacher on charts. Menus were written. One Puerto Rican child, using as many English words as she could, explained how to prepare *Tembleque,* a coconut custard. For weeks afterward the effects of the luncheon were felt. Some children compiled recipe books with accompanying pictures, and the Spanish-speaking youngsters checked the books for accuracy. There was a feeling of pride and a sense of acceptance in a mutually enriching social context. Learning to read begins with personal contacts, long before print is introduced and words are decoded.

The question of bilingual education is more than an issue of pedagogy. Whether to help non-English speaking youngsters become fluent in En-

[36]Joan Kaye, "Help! Pedro Can't Speak English," *Teacher* (October 1976): 78–80.

[37]Mary Finocchiaro, "Myth and Reality in Tesol: A Plea for a Broader View," *TESOL Quarterly* 5 (1971): 7.

glish while maintaining their native tongue or to create a situation in which there is no single common language is a political and educational question. To further complicate the issue, there is some evidence that children educated bilingually do as well in English as those educated monolingually. Obviously, there are no easy answers. As in the question of Black English, it is important to take a hard look at the world that non-English speaking youngsters will face outside the schools. In the United States the language of preferred jobs remains Standard American English. Our decision should be based upon the realities these youngsters will have to face.

READING AND THE LANGUAGE-DELAYED CHILD

By this time, you are aware that children who are slow language learners will have difficulty with the reading process. Children fail to use language competently for different reasons:

1. They may have an intelligence quotient below ninety-five and find it difficult to integrate new learnings.
2. They may have a learning disability that interferes with their intellectual functioning. A learning disability is frequently perceptual in nature and has often been associated with minimal brain damage.
3. They may be among the educable mentally retarded (with IQs below seventy) and thus experience general learning problems.
4. They may come from a deprived home environment.
5. They may be emotionally disturbed.

Many programs have been designed to meet the specific needs of these different groups of children. It is usually important for them to receive special instruction that is focused on their particular disability.

A generation ago, language-impaired children were not usually included in the average classroom. With the growing recognition, however, that all children learn from one another, many classes now include youngsters who have a variety of disabilities. As has been discussed, the integration of these children into regular classes is known as mainstreaming.

READING AND THE MAINSTREAMED CHILD

It is not unusual for the mainstreamed, handicapped child to exhibit reading difficulties. This is not surprising when we juxtapose the battery of skills necessary for efficient reading against the disabling features of particular handicaps. Reading is an aural, visual, intellectual, emotional, physical process. Any problem with vision, hearing, speech, body movement, conceptualization, and/or emotional adjustment has an effect upon the reading process. Very often, the handicapped child is the language-delayed child and difficulties are compounded. The classroom teacher who understands the reading process may consider the following emphases for the mainstreamed child:

1. An increase in time spent on reading readiness activities
2. Greater attention to concrete experiences before proceeding to abstractions
3. Development of positive experiences with language in a supportive interpersonal situation
4. Encouragement of spontaneous and relevant conversation
5. Frequent utilization of tape recordings and games
6. Special reading programs directed towards specific handicaps
7. Additional individualized instruction utilizing adjunct personnel and peers
8. Opportunities for drill and repetition with a variety of materials and strategies

Valuable assistance for the classroom teacher is provided in *Mainstreaming, the special child, and the reading process*, a handbook with instructional packets, by J. C. Harste and M. A. Terell.

Very often teachers may want to select a reading approach for mainstreamed children that differs from the one being used with other youngsters in the class. Figure 7-8 provides a general analysis of some reading programs taking into consideration the special needs of the mainstreamed child.

The growing body of children's literature about youngsters with handicaps is a valuable teaching resource. All children should be exposed to this literature, for it serves to enrich their emotional and intellectual perspective. A list of selected books follows:

Alan Brightman, *Like Me*. Little, Brown, 1976. (Mental handicaps.)

Joan Fassler, *Howie Helps Himself*. A. Whitman, 1975. (Cerebral palsy.)

Eloise Greenfield, *Darlene*. Methuen, 1980. (Physical handicap.)

Edith Hunter, *Sue Ellen*. Houghton Mifflin, 1969. (Learning disabilities.)

Ada B. Litchfield, *A Button in Her Ear*. A. Whitman, 1976. (Hearing deficiency.)

Palle Petersen, *Sally Can't See*. John Day, 1977. (Congenital blindness.)

Mary Beth Sullivan and Linda Bourke, *A Show of Hands*. Addison-Wesley, 1980. (Deafness.)

Programmed Instruction	1. The child is encouraged to proceed at his/her own pace with reinforcement provided at each learning step. 2. Continuous recording of the child's errors provides a learning profile for instructional planning. 3. Learning is designed for the individual child rather than for a group. 4. Instruction is provided in short units made up of many small segments.	1. Most EMR children are not self-directed learners and therefore cannot initiate and pace their learning. 2. Many EMR children lose their initial high motivation and become distracted. 3. The repetitive material often becomes boring and loses the child's attention. 4. Short frames do not allow the EMR child to experience the flow of written language. 5. It is difficult to program advanced comprehension skills within the short frame structure. 6. The instructional frames do not lend themselves to interesting stories. The child does not develop a desire for reading.
Alphabet	1. Simplifies reading by making a direct sound-symbol association. 2. Programmed for success which becomes both the reinforcer and the motivator. 3. There are no exceptions to the rule. Therefore children may learn to read more rapidly than by other approaches.	1. The child must make the transition from the alphabet approach (e.g., ITA) to the traditional orthography. This is often very difficult for the EMR child to do because of an inability to generalize. 2. The child sees the traditional alphabet outside of school and can become confused. 3. The program does not induce transfer from reading instruction to other academic areas.
Phonics	1. Emphasis upon word recognition leads to independent reading. 2. Increases interest in reading as the child learns to figure out new words. 3. Helps the child to associate sounds and printed letters representing them.	1. Isolation of speech sounds is unnatural. EMR children often cannot blend the sounds to form complete words. 2. Child learns to read word-by-word. The EMR child becomes frustrated by new sounds and their blending. 3. Emphasis on word recognition is often at the expense of comprehension. 4. There are many exceptions to every rule. The EMR child may become confused, unable to differentiate the rule from the exception.
Basal	1. A sequentially ordered, comprehensive approach from early readiness to advanced reading levels. 2. Skills are divided into small units for systematic teaching. 3. Establishes a basic vocabulary repeated throughout the sequence. 4. Provides diagnostic tools for pinpointing strengths and weaknesses. 5. Gives the individual teacher guidance in establishing the reading program focus. 6. Many basals emphasize a sight word learning method.	1. Organizes teaching reading for a group of children rather than for individual needs. 2. Limited vocabulary limits reading to only one basal series—de-emphasizes reading in content areas. 3. Stories and illustrations are often geared to the middle class child. A majority of EMR children do not fit that description. 4. The material is often too difficult for the children at the lower end of the learning continuum. Using books designed for younger students reduces motivation. 5. Workbooks for skill development result in isolated learning. The EMR student is often unable to make a transfer from skill practice to the reading text.

Linguistic	1. Stresses the transition from spoken to written language by showing the child the relationship between phonemes and graphemes. 2. Arranges learning from familiar, phonemically regular words to ones of irregular spelling. This encourages recognition of consistent visual patterns. 3. Child learns to spell and read the word as a whole unit. 4. Creates an awareness of sentence structure so child learns that words are arranged to form sentences. 5. Teaches reading by association with the child's natural language facility.	1. Most teachers are not skilled enough in linguistics to develop the necessary program for individual learners. 2. Vocabulary is too controlled and does not approximate the child's speaking skills so that the EMR child has difficulty relating to it. 3. Creates word reading, losing the flow of the sentence. 4. Use of nonsense words for pattern practice is irrelevant and reduces comprehension training. 5. Emphasizes auditory memory skills which many EMR children are deficient in.
Language Experience	1. Employs the child's current oral language abilities as the focus of the reading program. 2. Combines speaking, listening and writing skills into the reading program. 3. Utilizes direct experiences so the child can relate to the written language form. 4. Adaptable to individual or small groups according to learner and teaching needs. 5. Flexible in style as it may involve narratives, descriptions, and/or recordings of event sequences. This allows an expansion of the child's reading style.	1. Requires a prolonged attention span which is difficult for many EMR children. 2. May be limited to the child's speaking vocabulary and may not provide a structured enough approach to vocabulary development. 3. The LEA may not have enough consistency in vocabulary or control over syntax to teach and reinforce sequential skills for the EMR child. 4. Relies heavily upon the child's own experiences and ability to relate them.

7-8   **Reading Programs and Special Needs**   This analysis of the pros and cons of major reading programs in the teaching of the educable mentally retarded (EMR) raises points applicable to all mainstreamed students.

Table from "Selecting a Reading Approach for the Mainstreamed Child" by Sandra B. Cohen and Stephen Plaskon from *Language Arts*, Nov./Dec. 1978, pp. 969-70. Copyright © 1978 by the National Council of Teachers of English. Reprinted by permission of the publisher and the author.

In the discussion of mainstreaming, the emphasis has been on the language-delayed child. This youngster should not be confused with the child who is language-different because of dialect or non-English background. The language-delayed student is usually suffering from some cognitive, perceptual, and/or emotional difficulty. The problems surrounding the language of the non-English or dialect speaker are the result of vast discrepancies between home and school experiences. Though some of the teaching strategies for language-delayed and language-different children may be similar, the origin and nature of the language difficulties are not the same.

EVALUATION OF READING

As pointed out before, evaluation is not testing. Testing is only one means of evaluation, and it is usually a specific and very limited procedure. Evaluation is the more general, ongoing process of gathering different kinds of data about a student's growth toward specific goals. Neither evaluation nor testing should be ends in themselves. Ideally their purpose is to provide guidance to teachers and their students in the diagnosis, assessment, and improvement of learning Evaluation and testing should not be afterthoughts or follow-up procedures; they should be mechanisms built into a program at its inception.

The evaluation of reading skill is somewhat different from the evaluation of a student's command of a content area such as mathematics or history. Since reading is a process, it must be evaluated by observing the quality of the reader's use of the process in real reading situations.[38] We must first, therefore, understand what the process entails. How, for example, do children use context, or their personal language experiences, to decipher the words on a page? We want not only to identify an error, but to know why it occurs. As language arts teachers, we look to the role played by listening and speaking in the process of reading. At this point, you might want to refer back to page 166 for a discussion of how a child learns to read.

As a teacher, you have responsibilities that radiate beyond the classroom to the larger educational scene. You must make decisions not only about individual children but about the assets or liabilities of particular programs. Whether your input is direct or indirect and whether your opinion is generally responded to or not, as you teach you will always be asking yourself such evaluative questions as:

1. Is reading program X better than reading program Y?
2. Is reading test X evaluating reading or specific reading materials?
3. Which reading program is most effective with individual students? Why?
4. Would I recommend that we continue with reading program X?
5. Do my students seem more enthusiastic about reading after exposure to reading program X?
6. What are the liabilities of program X? What adjustments could be made?

Occasionally, a simple device may provide some insights. In recent years, for example, the cloze procedure has been used to shed light on how children go about getting meaning from the printed page. With this technique, children are asked to suggest what words are missing from one or more paragraphs. A number of possibilities may be offered

---

[38]Hall, Ribovich, and Ramig, *Reading and the Elementary School Child*, p. 282.

for each blank. Thus, in order to complete the sentence "The car was _____ down Sunset Boulevard," the students might offer *racing, cruising, driving, going,* or *hot-rodding.* The cloze procedure may be used as a teaching technique or an evaluative device. Children begin to see how context is altered by a word or how a sentence suggests a word. Used in several studies to determine how the analysis of context helps readers, the cloze procedure may provide clues to the elements that influence the understanding of language.[39]

Another important factor to consider in evaluation is whether we are testing the process of reading or the ability to handle a specific reading program. Most basal reading programs include a variety of evaluative devices designed to test the skills developed in that particular program. But sometimes the programs themselves are only reflections of the more popular standardized tests: the cart has come before the horse. As teachers of language arts, we must be particularly sensitive to this syndrome and ask whether we are developing in children the ability to take certain reading tests or the ability and desire to read.

Standardized, Criterion-Referenced Tests

Though you may not be involved in judgments about large scale evaluation schemes, you should be familiar with the most common evaluation procedures. Nationwide, millions of dollars are spent annually in the administration and scoring of standardized reading tests. Most of these formal measures can be categorized as criterion-referenced tests. That is, the efforts of the test takers are compared to those of a particular population chosen to serve as a standard. These tests tend to focus on the measurement of vocabulary and reading comprehension, and the results are usually expressed as grade-level equivalents. Among the commonly used reading achievement tests are the Metropolitan Achievement Test, the Standard Achievement Test, the Gates-MacGinitie Reading Tests, and the California Reading Test.

Many questions have been raised in recent years about the efficacy of these tests. Do they test reading, or cultural exposure? Or simply knowledge of specific reading materials? The implications of these questions are far too numerous to consider here, but certainly every teacher should consider what skills the standardized reading test is actually measuring, and administrators should be wary of relying on standardized tests for guidance in designing remedial programs.

[39]A good tape on the application of the cloze procedure is *Cloze Technique: A Classroom Tool,* by Judith Christensen and Barbara Taubenheim (Los Angeles: JAB Press).

Informal Reading Tests

Since standardized tests tend to give a picture of a pupil's maximum level, they often present an ability picture somewhat beyond a child's capacity and comfort. In contrast, an informal evaluation, since it may be given more frequently, can yield data about a youngster's most comfortable placement and progress. The materials for an informal assessment may be prepared by the teacher or provided by commercial publishers or local or state education departments. Figure 7-9 outlines a

7-9

Procedures for Giving Informal Tests

Reprinted by permission of the Board of Education of the City of New York from the curriculum bulletin: *A Guide for Beginning Teachers of Reading, Grades 1-4*, p. 92. New York City, 1967-68.

Testing At or Above Primer (1¹) Level

1. *Conditions.* Each test is to be administered individually. Other children should not hear the responses.

2. *Materials.* Obtain basal readers in a specific series, ranging from one year below to one year above the child's reading level, as noted on his Reading Record. Use, if available, the free Informal Textbook Test pamphlet prepared by the publisher of the series being used (this pamphlet indicates by page numbers the selections best suited for use in tests and provides suitable comprehension questions for each indicated selection).

Or, prepare an original test: (a) Select a passage of about 100 running words in a story without too many unfamiliar concepts. (b) Prepare four comprehension questions based on the selection, including literal meaning and finding details; getting main idea; drawing inferences; and reacting to the story.

3. *Procedure.* Choose a basal reader corresponding to the child's instructional level as noted on his Reading Record. Introduce the selection; establish rapport, tell a little about the story, tell the proper names, and ask the child to read *orally without previous silent reading.*

4. *Scoring.* Note and count errors as follows:

• *Nonrecognition Errors.* Each *different* word a child does not know (tell him the word after five seconds) or mispronounces counts as one error. Words mispronounced because of foreign accent are *not* counted as errors.

• *Addition Errors.* Count as one error all words the child adds, regardless of the total number of additions.

• *Omission Errors.* Count as one error all words the child omits, regardless of the number of omissions.

• *Endings Errors.* Count as one error all endings the child omits, no matter how many endings are omitted.

Interpreting the Informal Textbook Test

1. If a child makes fewer than 5 errors, repeat the test on a reader at the next higher level. Continue until the level at which he makes about five errors is reached.

2. If a child makes more than 5 errors, repeat the test on a reader at the next lower level. Continue until the level at which he makes about five errors is reached.

3. If the child makes about 5 errors, then ask the four comprehension questions. A score of 75 per cent or higher indicates that this is the child's instructional level. If he scores lower than 75 per cent, then:

a. Prepare another test of 100 running words from a story at the level on which he scored about five errors.

b. Have the child read the new selection *silently.*

c. Ask him four comprehension questions.

d. A score of 75 per cent or higher indicates that this is the child's instructional level; but if the comprehension score is lower than 75 per cent, then assign him the reader *one level below* the one used in this test, for this is the child's instructional level. Work closely with him on his comprehension skills.

Testing Below the Primer (1¹) Level

When testing below the primer (1¹) level, select 15 different words (no proper names) from the back of all pre-primers in the basal series being used for the test — perhaps every fifth word from a list of about 75 words.

Type (primer typewriter) or print (manuscript) the 15 words in a column or on separate cards. Ask the child to read the words aloud. Note his errors and evaluate:

1. If he does not know any of the words, provide him with a reading-readiness program.

2. If he recognizes between 1 and 12 words, then provide him with more pre-primer work, for this is his instructional level.

3. If he recognizes 13, 14, or 15 words (does not miss more than 2 words), then start him on the primer (1¹), for this is his instructional level.

procedure for giving an informal textbook test. The purpose is to determine the child's reading level and should be used along with other evaluative measures. Informal tests may take the form of inventories, teacher questions, basal reading tests at the end of a unit, reading attitude measures, informal textbook tests to determine reading level, or teacher check lists.

Perceptive teachers derive a wealth of information about their students through mere observation. The type of check list that appears below may be helpful in this regard.

STUDENT'S READING BEHAVIOR

General attitude toward reading

_____ Asks to read.

_____ Uses free time for reading.

_____ Asks to take home books.

_____ Shows involvement with a book, for example, laughing out loud.

Attention span

_____ Is easily distracted.

_____ Sits still.

_____ Waits turn.

Evidence of thinking while reading

_____ Asks questions.

_____ Anticipates what may happen.

_____ Relates to previous books and experiences.

_____ Sees further ramifications and problems.

Use of reading materials in content areas

_____ Utilizes reference materials.

_____ Handles word problems in mathematics.

_____ Follows charts, time lines, maps in social studies books.

General language ability

_____ Follows story line.

_____ Articulates ideas fluently.

_____ Listens attentively.

_____ Organizes and writes down main ideas.

AFTER EVALUATION: THEN WHAT?

Once the reading scores and teacher assessments are in, then what? Evaluation should provide an opportunity for adjustments. Should the reading program be altered, dropped, or reinforced? Should the curriculum be changed? Do the children enjoy reading and see it as a useful tool? For some teachers, the last question is most important. If children do not see reading as a unique and enjoyable way of knowing, it will never become their primary source of information. We cannot give children the impression that the only reason to read is to achieve higher grades on reading tests and still expect them to develop into practiced and voluntary readers.

TEST-TAKING SKILLS

Even if the ultimate goal is to develop a love for reading, all students will face certain realities. Testing is a fact of life. The ability to score high on tests is a lifelong asset. There are test-taking skills that children can be trained to develop. These skills may not make a child a successful or dedicated reader but they may enable the child to become a successful test taker.

Some teachers may find themselves caught in a dilemma. If they train children to become test-wise, they run the risk of reducing reading to a mechanical activity. Even dynamic material can become trivial when students are asked to distill its essence into an analysis of silent letters or word opposites. Very often the exercises to develop test-taking abilities are a series of isolated paragraphs which the student is instructed to skim for isolated facts—with or without understanding. This kind of activity is difficult for the child, and not infrequently a potential avid reader is lost forever. "If we want children to become proficient test-takers, then let us emphasize test-taking strategies. But, let us also be clear—such efforts have little to do with improving reading skills."[40]

Since hopes for future schooling or career can be undermined by poor test results, a proliferation of primers on standardized tests are now on the market. They instruct well-meaning parents on how to teach their children to read, take tests, increase IQ scores, and generally succeed with the evaluative devices that society has designed to measure, rate, and categorize people. But the reading process is elusive. It cannot be reduced to a recipe. The improvement of reading is a long and complicated procedure involving the whole child.

Since the teacher and the parent are bound to be confused in this situation, priorities have to be identified. If children can become better

[40]Ann Cook, "Reading Tests Vs. Reading." Taken from testimony presented at a public hearing on standardized reading tests held in New York City.

test-takers (if not better readers) with test-taking instruction, is it the teacher's responsibility to provide instruction in this area? It would appear that if we want to teach test-taking, we must set aside time for it at the expense of other studies. Teachers, parents, and school boards will have to ask themselves: Is such time well spent?

> **Afterview**   The more we learn about the reading process, the more we recognize its complexity. Teaching a child to read involves teaching a child to listen, speak, write, and think. Children learn to read when their bodies, emotions, senses, and intellects say "go." The "right" reading program, the "right" technique, and the "right" book do not exist in general terms. As in all educational matters, the central problem is matching program and child. Most significant in this "match" is the child's attitude and the teacher's competence (knowledge, skills, and attitudes).
>
> We are in the middle of a widespread public debate not only about what constitutes a good reading program, but even about what dialects or second languages should be taught in our schools. It is obvious that the solution is not a simple one and that educators will have to make special efforts to encourage all children to recognize the practical and personal rewards of reading. A good start is a rich language laboratory where the love for reading can grow along with the necessary skills.

WHEN YOU WANT TO KNOW MORE

1. Select a bilingual group in your area. Find out as much as you can about their cultural heritage and practices. Using your new knowledge, develop some readiness activities that could aid children in this group.

2. Compare the vocabulary in several first-grade readers. What similarities and differences do you note? Try to select readers from different regions of the country. How do you feel about the need for standardized vocabularies and the development of uniform word lists for beginning readers?

3. Develop some readiness activities for a child who has a limited experiential background.

4. Develop a list of books for an older child with limited reading ability. Try to match the child's interests and the books. A good source to begin with is *High Interest: Easy Reading,* edited by Marian E. White.

5. Reread the desert island example described in the section on the language-experience approach. Devise a similar example involving a different geographical setting. How would you teach the young child with you to read without the conventional tools? What will your environment provide in the way of experiences, materials, and strategies?

IN THE CLASSROOM

1. Plan and execute a pooling activity in individualized reading which will help children focus attention on an important story reading skill: the ability to predict outcomes. Be sure that your pooling activity can apply to many different books.

2. There has been evidence that a positive self-concept correlates with reading success. Plan and execute some activities that might enhance the self-concept of children in your class.

3. Try to identify the key vocabulary of one child. How will you discover these words? What activities will you develop to build on this vocabulary? What materials will you use?

4. Prepare a file of pictures that can be used to teach the following skills necessary for reading and language growth: sequence of events, details, left-to-right direction, noting differences and likenesses, making inferences.

5. Read some children's books written in Black English. Plan to use them to help Black children in your class bridge the gap between home and school.

SUGGESTED READINGS

Ching, Doris C. *Reading and the Bilingual Child.* Newark, Del.: International Reading Association, 1976.

Cullinan, Bernice E., ed. *Black Dialects & Reading.* Urbana, Ill.: National Council of Teachers of English, 1974.

Cunningham, Patricia Marr, et al. *Classroom Reading Instruction, K-5 Alternative Approaches.* Lexington, Mass.: Heath, 1977.

Durkin, Dolores. *Teaching Young Children to Read,* 3d ed. Boston: Allyn & Bacon, 1980.

Fox, Robert P., ed. *Teaching English as a Second Language and as a Second Dialect.* Urbana, Ill.: National Council of Teachers of English, 1973.

Hall, Mary Anne. *Teaching Reading as a Language Experience,* 2d ed. Columbus, Ohio: Merrill, 1976.

Kirk, Samuel A., and Gallagher, James J. *Educating Exceptional Children,* 3d ed. Boston: Houghton Mifflin, 1979.

Landeck, Beatrice. *Learn to Read/Read to Learn: Poetry and Prose from Afro-rooted Sources.* New York: McKay, 1975.

Mainstreaming Series. Boston: Teaching Resources.

Williams, Frederick, ed., *Language and Poverty.* Chicago: Markham Publishing, 1971.

Other Materials

Anderson, Betty. *Reading Readiness and the Mainstreamed Pupil.* Los Angeles: JAB Press. (One cassette tape.)

Barbe, Walter B. *Barbe's Reading Skills Check List.* New York: Parker Publishing, 1975.

Beginning Fluency in English as a New Language. Los Angeles: Bowmar/Noble. (Filmstrips, cassettes, records, booklets.)

Gould, Annabelle, and Schollaert, Warren. *Reading Activities for Primary and Intermediate Grades.* Dansville, N.Y.: Instructor Publications, 1972.

Greatsinger, Calvin, and Waeldner, Patricia Kelly. *Practice in Survival Reading.* Syracuse, N.Y.: New Readers Press, 1977. (Eight workbooks for students with limited reading skills. Books are titled: *Machine-Age Riddles, Signs Around Town, Label Talk, Read the Instructions First, Your Daily Paper, It's On the Map, Let's Look It Up, Caution: Fine Print Ahead.*)

Kachuck, Beatrice Levy. *Reading Comprehension Cognitive Strategies for Learning.* Los Angeles: JAB Press. (Four Cassette tapes.)

Raskin, Bruce, *The Reading Idea Book.* Palo Alto, Calif.: Education Today, 1978.

Russell, David H., and Karp, Etta E. *Reading Aids Through the Grades: Three Hundred Developmental Reading Activities.* New York: Teachers College, Columbia University, Bureau of Publications, 1963.

Spache, Evelyn B. *Reading Activities for Child Involvement,* 2d ed. Boston: Allyn & Bacon, 1976.

White, Marian E. *High Interest: Easy Reading for Junior and Senior High School Students.* New York: Scholastic Book Services, Citation Press, 1972.

CHAPTER **8**

Children's Literature

Preview Experiences with literature can make a difference in the lives of teachers and children. This chapter will identify the many ways in which literature may contribute to a child's intellectual and emotional growth. It will distinguish "what a book can be" from "what a book can do" and contrast the emotional powers of literature with its potential for developing a variety of intellectual skills. Through discussion of a great variety of books, the teacher will be assisted in recognizing how literature can be used to develop interest and fluency in all the language arts. Guidance will be given in identifying good books and setting up a literature program. A section will be devoted to a discussion of the new realism that has taken hold in children's literature, giving consideration to public reaction, questions of censorship, and the needs of today's children. Racism, sexism, and ageism in children's literature will be explored along with specific suggestions for incorporating nonstereotyped materials into the school curriculum. A class project in fantasy will be outlined to capitalize on the growing interest in science fiction. Finally, the specific competences necessary for those who teach children's literature will be identified.

You think your pain and your heartbreak are unprecedented in the history of the world, but then you read. It was books that taught me that the things that tormented me the most were the very things that connected me with all the people who were about, or who had been alive.

—James Baldwin

A book must be an ice-axe to break the seas frozen inside our soul.

—Franz Kafka

ON ONE OF THOSE soggy April days in New York City, when classroom morale floundered on the brink of disaster, I was determined to bypass the formal reading lesson so carefully prepared. The students and I were confined to our enclosure (known as the elementary-school classroom) and the mood both inside and out was gray, monotonous, and uninspired. A magical rescue was necessary. Too bad we didn't have a resident genie, a talking rabbit, or an horrific beast. None of these being readily available, I reached almost instinctively for the best substitute—a "dynamite" book. "Put your readers away," I said aloud. "Literature is why we learn to read anyway," I mumbled to myself. The beautiful, believable magic slowly began: "Once there were four children whose names were Peter, Susan, Edmund and Lucy. This story is about something that happened to them when they were sent away from London during the war because of the air raids."[1] After five minutes the students were captured by the mastery of C. S. Lewis and transported from Public School 167 to the wonderful world of Narnia.

How fortunate are those students whose teacher knows the witches, the dybbuks, the wee folk, and the clever animals of many heritages. Using the storyteller's art, the teacher can look into the students' eyes and embroider a tale in ways similar to those of traditional storytellers of old. Or, if choosing to read, the teacher may skilfully interpret the author's words and deftly maneuver the audience into another time and place that catches both their hearts and imaginations. What an exciting place classrooms would be if more teachers were able to match the myth to the moment, the hero to the child, the story to the situation.

But this is not a magical feat. The pleasure and power of literature are

---

[1]C. S. Lewis, *The Lion, the Witch and the Wardrobe* (New York: Collier Books, 1950), p. 1.

available to any teacher. This chapter will identify some basic information and content of children's literature for the elementary-school teacher. It will also suggest sources, guides, and other aids for further book selection.

WHAT DO YOU KNOW ABOUT CHILDREN'S LITERATURE?

> You may have tangible wealth untold
> Caskets of jewels and coffins of gold
> Richer than I you can never be—
> I had a Mother who read to me.
> —Strickland Gillilan

You probably know more about children's literature than you think you do. Your knowledge of it has been accumulating ever since some loving adult first sang, read, or told stories to you. Your first exposure might have been listening to a lullaby, a Mother Goose rhyme, a finger play, or a simple version of your family's favorite folktale. Whatever it was, you were learning to love the person and incidentally the story. Even if you didn't understand all the words, you had a sense of the rhythm, the sounds, and the many moods made possible by the spoken word. Your early experiences with literature might have involved listening to records or handling books that required you to "pat the bunny," or "open the door."

Take a moment and try to remember your early experiences with literature; relive a time of wonder. As you recall an incident, a character, or a title, you are probably remembering what Leland Jacobs refers to as a "feeling fact": your sadness because Wanda was forced to lie about her hundred dresses, your joy when Jack outwitted the giant, or your terror as young John Gunther fought his unsuccessful battle with death. Sometimes, it may be painful to remember things long past, but your recollections will help you to appreciate the power of literary experiences that you thought had long been forgotten.

WHAT CAN A BOOK BE?

> Teacher (aloud): "When you finish your book, I want you to write a report explaining the theme and the main characters."
> Scott (to himself): "Okay, I won't finish the book; then I won't have to write the report."

Can you recall a similar experience? Was your reaction the same as Scott's? The way a book is used in class may discourage young readers. But it can also turn them on so that they will believe that boysenberry pies float, dragons are bald, and elephants sit on nests. A good book has the power to make you sob or smile, fight or cringe. But unless you are a willing host, a book, no matter how great a work of art, can do nothing. Allow literature to enter your inner sanctum, and much enjoyment awaits.

Now enjoyment does not mean "liking." "Did you *like* the book?" is not a literary question. It is inappropriate to ask, "Did you like *The Diary of Anne Frank?*" "Were you involved?" is the literary question. Did you get personally caught up in the relationship between Anne and Peter? Were you one with the mood, the tone, the feeling created by the author? Were you moved by the story? Did it enter your life and make you cry? laugh? feel joy? discomfort? Did it "entertain" you by holding your attention—entertain you not in the sense of fun, but in the sense of involvement? In fact, did you not tacitly agree to be involved, even if the material was disturbing? Why is it that we are willing to consider literary experiences that deal with painful matters? Could it be that literature can serve as a kind of emotional compass pointing the way toward meaning? At times,

8-1

From *Horton Hatches the Egg,* by Dr. Seuss. Copyright 1940 and renewed 1968 by Dr. Seuss. Reprinted by permission of Random House, Inc. and William Collins Sons & Co. Ltd.

we turn to literature for the illumination of life which comes only from vicarious involvement. It has nothing to do with liking or disliking. Like life, it just is!

What can a book be, in the heart of a hospitable host?

(1) *A book can be an inspiration.* It can nurture and inspire human concern because it addresses feelings and brings the reader in direct contact with the deepest emotions of a character. Consider the feelings of Sylvester, a donkey transformed into a rock:

> He was scared and worried. Being helpless, he felt hopeless. He imagined all the possibilities, and eventually he realized that his only chance of becoming himself again was for someone to find the red pebble and to wish that the rock next to it would be a donkey. The chance was one in a billion at best.[2]

(2) *A book can be liberating.* Having the potential to educate and free the emotions, books can help young people understand their lives. Fairy tales in particular, according to child psychologist Bruno Bettelheim, may aid the young reader in the integration of personality. Beloved by all people, fairy tales present the message that life is a struggle—one that ends victoriously only if we respond with courage and steadfastness. The fairy tale

> . . . takes the existential anxieties and dilemmas very seriously and addresses itself directly to them: the need to be loved and the fear that one is thought worthless; the love of life, and the fear of death.[3]

(3) *A book can be a catalyst.* Books can help both children and adults increase their empathic and creative competence. As we experience another's reality, as we empathize with Edgemont the aging turtle, or worry with Wilbur the anxious pig, we simultaneously rethink our own lives. The characters' predicaments suggest choices for our own dilemmas.

Children should be encouraged to use reading experiences as springboards to new thinking. Rather than limiting discussions of literature to structural matters, the teacher should invite creative responses to reading material. Properly presented, a good book can give meaning to abstract concepts of courage, dignity, life, and love. In this sense, a creative encounter with literature may be likened to the first stage of a rocket; it can ignite a spark that transports the reader beyond the skies. Or as one writer says it: "For the creative readers, books are more than storehouses of thought—they are grist for their own thinking."[4]

[2]William Steig, *Sylvester and the Magic Pebble* (New York: Windmill Books/Simon & Schuster, 1960).

[3]Bruno Bettelheim, *The Uses of Enchantment: The Meaning and Importance of Fairy Tales* (New York: Alfred A. Knopf, 1976), p. 10.

[4]Robert L. Trezise, "Teaching Reading to the Gifted," *Language Arts* 54 (November/December 1977): 923.

(4) *A book can make us aware of the beauty, power, and fun of words.* Early on, children become aware of the repetitive and rhythmic quality of language. Most often, their experiences begin with some form of rhyme, jingle, or game; the Mother Goose rhymes are familiar to most school-age children. There are also modern versions of these rhymes. Like their traditional counterparts, they have a musical lilt and communicate the joys of language. *Father Fox's Pennyrhymes,* for example, delights young listeners and readers with verses like the following:

> Mister Lister passed his sister
> Married his wife 'cause he couldn't resist her:
> Three plus four times two he kissed her
> How many times is that, dear sister?[5]

Modern versions of folktales are also constantly rolling off the presses, and certainly much of their appeal is directly related to their style of language. These stories, like earlier folktales, are not meant to be read

The sky is dark, there blows a storm
Our cider is hot, the fire is warm
The snow is deep & the night is long:
Old Father Fox, will you sing us a song?

8-2

Illustration by Wendy Watson and text excerpt from *Father Fox's Pennyrhymes* by Clyde Watson. Text copyright © 1971 by Clyde Watson. Illustrations copyright © 1971 by Wendy Watson. By permission of Thomas Y. Crowell, Publishers, and Macmillan, London and Basingstoke.

[5]Clyde Watson, *Father Fox's Pennyrhymes,* illus. Wendy Watson (New York: Thomas Y. Crowell, 1971), p. 2.

silently. Often they feature a refrain that invites the listeners to chant along with the reader. Children enjoy serving as a chorus on the last lines of the Danish folktale *The Fat Cat*, for example:

> I ate the gruel
> and the pot
> and the old woman, too,
> And Skohottentot
> and Skolinkenlot.
> And now I am going
> To also eat YOU.[6]

The African folktale *The Adventures of Aku* also prompts children to chant and clap with its refrain:

> Kwaku, Kwaku
> Here comes Okraman
> Walking with Aku
> Just like a human.[7]

The fun of language is also revealed in the well-loved nonsense rhymes of poets Edward Lear, Ogden Nash, and others:

> There was an Old Man with a beard
> Who said, "It is just as I feared!
> Two Owls and a Hen, four Larks and a Wren,
> Have all built their nests in my beard!
> —Edward Lear[8]

THE OCTOPUS

> Tell me, O Octopus, I begs,
> Is those things arms, or is they legs?
> I marvel at thee, Octopus;
> If I were thou, I'd call me Us.
> —Ogden Nash[9]

THE PICKETY FENCE

> The pickety fence
> The pickety fence
> Give it a lick it's
> The pickety fence
> Give it a lick it's
> A clickety fence

[6]Jack Kent, *The Fat Cat: A Danish Folktale* (New York: Parents' Magazine Press, 1971).
[7]Ashley Bryan, *The Adventures of Aku* (New York: Atheneum, 1976), p. 15.
[8]Edward Lear, *The Complete Book of Nonsense* (New York, Dodd, Mead, 1958), p. 121.
[9]Ogden Nash, *Verses from 1929 On* (Boston: Little, Brown, 1959).

Give it a lick it's
A lickety fence
Give it a lick
Give it a lick
Give it a lick
With a rickety stick
Pickety
Pickety
Pickety
Pick.
—David McCord[10]

A book or poem can be a means to personal growth and exploration—if the reader permits the imagination to take over. Occasionally, a book can even release what Kafka calls the seas frozen inside our souls. But

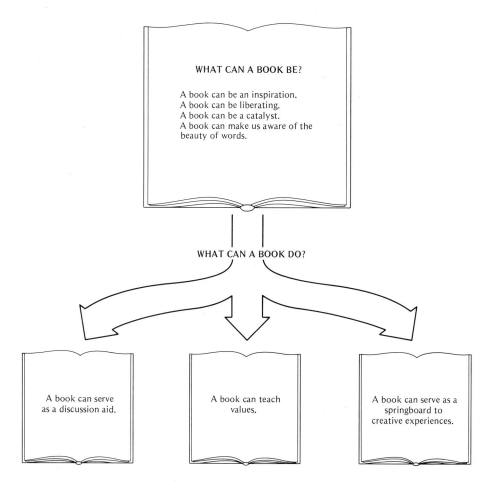

WHAT CAN A BOOK BE?

A book can be an inspiration.
A book can be liberating.
A book can be a catalyst.
A book can make us aware of the beauty of words.

WHAT CAN A BOOK DO?

A book can serve as a discussion aid.

A book can teach values.

A book can serve as a springboard to creative experiences.

[10]David McCord, "The Pickety Fence," illus. Marc Simont, in *Every Time I Climb a Tree* (Boston: Little, Brown, 1967).

the reader must be emotionally engaged. Without personal involvement, very little can happen. Assuming the presence and precedence of the emotional experience, teachers can then look to books for other values. The section that follows suggests a second stage, in which it is appropriate to ask, "What can a book do?"

WHAT CAN A BOOK DO?

(1) *Books can serve as discussion aids.* A third-grade teacher had just read her class an old Indian fable, "The Blind Men and the Elephant," the story of six blind men who have heard about elephants but never been near one. Their chance to touch an elephant comes when they visit the Rajah's palace. As each touches a different part of the elephant, each is sure he knows exactly what elephants are like. "Did any of them really know?" the teacher asks. Lively discussion follows as the children consider questions pondered since ancient times: Do people see only one side of a situation? Do those who are blind sometimes "see" more?

The students listen to each other's responses. Afterward, a small group decides to dramatize the story; they think it might lend itself to a reader's theater presentation. A few students decide to write their own Indian fables. The teacher suggests that they might first want to read "Usha, the Mouse Maiden," and other Indian tales.

Still other language-learning activities occur to the teacher. She could duplicate a copy of John G. Saxe's "The Blind Men and the Elephant," which translates the essence of the fable into poetic form. Maybe some children could do a puppet show or a choral reading based on the story. Others could develop their own poems.

The children were as involved as the teacher. They could approach this activity on many levels and from different vantage points. The power of language to open doors was evident and a book had been the catalyzing agent.

(2) *Books can teach values.* Even a cursory look at children's books of the past reveals many stories written expressly to instruct children in "the right way." A schoolchild in colonial America was exposed to books on manners, obedience to authority, and the dire consequences of misbehavior. The story line of a book served as a transparent disguise for the didactic content. As the country grew and attitudes changed, fear of retribution was no longer pressed as the reason for "moral" behavior. The appeal was to a child's sense of fair play, honesty, and the redeeming values of love. But we must ask along with Hughes Moir, "If we've had these good books for all these years, . . . why is the world in such lousy shape?"[11] Obviously, *how* children become moral, and even *what* is moral, is a complicated issue.

[11]Hughes Moir, "If We've Always Had Books That Taught All These Virtues Why Is Our Society in Such Lousy Shape?," *Language Arts* 54 (May 1977): 524.

Most parents do not wish to entrust the moral education of their children to the schools. What then is the role of the teacher in this area? If books can influence children's values and teachers are "book pushers," do they by association have a strong impact on the child's moral development?

A modern approach to this issue recognizes that although books do not have to provide moral instruction, they very often do. Similarly, teachers are visible role models of a didactic profession. Their presence, their body language, what they choose to say, and what they choose to be silent about serve as behavioral examples. Moral education, while not consciously taught by many teachers, is a kind of "hidden curriculum." Recognizing its presence in the schools is a step toward authenticity.

Teachers need some guidelines in this area, and they have been forthcoming from several sources, particularly the field of humanistic education and the studies of Lawrence Kohlberg. Humanistic education, in its search for personal knowledge, suggests strategies for helping children explore, question, and develop their own values. In this context, values orientation does not mean the inculcation of the teacher's values or those expressed in a particular literary work. The phrase refers to strategies used by teachers to help children recognize the moral alternatives implicit in a situation and the consequences of personal choice. Thus, for example, when a teacher asks students to consider the main ideas of a literary work or the behavior of a character, the purpose is to promote the students' thinking about the valuing process in general. Many contemporary works for children and adolescents have themes and resolutions that some adults consider ethically objectionable. There are those, therefore, who cry for censorship; others who proclaim their faith in the sophistication of today's children and suggest that youngsters be encouraged to use the literary experience for moral decision making. Indeed, the messages sent out by the popular culture on moral values are numerous. Gone are the clear-cut verbalizations of yesteryear, when the "good guys" and the "bad guys" got what was coming to them. And many children's books reflect this moral dilemma.

As teachers reflect on justice and moral values and their implications for the classroom, Lawrence Kohlberg's pioneering studies on moral decision making provide a helpful rubric. Kohlberg identifies three levels of moral development each of which has two stages.

Kohlberg's Stages of Moral Development

1. *Pre-moral level*
   Stage I: Punishment and obedience orientation. Rules are obeyed to avoid punishment.
   Stage II: Naive instrumental hedonism. The child conforms in order to obtain rewards.

2. *Morality of conventional role conformity*
   Stage III: "Good boy morality" of maintaining good relations. The child conforms to avoid disapproval.

Stage IV: Authority maintaining morality. The child conforms to avoid censure by authorities and resulting guilt.

3. *Morality of self-accepted principles*
Stage V: Morality of contract. A duty is defined in terms of contract, general avoidance of violation of the rights of others.
Stage VI: Morality of individual principles of conscience. The child conforms to avoid self-condemnation.[12]

When looking at his scheme, it is important to recognize that no ages are associated with the stages. There is, however, a readiness for moral decision making, as there is readiness for learning to read. Kohlberg's research further suggests "that changes in moral thinking go step by step through six stages, with children's development stopping or becoming fixed at any one of the six stages."[13] For children's literature, the major implication of Kohlberg's research is that prior to ages ten through twelve, children are rarely capable of Stage VI decision making.[14]

Kohlberg contends that "there are in fact universal human ethical values and principles." But these principles are not like those set down in nineteenth-century books for children. Rather than absolutes, they are guidelines controlled by a "principled sense of justice." For Kohlberg, justice is not everyone "doing his or her own thing."

Recognizing that the teacher of literature can easily be caught in the role of the teacher of morality, try to use Kohlberg's stages in the following ways:

1. Choose a book that suits the child's stage of moral development. A good example of a picture book that presents questions of justice for the very young is Russell Hoban's *A Bargain for Frances.*

2. Use literature that promotes a child's growth from one moral stage to another. For example, *The Cay*, by Theodore Taylor, presents the ethical dilemma of a young boy and helps the reader consider how he or she would respond in a situation in which self-gratification and expediency are in conflict.

3. Emphasis should be placed on meaningful open-ended discussions that encourage children to refine their moral sense and respond to ambivalence in characters who are both "good" and "bad." The characters in the stories in E. L. Konigsburg's *Throwing Shadows* are confronted with situations that suggestion moral alternatives. However, justice, in the sense of fairness and regard for the value and equality of all human beings, should be the ultimate principle. But this final level is arrived at, if ever, only after people go through a sequence of developmental stages.

[12]Laurence Kohlberg quoted in Norman Williams and Sheila Williams, *The Moral Development of Children* (New York: Macmillan, 1970), p. 83.

[13]Lawrence Kohlberg, "The Moral Atmosphere of the School" (Paper delivered at Association for Supervisors and Curriculum Development Conference on the "Unstudied Curriculum," Washington, D.C., 9 January 1969).

[14]Cheryl Gosa, "Moral Development in Current Fiction for Children and Young Adults," *Language Arts* 54 (May 1977): 530.

Clearly a word of caution is necessary. The prime purpose of literary experiences is not to teach moral behavior, but to provide the reader with meaningful encounters with life. The child who reconsiders his or her own values in the light of a character's dilemma is experiencing an important by-product of literary involvement.

(3) *Books can serve as springboards for creative growth.* The students in a fifth-grade class are learning to be themselves. Zelda has settled into the one comfortable chair in the room and is writing her own answer to the provocative question raised by Katherine Paterson in *Jacob Have I Loved:* "What would I do if I were the unloved twin?" A small group in front of the room is preparing an oral presentation of Randall Jarrell's prose poem *The Bat-Poet* after listening to the poet's recording of the story. Like the brown bat in the story, the students hope to find someone who will listen to them. Ari, a Greek-American boy, is at the easel working on a painting inspired by *Petro's War,* by Alki Zei, a vivid description of the Italian occupation of Athens during the Second World War. Some children are writing about real worlds; others are constructing imaginary ones. A small group is reading, oblivious to the activity around them. Are they all being creative? Probably not; but where children are invited to become involved, the possibilities for creative growth are always present. All creative growth is unique, and some children need more assistance than others. The creative process has discernible stages, and children should be allowed to proceed at their own pace.

The awareness that life may be seen from many viewpoints may serve as a creative catalyst. Books can help in this regard. Tana Hoban's *Look Again* and *Take Another Look* dare the young reader to recognize objects by showing only small sections of them. Different viewpoints are explored in another way in Charlotte Zolotow's *The Unfriendly Book* and in William Cole's *What's Good for a Three Year Old?* David MacCauley in *Unbuilding* takes a unique perspective when he challenges the reader to consider the dismantling of a structure such as the Empire State Building.

Some children, though extremely alert, are not quite ready to trust their own perceptions. These youngsters need further experiences rearranging old and familiar ideas into new relationships. Ask them to find different versions of the same fairy tale or cycle of poems about loneliness. Some might enjoy creating their own stories for wordless picture books. *Noah's Ark,* by Peter Spier, *Changes, Changes,* by Pat Hutchins, and *One Frog Too Many,* by Mercer and Marianna Mayer, are particularly well-suited to this activity.

The goal is to bring all children into the creative process. For those not inclined to dive in head first, literature can provide a safe remove. One can slowly get into the water and wade to a comfortable depth. There is surely no one best way for all children. Maybe the only answer is to make the books available, allowing the magic and mystery between the covers to weave its spell.

WHY SHOULD TEACHERS KNOW CHILDREN'S LITERATURE?

The teacher who can present children's literature warmly and intelligently can be a lasting influence on a student's attitude toward literature. Four principles provide the philosophical rationale for the elementary-school teacher's acquisition of knowledge about children's literature.

Principle I. Children who have personally enriching experiences with literature are more likely to appreciate the relationship that exists between life and literature. The enjoyment of literature remains a central reason for reading.

Principle II. Literature can play an important role in emotional development because it allows children to become aware of their own feelings as they respond to the feelings of others.

Principle III. Literature nourishes language development. There is an ongoing interaction between reading and facility with oral or written language.

Principle IV. Literature, like all art, strives to understand life: to bring order out of chaos, to explain the unexplainable, and to suggest alternative modes of response.

The principles identified above can provide some guidelines as teachers work with children. Knowledge of children's books, their authors, and the potential of the literary experience will place you in an advantageous position as a practitioner of the art of teaching. Here are some sample situations in which such knowledge could have practical value:

Situation A

In your classroom, peer group pressure is in full force. One child is being victimized; both you and he are rendered relatively helpless. Some books that address this problem are

—Taro Yashima, *Crow Boy.* Penguin, 1976. (For younger children.)
This Caldecott Honor Book sensitively relates the loneliness of a Japanese boy scorned by his classmates. For some time, "Chibi," as he is derisively named, continues to experience peer disapproval. In time, however, the children come to respect the "Crow Boy" for his "special" talents and abilities.
—Judy Blume, *Blubber.* Dell, 1978. (For the middle grades.)
The book's title is the nickname given to the main character, Linda, in fifth grade. Her classmates' cruelty is indeed believable, as is her anxious desire for acceptance. Readers will be surprised, possibly even comforted, when in the end Linda's principal tormentor gets a dose of her own medicine.

—Robert Cormier, *The Chocolate War.* Pantheon, 1974. (For older children.)

Jerry, the main character, goes to an all-boys' Catholic high school. The members of a gang that calls itself "The Vigils" frighten Jerry into following their orders. This means refusing to sell chocolates for a school fund-raising. At the moment of truth, "The Vigils" change their minds; but Jerry now has control of the situation and refuses to sell the chocolates. The gang is embarrassed and the reader soon realizes that punishment has been meted out to the guilty.

It cannot be assumed that books will solve a reader's personal problems. However, the awareness that he or she is not alone may help a youngster cope with the world. A book's relevance to a classroom situation does not have to be openly discussed. Sometimes it is best left to the private thinking of each reader. A fat student might be made self-conscious if mentioned in a class discussion of the book *Blubber,* for example.

Situation B

The students in your class seem to be selecting prose fiction that reduces life to simplistic terms. *Nancy Drew, The Hardy Boys,* and other books with simple narrative and relatively little character development are the staples of their literary diet. Although these series books are fine for the reluctant reader or for teaching speed reading skills, they do not teach the young reader to appreciate the real power of the literary way of knowing. Some books that might help sensitize students to literary merit are

—Maia Wojciechowsk, *Shadow of a Bull.* Atheneum, 1964.

Manolo, son of Juan Olivar, the most famous bullfighter in Spain, is afraid to fight bulls. The story builds to a climax as the boy questions what it means to be a matador. His thoughts become more confused as he worries about disappointing his father and the other men who have helped him. What obligation does he have to himself? How can he prove that he is not a coward? With the advice of an old doctor in the town, Manolo resolves the problem in a way that satisfies both his personal commitments and the faith of the townspeople.

Shadow of a Bull is a good example of effective plot development. After your students have read this award-winning book, let them consider these questions: Do the events of the story dramatize the theme? Do the tensions of the characters and events propel the story? Does each event add to our understanding?

—Robert Burch, *Queenie Peavy.* Viking, 1966. (To develop awareness of character.)

As children identify with fictional characters they begin to consider the possibility that people grow and change. Queenie, a thirteen year old, is a defiant youngster, desperately loyal to her father, who is in jail. As the story progresses, he is released, but only temporarily, for he violates his parole. During his stay at home, he is uncaring and distant. It becomes apparent to the young rebel that good will emerge only if she changes her own hostile attitudes and behavior. Set in a southern town, the story sheds light on how one's locality and personal experiences develop character.

After reading such stories, your students should begin to realize that the most important single element in a story is usually character. Plot develops as a result of the characters' behavior. In many books, plot exists to illuminate character.

—E. B. White, *Charlotte's Web*. Harper & Row, 1952. (To develop awareness of style.)

A variety of stylistic devices in *Charlotte's Web* assist the reader, both young and old, to accept the "truths" in this fantasy. The details, descriptions, and mood all serve to focus attention on a remarkable spider, Charlotte, who rescues Wilbur, the pig, from an early death. E. B. White meticulously delineates daily life in the farmyard, assisting the reader to identify with a host of animal characters.

In early summer, Wilbur's future is as hopeful as the "lilacs that bloom and make the air sweet." But as Charlotte's days wind down, the crickets sing in the grasses: " 'Summer is over and gone,' they sang 'Over and gone, over and gone. Summer is dying, dying.' "[15]

E. B. White is masterful in his use of seasonal changes to reveal future events and the technique of foreshadowing to create tension. His literary style heightens the dramatic effects and gives a multilevel meaning to the simple narrative.

WHAT IS A GOOD BOOK?

How do you determine the effectiveness or the value of a child's book? Consider for a moment the criteria you use in selecting and judging a book for your own personal reading. "I want something light and frivolous," you might say, or, "Can you suggest a book that deals with adolescent rebellion?" Or, "I need some pure escapism." Children have similar preferences determined by the current tempo of their lives.

Both children and adults should be given books appropriate to their moods and interests. Children's literature is not something apart from literature as a whole. As C. S. Lewis remarked,

> . . . no book is really worth reading at the age of ten which is not equally (and often far more) worth reading at the age of fifty.[16]

[15]E. B. White, *Charlotte's Web*, illus. Garth Williams (New York: Harper & Row, 1952), p. 113.

[16]C. S. Lewis, "On Stories," in *Essays Presented to Charles Williams* (London: Oxford, 1947), p. 100.

So there's the key! The criteria are the same—with one qualification. The adult brings a lifetime of experience to the printed page; some consideration must be given to the maturity of the language and concepts presented to children. Beyond that, however, adults and children ask the same questions about literature:

The Characters

Are the characters authentic?
Does the dialogue ring true?
Is their behavior consistent?
Do they appropriately suggest the qualities and limitations imposed by the author?
Can you get inside the characters, feel *with* them, and understand their motivations?

The Plot

Is the plot well-paced?
Does the narrative create enough tension to hold your interest?
Is the sequence of incidents logical?

The Details

The details selected and described in a story contribute to the reader's appreciation of character, plot, and place. For details help to create the illusion. Consider the following when evaluating a story:

Are the details accurate?
Do the details contribute to the reader's visualization of the story?
Do the details help to explain causality?
Are the details consistent?
Do the details help to create the mood?

The Style

Is the style appropriate to the content?
Is a mood created that engulfs the reader?
Is the language of the story forced, or does it evolve naturally?
Is the author preachy? Overly moralistic?

The Value

Was it worth the time?
Were there any universal qualities of human experience illuminated?
Was the theme worthy of the book? Was the book worthy of the theme?
Did you respond imaginatively?
Did it provide personal insight?
Do you remember more than the story?

SETTING UP A LITERATURE PROGRAM

As a teacher of literature, you will have to begin where you feel most comfortable. Are there books from your childhood that you recall with special joy? What books have you read or heard about recently that you would like to share with your students? Getting today's children to be enthusiastic about print is not easy. But it certainly can be done, as many teachers will testify. Here are some initial suggestions:

(1) *Become a reader of children's books.*

If you did not have the good fortune to meet the Biggest Bear, the Velveteen Rabbit, or Rosa-Too-Little when you were a young one, a happy time awaits you. Good literature knows no age. Here are some ways to begin:

a. Make friends with the school or local librarian and talk about children and books.

b. Consult lists of award-winning children's books (see pages 257–60) and read several of these books

c. Subscribe to a professional journal that is devoted to books for children and young adults. Some of these are

> *The Horn Book*
> *The School Library Journal*
> *The Lion and the Unicorn*
> *Children's Literature in Education*

d. Read reviews of the latest children's books in newspapers and magazines. The *New York Times* publishes an excellent semiannual review of children's books. The *Washington Post* and *Publishers' Weekly* also print a children's books issue. *Saturday Review* provides extensive coverage of children's books.

e. A variety of excellent books and general booklists about children's books are available in most libraries. Some particularly helpful references with comprehensive annotated bibliographies are

> Charlotte Huck, *Children's Literature in the Elementary School.* Holt, Rinehart & Winston, 1979.
> Abby Campbell Hunt, *The World of Children's Books: A Parent's Guide.* Sovereign Books, 1979.
> Nancy Larrick, *A Parents' Guide to Children's Reading.* Bantam, 1975.
> Sheldon Root, *Adventuring with Books: 2400 Titles for Pre-Kindergarten–Grade 8.* Citation Press, 1973.
> Zena Sutherland and May Hill Arbuthnot, *Children and Books.* Scott Foresman, 1977.

f. A new focus is being placed on nonprint media. Consult one of the guides that list films, records, and other nonprint media dramatizing children's books.

> Flossie L. Perkins, *Book and Non-Book Media: Annotated Guide to Selection Aids for Educational Materials.* National Council of Teachers, 1972.
> Ellin Greene and Madalynne Schoenfeld, *A Multimedia Approach to Children's Literature.* American Library Association, 1977.
> Catalogs from Weston Woods Studios, Weston, Ct. (A good listing of films and filmstrips.)

g. Read some children's books that have a special meaning for adults. Frequently, simple language and an uncomplicated plot disguise a sophisticated theme. Among the books that speak on several levels are:

> Hans Christian Andersen, *The Ugly Duckling*. Harcourt Brace Jovanovich, 1979.
>
> Albert Cullum, *The Geranium on the Window Sill Just Died and Teacher You Went Right On*. Harlin Quist, 1971.
>
> Robert Kraus, *Leo, the Late Bloomer*. Dutton, 1973.
>
> Antoine de Saint Exupéry, *The Little Prince*. Harcourt Brace Jovanovich, 1968.
>
> Shel Silverstein, *The Giving Tree*. Harper & Row, 1964.
>
> James Thurber, *The Last Flower*. Harper & Row, 1971.
>
> Kit Williams, *Masquerade*. Schocken, 1980.

The message is *read, read, read*. Consider the criteria suggested earlier regarding character, plot, language, and theme, but don't be overly critical. Let the literary experience overtake you.

(2) *Create a classroom climate in which literature is an integral component.*

a. The room should be physically conducive to reading. If necessary, beg or borrow some comfortable chairs, an old rug, and bookcases.

b. Start a collection of books. Suggest that some money be transferred from basal reader to trade book purchases. Plan a fund-raising event to help pay for new books. Invite children and parents to bring books from home and the library. Then organize a system for returning library books on time.

c. Use books, their jackets, advertising, and illustrations to decorate the room. Strategically place provocative questions based on popular children's stories: "Have you met Amos and Boris?" "What's going on in Salem Village?" "Do you think that Ramona is really a pest?"

d. Talk about books whenever possible. Refer to "Dandelion's mistake" and "Mr. Popper's problems." Encourage the students to share their reading experiences with each other, both formally and informally.

e. Start reading and telling stories to your class daily. The art of storytelling does not have to be reserved for the professional. We all have a special quality to bring to children, and often a good story enables us to share ourselves in a very personal way. Remember body language and intonation communicate the mood of a story as much as the spoken word. We cannot all be magnificent storytellers, but we can each develop a style that will make children look forward to story hour. Dewey W. Chambers' *Storytelling and Creative Drama* suggests that the beginning storyteller must first attempt to analyze his own uniqueness—that is, his own personality, his own style:

> He needs to ask himself, "What kind of stories am I able to tell effectively and well? How can I match my own personality with a tale so that both are able to communicate to the listener?"[17]

---

[17]Dewey W. Chambers, *Storytelling and Creative Drama* (Dubuque, Iowa: William C. Brown, 1970), p. 15.

    f. Give students sufficient time to read. Consider Aidan Chambers' view on this matter:

> In the end Johnny cannot read because Johnny is not allowed to read and not allowed to become a reader. . . . How much time is Johnny given in school in which to read for reading's own sake? How many books is he given to choose from? How far is his reading no more than a tool he is required to use before answering routine questions of a pointless and book-killing kind?[18]

(3) *Try to match the child and the type of book.*

If a Ten Commandments were created especially for teachers, "Know Thy Student" would be at the top of the list. The teacher who knows his or her students and books can frequently arrange a meaningful union between the two. Charlotte Huck's "Books for Ages and Stages" (a section in her book *Children's Literature in the Elementary School)* and similar references are valuable basic tools for the teacher trying to determine which literature is suited to his or her students. It is not that there is one book but rather a type of book particularly appropriate at a given time.

    However, common sense tells us that even well-documented general-

[18]Aidan Chambers, "Letter from England: Talking About Reading: Back to Basics? Part II," *The Hornbook Magazine* 53 (December 1977): 708.

izations such as these have to be tempered by the teacher's judgment. There is no substitute for on-the-spot, firsthand observation of behavior viewed in the light of the child's background.

(4) *Capitalize on children's attraction to fairy tales.*

In a recent study, F. André Favat investigated the appeal that fairy tales have among children. A key conclusion was that fairy tales embody a child's conception of the world. For children younger than eight years, the form and content of fairy tales serves to reaffirm a simplistic conception of the world as a stable and ultimately gratifying universe.[19]

No adult should feel uneasy about selecting fairy tales for children, despite the sometimes fearful content. The stories are usually placed in an indefinite place (a land far away), a remote time (a long time ago), and the resolution is usually in favor of children. In general, fairy tales allow the young mind temporary escape from the restrictions of the real world, where children often feel powerless and unfairly treated.

Some educators and psychologists also contend that most fairy tales are instructive and consoling.

> From them a child can learn more about the inner problems of man, and about solutions to his own (and our) predicaments in any society, than he can from any other type of story within his comprehension.[20]

The tone of most well-known fairy tales is basically optimistic. *Cinderella* presents the assurance that kindness triumphs; *Jack and the Beanstalk* suggests that even the lowliest can succeed. But fairy tales can prompt understanding only when a child is ready to perceive their situations as personally meaningful. The implications of fairy tales should be caught, not taught. Bettelheim notes that, "It is always intrusive to interpret a person's unconscious thoughts, to make conscious what he wishes to keep preconscious, and this is especially true in the case of the child."[21] The personal discovery of meaning belongs to the child.

(5) *Delight in humor together.*

"I love to laugh," scream the characters in E. L. Travers' *Mary Poppins*, as they float on the ceiling. We all love to laugh, but we tend to do it less and less as we get older. Some adults need to relearn laughing; most children do it instinctively. They laugh at themselves and at literature. When they read about the fools from Chelm who confuse "your boots" and "my boots," or the members of the Stupid family who devour mashed potato sundaes, children laugh and are comforted by the characters' imperfections. They realize that one can be a "fool" and still be loved. Children are not afraid to identify with fools, for they themselves

---

[19]F. André Favat, *Child and Tale: The Origins of Interest* (Urbana, Ill.: National Council of Teachers of English, 1977).

[20]Bettelheim, *The Uses of Enchantment*, p. 5.

[21]Bettelheim, *The Uses of Enchantment*, p. 18.

so often do things considered foolish by the adult world. Francelia Butler, in *Sharing Literature With Children,* suggests that teachers do a
whole unit on "fools in literature." As children laugh and identify with
the comic antics of the fool, they are being given a chance to reflect on
their own lives. "The literature about fools . . . is appealing because fools
are, above all, human—and therefore tales about fools bring with them
always a certain joy and delight in the human condition."[22]

Talk about fools with your class: the Charlie Chaplins, the Laurel and
Hardys, and other talented mimes with whom children can easily identify.

The folklore of almost every culture will provide you with additional
material. I particularly like *The Funny Little Woman,* a tale from old
Japan retold by Arlene Masel, about an old lady who runs after her rice
dumpling into a hole in the ground. After much difficulty and much

8-5   Illustration by James Marshall from THE STUPIDS STEP OUT by Harry Allard.
Illustrated by James Marshall. Copyright © 1974 by James Marshall. Reproduced
by permission of Houghton Mifflin Company.

[22]Francelia Butler, *Sharing Literature with Children* (New York: McKay, 1977).

laughing, she returns safely to her own house. The rewards are such that the reader is convinced that the funny little woman has not been so foolish as originally thought. In another humorous tale, from Lebanon, "Don't Beat Your Children Before They're Born," a foolish shepherd makes himself miserable over difficulties with imaginary children. The descriptions of his troubles with his imaginary sons are hilarious. No wonder he decides, "If sons are this much trouble . . . I guess I won't bother to get married after all."[23]

Contemporary realistic fiction has its share of children who do seemingly foolish things but learn from their experiences. Homer Price's difficulties with his uncle's new doughnut machine is a favorite. Such well-loved characters as Ramona, Encylopedia Brown and Benjie all have their share of problems but manage to overcome them.

There are also a great variety of foolish, but well-meaning, animals who are ultimately appreciated. Have your children meet Horton, the likeable, farcical elephant who sits on Mayzie Bird's nest; Lyle, the crocodile who can't believe that everyone does not love him; and Dandelion, a narcissistic but likeable lion who learns to be himself.

As teachers of young children, we are in an enviable position. Our funny bones can be tickled daily. Great writers of tragedy from William Shakespeare to Arthur Miller have recognized the importance of punctuating their plays with comic relief. After a while even suffering loses its sting and becomes boring. With your students, it is an easy matter to recognize your own capacity for laughter. Children's literature offers a noble beginning; it is rich in laughable characters and situations and the fun of sheer and utter nonsense.

CLASSIFYING BOOKS

There are children's books about everything from A to Z—from anatomy to zithers. It is helpful for teachers to be aware of the kinds and types of books written for children. Children's books are usually divided into the following categories.

Picture Books

Picture books are books that rely heavily on illustrations to tell their stories. A successful picture book blends illustrations and text so that they are mutually enhancing. Many children can recognize an illustrator's techniques long before they can identify the writing style of a spe-

---

[23]Gloria Skuryzynski, "Don't Beat Your Children Before They're Born," in *Two Fools and a Faker*, illus. William Papos (New York: Lothrop, Lee and Shepard, 1977), p. 14.

cific author. Illustrators Maurice Sendak, Barbara Cooney, William Steig, and Uri Shulevitz are only a sampling of the many perennial favorites with youngsters.[24]

Picture books can play an important role in developing the child's aesthetic sensibilities. They are particularly important for those youngsters who are exposed to almost no other art in their early years. The Caldecott Medal given each year to the most distinguished American picture book for children will suggest many familiar titles (see page 257).

Traditional Literature

Much of children's literature is heavily indebted to the oral tradition. Folktales (fairy tales are included in this category), myths, legends, epics, and fables re-created and embroidered in speech by several generations survive today in stories written for children. Like their sources, these stories are usually simple and direct. The characters are usually one dimensional, and the resolution of plot is quick and complete. In the integration of literature into the curriculum, it is sometimes helpful to further classify traditional literature into ethnic or national categories.

Fantasy

Although they present imaginary worlds, strange behaviors of people and animals, and intriguing machinations with time perception, books of fantasy remain grounded in certain realities. Fantasy is only "a small step from reality . . . one elf, one accelerated trip through time, one child who can fly."[25] Any imaginative youngster can conceive of these possibilities. However, in order for the reader to accept the "fantastical" notion, certain realities must be maintained. For example, once the mythical land of Narnia has been established and the reader accepts its magic, the author is obliged to remain faithful to the original elements of the fantasy. There are also limits to this story world—for example, the children in Narnia cannot fly and Wilbur the pig cannot spin a web. The integrity of the fantasy has to be maintained. Interest in fantasy runs very high in many youngsters for it provides a vent for the imagination. This interest frequently increases with age. College bookstores report that books of fantasy are their best sellers.

---

[24]Children's book illustration is achieving a new prominence with the publication of *The Art of Maurice Sendak*, by Selma G. Lanes. (New York: Harry N. Abrams, 1980.)

[25]Joan I. Glazer and Gurney Williams III, *Introduction to Children's Literature* (New York: McGraw-Hill, 1979), p. 258.

Realistic Fiction

Fiction has been described as "the truth of life embroidered by the imagination." Another definition describes fiction as something that did not happen but could have. Children in the middle grades are very interested in books of realistic fiction. It is almost as if they are searching for a personal reflection between the covers of a book. A broad range of topics is covered in realistic fiction. In an attempt to reflect modern society, many new books of fiction for children confront disturbing subjects. The wisdom of this tendency will be explored in a later section of this chapter.

Historical Fiction

Through authentic stories of the people, places, and experiences of yesteryear, young readers begin to realize their connection to the past. Though it may require a more mature mind to recognize that we cannot live apart from our history, meaningful encounters with historical fiction can help a child bridge the gap between the concrete "now" and the more abstract "then." Social studies lessons are given an added dimension when an era, an event, or a famous person is seen through the eyes and, most important, the sensibilities of a character "who was there." Discussions of historical fiction provide the teacher with an opportunity to raise questions about content and develop an inquiry-oriented approach to historical fact and fiction. In this way, literature can also help the young reader to read more critically and to understand that a writer's values influence what is included and excluded in an historical accounting. Hopefully, students may come to realize that popular history does not necessarily record the past in its entirety. This perception is particularly important as youngsters consider questions involving racial, ethnic, and sexual stereotyping. The history of our country is told in many fine books for children. Some use inventive formats, as did a recent Newbery Medal Book, *A Gathering of Days: A New England Girl's Journal, 1830-32,* by Joan W. Blos.

Nonfiction

In the nonfiction category, there are thousands of books that reflect the current interests of children. Some of the newest titles illustrate this variety: *Kid Camping from Aaaaiii to Zip, Care of Uncommon Pets, Tutankamen's Tomb, The Age of Aquarius, The Best of Rube Goldberg's Inventions,* and *Energy for America.* Much of the nonfiction written for children consists of biographies and autobiographies. Particularly popular are the stories of present-day superstars in sports or entertainment.

The best of these transcend the subject's struggle and provide a model for human behavior.

Well-written, accurate, attractively illustrated nonfiction trade books may be more effective than textbooks in catalyzing children's enthusiasm for a subject. One fifth-grade girl who wanted to read everything that she could on ants found that a large number of excellent trade books are published on this topic. In searching them out, she not only learned about the ants, but developed a variety of reference skills.

Poetry

Many books of poetry for children, both anthologies and works devoted to individual poets, are published annually. The National Council of Teachers of English has identified a number of poets who have made outstanding contributions to the field. Among these are David McCord, Aileen Fisher, Myra Cohn Livingston, and Lillian Moore. (See page 260.) The potentialities of the poetic mode and suggestions for reading and writing experiences with poetry are provided in Chapter 11.

THE NEW REALISM IN CHILDREN'S BOOKS: A REVOLUTION

A new realism has taken hold in children's literature. Topics that were formerly taboo are being explored in a wide variety of contemporary books for children. Children's books now deal with such subjects as death, one-parent families, pregnancy, adolescent physical changes, sexual identity, drugs, alcoholism and emotional disturbance. Educators and parents are asking whether these are appropriate topics for youngsters, and because opinions vary, problems do arise.

Public reaction to the new realism has ranged from enthusiastic acceptance to demands that certain books be removed from the shelves. In many ways, because of the increasing publication of a wide variety of controversial books for children, the gulf between differing views seems to have widened. Do we, should we, dare we, limit young people's access to certain printed materials? Does reading "bad" things necessarily make "bad" people? Or more discriminating ones? Are objective answers to these questions possible? Or are our views always conditioned by a host of societal, cultural, and generational prescriptions?

As a teacher, you will be required to make decisions about these controversial materials. Your judgments may be more objective and responsible if you understand the factors that contributed to this revolution in books for children.

Since the Second World War, American society has repeatedly experienced traumatic shocks. The war itself awakened us to certain realities of human nature. We became a more mobile people, and there was a real

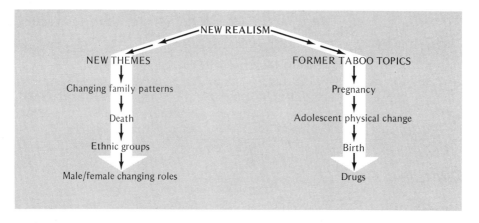

8-6   Diagram by Dr. Lee Rinsky and Roman Schweikert, Xavier University.

need for women to enter the job market. All of which laid the groundwork for the powerful Women's Movement. As a result of the increasing mobility and changing sexual roles, family life was altered. The divorce rate doubled, premarital sex was acknowledged as a fact of life, and alternate life styles emerged. Children were eyewitnesses to the new realism. They experienced it in their homes, and viewed it on television. Juvenile literature would soon catch up.

The cataclysmic Sixties intensified the social change. Newspaper headlines daily documented student revolts spurred on by the Vietnam War, the Women's Movement, and the thrust for equality by ethnic groups. The battle cry was "liberation," and there was concern about the growing dehumanization of society. There were those who were satisfied with the status quo, but the restlessness showed itself in the growing incidence of divorce, draft evasion, and political unrest. A new freedom to question had emerged. The titles of books for adults reflected the anxiety, among them J. Anthony Lukas' *Don't Shoot, We Are Your Children,* Alvin Toffler's *Future Shock,* and Charles Reich's *The Greening of America.* Literature for children was also concerned with these social issues. In *The Man in the Box: A Story from Vietnam,* Mary Lois Dunn expressed the misery and absurdity of war. The concern for human liberation emerged in *Durango Street,* by Frank Bonham. This book confronted the question of social equality, a topic not openly discussed in earlier works for children.

It is not that these issues are new to the literary scene. Good literature has always been a reflection of reality. However, in an attempt to protect children from some of life's realities, children's books have heretofore avoided many themes. The list on page 246 suggests a number of books on so-called controversial issues that have been used in many schools.

Even if we desire to do so, we are no longer able to protect children from the new realism. This does not mean that adults should abdicate all responsibility in judging which material is suitable for youngsters. Rather, the suggestion is that decision making should reflect a society that confronts the young child with heretofore unprecedented possibilities.

The New Realism and the New Child

> Childhood as we have known it for the past 200 years, is rapidly disappearing. The days when children are increasingly nurtured and sheltered before being inducted into the real or adult world are almost over.[26]

There is a new child on the scene, one who openly discusses racial tensions, sex, and drugs. Many elementary-school children are presently confronting what literary critics call the new realism. Faith is living in a one-parent family. Jennie, a third grader, has experienced the death of a loved one. Jamie's mother and father are in the process of getting a divorce, and Richard's unmarried sister is pregnant. Steven, only a kindergartner, already expresses the cultural stereotypes about what boys and girls *should* do. Emily, his sister, wants to be an engineer when she grows up.

In other ways as well, children learn about the taboo topics of our time. Peter gets information about drugs from listening to conversations among older siblings. Susan internalizes attitudes about violence from television. Janet hears her parents discussing a hopelessly alcoholic uncle. All children need help in determining what their attitudes and feelings are about life's crises. Realistic fiction may provide some perspective in this regard since children very often accept what they read as an accurate portrayal of life. Contemporary realistic fiction gives youngsters the chance to consider experiences from a perspective different from their own. The "safe remove" of literature can be comforting.

This is not to suggest that books should serve a therapeutic function. Bibliotherapy, the use of literature to work through emotional problems, is yet to be documented with research. Yet the theory underlying bibliotherapy is worthy of consideration. Through emotional identification with characters and story, readers may add to their self-understanding.

"Bibliotherapy does not refer to the use of didactic literature that hammers home a moral lesson, but rather it takes advantage of books in which true-to-life people (or animals as people substitutes) resolve conflicts, overcome handicaps and make satisfactory adjustments to life. If the reader is able to learn something from their experiences, well and good."[27]

[26]Sheldon Root, "The New Realism—Some Personal Reflections," *Language Arts* 54 (January 1977): 20.

[27]Betty Coody, "Bibliotherapy: Using Books to Meet Needs," in *Teaching in the 70's*, ed. Kenneth Briggs (Dubuque, Iowa: Kendall Hunt Publishing, 1971), p. 61.

BOOKS ON CONTROVERSIAL ISSUES

(Recommended ages are given in parentheses.)

Death

Bernstein, Joanne, and Gullo, Steven. *When People Die.* Dutton, 1977. (6–8)

Byars, Betsy. *Good-bye, Chicken Little.* Harper & Row, 1979. (8–11)

———. *Summer of the Swans.* Viking Press, 1970. (10–12)

Cleaver, Bill, and Cleaver, Vera. *Grover.* Lippincott, 1970. (9–11)

Clifford, Eth. *The Killer Swan.* Houghton Mifflin, 1980. (10–13)

Hunter, Mollie. *A Sound of Chariots.* Harper & Row, 1972. (12 and up)

Miles, Miska. *Annie and The Old One.* Little, Brown, 1971. (6–8)

Viorst, Judith. *The Tenth Good Thing About Barney.* Atheneum, 1975. (5–9)

Wersba, Barbara. *The Dream Watcher.* Atheneum, 1968. (10–12)

Aging

Blue, Rose. *Grandma Didn't Wave Back.* Watts, 1972. (8–10)

Irwin, Hadley. *The Lilith Summer.* Feminist Press, 1979. (10–12)

Kantrowitz, Mildred. *Maxie.* Scholastic Book Service, 1980. (5–8)

Langner, Nola. *Freddy, My Grandfather.* Scholastic Book Service, 1979. (6–8)

Mazer, Nora. *A Figure of Speech.* Delacorte, 1973. (12 and up)

Sharmat, Marjorie. *Edgemont.* Coward, 1976. (5–8)

Skorpen, Liesel. *Old Arthur.* Harper & Row, 1972. (6–8)

Divorce

Blue Rose. *A Month of Sundays.* Watts, 1972. (8–10)

Blume, Judy. *It's Not the End of the World.* Bantam, 1980. (10–12)

Bunting, Eve. *Blackbird Singing.* Macmillan, 1980. (10–13)

Cohen, Barbara. *Queen for a Day.* Lothrop, 1980. (10–13)

Donovan, John. *I'll Get There: It Better Be Worth the Trip.* Harper & Row, 1969. (12 and up)

Goff, Beth. *Where is Daddy? The Story of a Divorce.* Beacon Press, 1969. (4–7)

Mann, Peggy. *My Dad Lives in a Downtown Hotel.* Avon, 1974. (9–11)

Drugs

Anonymous. *Go Ask Alice.* Avon, 1972. (13 and up)

Childress, Alice. *A Hero Ain't Nothin' But A Sandwich.* Avon, 1977. (12 and up)

Gilbert, Sara. *Trouble at Home.* Lothrop, 1980. (12 and up)

Kerr, M. E. *Dinky Hocker Shoots Smack.* Dell, 1973. (12 and up)

Pope, Elizabeth. *The Perilous Guard.* Houghton Mifflin, 1974. (12 and up)

Wojchiechowska, Maia. *Tuned Out.* Harper & Row, 1968. (12 and up)

Sexuality

Blume, Judy. *Are You There God? It's Me, Margaret.* Dell, 1974. (10 and up)

Hall, Lynn. *Sticks and Stones.* Dell, 1972. (13 and up)

Neufeld, John. *Freddy's Book.* Random House, 1973. (8–10)

Zindel, Paul. *My Darling, My Hamburger.* Bantam, 1971. (12 and up)

War

Collier, Christopher, and Lincoln, James. *My Brother Sam Is Dead*. Scholastic Book Service, 1977. (12 and up)

DeJong, Meindert. *The House of Sixty Fathers*. Harper & Row, 1956. (9–11)

Kerr, Judith. *When Hitler Stole Pink Rabbit*. Dell, 1973. (8–10)

Pelgrom, Els. *The Winter When Time Was Frozen*. Morrow, 1980. (11–13)

Ryan, Cheli D. *Paz*. Macmillan, 1971. (6–8)

Thurber, James. *The Last Flower*. Queens House, 1977. (9 and up)

Uchida, Yoshiko. *Journey to Topaz*. Scribner, 1971. (11 and up)

Walsh, Jill. *Fireweed*. Avon, 1972. (12 and up)

Zei, Alki. *Petro's War*. Dutton, 1972. (10 and up)

Alternate Life Styles

Adler, C. S. *In Our House Scott Is My Brother*. Macmillan, 1980. (11 and up)

Cleaver, Bill, and Cleaver, Vera. *I Would Rather Be a Turnip*. New American Library, 1976. (12 and up)

Gripe, Maria. *The Night Daddy*. Delacorte, 1971. (8–11)

Klein, Norma. *Mom, The Wolf Man and Me*. Avon, 1974. (10 and up)

Little, Jean. *Home from Far*. Little, Brown, 1965. (10–12)

Mearian, Judy, *Someone Slightly Different*. Dial, 1980. (11–13)

Handicapping Conditions

Byars, Betsy. *The Summer of the Swans*. Viking Press, 1970. (10–12)

Colman, Hila. *Accident*. Morrow, 1980. (12 and up)

Cookson, Catherine. *Go Tell It to Mrs. Golightly*. Lothrop, 1980. (10–12)

Hermes, Patricia. *What If They Knew?* Harcourt Brace Jovanovich, 1980. (9–12)

Lasker, J. *He's My Brother*. A. Whitman, 1974. (6–8)

Levine, E. S. *Lisa And Her Soundless World*. Human Science Press, 1974. (6–8)

Slepian, Jan. *The Alfred Summer*. Macmillan, 1980. (8–11)

Young, Helen. *What Difference Does It Make Danny?* Andre Deutsch, 1980. (9–12)

Utilizing the Literature of the New Realism

The teacher who wishes to deal with some of the controversial issues that comprise the new realism in children's literature should proceed cautiously—not out of fear (there is always a commitment to one's professional judgment), but out of respect for the students, their families, and the community. The concept of readiness should be applied. Parents as well as children have a point at which they are prepared to deal with "controversial" issues. Cultural, religious, and educational experiences condition human responses and explain why some people are trail blazers and others adopt a more conservative stance.

I always suggest meeting with parents of the children in a class before embarking on a literary unit that deals with a controversial issue. The session is as enlightening for the teacher as for the parents. You might apply the following format for a parents' discussion of a unit of death to other controversial issues.

What the Teacher Wants to Know:

How do they (the parents) feel about the subject?
Do they have any religious attitudes that should be considered?
What are their personal attitudes about the subject?
Have any of their children had recent experiences relevant to the subject?

What the Parents Want to Know:

How does the teacher feel about the subject?
Will the teacher's religious convictions be allowed to influence the discussion?
What subject matter will be covered?
How will the teacher answer the children's questions?

I usually tell parents how I will proceed, stressing that learning has to begin where the children are. To what extent do the children have erroneous conceptions? I may begin with a questionnaire, a class discussion, a television program, a news event. My major concern, as in all the issues, is to help the children accept their own feelings about the topic.

What parents seem to want more than anything else is the reassurance that a teacher will not impose his or her personal views on controversial topics, but will discover how the children perceive the subject. There is also a concern that the teacher be sensitive to evidence of anxiety provoked by a particular issue. Frequently, there are one or two parents who do not want their children exposed to the material. Such wishes should be respected. Children whose parents object to a discussion can be discretely scheduled for another activity during that time.

Sometimes, parents want to know what they can read on the topic. The teacher should suggest a variety of adult and children's books, and encourage parental participation.

Selection Criteria for the New Realism

In the rush to conquer the market place of "relevant" topics, a number of titles have emerged that do not adhere to the standards of good writing. A teacher has to consider how much graphic detail is necessary, how much violence is appropriate. Somewhere lies a balance between the rejection of any book that is candid, and the acceptance of any book that braves a controversial issue. When selecting and recommending contemporary realistic fiction, the teacher should take into account a number of factors:

1. Does the book make the reader aware of the resulting human suffering of people's inhumane acts? (This may be established by having another character respond sensitively and show concern for a brutal act.)

2. Does the book provide a perspective on the pain and suffering of people? Do the details of harsh realities serve a purpose? Are they there only for shock value? (Does the author present full human beings so that their behavior and motivation can be understood and viewed empathically?)

3. Does the book offer hope? Does it suggest the possibility that human courage and effort can make a difference?[28]

Sheldon Root sums it up well when he says, "We must insure that our children have access to, and are encouraged to read from, new realism that not only 'tells it like it is,' but tells it with moral integrity."[29]

STEREOTYPING IN CHILDREN'S LITERATURE

A stereotype is a fixed or conventional notion about a person or group. It may be widely accepted but not necessarily true. Stereotyping is often perpetuated through language and frequently provides an inaccurate interpretation of reality. In children's books, this is particularly serious, for many youngsters believe what they read. Many accept any statement "frozen in print" as gospel truth. Since minority groups have suffered most deeply from stereotypic portrayals, it is necessary to redress the situation and expose children to books that are unbiased and provide positive multicultural experiences.

In recent years, materials have appeared that reflect a real attempt to portray minority groups and women with fairness. Stereotypes in the new children's books are less evident, but subtle distortions still exist. Minority groups are still often under-represented or simply stereotyped into new roles. Language as well may reflect a stereotyped perspective. Female role models are still limited, and many women's contributions to society remain ignored.

Racism

Reading and discussing literature by and about other racial groups can provide a valuable appreciation of their experience. Literary works can also encourage cultural identification and promote intense personal growth.

The controversial nature of the area of race relations may have pre-

---

[28]Items 1 and 2 in this list paraphrase Charlotte S. Huck's suggestions in *Children's Literature in the Elementary School* (New York: Holt, Rinehart & Winston, 1976), pp. 395–98.

[29]Root, "The New Realism," p. 24.

cluded some teachers from including anything other than conventional materials. It is anticipated that with the guidelines in this chapter and a growing acquaintanceship with nonstereotypic books, teachers will feel more comfortable with this literature. Furthermore, the kind of group discussion that should evolve will provide a positive model for all children. In a climate where a wide range of personal reactions is acceptable, children will be able to test and clarify their own feelings.[30]

The question of what one can learn from reading ethnic literature is pivotal. The sincere reader can gain the following:

1. An awareness of how a writer from a minority group views the group's experience.
   Anpao, by Jamake Highwater, is a fine story about the conflicts of American Indians.

2. An appreciation of what it "feels like" to be a member of an ethnic minority.
   To Be a Slave, by Julius Lester, recounts in oral biography form the feelings and experiences of Afro-Americans who were brought to America.

3. An insight into the contradictions between democracy and racism through the eyes of characters.
   Without being didactic, in *Childtimes: A Three-Generation Memoir*, Eloise Greenfield and Lessie Jones Little place in bold relief the hypocrisy of racism as three black women describe their struggles to stay alive.

4. A knowledge about certain "truths" in the lives of people from ethnic minorities, by opening the gates to a flood of information.
   Lupita Mañana, by Patricia Beatty, is the story of two young Mexican immigrants who illegally enter the United States. Their dramatic adventures paint a disturbing but realistic picture of cultural conflicts and the immigration issue.

5. An appreciation of the varied insights provided for all students by ethnic literature.
   In Alice Childress's *A Hero Ain't Nothin' But a Sandwich*, we look at thirteen-year-old Benjie's drug problem through the eyes of many characters. The story has a universal quality and one with which young adolescents of different backgrounds will identify.

Sexism

"In due time, the prince carried his bride away to his own kingdom where they lived in great happiness ever after." And so ends the centuries-old fairy tale *The Sleeping Beauty*. Countless modern "realistic" stories end in much the same way. In these contemporary renditions of reality the characters are not enchanted or supernatural beings, but they are frequently personifications of the American Dream. The adult female is

---

[30]Karel Rose, *A Gift of the Spirit: Readings in Black Literature for Teachers* (New York: Holt, Rinehart & Winston, 1971).

JUDGING A BOOK FOR RACISM, SEXISM, OR AGEISM

The "ism"	What to look for
Racism A belief that color of skin or ethnic origin is the basis for judging individuals and their behavior. Racism usually involves the idea that one's own race is superior	1. A denial of the distinctive qualities of the minority group. ("All Italians like spaghetti.") 2. Language that is demeaning or insulting by implication ("All you people . . . .") 3. The absence of minority characters when it is appropriate to the text for them to be present. 4. Pictures that are not authentic. (Black faces with Caucasian features.) 5. The accuracy of the cultural representation. ("The highlight of Chinese life is the New Year celebration.") 6. The date of publication. (Ideas reflect the society of the time.)
Sexism The assignment of characteristics, roles, and occupations according to sex, with the implication that deviation from the standard is bizarre. Sexism prevents boys and girls and men and women from realizing their potential.	1. Females consistently subordinate to males. (Male doctor, female nurse.) 2. Females less visible than males. (Males are main characters and do a variety of exciting things; females are minor characters and are rarely active.) 3. Activities for males and females typed by sex. (Men go to work and women do household chores.) 4. Language that reflects a sexist bias. ("Using feminine logic, Norma figured out that she would win.") 5. The absence of one-parent families. (All families reflect the traditional scene of mother, father, and children.) 6. Both males and females have a variety of choices and goals. (Females independently meet challenges and find solutions to them.)
Ageism The categorization of people on the basis of being elderly without appropriate consideration of individual differences.	1. Provision for individual differences. (Elderly characters are exciting, diverse, and have a variety of abilities and interests.) 2. The subordination of the elderly. (Old people are not trusted with responsibility.) 3. Illustrations that present the same physical stereotype. (Old people identified by their bears, silly bonnets, and rocking chairs.) 4. Accuracy of personal relationships. (Situations that reflect meaningful interactions with younger people as well as with the elderly.)

usually a homemaker who does her mothering and housekeeping 24 hours a day, 365 days a year, for 70 years. Her efforts almost always commit her to the walls of her house. Until recently, it was most unusual to see mothers doing many of the things that they really do: driving, reading, weeding the garden, going to school, voting, engaging in political activities, or working at a non–home-related job. Mothers, for a long time, have been fairy-tale characters in realistic children's books.[31]

Males as well have been mythologized. Boys and men have been depicted with little emotional range and few home responsibilities. Boys were taught the intricacies of airplanes, while girls were given jobs related to cooking and cleaning the house. For the boy whose home life did not follow this pattern—the boy who assisted in cleaning the house as well as the family car—the characters in many realistic children's books were as fanciful as Rumpelstiltskin. The fact is that children's trade books and textbooks have been permeated by an unreality that has far-reaching influences on intellectual achievement and social functioning.

Several studies of children's books have revealed that female characters, if not invisible, are usually dependent upon others and consistently take an inactive role. Females are not called upon to make important decisions. Lenore Weitzman's study of Caldecott Medal books notes that the overwhelming number of female characters in these children's books are passive and helpless, often needing to be rescued by a man or boy.[32] Men, boys, and even male mice have adventures, intelligence, and magical powers. The female characters in these prize-winning books are less flattering caricatures. Their clothing is restrictive and cumbersome, their setting is usually indoors, and their activities and excitements are those of spectators. Other research has had similar findings.

Responsibility, resourcefulness, ingenuity, and persistence—these are some of the qualities which assist youngsters to function effectively, and prepare them to participate in a democratic form of government. Yet, the females—young and old—in children's books have for the most part, been denied these attributes. *Dick and Jane as Victims*, a study of sex stereotyping in children's readers, reported that

> in studying 2,760 stories in 134 books, clever girls appear 33 times, clever boys 131 . . . Persevering boys are a dime a dozen. Persistent girls are a rare specimen. The actual score is 169 for the boys to 47 for the girls . . . Nothing in the readers encourages girls to persevere.[33]

In the readers studied, the leadership roles and all the concomitant intellectual and emotional growth, usually belonged to males.

---

[31]Karel Rose, "Sleeping Beauty Awakes: Children's Literature and Sex Role Myths," *Research in Education*, August 1974. (ERIC ED 089 322, CS 201 132).

[32]Lenore Weitzman, Deborah Ekfler, Elizabeth Hokada, and Catherine Ross, "Sex-Role Socialization in Picture Books for Pre-School Children," *American Journal of Sociology* 77, no. 6 (May 1972) 1125–50.

[33]*Dick and Jane as Victims: Sex Stereotyping in Children's Readers* (Princeton, N.J.: Women on Words and Images, 1970).

But there is evidence that times and attitudes are changing, especially certain ideas about sex roles. Both men and women are choosing roles on the basis of personal preferences rather than societal prescription. Even a new kind of fairy tale is being written. In *The Trouble with Dragons,* written with ingenuity and wit by Oliver G. Selfridge, the princess must slay the dragon in order to win the hand of the prince in marriage.

The qualities of courage, perseverance, and creativity, traditionally attributed to boys in children's literature, are now being considered valuable traits for girls as well. A new genre of book is developing, one in which both boys and girls are encouraged to achieve, to pursue intellectual activities, and to consider a variety of options.

More recent studies of basal readers indicate that there has indeed been improvement. Females are becoming more humorous; many are active, resourceful, and brave, and some work outside the home.[34] Sensitive to the sexual bias reflected by language, many publishers of children's readers have developed guidelines for equal editorial treatment of the sexes. But while appreciative of the efforts made by authors and publishers to improve their presentations of the sexes, many studies suggest that subtle forms of sexism remain in many children's readers.

Trade books for children are far ahead of the basal readers when it comes to freedom from sex bias. Consideration is given to opening options for both sexes. A number of excellent books now picture mothers in a variety of nontraditional roles. Joe Lasker's *A Terrible Thing Happened at Our House* and Eve Merriam's *Mommies at Work* are among those that enumerate the many possibilities for women who are parents. Fathers are more likely to be shown in a nurturing role, as in *Martin's Father,* by Margaret Richler. And stories such as Eleanor Clymer's *Luke Was There* discard the notion that it is inappropriate for males to show certain emotions.

Another indication that things are changing, at least in the literary world, is the fact that books about women who succeed because of their own ingenuity and humanity are winning coveted awards. In 1973, the Newbery Medal was won by Jean George's *Julie of the Wolves,* the story of a woman's survival in Alaska. The Newbery Medal was won in 1977 by Katherine Paterson's *Bridge to Terabitha,* and by the same author once again in 1980 for *Jacob's Dream.* Both books depict young women of intelligence and insight. Many new books are biographical and relate heretofore untold stories about girls and women. *Flora Tristan,* by Joyce Anne Schneider, is the story of the grandmother of the artist Paul Gauguin whose ideas earned the respect of nineteenth-century Europe. Attention is given in three separate books to women in politics, religion, and literature in a new series, *Breakthrough,* published by Walker.

The meaningful relationships that develop between parents and their children of the opposite sex are also being explored more realistically:

---

[34]*Sexism and Racism in Popular Basal Readers: 1964-1976* (New York: Council on Interracial Books for Children and the Foundation for Change, 1976).

see Beverly Cleary's *Ramona and Her Father,* Lucille Clifton's *Don't You Remember?,* and *Sam, Bangs and Moonshine,* by Evaline Ness.

Several helpful bibliographies of nonsexist materials are now available. A highly recommended reference is *The Liberty Cap,* by Enid Davis.[35]

The teacher should be able to recognize the trappings of sexual myth making and the gross and subtle evidences of sexism in reading materials. To some extent, the vision of what books can do must be tempered by the recognition that what children read is only one step on the staircase to identity. Books neither create nor abolish stereotypes, teachers must remain alert to any limitations on freedom.

Ageism

The elderly in American society have not enjoyed the respect accorded the elderly in many other cultures. In recent years, however, partially because of increased longevity, vitality, and political power, the nation's attitude toward the elderly has been changing. It is no longer credible to imply that all old people have a dull sameness. They need not be victims of the "rocking chair syndrome," wear old baggy sweaters, or speak in high squeaky voices. Without romanticizing the later years, health professionals have begun to emphasize the individual differences in aging. And many people agree with Bernard M. Baruch that "old age is fifteen years older than I am."

Ageism in books has also begun to ebb. There are a variety of very fine books that present the elderly as vital and dynamic. Sometimes a compassionate and individual picture of an old person is presented through an alliance between the young and the elderly. This is the case in *When Grandfather Journeys into Winter,* by Craig Kee Strete. In this tender story, both the aged Indian grandfather and his young grandson discover how important they are to each other. In *How Does It Feel to be Old?* by Norma Farber, a young girl and an elderly woman honestly explore the realities of aging. A meaningful relationship between the two is the result. *Jessie and Abe,* a recent book by Rachel Isadora, depicts the relationship between a young boy and his grandfather, using the 1920s and the vaudeville era as a backdrop. In *William's Doll,* by Charlotte Zolotow, the grandmother is the character with the fresh perspective. Defending her young grandson's right to have a doll, she argues, "He needs it . . . to hug and to cradle . . . so that when he's a father like you, he'll know how to care for his baby."

The universal need to be needed is emphasized in many new children's books about the elderly. In *Maxie,* by Mildred Kantrowitz, the emphasis is on how the daily habits of an older woman help people who live in her apartment house. And in *Edgemont,* by Marjorie Weinman Sharmat, an

---

[35]Enid Davis, *The Liberty Cap: A Catalogue of Non-Sexist Materials for Children* (Chicago: Academy Press, 1977).

8-7

From SPECIAL FRIENDS by Terry Berger
and photos by David Hechtlinger.
Copyright © 1979 by Terry Berger. Photos
copyright © 1979 by David Hechtlinger.
Reprinted by permission of Julian
Messner, a Simon & Schuster division of
Gulf & Western Corporation.

old turtle, stereotypically attired in baggy sweater and argyle socks,
spends his days dreaming of being needed and having fun. When he
meets another turtle, Blanche, who is also old, wonderful things begin to
happen. The turtles and young readers discover that you are never too
old to be needed and to have fun.

A candid approach to aging is reflected in many books for adolescents,
and one of the common subjects is the old person who is not wanted in
the family setting. Among the best of the books on this topic is *A Figure
of Speech*, by Norma Fox Mazer, a dolorous novel about the physical
decline of a "senior citizen," the arrangements for moving him into an
old folks' home, and his granddaughter's devotion. In *The Lilith Summer*,
by Hadley Irwin, the relationship between seventy-seven-year-old Lilith
and Ellen, a twelve year old, is also sensitively portrayed. The bond between young and old is well expressed when Lilith says to Ellen, "We are
very vulnerable, you know. You and I. You because you're so young. I,
because I'm so old."[36] Like *A Figure of Speech*, this book confronts the

---

[36]Hadley Irwin, *The Lilith Summer* (Old Westbury, N.Y.: The Feminist Press, 1979), p. 17.

problems of aging honestly. From such books, young readers can learn how the elderly face their lives, not unflinchingly, but as real people do, with mixed emotions: denying, blaming, fantasizing, sometimes accepting.

A good bibliography of books about death and old age can be found in *Children's Literature: An Issues Approach*, by Masha Rudman.

HOW CHILDREN SHARE THEIR BOOKS

Whether children have read about rabbits or princes, old people or babies, failure or success, they will usually want to share the experience with others. And nothing sells a book quite so well as the recommendation of a peer. Teachers should permit children to share their responses to literature in a variety of creative ways.

Since conventional book reporting has come under a cloud—millions of children having been forced to churn out artificial, unemotional responses to books—let us look at some alternate ways of sharing a book:

1. Present a puppet show depicting a favorite scene.
2. Cook one of the foods suggested in a book:
   —make Stone Soup (Marcia Brown, *Stone Soup*)
   —bake the cake that the Duchess did (Virginia Kahl, *The Duchess Bakes a Cake*)
   —prepare a natural food recipe (Lila Perl, *Junk Food, Fast Food, Health Food: What America Eats and Why*)
3. Create a mural that highlights some of the fascinating facts about the ways of wolves (Scott Barry, *The Kingdom of the Wolves*).
4. Prepare a choral reading of favorite poetry by Langston Hughes.
5. Develop a genealogical table of all the characters from books in a series, such as *The Borrowers, The Moffats, All-of-a-Kind Family,* and the Ramona books.
6. Stage a readers' theater presentation. This involves a narrator and as many readers as there are characters. A good discussion of readers' theater is provided in *Creative Drama in the Classroom*, by Nellie McCaslin. Excerpts from the following books have been used successfully: *Charlie and the Chocolate Factory*, by Roald Dahl, *My Father's Dragon*, by Ruth S. Gannett, *Nobody's Family Is Going to Change*, by Louise Fitzhugh, and the Miss Pickerell Books, by Ellen MacGregor.

A CLASS PROJECT IN CHILDREN'S LITERATURE: FACT OR FANTASY?

Children and adults are tantalized by the possibility of strange worlds, hidden empires, space odysseys, and spiritual forces out of control. Such films as *Star Wars, The Exorcist, 2001: A Space Odyssey,* and *The Empire Strikes Back* have been runaway media events. Classroom teachers can capitalize on this natural interest in worlds beyond by developing a class project on present-day fantasies. Children can consult newspapers and books for "documentation." Some popular topics that can enmesh even the most resistant realist include the Loch Ness Monster, the Bermuda Triangle, UFO's, Atlantis (the hidden continent), and Big Foot (Sasquatch or The Abominable Snowman).

Through the consideration of fantasy, children feed both their intellect and imagination. The fantasy must be sufficiently earthbound to make the story believable. In the case of contemporary events, this is accomplished through real or fictional documentation. Children will expand their thinking as they compare newspaper "testimonies" with accounts in full-length books. Bulletin boards can be devoted to the photographs and drawings that are gathered. Book jackets, newspaper clippings, blurbs, and book reviews can be displayed. Children can write their own accounts based on research.

Children can further appreciate the fact-fantasy continuum by preparing charts and time lines that identify the distinctions. What evidence indicates fact? Fantasy? They will begin to focus on details, documentation, and consistency. At what point can we comfortably surrender to the "I don't know" response?

A project on fact or fantasy may lead to other literary experiences that encourage the sense of wonder. After reading a few fantasies, they may achieve a new perspective on reality. In some of the best-loved tales, ordinary people develop remarkable powers and gain control of their lives. For example, a young girl triumphs over evil forces in Frank Baum's *The Wizard of Oz.* The usual tone is one of affirmation. How refreshing this can be! Children's literature is replete with problems that youngsters face, some of which render them helpless and insignificant. Balance this with the power of possibility in fantasy. When the imagination is properly fed, a sense of vision develops.

Introduction to Children's Literature, by Joan Glazer and Gurney Williams III, has an excellent bibliography of fantasies.

BOOK SELECTION AIDS

Children's Book Awards

The Caldecott Medal   The Caldecott Medal is awarded annually by the Association for Library Services for Children of the American Library Association to the artist of the most distinguished American picture book for children published in the United States during the preceding year.

1981   *Fables*
        Lobel (Harper)
1980   *The Ox-Cart Man*
        Cooney (Viking)
1979   *The Girl Who Loved Wild Horses*
        Globe (Bradbury)
1978   *Noah's Ark*
        Spier (Doubleday)
1977   *Ashanti to Zulu: African Traditions*
        Dillon (Dial)
1976   *Why Mosquitoes Buzz in People's Ears*
        Dillon (Dial)
1975   *Arrow to the Sun*
        McDermott (Viking)
1974   *Duffy and the Devil*
        Zemach (Farrar)
1973   *The Funny Little Woman*
        Lent (Dutton)
1972   *One Fine Day*
        Hogrogian (Macmillan)
1971   *A Story—A Story*
        Haley (Atheneum)
1970   *Sylvester and the Magic Pebble*
        Steig (Windmill/Simon & Schuster)
1969   *The Fool of the World and the Flying Ship*
        Shulevitz (Farrar)
1968   *Drummer Hoff*
        Emberley (Prentice-Hall)
1967   *Sam, Bangs and Moonshine*
        Ness (Holt)
1966   *Always Room for One More*
        Hogrogian (Holt)
1965   *May I Bring a Friend?*
        Montresor (Atheneum)
1964   *Where the Wild Things Are*
        Sendak (Harper)
1963   *The Snowy Day*
        Keats (Viking)
1962   *Once a Mouse*
        Brown (Scribner)
1961   *Baboushka and the Three Kings*
        Sidjakov (Parnassus)

1960   *Nine Days to Christmas*
        Ets (Viking)
1959   *Chanticleer and the Fox*
        Cooney (Crowell)
1958   *Time of Wonder*
        McCloskey (Viking)
1957   *A Tree Is Nice*
        Simont (Harper)
1956   *Frog Went A-Courtin'*
        Rojankovsky (Harcourt)
1955   *Cinderella*
        Brown (Scribner)
1954   *Madeline's Rescue*
        Bemelmans (Viking)
1953   *The Biggest Bear*
        Ward (Houghton Mifflin)
1952   *Finders Keepers*
        Mordvinoff (Harcourt)
1951   *The Egg Tree*
        Milhous (Scribner)
1950   *Song of the Swallows*
        Politi (Scribner)
1949   *The Big Snow*
        Hader (Macmillan)
1948   *White Snow, Bright Snow*
        Duvoisin (Lothrop)
1947   *The Little Island*
        Weisgard (Doubleday)
1946   *The Rooster Crows*
        Petersham (Macmillan)
1945   *Prayer for a Child*
        Jones (Macmillan)
1944   *Many Moons*
        Slobodkin (Harcourt)
1943   *The Little House*
        Burton (Houghton Mifflin)
1942   *Make Way for Ducklings*
        McCloskey (Viking)
1941   *They Were Strong and Good*
        Lawson (Viking)
1940   *Abraham Lincoln*
        d'Aulaire (Doubleday)
1939   *Mei Li*
        Handforth (Doubleday)
1938   *Animals of the Bible*
        Lathrop (Lippincott)

The Newbery Medal   The Newbery Medal is awarded annually by the Association for Library Services for Children of the American Library

Association to the author of the most distinguished contribution to American literature for children published during the preceding year.

1981 *Jacob Have I Loved*
Paterson (Crowell)

1980 *A Gathering of Days: A New England Girl's Journal, 1830–32*
Blos (Scribner's)

1979 *The Westing Game*
Raskin (Dutton)

1978 *Bridge to Terabitha*
Paterson (Crowell)

1977 *Roll of Thunder, Hear My Cry*
Taylor (Dial)

1976 *The Grey King*
Cooper (Margaret K. McElderry/ Atheneum)

1975 *M. C. Higgins the Great*
Hamilton (Macmillan)

1974 *The Slave Dancer*
Fox (Bradbury

1973 *Julie of the Wolves*
George (Harper)

1972 *Mrs. Frisby and the Rats of NIMH*
O'Brien (Atheneum)

1971 *Summer of the Swans*
Byars (Viking)

1970 *Sounder*
Armstrong (Harper)

1969 *The High King*
Alexander (Holt)

1968 *From the Mixed-Up Files of Mrs. Basil E. Frankweiler*
Konigsburg (Atheneum)

1967 *Up a Road Slowly*
Hunt (Follett)

1966 *I, Juan de Pareja*
Treviño (Farrar)

1965 *Shadow of a Bull*
Wojciechowska (Atheneum)

1964 *It's Like This, Cat*
Neville (Harper)

1963 *A Wrinkle in Time*
L'Engle (Farrar)

1962 *The Bronze Bow*
Speare (Houghton Mifflin)

1961 *Island of the Blue Dolphins*
O'Dell (Houghton Mifflin)

1960 *Onion John*
Krumgold (Crowell)

1959 *The Witch of Blackbird Pond*
Speare (Houghton Mifflin)

1958 *Rifles for Watie*
Keith (Crowell)

1957 *Miracles on Maple Hill*
Sorensen (Harcourt)

1956 *Carry On, Mr. Bowditch*
Latham (Houghton Mifflin)

1955 *The Wheel on the School*
De Jon (Harper)

1954 *And Now Miguel*
Krumgold (Crowell)

1953 *Secret of the Andes*
Clark (Viking)

1952 *Ginger Pye*
Estes (Harcourt)

1951 *Amos Fortune, Free Man*
Yates (Dutton)

1950 *The Door in the Wall*
de Angeli (Doubleday)

1949 *King of the Wind*
Henry (Rand McNally)

1948 *The Twenty-One Balloons*
du Bois (Viking)

1947 *Miss Hickory*
Bailey (Viking)

1946 *Strawberry Girl*
Lenski (Lippincott)

1945 *Rabbit Hill*
Lawson (Viking)

1944 *Johnny Tremain*
Forbes (Houghton Mifflin)

1943 *Adam of the Road*
Gray (Viking)

1942 *The Matchlock Gun*
Edmonds (Dodd, Mead)

1941 *Call it Courage*
Sperry (Macmillan)

1940 *Daniel Boone*
Daugherty (Viking)

1939 *Thimble Summer*
Enright (Holt)

1938 *The White Stag*
Seredy (Viking)

1937 *Roller Skates*
Sawyer (Viking)

1936 *Caddie Woodlawn*
Brink (Macmillan)

1935	*Dobry* Shannon (Viking)	1928	*Gay-Neck* Mukerji (Dutton)
1934	*Invincible Louise* Meigs (Little Brown)	1927	*Smoky, The Cowhorse* James (Scribner)
1933	*Young Fu of the Upper Yangtze* Lewis (Holt)	1926	*Shen of the Sea* Chrisman (Dutton)
1932	*Waterless Mountain* Armer (McKay)	1925	*Tales from Silver Lands* Finger (Doubleday)
1931	*The Cat Who Went to Heaven* Coatsworth (Macmillan)	1924	*The Dark Frigate* Hawes (Little, Brown)
1930	*Hitty, Her First Hundred Years* Field (Macmillan)	1923	*The Voyages of Doctor Dolittle* Lofting (Lippincott)
1929	*The Trumpeter of Krakow* Kelly (Macmillan)	1922	*The Story of Mankind* Van Loon (Liveright)

The National Council of Teachers of English Award for Excellence in Poetry for Children   Each year the National Council of Teachers of English honors a living American poet for his or her entire body of work. Recipients of the award include David McCord, Aileen Fisher, Myra Cohn Livingston, and Lillian Moore.

Annotated Bibliographies

Children's Choices. The reading preferences of several thousand children throughout the country are reflected in this bibliography published annually by The International Reading Association and the Children's Book Council. (Children's Book Council, 67 Irving Place, New York, New York 10003.)

Notable Children's Trade Books in the Field of Social Studies. This is an annual compilation by a committee of educators working with the National Council for the Social Studies-Children's Book Council Joint Committee. (Same address as above.)

Outstanding Science Trade Books for Children. This bibliography is annually compiled by a committee of educators and librarians with the National Science Teachers Association-Children's Book Council Joint Committee.

TEACHER COMPETENCES

This chapter has suggested that the utilization of children's literature requires specific knowledge, skills, and attitudes on the part of the teacher. Fortunately, many of these competences may be acquired as the teacher shares the richness of children's books with students. The teacher who wishes to discover the joys of literature must make an emotional commitment as well as an intellectual one.

Teaching Literature

Knowledge	Skills	Attitude
The teacher will have knowledge of	*The teacher will be able to*	*The teacher will be ready to*
1. The characteristics and abilities of children and their interests.	1. Help children to identify and utilize the essential aspects of story: plot, characterization, mood, setting, point of view, and language.	1. Identify and utilize books that have the potential for empathic views of a variety of emotional situations: death, aging, ethnic, racial and sexual inequalities, alternate life styles.
2. The many genres of children's books; fairy tales, folktales, poetry, biography, realistic fiction, historical fiction, and informational books.	2. Assist children in identifying stereotypes in their literature (racism, sexism, ageism).	2. Encourage the imaginative functioning of children through literary experiences.
3. Interpretations of children's literature in other media.	3. Prepare children to use criteria in judging books.	3. Prepare time for reading as well as reading instruction.
4. Criteria for evaluating "what is a good book."	4. Share books through affective storytelling or reading.	4. Focus sensitively on controversial issues.
5. Criteria for evaluating and utilizing artwork in children's books.	5. Use literature to develop story reading abilities, for example, seeing sequence of events, making inferences, recognizing the fact-fantasy continuum.	5. Use literature to encourage positive self-concepts.
6. The many local resources that encourage children's literature: libraries, museums, children's theater groups.	6. Utilize many approaches for turning children on to books.	6. Use literature to encourage positive self-concepts

Knowledge	Skills	Attitude
The teacher will have knowledge of	*The teacher will be able to*	*The teacher will be ready to*
7. The "classics" of children's literature.	7. Suggest a variety of strategies for the sharing of books.	7. Critically evaluate the literature by or about ethnic minorities, for authenticity and fairness.
8. A variety of books and media interpretations of books that provide a non-stereotypic role model and perspective.	8. Develop a classroom environment that encourages positive experiences with books.	
9. The way an author uses language to suggest mood, to foreshadow, to create tension, and to express character.	9. Determine whether students are developing an interest in literature.	

Afterview   To paraphrase epicure Brillat Savarin—the discovery of a new book may do more for your happiness than the discovery of a new star. In this chapter, the focus has been on personalizing the literary experience for both teacher and child. The process of bringing children and books together is a complicated one, for there are many forces that might break the connection: the generation gap (adults writing for children), the impact of television, the pace of modern life, and highly individual tastes. Nevertheless, knowledgeable, enthusiastic teachers are in a position to show children how to use imaginative literature to contemplate the universal dilemmas that concern us all.

Literature, to use Esther Rauchenbush's term, is an individual education. It is very much a private affair. No formula exists to tell us how to experience another's reality. It is not possible to command, legislate, or even teach literary response. Readers vary in their reactions, and the same reader will have different responses at different times. Teachers can best appreciate the highly individual nature of the literary encounter by experiencing many books. It is this personal discovery of the power of literature that prepares the teacher to guide children in their own quest toward maturity.

WHEN YOU WANT TO KNOW MORE

1. Read one of the following books on the special problems of the handicapped child:

   Betsy Byars, *Summer of the Swans*. Viking, 1970. (Retardation.)
   Eloise Greenfield, *Darlene*. Methuen, 1980. (Physical disability.)
   Edith Hunter, *Sue Ellen*. Houghton Mifflin, 1969. (Learning disabilities.)
   Ken Platt, *The Boy Who Could Make Himself Disappear*. Dell, 1971. (Emotional retardation.)
   Helen Young, *What Difference Does It Make, Danny?* Andre Deutsch, 1980. (Epilepsy.)

   What insights did you gain? How would you use this book with both normal and disabled children?

2. Consult one of the many guides for detecting racism in children's books—those of the Council for Interracial Books, for example—then develop personal criteria for judging stereotyping in children's books using your own racial, religious, or ethnic group as the focus.

3. Read some modern fairy tales—for example, the works of Phyllis McGinley, James Thurber, Ionesco, Dr. Seuss. Compare them to traditional fairy tales. Consider subject, theme, plot, and character development.

4. Read a selection of poetry that children have written. What topics seem to be of greatest interest to young poets?

5. Keep an annotated children's book file organized according to genres of literature. Be sure that there is a representation of books from your geographical area.

6. Analyze any two Caldecott Medal books not mentioned in the chapter with respect to the following: roles of males and females, representation of males and females in illustrations, occupations of males and females. What might be the effects of these presentations on a child's self-image and aspirations?

7. Find several books that are easy reading but contain mature content that would interest slow readers in your class. A good source is *High Interest: Easy Reading for Junior and Senior High School Students,* edited by Marian E. White.

8. Compare the treatment of death in several books for children. Which books would you recommend for classroom use? Why?

IN THE CLASSROOM

1. Display a number of wordless picture books. Some are listed below and noted in the chapter. Have a small group of children share them. Then ask

individual children to write or tell their own story about the content of one of them. See if the others in the group can guess which book was used.

John S. Goodall, *Paddy's New Hat*. Atheneum, 1980.
Diane De Groat, *Alligator's Toothache*. Crown, 1977.
Pat Hutchins, *Rosie's Walk*. Macmillan, 1971.
Graham Oakley, *Magical Changes*. Atheneum, 1980.

2. Read many versions of a well-known folktale. Share these interpretations with a group of children. What is their reaction to the variations? What insights can you discover about children's preferences? Use the experience to discuss why different versions developed.

3. Conduct your own "Children's Choices" project. Ask children to rate books that they have read on a scale from five (the high) to one. Have class discussions and help students focus on the reasons for their ratings.

4. Using a trade book, plan a lesson that instructs children on how to: (a) follow a sequence of events, (b) make inferences, and (c) heighten their awareness of details.

5. Collect several illustrated versions of the same story. Ask children to discuss how different artists present the story. What values might this activity have for children?

6. Collect and share with children a cycle of poems about one particular subject—for example, the city, sadness, secrets, the circus.

SUGGESTED READINGS

Children's Books: Awards and Prizes. New York: The Children's Book Council, 1976.

Chukovsky, Kornei. *From Two to Five*. Translated and edited by Miriam Morton. Berkeley: University of California Press, 1971.

Coody, Betty. *Using Literature with Young Children*. Dubuque, Iowa: William C. Brown, 1973.

Cullinan, Beatrice E., and Carmichael, Carolyn, eds. *Literature and Young Children*. Urbana, Ill.: National Council of Teachers of English, 1977.

Egoff, Sheila, et al., eds. *Only Connect: Readings on Children's Literature*. 2d ed. New York: Oxford University Press, 1980.

Huck, Charlotte S. *Children's Literature in the Elementary School*. 3d ed. New York: Holt, Rinehart & Winston, 1976.

Jackson, Miles M., Jr., ed. *A Bibliography of Negro History and Culture for Young Readers*. Pittsburgh, Penn.: University of Pittsburgh Press, 1968.

Jacobs, Leland B., ed. *Using Literature with Young Children*. New York: Teachers College Press, 1965.

Laubach, David C. *Introduction to Folklore*. Rochelle Park, N.J.: Hayden Book Company, 1980.

Rudman, Masha Kabakow. *Children's Literature: An Issues Approach*. Lexington, Mass.: D. C. Heath, 1976.

Megna, James. "Non-White Ethnic Literature." *English Journal* 70, no. 1 (January 1981): 46–48.

Sebesta, Sam Leaton, and Iverson, William J. *Literature for Thursday's Child*. Chicago: Science Research Associates, 1975.

Sexism in Children's Books: Facts, Figures and Guidelines. London: Writers and Readers Publishing Cooperative, 1976.

Sloan, Glenna Davis. *The Child as Critic: Teaching Literature in the Elementary School,* New York: Teachers College Press, 1975.

Stewig, John Warren. *Children and Literature*. Chicago: Rand McNally College Publishing Company, 1980.

Sutherland, Zena, and Arbuthnot, May Hill. *Children and Books*. 5th ed. Glenview, Ill.: Scott Foresman, 1977.

Other Materials

Ellin Green and Madalynne Schoenfeld. *A Multimedia Approach to Children's Literature: A Selective List of Films, Filmstrips and Recordings Based on Children's Books*. Chicago: American Library Association, 1972.

The organizations listed below distribute many filmstrips, films, cassettes and records in the field of children's literature:

Instructional Media
Coronet
Encyclopedia Britannica
McGraw-Hill Publishers
Miller-Brody Productions
National Council of Teachers of English
Troll Associates
Weston Woods Studios

PART III

EXPRESSING
LANGUAGE

CHAPTER 9

Oral Language

Preview This chapter will focus on seven considerations in the teaching of speaking: classroom climate, spontaneous language, natural style of talking, oral language appreciation, dialect, Standard American English, and purposive oral communication. In each area, classroom activities will be suggested that increase student/teacher awareness of the scope, variety, and potential of oral language experiences. Conversations, chalk talks, brainstorming, private conferences, creative drama, and group discussions will be among the activities analyzed. The teacher will be provided with guidelines for reviewing his or her role as a facilitator of oral language and advised on how to prepare students to do their own self-evaluations. It will be assumed throughout the chapter that oral language is an expression of self and a vehicle for expressing individuality. The recognition that oral language is an expression of the speaker's uniqueness will also guide the discussion of dialect and Standard American English. The importance of the teacher's attitude toward a foreign speaker or a youngster whose native language is not the standard dialect will be examined. Activities aimed at providing a rich classroom language environment for dialect users and non-native speakers without minimizing the linguistic contributions of their backgrounds will be outlined. The emphasis is on the development of a variety of speech presentations for situations such as interviews, panel discussions, oral reports, puppetry, and choral speaking. The chapter will close with a list of competencies for the classroom teacher of oral language.

O N APRIL 27, 1979 , a pump failed at a nuclear power plant in Pennsylvania. After days of suspense, people within a twenty-mile radius of Three Mile Island were considered to be in danger; and most of the women and children were evacuated. Throughout the crisis, countless Americans turned on their radios and television sets to get "the word" about what was being done to prevent nuclear leakage. For in any emergency situation the public depends upon the media to find out what is happening.

Have you ever stopped to consider how decisions are made in broadcast journalism about what should be told, when and how it should be told, and by whom? Though critical situations serve to highlight the importance of listening and speaking in our daily lives, our concern for what and how we communicate should not be limited to crises. Critical listening and clear verbal expression are relevant social skills at all times.

In an increasingly oral society, both teachers and students have to recognize the relationship between the spoken word, whether live or electronic, and the audience for whom it is intended. The students in your classes are tomorrow's voters, lobbyists, workers, labor leaders, and corporation presidents. They all hope to find a dignified and comfortable place in society. Whether this goal is realized may depend upon their ability to articulate their needs in a pluralistic culture. As teachers, we have a responsibility to help students develop their potential for self-expression. When people cannot tell their own story, someone tells it for them. They then run the risk of being misinterpreted or not heard at all.

CRITERIA FOR EXCELLENCE IN TEACHING SPEAKING

Teacher education programs should be planned around criteria of excellence and should foster teaching behaviors that bridge the gap between educational research and classroom learning. Consequently, the framework of this chapter will reflect the categories and criteria that evolved from the research of the National Conference on Research in English.[1] A variety of classroom experiences designed to promote oral language growth will be suggested for each category.

[1]H. Alan Robinson and Alvina Treut Burrows, *Teacher Effectiveness in Elementary Language Arts: Progress Report* (Urbana, Ill.: ERIC Clearinghouse on Reading and Communication Skills and National Council of Teachers of English, 1974). A debt of gratitude is expressed to the authors of this report. Their findings contributed in a very real way to the organization of this chapter.

There is, however, something of a Catch-22 here. Teaching is a practical activity, and classrooms are action-oriented laboratories. It would be tempting to take whatever experience and research has told us and place criteria and teaching behaviors on a cause-and-effect grid that would guarantee success. But the teaching/learning process is too complex for such a neat arrangement.

Teaching is not an exact science—many call it an art—criteria cannot always be clearly identified. Some important teaching behaviors cannot be neatly categorized or even described. How do we define, for example, the effective teacher? Everyone thinks they know what an effective teacher is, but there is a startling lack of agreement on how to define operationally the behaviors of an effective teacher. This does not mean, however, that we should abandon the effort. Teaching criteria are helpful, but individual practitioners should always reevaluate and alter them based on personal experience in the classroom. Whatever the limitations or benefits of criteria, it is not assumed that any one teacher will demonstrate them all at a high level of artistry and power. As the National Conference study noted, such an individual would be a paragon beyond description.[2]

Teaching is not a discrete set of behaviors; therefore, the activities suggested in each category are neither exhaustive nor mutually exclusive. Teaching behaviors that develop language power may occur during a science lesson or during recess. In like manner, experiences with puppets may be appropriate to several categories—establishing a classroom climate of respect, developing appreciation of oral language, facilitating the acquisition of Standard American English, and so on. Though a particular activity may be mentioned in only one context, you are encouraged to integrate the information on the basis of your own training and experience and flexibly make a professional judgment about the appropriate placement of a learning experience. The teaching of language goes on all day. The assumption that language arts lessons are the only nurturers of linguistic growth is false. Such lessons are only one organizing framework for this fundamental human activity.

CLASSROOM CLIMATE

Norma Greene is a gifted third-grade teacher who values children's self-expression. She recognizes that language cannot flourish in a setting that is restrictive, judgmental, or personally threatening. Recently, this teacher has been reading some of the contemporary research on speaking and has been wondering about its application to the activities in her classroom. One of the most obvious current trends has been the growing acceptance of the classroom as a language laboratory. The classroom is

[2]Robinson and Burrows, *Teacher Effectiveness*, p. 89.

not the place to hang a "no talking" sign, real or implied. There is much evidence that the encouragement of classroom talk is food for children's conceptual development as well as for their language and emotional growth. Quantity can lead to quality.

It is now understood that teaching children to speak effectively is as important as teaching them the skills of reading and writing. The conceptual processes involved in the acquisition of all these skills are related. Interactive classrooms with a wealth of speaking opportunities nourish every aspect of language growth.

Recent studies have focused on children in the process of learning language. Rather than *prescribe*, many researchers now *describe* what goes on as youngsters grow linguistically. Since for centuries parents and caretakers of children have been reasonably successful at helping them acquire the initial stages of language, the nature of this interaction is being carefully monitored for its implications for the classroom teacher. Carole Edelsky reports that parental success with very young children may result because adults outside the classroom are rarely anxious about language acquisition.[3] The attitude of these adults shows the implicit understanding that some children will learn slower than others. There is the confidence, however, that the learning will eventually occur. The message transmitted to the child is, "I know that you can do it. I'm not worried." The "self-fulfilling prophecy" in this situation suggests success and encouragement. Most children respond as expected; they learn to speak a language, although not always with great proficiency. What is made evident by this study and similar ones (see Chapter 2) is that the cognitive and emotional growth of children are primarily natural happenings.

The Role of the Teacher

Relating these findings to the classroom situation, Ms. Greene can readily see the importance of a supportive and interactive climate for developing speaking skills. Aware of the research, she has begun to develop an increasing respect for her own experiences both as teacher and learner. She sinks taps into her background, juxtaposes her experiences against the research findings, and begins to appreciate in a personal way the Rogerian theory that "The only learning which significantly influences behavior is self-discovered, self-appropriated learning."[4] This suggests that a primary teaching role is one of facilitator in a climate that encourages learning that is personally valuable. The work of Sara W. Lundsteen supports this perspective. In analyzing the teacher's role in discussion groups, Lundsteen suggests that teachers should participate

[3]Carole Edelsky, "'Teaching' Oral Language," *Language Arts* 55 (March 1978), p. 293.
[4]Carl R. Rogers, *Freedom to Learn* (Columbus, Ohio: Merrill, 1969), p. 153.

mainly as guiders of process—not as content givers.[5] Eventually, the most skillful teachers, through careful organization, eliminate the need for teacher guidance at all.

The problem this raises is, "Does a supportive climate require that the teacher assume a nondirective role?" James Moffet poses the crucial question "How much should the teacher lead; how much should be left alone?"[6] As in most important questions, issues are raised for which there are no simple answers. The degree to which you structure classroom language activities, either directly (by being there) or indirectly (through materials and organization) cannot be prescribed. Some teaching behaviors are by necessity determined "on the spot," largely on intuition and experience. Other teaching behaviors are prestructured by the teacher based on his or her ultimate objectives. Teachers should play many roles as they react to children's language. These roles range from nondirective to controlling, but there should always be respect for each individual's speech and the opportunity for pupil talk to exceed teacher talk. The goal of verbally responsive, articulate students is not easy to accomplish but exceedingly important. "For verbal language permits [the child] to try out ideas and play with possibilities unlimited by empirical reality . . . to test belief against the world."[7]

What are some means toward this end? Teachers have found that encouraging a wide variety of speaking activities among the pupils themselves is productive. Giving over large blocks of time to this type of interaction demonstrates the teacher's respect for peer interactions as contributors to learning. The children, in turn, seem to show more respect for each other's responses. Too often in the classroom the teacher has been seen as the only source of knowledge, perhaps leading many students to an unquestioning acceptance of authority in adulthood—an attitude that a democratic society can ill afford in its citizenry.

All teachers must ultimately look as critically as possible at their own teaching styles. An examination of the climate in their classrooms as well as their own attitudes and teaching behaviors in the area of speaking is a good place to begin.

It is the teacher's reaction to individual student-speakers, the amount of time given over to students' talk, and the kinds of speaking activities provided that control not only the quantity of students' language but the quality. Some of the speaking activities that encourage linguistic initiative while taking into account developmental capacity will be discussed in the following sections.

[5]Sara W. Lundsteen, *Children Learn to Communicate* (Englewood Cliffs, N.J.: Prentice-Hall, 1976), p. 154.

[6]James Moffett and Betty Jane Wagner, *Student-Centered Language Arts and Reading, K-13: A Handbook for Teachers*, 2d ed. (Boston: Houghton Mifflin, 1976), p. 71.

[7]Marvin L. Klein, *Talk in the Language Arts Classroom* (Urbana, Ill.: ERIC Clearinghouse on Reading and Communication Skills and National Council of Teachers of English, 1977), p. 5

EXAMINE YOUR TEACHING STYLE

How pervasive is my role in the classroom? Do I come on too "heavy"?

Am I comfortable taking a "back seat" in certain aspects of classroom life?

Do I usually tilt the scales in favor of too much participation on my part?

Do I feel that I am not doing my job if I am not talking?

Do I assume responsibility for assisting the reluctant speaker? Serving as mediator? Dealing with the child who monopolizes discussion?

Am I prepared to assist children to clarify their direction, organize their thinking, and set realistic limits?

Conversations

Conversation, the informal verbal exchange of ideas between two (or more) people, usually has no formal structure imposed upon it. However, recognizing that conversations require both listening and responding, the teacher facilitates conversational interactions in the following ways:

1. Small groups are encouraged to speak in settings in which children feel physically and emotionally close to one another.
2. Topics are not predetermined. Children converse about whatever they wish and the teacher is not usually included.
3. Spontaneous talk is not discouraged. Since doing and talking go together, some conversations emerge quite naturally. For example, two children who are painting in close proximity will often discuss their work.

Classroom conversations can cover a wide range of topics. Students can talk about television programs, something noticed on the way to school, a new toy, or an event at home. Even the telling of jokes and riddles can be used as a form of classroom conversation. And research findings suggest that classroom talk is never valueless. The talk of children in the classroom serves a variety of useful functions in their development.[8]

Chalk Talks

For some reason, the use of chalk talks as a means of improving oral expression is not widely practiced. Yet the chalk talk is a simple procedure. Here is an example—using colored chalks, a teacher drew the following design on the chalkboard:

[8]M. A. K. Halliday, "The Functional Basis of Language," in *Class, Codes and Control: Applied Studies Towards a Sociology of Language*, vol. 2, ed. Basil Bernstein (Boston: Routledge and Kegan Paul, 1973).

"What do you think I'm drawing?" she asked the class. There were a variety of responses: an electric current, a snake, a telephone cord. "Tell me a story about one of them" she said, "and then I'll complete the picture." Ralph told the tale of a snake sneaking up on an elephant in tall grasses. The picture looked like this:

Then Yvonne spoke about an electric current that had lost its way and wandered into the water, and she drew her picture on the chalkboard. Mike saw a telephone cord attached to telephones around the world, and he also illustrated his story.

In interpreting the wiggly line, students were given the chance to be imaginative and use language creatively. Throughout, they were inspiring each other to think up new ideas. Very soon the children were guiding their own chalk talks.

Group Discussions

Group discussion, like conversation, serves many purposes; however, it involves talking about something in a more deliberative fashion than usually occurs in conversation. In discussion, a format, albeit a flexible one, is usually implied in order to permit equal participation. There is often a specific goal in mind: to decide on a class project, to settle a controversy, and so on.

Group discussion provides varied opportunities to use language and to learn to respect the sharing process and the values of a "group think." For these reasons, it is useful in improving classroom climate. The relationship between verbal interaction and other curriculum areas is also apparent during group discussion. Precise language can clarify basic concepts in any subject.

Group discussion teaches language by indirection. It may not always be apparent to the student that he or she is learning linguistic skills. The most effective classroom group discussions, particularly in the younger grades, are goal oriented. They are directed toward getting something done: how to start a shell collection, where to store the audio-visual equipment, what to do for recreation on the weekends. Verbal interaction becomes the means to the end.

A group of children in a Great Neck class were confronted with the problem of how to set up and exhibit their inventions. There were some delightful and creative products: a unique pinball machine, a building buster, an automatic flag raiser, a peanut opener. An attractive display was important. Many things had to be discussed. How large a space would be available? Would everyone's invention be displayed? What materials would be needed? What explanations would have to be written? Would other classes be invited? Would there be an admission charge for parents? Who would assume specific responsibilities? The emphasis was not on discussion skills, but the teacher felt confident that they were being developed. Though not all children in the group participated equally or at the same level, there were a variety of interactions, enabling most children to function comfortably.

The Teachers Role During Group Discussion   Although most children should be allowed to learn about the discussion process through voluntary involvement, the teacher has a responsibility to encourage the participation of specific children. The reluctant speaker may respond to a personalized invitation: "Sondra, I know that you have had some experience with pets. What do you think about the class adopting a guinea pig?"; "Richard, tell us how you think we might celebrate the birthday of Martin Luther King"; or, "David, I heard that you built some shelves at home. Do you have any suggestions where we might get the wood for our bookcases?"

The teacher may also serve as mediator between two children: "I can see your point of view, Nicole, but I also understand why Linda is concerned about inviting senior citizens to class. How do you girls think we might resolve the situation?" By directing attention to a solution, the teacher models behavior that focuses on the problem rather than the personalities.

Every teacher will eventually have to deal with the child who monopolizes discussions. The teacher must first determine why the child exhibits this behavior. The most effective way is to discuss the matter with the child. Does the child think that his or her good ideas will be forgotten if he or she has to delay a response? Does the child always need to prove that he or she knows the right answer? Has the child ever been taught how to respect and respond to the ideas of peers? Is it possible that the child is unaware of other ways of responding? An aggressive monopolizer might be given the role of recorder.[9] In stepping back from the discussion to take notes or record, the monopolizing child may see his or her disturbing behavior from a different perspective. Altering the behavior of the over-talkative child is a delicate matter for the teacher. Sometimes, the student's peers will be more successful. The important thing is that the child be made to recognize the problems created by such egocentric behavior.

The behaviorial change is made easier by a classroom climate that allows children to admit mistakes and inadequacies. Unfortunately, "to err is human" is a philosophy not always practiced in classrooms.

The teacher who views group discussion as a valuable growth process will communicate to children that its success is dependent upon the combined energies of teacher and students. The teacher's expertise may be used to give direction to the discussion from time to time. For example, it may be helpful for the teacher to clarify a word, a concept, or a basic misunderstanding: "I'm not sure that we're all talking about the same thing. When you speak about 'man's contribution,' are you referring to both men and women? What kinds of contributions were you thinking of?" The teacher can also help to organize and set the limits of the discussion: "Let's identify our priorities. Setting up a newspaper is a big job. What are some of the most important things to decide at this point?"

In the course of developing group discussions with a class, perceptive teachers may find that there is a decrease in the students' interest at certain points. When students are asked why this is so, their answers often provide valuable insights into attitudinal and developmental factors. Some children have said that

- —they feel that they cannot and should not learn from their peers. (Is this because their experiences have been in teacher-dominated classrooms where the teacher is the source of all "important" knowledge?)
- —they are not interested in the topics brought up for discussion. (Has there been inadequate lead-in and motivation? Were discussion topics imposed by the teacher?)
- —they are unable to contribute to the discussion. (Are they not capable of serious discussion on abstract levels? Some may need more opportunities to converse about concrete situations in their own experience.)
- —they are not comfortable when the teacher is not in charge. (Are they overly dependent on adult authority because they have had few opportunities to assume reponsibility and to make mistakes?)

Pupils carefully watch a teacher's behavior, sometimes more than they listen to what he or she says. In order for the group discussion process to grow and serve useful purposes for the individual and the class, the

[9]Lundsteen, *Children Learn to Communicate*, p. 149.

teacher, as a model, must demonstrate faith in the process. This is sometimes accomplished by the teacher's seeming retreat from center stage.

Discussion Topics   A large variety of problems, events, and ideas may serve as catalysts for classroom discussions. In the early grades, task-oriented discussions on relevant topics are most successful, their direction and boundaries being clearly defined. The following are examples of topics that deal with the concerns of young children:

Setting up a class store
Planning a program for parents
Organizing a trip to Golden Gate Park
Celebrating holidays
Sharing class responsibilities
Television shows
Organizing a class breakfast
Sports
How to handle school yard problems
Who should bring up children? Fathers? Mothers? Both?

As children mature and become more skilled in discussion, they are ready to consider a broader range of problems, such as

My feelings about older people
The main problem with school
A "panicky" moment
Kids who scare me
Mixed feelings about my brother
Predictions for the 1980s
Future travel
The assassinations of the 1960s
Inflation

A whole range of topics fall into the category of "Let's pretend":

What I would tell the President of the United States about energy.
If I were the teacher
A week in the desert
If I were the mayor
Climbing the Himalayas
When I met the Abominable Snowman
If I were invisible
In my next life
The year 2000

SOME QUESTIONS TO ASK ABOUT A DISCUSSION

1. Should the topic be discussed? Is it big enough? Worthy of discussion?
2. Is the purpose of the discussion clear? Is it understood what can be accomplished?
3. Do the participants have enough information, experience and/or interest in the topic?
4. How is respect shown for another's contributions?
5. Is the physical setting conducive to the discussion? Are distractions minimized?
6. Are the participants staying with the topic?
7. Are there too many people in the discussion group?
8. Is listening as well as speaking a part of the discussion?
9. Are provisions made so that the discussion can proceed in an orderly way (one person speaking at a time, checks on time, and so on)?

Remember, the best classroom discussions are not teacher-controlled question and answer sessions. Try to create schedules that can absorb worthwhile spontaneous discussion.

Brainstorming

Brainstorming, the nonevaluative pooling of ideas best known as a means of solving problems, can be used as a catalyst to general classroom discussion. Children can easily become so accustomed to the technique that they practice it quite independently. Brainstorming initially places the emphasis on quantity rather than quality. Since judgment of suggestions is deferred, many children feel more comfortable about participating. Brainstorming may seem to be a rather superficial activity, but as one idea generates another, each student has the opportunity to become a link in an intellectual chain reaction.

One educator has developed four basic rules for brainstorming: (1) criticism is ruled out; (2) free wheeling is welcome; (3) quantity is wanted; and (4) combination and improvement are sought.[10] At the beginning of a brainstorming session, a student should be appointed to write down *all* suggestions. At this point, the goal is the largest number of ideas possible; no idea should be rejected. For example, in a discussion of how to increase the physical comfort of the classroom, the ideas offered went

[10]A. F. Osborn, *Applied Imagination*, 3d. ed. (New York: Scribners, 1963), p. 156.

from the practical to the impractical, the sublime to the ridiculous: make curtains for the windows, ask people for old furniture, paint the room, throw out the desks and chairs, change the lighting, buy cushions for the floor, have a raffle to raise money for a rug, and so on. Since the teacher wanted the many ideas from the first brainstorming session to percolate in the children's minds for a while, a second session was not held until the following day. At the start of this session, the ideas from the day before were read and before any judgments were made, additional suggestions were invited. Questions were then raised about each idea: Can we do it? How much will it cost? Are we violating any rules about school property? Will it take too long? Does it serve our purpose? How will it look? The chalkboard was used by several recorders to discard or retain ideas. It was a noisy time. The decisions that the class finally made were based upon a wealth of ideas. After many experiences with this technique, children can appreciate that all ideas have value, if only because they suggest others. Here are some brainstorming topics that elementary-school students have discussed:

How to entertain the people at the senior citizen's home

Uses for things that people throw away

Ideas for a class play

Ways to save money

Alternatives to television

Problems between parents and children

How each person can contribute to the conservation of energy

How to prevent stereotyping

How we can make a robot

Materials for making puppets

The forgotten contributions of women

What we can put in our time capsule

Private Conferences

The private conference between the teacher and the student is one means by which the teacher can show pupils that what each has to say is valued. Furthermore, it enables those children who are not comfortable expressing themselves in a group to share their thoughts and ideas in a completely one-to-one situation. The following ground rules may encourage and enrich the private conference:

1. Either a student or the teacher can initiate a private conference.
2. The major objective of the conference is to assist the student.
3. Authenticity and honesty are expected of the student and the teacher.
4. Evaluative devices, such as written or oral tests, are never given during a conference.

5. Students are encouraged to prepare for the conference by rethinking and writing down what they wish to discuss.

6. It is understood that conferences are not limited to school subjects or academic matters.

7. Both teachers and pupils should try to provide evidence to support their positions.

Talking is a creative response to outside stimuli. Talk should not be "commanded." The best way to unleash words is to encourage children to tell about their experiences and reactions to life. By the time children come to school, they have done a lot of living. They have much to say. In the supportive, nonthreatening classroom, they will say it.

CHILDREN'S SPONTANEOUS LANGUAGE

Children are innovative in their speech. The verbal constructions they create often contain surprising and delightful metaphors. Piaget reported that his daughter at four years of age described the sand hills etched by the ocean on a beach as "like a little girl's hair being combed." Not only are existing words used in unique ways, but children propelled by the tremendous desire to express often create their own words. Teachers do not have to move outside their classrooms to find evidence of children's imaginative, spontaneous speech. Once having recognized and appreciated some of these marvelous creations, however, the teacher has a responsibility to help students funnel such responses into new verbal challenges. This means helping students acquire more words and creating situations in which spontaneous and new language is seen to be a valuable asset.

DRAMATIC ACTIVITIES

Dramatic activities provide children with many opportunities to use language inventively. Yet for a long time educators tended to ignore drama. Creative drama, particularly, was not considered worthy of academic consideration and was generally discouraged in most schools. At best, dramatics were relegated to an extracurricular activity or used as a vehicle for assisting children with behavioral problems. It was not until the 1950s, when an innovative teacher Winifred Ward persuaded the Illinois school system to have creative drama activities, that their value began to be recognized. Fortunately, Ward was followed by Geraldine Siks who took up the case for creative drama in the excellent book *Children's Theater and Creative Dramatics*. Siks maintained that creative drama is important in education because every child has a basic need for self-expression, for ways to get out anger, hatred, joy, loneliness. Teachers have since come to accept such expression as a necessary part of human development and creative drama as one avenue though which it can be accomplished by students.

There has been some confusion regarding terminology in this field. For present purposes, let us use the following definitions:

Pantomime is the body's silent translation of the verbal reality. It is the foundation of drama. Though wordless, pantomime can be pregnant with meaning.

Dramatic Play refers to the unplanned, spontaneous dramatic activity, usually of very young children. There may be some preplanning in the assignment of roles or the use of the props, but this is always determined by the children themselves. When youngsters play house, go to the moon, act as the "The Incredible Hulk," or breathe life into their stuffed animals, they are engaging in dramatic play.

Creative Drama is more structured than dramatic play for it involves some preplanning and evaluation. It is sometimes referred to as improvised drama or playmaking. Any experience may serve as the catalyst for creative dramatics: a favorite story, a problem, a television program, an ordinary or unusual event. Though written scripts are not used, the individual actors have definite roles to play. The children may decide to use costumes, props, or scenery, but these are limited to what can be spontaneously found at the last moment: "Let's use the eraser for Cinderella's slipper"; "Ellen can wind the scarf around her head and she'll look like a genie"; "Linda's slicker can be the yellow brick road."

Creative-drama activities do not require an audience; it is sufficient for the actors to perform for each other. The emphasis is on the process. Creative self-expression is the objective.

Creative-drama situations are evaluated and often repeated with variations and a changing cast. The teacher, while providing a minimum of direction, should encourage the children to preplan and evaluate what they have done. The teacher's role is an elusive one. Kornei Chukovsky, the celebrated Russian author of books, suggests that children's speech is best nurtured "by teachers who will act indirectly, with restraint, not too persistently—almost imperceptibly."[11]

Theatre is the formal presentation of a play most often involving a written script and memorized lines. Several rehearsals usually characterize theatre and the audience is an important consideration in planning the presentation.

CREATIVE DRAMA IN THE CLASSROOM

Creative drama has a particularly high potential for encouraging spontaneous language; it provides a reason for dialogue and a setting in which children can speak and think effectively. As you use creative-drama activities in the classroom, you will begin to sense the delicate

[11]Kornei Chukovsky, *From Two to Five* (Berkeley, University of California Press, 1968), p. 18.

balance that exists between the encouragement of spontaneous language and new learnings. Timing, tone, and readiness must all be considered. If you are too critical, you risk stilted, unimaginative expression. On the other hand, it is important that the "teachable moment" not be lost and an opportunity for growth not be missed. You will sense what to do as your experience increases. Trust your intuitive sense as much as your intellectual abilities. Take your clues from the children, allowing them to point the way and showing what they are able to do and what they need to learn to do. With creative drama, it is more desirable to err on the side of doing too little rather than too much. Remember that in giving creative drama a place in your students' busy day, you are building language power as well as making an important statement about your values.

The typical elementary school classroom is an ideal culture for propogating creative-drama activities. No materials are necessary, minimal space is required, and the number of students needed is flexible. All that is required is an emotionally supportive environment with a teacher and students who see the relevance of the activity. Probably most significant is the fact that drama is one of those rare classroom activities in which the standards of conventional academic achievement are not emphasized. A new group of youngsters have a chance to become the best in class. Failure is easily avoided in creative drama for the main criterion is a "feelingful" response.

The Warm-up

Initially, creative-drama activities may meet with some resistance, particularly among less venturesome children. Overcome with shyness, many youngsters are not prepared to perform alone in front of their peers. Therefore, before launching into creative-drama activities, it is important to have what is traditionally referred to as the warm-up. During this period, the class should be given opportunities to move the body in different ways and to recognize the infinite number of movements that are possible. Give the youngsters all the time they need at this stage. A successful warm-up allows children to slip effortlessly into creative drama without the pressure of being observed by others. Here are some sample warm-ups:

1. Use one of the seasons as the theme for dramatic responses. In autumn, the children can be the leaves falling from the trees; in winter, snowflakes; in spring, grass growing; in summer, a gentle breeze.

2. Try some body movement activities. Children can lie down on the floor and close up like a flower at night, then open up and turn their faces to the sun. Other movements might be falling off a bicycle, jumping rope, or stretching like a cat.

3. Create a zoo. Let the children use their bodies to suggest snakes, elephants, gorillas, ducks, or rabbits.

Getting Creative Drama Started

The creative-drama activities that follow the warm-up may be group or solo situations:

Group Situations
1. Children can build a machine with their bodies, for example, an airplane, a lawnmower, a derrick.
2. Play the pantomime game "Can You Guess Who I Am?," miming some of the following: a fireman, an eggbeater, the teacher, a cat.
3. Have children add movement to a choral reading of a poem. The record "Free to Be You and Me," by Marlo Thomas, is a good source of material.

Solo Situations
1. With the children seated in a circle, each child acts out an object that begins with a specified letter of the alphabet. The rest of the group try to guess the object (automobile, banana, church, and so on). Many variations on this charade game may be played; the children can act out making a snowman, climbing a tree, flying a kite, lying on the beach. Encourage the students to suggest situations.
2. Pass a ball from child to child, pretending it is a hot potato, a cuddly puppy, an ice cube, or a very special present.
3. Introduce a situation in which children talk to the person sitting next to them while acting as a make-believe character, for example; a cat trying to be friends with a dog, a country mouse telling a city mouse about life, a Martian explaining the universe to a person from earth, Little Orphan Annie meeting Batman.

Dramatic Stimuli

Objects   Objects are helpful for increasing concentration and distracting children from themselves.

1. Bring to class the following objects: a ring, a key, a tooth, an odd hat, a broken cup. Divide the children into small groups and have each group create a dramatic tale about their object.
2. Place a variety of objects in a paper bag. Spill the objects out together or have them selected one at a time. Encourage children to develop a story using the objects. Try to select objects with "dramatic potential," such as an empty medicine bottle, an old fur, a foreign coin, a torn shirt, an outdated newspaper, a raggedy broom.

Music   For many people, music is a spur to feeling. Provide opportunities for your students to listen to "mood music"; for example, "Nutcracker Suite," "Sorcerer's Apprentice," "2001: A Space Odyssey," "Star Wars," "Grand Canyon Suite," "Gayne Ballet Suite," "Pictures at an Exhibition." The students can then create a drama that reflects the musical emotion.

Disasters   Pamela Blackie, an eminent teacher of drama in Great Britain, suggests that disasters have excellent dramatic possibilities for older children.[12] Children can play themselves in earthquakes, erupting volcanoes, shipwrecks, fires, floods, and avalanches. After this experience, they may want to act out the roles of professionals associated with these situations—fire fighters, sea captains, rescue parties, and so on.

Mixed-up Meetings   Help the children bring together characters who could never meet but might enjoy each other. In this dramatic exercise, fictional and real characters may be mixed:

> Mork and John Glenn
>
> Mickey Mouse and the Beatles
>
> The New York Yankees and Superman
>
> President Reagan and Christopher Columbus

Encourage the students to select their own characters for mixed-up meetings.

Historical Events   An excellent source of drama is the well-known historical event. Some historical events with dramatic potential are

> The first landing on the moon
>
> The San Francisco earthquake
>
> The first Thanksgiving
>
> The signing of the Declaration of Independence
>
> The assassination of Abraham Lincoln
>
> Babe Ruth hitting his sixtieth home run
>
> The sinking of the Titanic

Allow the children to suggest other events. Sometimes a prop or two may be desirable.

Children's Literature   Children's literature can be a rich source of creative dramatics for the classroom. Folktales are particularly valuable in this regard. In most of them, the plot is simple, the characters are clearly defined, and the sequence of events is clear. Some old favorites with a history of dramatic success are

> For Younger Children:
>
> *The Five Chinese Brothers*
>
> *Three Billy Goats Gruff*

---

[12]Pamela Blackie, Bess Bullough, and Doris Nash, *Drama* (New York: Citation Press, 1972), p. 19.

DRAMATIZING PROBLEM SITUATIONS

Suggest one of the following problem situations as a start for a dramatic activity:

1. You are waiting in a long line at the hamburger stand, and you are very hungry. On two occasions, people manage to get ahead of you. What do you do the third time it happens?

2. You breathlessly run into the police station to report that your bicycle has been stolen. The police seem to doubt your story.

3. You have just broken your mother's expensive pearl necklace and the pearls are scattered all over the floor. You are busily picking them up when your mother enters the room.

4. Your best friend wants to try your new skate board. He has never been on one before. Your parents have asked you not to lend it to anyone. Your friend keeps asking you as others stand by. How will you handle the situation?

5. You have been called at school to go home immediately.

6. It is late at night. You are alone in your apartment. Suddenly you hear a strange noise.

The Three Bears
Henny Penny
The Elves and the Shoemaker

For Older Children:
The Emperor's New Clothes
Stone Soup
The Golden Touch
The Four Musicians
East of the Sun and West of the Moon

For further suggestions, see Chapter 8 on children's literature.

Evaluating Creative Drama

Evaluation is an integral part of creative drama in the classroom. Students should be encouraged to judge their own dramatic efforts. Questions to serve as the framework of an evaluation session can be developed in advance by the students themselves. Here is one list of questions developed by fifth graders:

Did the characters seem believable?

Were they the kind of people that you had hoped to portray?

Did the words sound convincing?

Was the speech clear?

Could you tell what the characters were like from what they said?

The evaluation of creative drama can be overdone, however. A rigorous analysis of this improvisational art form may discourage spontaneity in future participants.

If students are acquainted with the essentials of evaluation before the dramatization, they will know on what aspects to focus their attention during the drama and will probably come up with better assessments. If they also know that some of their creative dramas may be replayed and possibly even recast, they will show more motivation in considering how a particular drama might be improved. The teacher should always attempt to get the evaluation started on a positive note: "Linda certainly was an effective Rapunzel"; "Couldn't you just see the Emperor walking down the street without any clothes?" If the teacher's input is supportive and kept to a minimum, the need for it should soon decrease. The evaluation of classroom drama should soon become an activity directed by the students themselves.

Classroom dramatizations provide a unique opportunity for children to use language spontaneously and creatively. Indeed, the acting they involve is not their only contribution to language training. The planning and evaluative stages of a drama can also be rich in verbal learning.

EVALUATING CREATIVE DRAMA

Winifred Ward, author of *Playmaking with Children,* suggests that the evaluation of children's dramas concentrate only on essentials. She notes that the vital aspects of story dramatization are

Story—Was the story clear?

Characterization—Were the characters real for the story?

Dialogue—Did it make the story progress?

Teamwork—Did the characters play together?

Timing—Did the scene move?

Voice and *diction*—Could everyone be heard?

Making believe is as natural and absorbing for children as dealing with life's daily realities. Most children want to transform reality at some time. For them, creative drama is an easy way to discover the body, the emotions, the imagination, and the cognitive processes.

ORAL LANGUAGE APPRECIATION

People tend to demonstrate their joy in listening to language in many ways. They smile, clap their hands, stamp their feet, or just sit silently enraptured. Some of these reactions have been learned through observation of others engaged by the sounds of language. At a very young age, children recognize that the spoken word may soothe, entertain, confer power, satisfy needs, and give form to feelings.

Children can be helped in their appreciation of oral language by exposure to activity in which language is used to entertain. The child may participate as listener or speaker. Not only may the language of literature create a sense of connection with the past (as in traditional folktales), but those sharing the same pleasurable experience may develop a special bond.

Other oral language forms that the teacher may utilize to develop children's appreciation of the spoken work include puppetry, choral speaking, oral interpretation, and theatre presentations.

Puppetry

Puppetry is an old art form. The early Egyptians buried marionette-like figures in their tombs; puppets could be seen on the streets of ancient Greece and Rome; and in England puppetry has flourished since medieval times. Contemporary Punch and Judy's are not very different from their eighteenth-century English predecessors. Traditional American Indians use puppets in their rituals. Puppetry is practiced today by professional theatre groups at fairs, carnivals, and parades, providing a special kind of enjoyment for both young and old.

Many teachers are now recognizing that puppetry can be a dazzling addition to their classrooms. Through puppets, children may express what they would hesitate to say more directly. Acting through a puppet permits the shy child to become a ferocious lion or a formidable giant. Protected by a disguise and busily engaged in manipulating strings, paper bags, or fists, children lose some of their self-consciousness and feel freer to express their feelings. Courage creeps up on the puppeteer as he or she identifies with the puppet character. What the puppet will say is seldom a problem as long as the situation reflects the interests or experiences of the students.

Getting Puppetry Started   Most young children have had limited exposure to puppets, and even some teachers may not recall any school experience involving this art form. Your first job is to expose your students to a variety of puppets and forms of puppetry so as to stimulate their enthusiasm. For example:

1. Take the class to a professional puppet show. (Street fairs and children's theaters are the usual sources.)
2. Have the students visit a museum to see its collections of puppets, marionettes, and traditional masks.
3. Plan a classroom display of puppets borrowed from museums, libraries, other teachers, a local puppeteer.
4. Encourage the students to bring puppets from home that can be used in the classroom.
5. Suggest the viewing of television shows that use puppets effectively, such as "The Muppets" and "Sesame Street."
6. Invite someone with expertise in puppetry to be a guest speaker at the school.

The most effective way to heighten interest in puppetry is to have students create their own puppets. Most puppets are quick and inexpensive to make, and durable. If you have not constructed puppets be sure to take the opportunity to do so. But try not to display your own puppets as models. Young students tend to copy the teacher too closely. They may feel freer to improvise if given anonymous examples. Once started, it is almost a certainty that each child's puppet will bear an individual stamp.

There are many types of puppets suitable for the classroom. *Hand puppets* are perhaps the easiest to construct. The simplest form involves only the fingers. The students can roll construction paper into cylinders and tape them to fit the tips of their fingers. Before being taped, these pieces of paper can be decorated with drawings or features done in crayon. Three-dimensional interest can be achieved by adding bits of construction paper, feathers, fabric, or whatever materials can be made to adhere.

A simple hand puppet may be made without any props. Features are created by drawing with magic marker directly on the hand. Another popular form of hand puppet is made from a sock, with yarn, buttons, paper, and so on used for features. Frequently, a long sock is used so that the puppeteer's arm serves as the puppet's body. Hand puppets can also be made from a rubber, or styrofoam, ball. Cut a hole in the ball just large enough to fit it firmly over the index finger. Features, hats, or jewelry may be painted or pasted on with glue. Clothes may be made from a large handkerchief or piece of fabric and secured with a rubber band.

Paper bag puppets are also possible, requiring only the ordinary large brown supermarket paper bag. Stuffing such a bag with paper and slipping another over it provides a three-dimensional standing form. Details may be added with paper, foil, paint, or reflector tape. If you push a length of broomstick or long stick into a paper bag puppet and then tie and tape it, you have the makings of a very dramatic form.

The *stick puppet,* sometimes referred to as the rod puppet, is made using tongue depressors, clothespins, or any type of stick as support. Oak tag, sponges, cardboard, or paper may be stapled to the stick and decorated or dressed. For a more dramatic stick puppet, use a longer length stick.

Empty boxes, cans and paper plates provide excellent beginnings for *box puppets.* Small cereal boxes are usually particularly successful. Abe Lincoln can come to life through a tall tin can: accentuate the height with a black fabric top hat, a black paper beard, bow tie, and black paper suit. Paper plates have a variety of uses for the puppeteer. Simple caricatures can be drawn onto the plate or they can be lavishly decorated and textured.

Because of the variety of shapes and the potential for unusual transformations, *junk puppets* provide an unusual challenge to the youngster's imagination. An empty large plastic bottle can become a pig; a milk container can be transformed into Little Toot, the tugboat; the roller from paper towelling can become a giant.

Vegetables and fruits make fascinating puppets; some of the most effective are apples, carrots, potatoes, bananas, walnuts, and oranges. Again, the shape will suggest the puppet. One popular type is the yam animal puppet (Figure 9-1). Children select a yam with a shape that resembles a particular animal and scoop out a hole to fit their index fingers. Tusks or horns may be made from toothpicks with frilled ends, match sticks, or old knitting needles. Cloves or raisins on toothpicks serve as eyes. Fingers from old gloves can be used for ears. The shape of the yam will determine the placement and shape of the mouth. A simple slit or painted line may suffice. If desired, the body may be dressed using cloth or paper. Wool or pipe cleaners make an effective tail. Remember that vegetables and fruits are perishable, and therefore not suitable for puppets that will be handled a great deal or used for a long period of time.

Though time consuming, *papier maché puppets* are not difficult to construct. A popular method is to use an inflated balloon as a base, covering it with strips of newspaper that have been dipped in a paste of flour and water and layered onto the balloon. After the puppet has dried it can be painted and attractively decorated.

Marionettes require considerable time and skill to construct and manipulate, but the art of constructing them provides multiple opportunities for using language in purposeful ways. Individual children who are particularly interested in constructing this type of puppet should certainly be encouraged to do so.

Every classroom should own one or two well-illustrated books on

9-1   **Vegetable (Yam) Puppets**

Constructed by Yvonne Steiner Gerin and Stephen Saxe. /HBJ Photo.

puppet construction. They need not be expensive. Some particularly good references with simple directions are *Making Puppets Come Alive*, by Larry Engler and Carol Fijan; *The Shari Lewis Puppet Book*, by Shari Lewis; and *Puppet Fun*, by Nellie McCaslin.

Using Puppets   Now that the children have made their puppets, what can be done with them? Students should be allowed to devise spontaneous plays based on their own experiences. Adam's paper-bag puppet was meant to be his Aunt Tillie at her seventy-fifth birthday party. Lillie's finger puppets are a family of birds who have made their nest in the tree outside her window. Richard had made a puppet of the policeman on the corner, and Anne's sock puppet bears a striking resemblance to her dachshund. In the primary grades, puppets can be used to act out stories about personal experiences or favorite fictional characters. Older children may wish to reenact great scenes from history, such as

Christopher Columbus landing on the American continent

Lewis and Clark discovering the Pacific Ocean

Alexander Graham Bell's invention of the telephone

Admiral Peary landing on the North Pole

The Wright brothers' flight at Kitty Hawk

The use of puppets in language development should give students an opportunity to respond to experiences spontaneously. In most situations, scripts should not be used and, as in creative dramatics, the characters and sequence of action should be planned but not memorized. If a stage is used, it should be kept simple: a sheet thrown over a table behind which the puppeteers are hidden, or a few pieces of cardboard glued together for the puppets.

Most puppetry activities should begin simply. Initially, only one puppet may be involved as the child introduces the puppet to another child or a group, telling its names, where it came from, how it was made, why it's here, how it feels. The following rules should be observed by each puppeteer:

1. Be prepared. Know what you are going to say.
2. Speak in a voice that communicates the puppet's mood.
3. Look at the puppet, not at the audience.

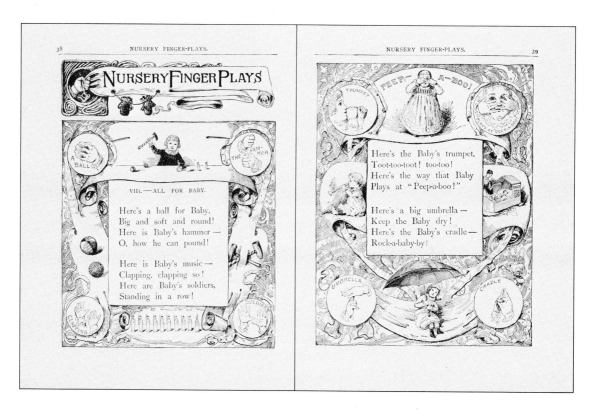

9-2   From FINGER AND ACTION RHYMES. Used with permission of the publisher, The Instructor Publications, Inc., Dansville, New York, 14437.

GRANDPA'S BARN

Grandpa's barn is wonderful
Make a "roof" with fingertips of both hands touching.
On a rainy day;
Make a motion of falling rain.
When we can't be out of doors
We all go there to play.
Make index and middle fingers of both hands "run for the barn."

The bantam hens run in and out,
Scratching through the grain.
Scratch with all fingers.
The cats chase mice with might and main
But never out into the rain!
Fingers of right hand "chase" fingers of left hand.

The horses stamp their feet and switch
Their tails at buzzing flies.
Pantomime stamping foot as horse does. Put hands together behind back; move them like a switching tail.
The cows contentedly chew their cuds
And drowsily roll their gentle eyes.
Pantomime chewing and roll eyes.

Climbing to the rafters,
Jumping down again,
Right index and middle fingers "climb" fingers of left hand and "jump" off.
Sliding down the haymow—
These are favorite games.
Index and middle fingers of right hand "climb" to left elbow from wrist and "slide" back down.

Grandpa's barn is wonderful
On a rainy day.
Repeat symbols for barn and for rain.
Don't you wish you could go there
With me some day to play?
Point to "you"; point to "me."

9-3 Taken from FINGER PLAYS FOR NURSERY AND KINDERGARTEN by Emilie Poulsson. Dover Publications, Inc. NY 1971.

4. Move the puppet as a person would move his or her face and body when speaking.
5. If possible have the puppet address a question to the audience or a particular person.

Puppets need not have one life, especially if the students have invested much time and emotional energy in making them. The puppet who played King Midas this week can become King John next week and sign the Magna Carta. Take off the crown and the king is transformed into Bartholomew Cubbins. Dick Whittington's cat can become the Cat Who Went to Heaven. The puppet that was Peter Rabbit yesterday can be the Velveteen Rabbit today, and the Runaway Bunny tomorrow. Magical transformations can be accomplished through a new hat, a moustache, or a bow tie.

Puppets are language springboards. They may serve as a stimulus for creative writing, or they may be utilized as visual aids when children tell stories. Some teachers report that they have prerecorded on tape the sound track of puppet presentations and then used it during the live performance. Though this is a debatable procedure since the child may lose concentration during the presentation, prerecording removes the pressure of having to do gestures and dialogue at the same time.

Finger Plays   When children engage in finger plays, they use their fingers as puppets. This is not a new activity for primary-school children because they have found their fingers fascinating since infancy.

Develop a repertoire of finger plays and children will have many chances for both verbal and body activities. While doing finger plays, mistakes are quickly corrected and youngsters can practice difficult sounds in a most delightful way. With some assistance from the teacher, children can create their own finger plays and "dress up" their fingers with gloves, paper, ribbons, and so on. The ideas for finger plays may be suggested by nursery or jump-rope rhymes, folktales, or the children's own stories. Figures 9-2 and 9-3 show some finger plays that rank among children's favorites.

Choral Speaking

Choral speaking is the recitation of poetry, dramatic pieces, or stories by speakers acting as a group. It is a wonderful way for children to express their emotional response to a work of art. Since the success of these expressions depends not on one voice but on the group, many children lose their self-consciousness and throw themselves into the activity. Poems are particularly well-suited to choral work because of their intrinsic rhythm and melody. The rules are simple:

1. Let it be a fun experience.

2. The pleasure of the participants, not the audience, is the objective.

3. Select poems that are appealing (rhythmic, humorous, tuneful, imagistic, clever).

4. Let the children decide on the choral arrangement (who says what and how).

5. Have a student leader start, cue, and direct different responders.

6. Initially select poems which are simple and familiar. Try to choose selections that children like rather than what you think they like.

7. Have frequent choral reading experiences.

Once you have a climate in which choral speaking has been established, the teacher can provide the materials and stimuli to keep it going:

1. Have a variety of appropriate selections available in multiple copies:

   For Younger Children (Grades 1–3):
   Jump-rope rhymes
   Nursery rhymes ("Three Little Kittens," "There Was
     an Old Woman," and so on)
   "The Milkman's Horse,"
   Leland Jacobs, "The Merry Robin"
   Evelyn Beyer, "Jump or Jiggle"
   Marchette Gaylord Chute, "Presents"
   A. A. Milne, "Lines and Squares"
   "Mister Frog Went A-Courtin' "
   "Get On Board Little Children"
   "Ha-Ha, This-a-Way"

   For Older Children (Grades 4–8):
   D. K. Stevens, "The Cautious Cat"
   Bliss Carmen, "A Vagabond Song"
   Charles Carryl, "The Camel's Complaint,"
   "Poor Old Woman"
   John Masefield, "Sea-Fever"
   Christopher Morley, "Smells"
   Rachel Field, "Roads"
   "Don Gato"
   Agnes Maxwell-Hall, "Jamaica Market"
   Claude McKay, "The Tropics in New York"

2. Stress the importance of the group in selecting and interpreting the selection. Encourage them to try out many suggestions before coming to a final decision.

3. Encourage the children to interpret and reinterpret a selection. (This does not mean it should be honed to perfection. Rather, it should reflect a number of possible interpretations.)

4. Suggest that the children assign roles.

5. Have a student leader direct their efforts during the speaking.

Start by developing a sense of the group as well as an appreciation of rhythm: "Jonathan King, clap out your name." "Good." "Now let's all clap out Jonathan's name." "Who else would like to clap his/her name?" After several children have participated, try clapping the rhythms of two different names, dividing the class in half.

Proceed to clapping out other rhythmic patterns: rain falling, clocks ticking, waves crashing.

Clap out a rhythmic story of a storm, assigning different parts: raindrops, thunder, lightning, wind, people running. Later on, rhythm instruments may be used.

When you use poems, initially select those that are short, familiar, and easy for the children to understand and interpret. Have copies available for each child to follow as you or a student read the poem. Ask questions like: "How did the poem make you feel?" "What line did you like best?" Don't ask: "What did the second line mean?" or "What did you learn from that poem?" Discuss how the poem might be arranged for class participation and then have the children volunteer for specific lines, couplets, or sections. Have them mark their copies so they know when to participate. After reciting the poem once, the children may decide to make some alterations. In the process of marking the interpretation, children will begin to use terms that can describe voices: light, heavy, dark, and so on. Some teachers even encourage the use of musical terms (piano, forte), helping children to see the kinship between music and poetry.

Here are two easy-to-do selections for choral speaking that have been used widely in the schools:

OUR DRUMS

My father bought me a big bass drum.
(Boys) Boom! Boom! Boom!
He bought my sister a little snare drum.
(Girls) Boom! tee dee dee dee Boom!
We took our drums and we went for a walk.
(Boys) . . .
We didn't take time to look or talk.
(Girls) . . .
All the people came out to see,
(Boys) . . .
What all the terrible noise could be.
(Girls) . . .
Of course we didn't mind that, you know,
(Boys) . . .
Until a big man said, "Go! Go! Go!"
(Girls) . . .
We took our drums and ran right back,
(Boys) . . .
Now I carry my drum in a sack.
(Girls) . . .

HICKORY, DICKORY, DOCK

(Rhythmic "clicking" sound of the tongue
 and delicate, precise "Tick-Tock")

Hickory, Dickory, Dock!
The mouse ran up the clock,
The clock struck one, (Solo) "Bong!"
The mouse ran down, (Light Solo) "Squeak!"
Hickory, Dickory, Dock!
Hickory, Dickory, Dock!
Tick-Tock, Tick-Tock, Tick-Tock, Tick-Tock, . . .

Choral speaking, like creative drama, is a good example of process being more important than product. Since many interpretations are "right" and a perfect performance is not the goal, the teacher and the students can relax and enjoy the activity. Some evaluative statements may be interjected by the teacher, such as, "We need a group to break the monotony of single voices," or "This line needs heavier voices." However, the dominant role should be assumed by the children. If the teacher has a role after the initial preparation, it is to call attention to the pleasure of the process. Two good references for choral speaking are: *Oral Interpretation of Children's Literature*, by Henry A. Bamman, Mildred A. Dawson, and Robert J. Whitehead, and *Storyteller*, by Ramon R. Ross.

Oral Interpretation

Oral interpretation is the individual reading aloud of literary materials. Children can start out reading short selections. Previous experience with choral reading and group recitation of poetry are usually an asset for the beginning interpretive reader. Bamman, Dawson, and Whitehead suggest that children need experience plus proper training to be successful oral readers. Toward this end they suggest training for clear and distinct enunciation, tempo regulation, and good phrasing.[13]

Theater Presentations

Theater presentations have a place in the elementary-school curriculum. Besides increasing the child's awareness of audience, formal stage presentations may sensitize both the listeners and the speakers to the multifaceted ways in which language may be interpreted. Stage presentations have sometimes been considered creative-drama activities, but this

[13]Henry A. Bamman, Mildred A. Dawson, and Robert J. Whitehead, *Oral Interpretation of Children's Literature*, 2d ed. (Dubuque, Iowa: William C. Brown, 1973), p. 16.

is somewhat misleading. The focus of creative drama is the self-awareness of the participant; theater presentations emphasize audience awareness.

For some children, "all the world's a stage," and they perform without
benefit of the proscenium arch, props, or audience. For others, drama, on
or off a formal stage, is painful. However, all children if they so desire,
should have the opportunity to try this type of presentation.

A word of caution: theater presentations should not occupy large
blocks of classroom time, with many children playing insignificant roles.
One man expressed to me his current disdain for the theater because he
was required as a youngster to be present and motionless at countless
rehearsals of an elementary-school play in which he acted the part of a
tree. If the teacher's objective in planning a theater presentation is to
provide children with the opportunity to work cooperatively on a long-
term goal, many other projects can be developed such as a class exhibit,
a newspaper, a mural, and so on.

DIALECT AND STANDARD AMERICAN ENGLISH

Wherever you teach in the United States, you will probably encounter at
some point, if not on a daily basis, English-speaking children whose dialect is not Standard American English (see Chapters 6 and 7). How can
a teacher help these students develop their command of standard English? The first factor to consider is your attitude; techniques come later.
Remember that a nonstandard dialect is a rule-governed language system that is as legitimate, complex, sensible, and arbitrary as Standard
American English. Widespread ignorance of this fact has helped to foster
language prejudice.

The acceptance of teachers is important to speakers of nonstandard
dialects, for it allows the positive self-concepts necessary for language
growth. For teachers, acceptance of nonstandard English means

—awareness that language is a reflection of the attitudes, prejudices, and
values of the speaker's culture.

—focusing on what is said rather than how it is said: listening.

—appreciating that language is linked to self-identity.

This acceptance of nonstandard dialects does not necessarily mean that
any child in this society should not learn Standard American English.
Nor does it mean that children should not be made aware of the relationship between the use of language and academic and economic success.

Acknowledging and even behaving in a positive way toward children
who do not speak the standard dialect is not enough. Teachers must be
more than well-meaning adults; they must be professionals with specific
skills. What techniques can the teacher use to help children recognize

the importance of Standard American English and incorporate it into their daily usage?

Exposure to much classroom talk and opportunities to respond verbally are an excellent beginning. The activities suggested in the beginning of the chapter for formal and informal talks, discussions, and creative drama experiences can all contribute to the linguistic growth of a child who may not yet be comfortable with the standard dialect.

Since all language ability builds upon a rich oral language foundation, children should be given many opportunities to hear and express themselves orally. There are differing perspectives on how this can best be accomplished with children whose first dialect is not Standard American English. But regardless of which strategy is suggested, most researchers find it valuable to build on the youngster's oral tradition.

Developing Standard Dialect Skills

1. *Provide opportunities for much interactive talk.*
   Children should speak to small groups, larger groups, talk in teams of two, and engage in teacher conferences.

2. *Recognize the importance of models.*
   Expose students to live and recorded examples of Standard American English that stimulate responses. Children's literature with repetitive refrains and Mother Goose rhymes are good beginnings. The speech of the teacher as well as adjunct classroom personnel serves as a model, assisting students to reach out beyond their usual oral responses.

3. *Highlight and practice situations in which students recognize the appropriateness of language levels.*
   Structure role-playing situations in which students explain why they didn't do their homework to their best friend, their mother, their teacher, the principal. They can then consider whether they changed their language when they spoke to different people. Another good situation for role playing is telling a friend, a parent, or a prospective employer why you want a certain job.

   The recognition that the situation may dictate not only vocabulary but linguistic style is an important one for language expansion. The casual, vernacular style adopted with friends may not be effective with someone who is not part of the group. "Appropriateness is the standard for good language."[14]

4. *Use pictures.*
   Many teachers have found that the use of exciting and dramatic pictures or photographs starts a flow of language. Encouraging closer observation prods the student into thinking. Use pictures that are highly emotional and in which details are important. Encourage conversations—not test situations—about pictures. Use pictures of children, sporting events, disasters, conflicts, extreme situations, humorous occurrences, and unexpected events.

[14]Walter Loban, Margaret Ryan and James R. Squire, *Teaching Language and Literature, Grades 7-12* (New York: Harcourt Brace and World, 1961), p. 544.

5. *Use the tape recorder frequently.*

   The tape recorder may be used to provide private feedback. Children can listen to their own speech, identify errors (with or without the teacher), and then make improved recordings.

6. *Focus on the activity.*

   Structure situations in which the emphasis is on the activity rather than talk itself. When children plan cooperatively for a class party or build sets for a play production, they interact un–self-consciously through language. Problem solving situations, demonstrations, and simple show-and-tell situations provide subtle opportunities for language growth. The child who is enthusiastic about what is to be communicated will be less concerned with the form that his or her language takes.

7. *Minimize teacher corrections.*

   Try not to correct the child's speech in front of other children. In fact, a body of research suggests that these superficial corrections ("It's not I'se but I'm") have very little impact and are perhaps even counterproductive. They are discouraging and make the child uncomfortable. When children are ready to alter these surface features of language, they will do so.

ORAL COMMUNICATION FOR DIFFERENT PURPOSES

Children can best appreciate the power of the spoken word when they recognize its many purposes. In a world that bombards us with oral messages, teachers should provide opportunities for students to become more critical.

Attention will be directed in this section to situations in which children themselves can use language to persuade, explain, secure information, and share feelings. These purposeful aspects of language should be viewed in the context of Michael Halliday's research referred to earlier in this chapter.

Interviews

Everyone should know something about interview technique. Long associated with the print media, it is today also a staple of electronic broadcasting. Skilled interviewers are particularly sought after and highly prized by television.

Since children have many opportunities to hear interviews on television, the teacher should utilize these experiences constructively in the classroom. Select an effective interviewer as a model and have the students analyze his or her work in terms of the following questions:

1. What do you think the interviewer did in preparation for the interview?
2. How did the interviewer make the subject feel comfortable?
3. How did the interviewer keep talk from straying from the topic?

    4. How did the interviewer show awareness of time?

    5. How did the interviewer clear up any confusing points?

    6. How did the interviewer conclude the interview?

After observing several interviews, the students can proceed to establish some guidelines of their own. Here are some developed by a sixth-grade class:

    1. Prepare for the interview. Find out about the topic and the background of the person to be interviewed. Develop some questions. Give special attention to your opening question.

    2. Introduce yourself in a pleasant manner to the individual whom you are interviewing.

    3. If you are taping the interview ask the individual's permission to do so.

    4. Try to stay with your topic.

    5. Keep your eye on the clock so that the interview is not too long.

    6. Ask for clarification on points that you do not understand.

    7. Show your appreciation for the interview.

Some teachers have children interview each other. This is a particularly good technique to use at the beginning of the term with students who do not yet know each other. Sensitively handled, it can facilitate the introduction of a new classmate. Two students can hold an interview as the other children observe. It can then be discussed by the class.

Interviews may also be attempted with nonclassmates. Before conducting an outside interview, the student should answer the following questions:

How will I arrange for the interview?

What do I want to find out?

How will I introduce myself (without beginning, "My teacher said . . .")?

How will I end the interview?

How will I use this information?

Interviews need not be limited to the gathering of factual information. Encourage children to ask questions that begin with "How do you *feel* about . . .? Here is a series of questions a fourth grader devised for interviewing her jogging classmates.

Do you like jogging?

How do you usually feel just before you jog? Right after?

What do you think about when you jog?

Why do you jog?

Do you feel that jogging is healthy?

Do you feel that most people should jog?

How do you feel about nonjoggers?

INTERVIEWS WITH LOCAL PEOPLE

Your local area contains a number of interesting people with whom an interview could be arranged. Some might include

—a neighborhood tradesperson
—the school custodian
—the sergeant at the neighborhood precinct
—a senior citizen
—a person with musical talent
—a person from a foreign country
—the owner of a pet store
—a member of your family

Children should be encouraged to ask questions that are open-ended and cannot be answered with a "yes" or "no." Here are some questions that might be asked of local business people:

At the gas station: How do you get your gasoline?
At the supermarket: What do you do with the products from the time they are delivered till they are placed on the shelves?
At the bowling alley: How do the bowling pin machines work?
At the bank: Where does all the money come from?
At the plant store: What kind of care do you have to give to the plants?
At the produce store: How do the fruits and vegetables get to the store?
At the electric company: How do you know when the city is low on electricity?
At the firehouse: What happens when an alarm sounds?

Children in one class did a kind of saturation interviewing of their neighborhood. After all the interviews were presented, these fourth-grade students had a much clearer idea of life in their community.

Panel Discussions

The panel discussion is an extended interview, usually involving three or more people. It is conducted by a leader or moderator who usually poses open-ended questions that are answered in turn by each member of the panel. Often, a brief time is allowed for panelists to respond to the comments of other panel members. Children should be given the opportunity to serve as panelists as well as moderators. In each situation, the importance of advanced preparation is stressed. Panelists should be aware of the questions before the discussion begins and the time alloted for presentation, but there should be no set speeches.

As in interviewing, students can be asked to watch a panel discussion on television. If possible, have all the students watch the same program. From this shared experience, students should begin to appreciate the roles of the moderator and panelists. The effective moderator, they will discover,

Introduces the panelists

Selects good questions

Steers the discussion

Prevents discussion from going off the track

Summarizes

and effective panelists

Support points of view with facts

Behave courteously to moderator and other panelists

Are well prepared

After class panel discussions, time should be devoted to audience responses to the issues. Since not all students will be comfortable with the panel discussion format, the participants should be volunteers. The teacher should, however, encourage a slightly reluctant child who simply needs some additional confidence.

TOPICS FOR PANEL DISCUSSION

Though panel discussions are usually most effective in the upper elementary grades, simplified variations have been successful with younger children. The age level of the participants should guide the selection of issues.

For Younger Children:

What can you do when you are feeling unhappy?
How can we have a better class?
What are the best ways to use an allowance?
Is television a good thing?
What should we do about people who destroy school property?

For Older Children:

How much television should we watch?
What can we do about pollution?
Can we play a part in crime prevention?
How can we handle the energy crisis?
In what ways can we be of help to the handicapped?
How can the school cafeteria be improved?
Should nuclear reactors be outlawed?
Should girls and boys play on the same teams?

Informal Oral Reports

Throughout the grades, there are many opportunities for children to do oral reporting, both formally and informally. The informal oral report is usually a spontaneous brief recounting of an experience. In the lowest grades, it may be as simple as: "My tooth fell out last night and here it is," or "Today is my grandma's birthday." As children become more fluent and more at ease before the class, their oral reports will lengthen. A "sharing time" can be set aside, a time during which the students are encouraged to make informal reports and recount experiences. Teachers need not always structure these sessions, but they should offer students guidance on what materials are appropriate for sharing, on how to make use of illustrative materials, and on the importance of including only relevant details. They may also remind students of time considerations. The topics of oral reports made by students in one third-grade class show the great variation that is possible:

A trip to Washington, D.C.

A pet snake

A coin collection

"Star Wars" cards

A fire on my block

Making pretzels at home

The Memorial Day Parade

Yesterday's Little League game

How I broke my arm

When these reports are spontaneous, allow the children to use informal language as well as the more formal language promoted in school. One child describing a frightening experience said it this way: "I was standing on this gooky corner waiting for my uncle when this creepy guy came up to me. He looked dirty and icky. 'Do you have any money?' he asked. I ran away."

Formal Reports

Formal reporting is a frequent practice in elementary schools, particularly in grades three through six. Unfortunately, very often these reports are dull or poorly executed. Sometimes the topic is the problem, having been of limited interest to both the reporter and the audience. Thus, whenever possible, the final topics should be selected by the students themselves. An interest in the topic usually aids its presentation.

Too often, the child who is reporting has not been *taught* the appropriate skills, merely *told* what they are. Effective formal reporting is also impeded by self-consciousness and overconcern for what classmates will think. Having the children report to small groups rather than to the whole class may minimize this anxiety.

Students doing their first formal reporting should explain material that is very familiar to them, rather than the results of research. But even when these beginning reports are about firsthand experience, they should differ from informal "show and tell" activities in length and level of sophistication. Accordingly, the student may need to use notes. The following guidelines may also prove helpful to the reporter:

1. Give the report in your own words.
2. Plan an interesting opening sentence. (Memorize it if you wish.)
3. Use illustrative or audio-visual material. Arrange for someone to assist you in showing it (if help is necessary), and give that person written instructions on what to do.
4. Include a summary of important points.

It is assumed, of course, that if the report requires research, the students will have been given appropriate instruction in the use of reference materials.

The teacher should be available to confer with students who are planning reports. At these conferences, pupils might do a "dry run" of sections of their report and discuss their plans. A conference is also an opportunity for the teacher to assess the student's personal readiness for reporting and the accuracy of the information gathered thus far. If the student is a reluctant reporter, this time might well be spent building confidence; it can be a kind of rehearsal for coping.

In some cases, the teacher may judge that the student is not yet ready to do this type of oral report and will suggest that the report be shortened or temporarily postponed; or the teacher may suggest that the student do the report with a classmate. Allowing students to approach the task gradually increases their receptivity to future presentations. Too frequently, throwing a frightened nonswimmer into the water only ensures a continuing anxiety about swimming.

Evaluation of Oral Reports

Children can be rather ruthless in evaluating oral reports, and the student who is an ineffective speaker may have to endure considerable discomfort. Some of this discomfort can be avoided if guidelines for evaluation are discussed with the class before reporting sessions begin. These discussions should generate not only evaluative criteria related to content and delivery, but suggestions on how to respond to an oral report in a manner that reflects sensitivity to the feelings of others. Several class sessions may have to be devoted to developing this heightened consciousness, but a teacher who understands the relationships between a caring environment and the learning process will consider the time well spent.

GUIDELINES FOR RESPONDING TO ORAL REPORTS

(These two sets of guidelines were established by a fifth-grade class.)

How to criticize a report:
1. State positive aspects before giving negative comments.
2. Provide constructive suggestions.
3. Speak about the report not the person.
4. Look at the person when you make your comments.
5. Try to put yourself in the place of the person who has reported.

Answer these questions when evaluating reports:
1. Was the report clear?
2. Was information presented from different reference sources?
3. Did the speaker stay with the topic?
4. Did the speaker summarize the information?
5. Were visual or electronic aids used effectively?

The tape recorder, a machine fast becoming commonplace in the classroom, can be used in the building of reporting skills. Children can practice reports and get instant feedback through this device. Unlike the live audience, a tape recorder is nonjudgmental and allows the speaker a second chance. Using guidelines similar to those noted on p. 000, the student can listen to a playback and make a personal evaluation of his or her report, identifying weak spots and gaining confidence from the practice.

Announcements

Experience at making announcements tends to improve students' communication skills. Usually brief and involving very specific objectives, school announcements are ideal as a student's first form of oral presentation. Since an element of prestige may be associated with making announcements, the teacher should make sure that every student has a chance at it. The reluctant speaker can be allowed to read the announcement. Here are some typical classroom or schoolwide announcements:

1. Class agenda for the week: "There will be no show-and-tell on Friday; we will be in the auditorium all afternoon."

2. Commemorative days and special projects of interest to the whole school: "Tuesday is Grandparents' Day"; "The fourth grade will sponsor a plant sale in the gym on Friday."

3. Notice of articles lost or found.

4. Distinctions earned by students or faculty members: "Our art teacher, Ms. Helfant, is the subject of an article in today's *Washington Post.*"

5. Community events: "The Lenox Library is having a 'please touch' exhibit of important simple machines."

Role Playing

Role playing provides a good beginning in helping children to recognize the different ways in which they can use language and abstract thinking. Recognizing that a variety of language levels are natural for each person, take the time to provide role-playing experiences and encourage children to interchange roles in order to increase their understanding and empathy with one another.

For Younger Children   First and second graders, even preschoolers, are ready to participate in simple role-playing situations. The situations may be drawn from literature or real life. Here is a sample role-playing exercise, "Superheroes: Help Us," suggested for preschoolers. It can also be used, with slight revisions, for older children.[15]

Children are asked to prepare a costume for the character they would like to pretend to be (perhaps Superman, Wonder Woman, or Batman). They are presented with a dangerous situation. For instance: The Riddler and The Penguin have kidnapped somebody important. The superheroes are asked to figure out a solution to the crime and act out the rescue for the class. They must first plan a strategy, and students are told to discuss in small groups why the person was kidnapped and where they should look to find the criminals. Other role-playing situations for younger children might include

A mother and daughter argue about what the daughter should wear to a family party.

A scene from *Where the Wild Things Are*—Max's mother sends him to bed without any dinner.

For Older Children   Barbara Sundene suggests another role playing situation for children in grades four through six in which the "typical" behaviors of children and adults are enacted in a restaurant setting. The roles assumed are Mom, Dad, Susie, the dreamer, Crabby Jimmy, the busy waitress, and the harried hostess.[16] In this situation, the personality characteristics suggest the plot. However, variations can be developed

[15]Barbara Sundene Wood, ed., *Development of Functional Communication Competencies: Pre-K-Grade 6* (Urbana, Ill.: ERIC Clearing House on Reading and Communication Skills and Speech Communication Association, 1977), p. 16.

[16]Wood, *Development of Functional Communication Competencies*, p. 29.

by changing the scene and the personalities, or by adding a conflict. Other possibilities for role playing follow:

> A confrontation between a girl and her neighbor after the ball she has just thrown has broken his front window.

> A boy tries to convince his parents to send him on a bicycle trip.

The Follow-up

The follow-up is a vital aspect of role playing and can be a lead-in to a reenactment of the same or other situations. The purpose of the follow-up is to share rather than evaluate. Unlike the discussion which follows creative drama, performance is not considered. The focus is on the players' explanation of their behavior. The observers may participate but the emphasis is on what was or might be said rather than on how.

Role playing should not be judged for accuracy or truthfulness. It's purpose is not authentic reenactment but the playing out of personal responses to conflict. As children step into someone else's world, they can appreicate the duality of their feelings. Role playing is a fertile ground for building empathic competence as children begin to recognize the variety of reactions and verbal responses generated by each circumstance.

Developing Audience Antennae

Oral communication is a social activity. It requires people other than the speaker. Even if silent, these "others" can influence the way in which a speaker uses language. As children grow conceptually and linguistically, they recognize that communication styles change with the situation. A heightened awareness of "others"—whether an individual, a small group, or a large one—helps to increase a youngster's sensitivity about what should be said.

How can a teacher help students develop a sense of audience? While this awareness usually comes with maturity and experience, children can still profit from some guidelines. Here are a set developed by a small group of sixth graders determined to improve their audience antennae.

> I always try to look at the eyes of two or three people.

> I look for body movements in the audience. Are they moving around a lot? Are they slumped down in their chairs?

> When I plan my talk, I try to think of my audience.

> If the audience doesn't seem interested, I think about possible reasons. I may be one reason, but not the only one.

The suggestions above are appropriate to speakers of any age. In all grades, give children an opportunity to discuss these questions: Who is the audience? How will I know if they are interested? It is through such discussions that many children lose their self-consciousness about public presentations.

A Word about Speech Problems

It is not assumed that the elementary language arts teacher will be a speech therapist. But while not prepared to treat speech defects, the teacher is in a position to identify chronic speech problems and refer children who need assistance to a specially trained professional. For this reason, it is important that all teachers be able to distinguish between speech faults or articulation problems and speech disorders. Some of the more common speech disorders are:

Stuttering

Cleft-palate speech

Hearing-impaired speech

Delayed speech (resulting from psychological or physical difficulties)

Early recognition and expert treatment will be of immeasurable assistance to the child who exhibits speech disorders. Obviously, it is the responsibility of the classroom teacher to help the child with a speech disorder feel as comfortable in speaking as possible. Anything that the teacher can do to keep other students from focusing on the youngster's defect is valuable.

The elementary classroom teacher encounters more simple problems in articulation than speech disorders—that is, careless or slurred speech, substitutions and omissions of letters, and distorted sounds. Though not able to do the work of a speech therapist, the average teacher should be able to help students recognize their speech faults and to provide them with a few helpful exercises. For example, here are some exercises that can be used to assist children who have difficulties with the *s* sound:

1. Read this poem aloud:

Seashell

Here is a seashell
Put it to your ear.
Listen! Listen!
What do you hear?
The sound of the ocean,
The sound of the sea,
A sing-song sea song
The shell sings to me.
—Ivy O. Eastwick

2. Read a comic strip, such as "Peanuts," underlining all the *s* sounds.

3. Write down and then say all the baseball words that you can think of that begin with *s*. (Words from the kitchen, the pet shop, the zoo may, of course, be substituted for baseball. The emphasis may also be changed to words that have *s* in the medial or the final position.)[17]

Some minor speech problems manifest themselves in the quality of voice. The pitch or the volume of the voice may be unpleasant—in some cases rendering it inaudible. If the child has been seen by a physician and no handicapping condition has been discovered, a variety of classroom exercises may be utilized. However, it should be remembered that the child's difficulties may be emotional; if this is the case, relaxation activities are highly recommended. Problems such as nasality, inaudibility, and stridency can be reduced with regularly practiced relaxation exercises.

Sloppy speech can be cured, but the speaker must first recognize the need for care. The American Medical Association recently noted that millions of Americans are handicapped because they unthinkingly slur, mumble, and swallow word endings.

The tape recorder can be a valuable aid in improving minor speech faults and should be used frequently by children—working individually or in pairs. Recording of their own speech can help students identify articulation problems, inaudibility, hoarseness, lisping, and inappropriate volume. Self-awareness is more than half the battle in sloppy speech.

TEACHER COMPETENCES

Satisfying all of these criteria for teaching oral language requires considerable talent and experience, if not a super being. What competences is it reasonable to expect of the classroom teacher of language arts who is in the process of working toward excellence in teaching speaking? Some suggestions follow:

1. The teacher is able to assess his or her own speech patterns.

2. The teacher is able to structure a supportive classroom environment in which children feel permitted to speek freely.

3. The teacher is able to plan for a variety of speaking activities at the child's developmental level.

4. The teacher is aware of those children who speak too little or too much and tries out a number of strategies to improve the quality of their participation.

[17]The suggestions in this section resulted from informal talks with Mrs. Rhonda Galucci, a speech therapist in the Great Neck school system, Great Neck, New York.

5. The teacher utilizes a number of teaching methods that capitalize on children's creative use of language.

6. The teacher uses a variety of creative drama activities as an expressive art form.

7. The teacher devises situations in which the students can practice using speech to inform, instruct, convince, and entertain.

8. The teacher uses positive measures to encourage children who do not speak the standard dialect to recognize its importance and make it their principal dialect.

9. The teacher identifies speech disorders and makes appropriate professional referrals.

10. The teacher devises appropriate exercises for those students with common speech faults.

Afterview   Who ever said that classrooms should be quiet? The quiet classroom is a luxury that we cannot afford if children are to become prepared for the real world. In an increasingly oral society, verbal fluency is a survival skill. Speech competence is not only a matter of personal communication, it is a vital capacity for responding critically to the mass media and the variety of persuasive strategies that bombard us. This chapter has suggested many speech communication strategies to assist children in their development of verbal skills. Though directed toward speech improvement, these strategies reflect the inextricable bonds that exist among language, concept development, and the sense of self.

WHEN YOU WANT TO KNOW MORE

1. Listen to a professional actor read a poem or story. Identify those factors that contributed to the effectiveness of the presentation. Do you see any implications for the teaching of effective speaking?

2. Consult appropriate written materials and the school or district speech consultant to discover what speech exercises would be most helpful for youngsters who slur letters and words.

3. Find out as much as you can about finger plays. Develop a repertoire of at least ten. Consult a reference such as Bernice Carlson's *Listen and Tell the Story*.

4. Prepare an annotated list of records, films, and filmstrips that would be helpful in the development of various oral language abilities in young children. Some suggested sources: *Oral Aids Through the Grades* (SPICE); *Using Media in the Language Arts* by Michael C. Flanigan and Robert S. Boone.

5. With a colleague, experiment with a series of dramatic warm-up exercises similar to those described in this chapter. Begin by using only body movements so that you can explore the potential of nonverbal communication.

IN THE CLASSROOM

1. After perusing a few art books, select a painting and use it to develop the discussion skills of children in the upper elementary grades.

2. Plan lessons in which children from different ethnic groups have the opportunity to share selections from their oral tradition.

3. Develop a series of lessons in which children have the opportunity to practice the social amenities, for example, introductions, telephone conversations, oral invitations, polite refusals.

4. With a group of children, develop a pupil self-evaluation form for different kinds of oral expressions—reporting, discussion, storytelling, and so on.

SUGGESTED READINGS

Baker, Augusta, and Greene, Ellin. *Storytelling: Art and Technique.* New York: R. R. Bowker, 1977.

Bamman, Henry A.; Dawson, Mildred A.; and Whitehead, Robert J. *Oral Interpretation of Children's Literature.* 2d ed. Dubuque, Iowa: William C. Brown, 1971.

Chambers, Dewey W. *Storytelling and Creative Drama.* Dubuque, Iowa: William C. Brown Company Publishers, 1970.

Cheney, Arnold B. *Teaching Children of Different Cultures in the Classroom, A Language Approach.* 2d ed. Columbus, Ohio: Merrill, 1976.

Cohen, Sandra B., and Plaskon, Stephen P. *Language Arts for the Mildly Handicapped.* Columbus, Ohio: Merrill, 1980.

Engler, Larry, and Fijan, Carol. *Making Puppets Come Alive: A Method of Learning and Teaching Hand Puppetry.* New York: Taplinger Publishing, 1973.

Hoetker, James. *Theater Games: One Way Into Drama.* Urbana, Ill.: ERIC Clearinghouse on Reading and Communication Skills and National Council of Teachers of English, 1975.

McCaslin, Nellie. *Creative Drama in the Classroom.* 3d ed. New York: Longman, 1980.

McIntyre, Barbara M. *Creative Drama in the Classroom.* 3d ed. New York: Longman, 1980.

McIntyre, Barbara M. *Creative Drama in the Elementary School.* Itasca, Ill.: Peacock Publishers, 1974.

Paludan, Lis. *Playing with Puppets.* Translated by Christine Crowley. Boston: Plays, 1975.

Ross, Ramon Royal. *Storyteller.* 2d ed. Columbus, Ohio: Merrill, 1980.

Siks, Geraldine Brain. *Drama with Children.* New York: Harper & Row, 1977.

Ziskind, Sylvia. *Telling Stories to Children.* New York: H. W. Wilson, 1976.

Other Materials

Carlson, Bernice Wells. *Listen! And Help Tell the Story.* Nashville, Tenn.: Abingdon Press, 1965.

Cullum, Albert. *Aesop in the Afternoon.* New York: Citation Press, 1972.

Gerbrandt, Gary L. *An Idea Book for Acting Out and Writing Language.* Urbana, Ill.: National Council of Teachers of English, 1974.

Hutson, Natalie Bovee. *Stage: A Handbook for Teachers of Creative Dramatics.* Stevensville, Mich.: Educational Service, 1968.

Lewis, Shari. *The Shari Lewis Puppet Book.* Secaucus, N.J.: Citadel Press, 1958.

McCaslin, Nellie. *Act Now! Plays and Ways to Make Them.* New York: S. G. Phillips, 1975.

McGuire, Mabelle B. *Finger and Action Rhymes.* Dansville, N.Y.: Instructor Publications, 1966.

Poulsson, Emilie. *Finger Plays for Nursery and Kindergarten.* New York: Dover, 1971.

CHAPTER 10

Writing: A Growth Process for Teachers and Children

Preview   This chapter will discuss the strong relationship that exists between writing, living, and growing. We are all aware that before we can write we have to have something to say. The richer the life, the deeper the experience, the greater the odds that expression will be enhanced. Writing is an organismic reaction that simultaneously makes demands upon our cognitive, physical, and affective selves. Unlike reading, which may be mechanical or passive, writing requires our active participation. Compare reading and writing to viewing and painting a picture. Reading and viewing are intake procedures, whereas writing and painting exact a harvest.

Before teachers can improve the quality of children's writing, certain realities must be faced. Among these are the teacher's own attitude and skills in the composing process. This chapter will therefore explore the stages and developmental levels in writing of both teachers and children. Many suggestions will be provided for sharing writing with the class and the school community. A section will be devoted to the teacher's need to write, and the competences near the end of the chapter will focus on the ability of teachers to develop students' writing abilities as well as their own.

"Had I been blessed with even limited access to my own mind there would have been no reason to write. I write entirely to find out what I'm thinking, what I'm looking at, what I see and what it means."

—Joan Didion

OUR ERA HAS been described as an age of diminishing expectations, an age in which we allow others to define our needs.[1] Long hours in front of the television screen passively participating in another's reality may indeed be a contributing factor to this decline. Previous sections in this book have identified the probable influences of televiewing on the language arts; writing skills, we may discover, atrophy the most. Writing is a demanding and rigorous encoding process; it requires output. The writer must ferret out and put together pieces of experience carefully stored away. How do we go about convincing children that this task is worth the struggle? Perhaps our main hope lies in appealing to the basic human need for self-actualization and growth. Many of life's satisfactions require effort. Learning to play the piano, gardening, acquiring a college degree—all demand effort and generally involve periods of frustration and delayed gratification. But when people believe that what they are doing will increase their competence and help them cope in a complex world, effort takes on a new meaning. That which is self-serving cannot be burdensome. Teachers should promote writing as an instrument of personal growth.

> Writing is extolled, worried over, cited as a national priority, but seldom practiced. The problem with writing is not poor spelling, punctuation, grammar, and handwriting. The problem with writing is no writing.[2]

The principle is a simple one, "The more writing you do, the better you get." But with the popularity of the telephone company, Western Union, and the television networks, the opportunities to practice writing appear to be shrinking. Adults with deficient writing skills are handicapped. Functional writing competence is necessary when applying for jobs, writing business and personal letters, recording experiences, presenting convincing arguments, and in a host of other important situations in our daily lives. Furthermore, and possibly of primary importance, writing

---

[1]Christopher Lasch, *The Culture of Narcissism: American Life in an Age of Diminishing Expectations* (New York: W. W. Norton, 1978).

[2]Donald H. Graves, "We Won't Let Them Write," *Language Arts 55* (May 1978): 636.

serves to generate further thinking. When we have to write, we have to mentally compose, filter through ideas, and generally get our heads in order.

Most students have experienced the chain-reaction phenomenon in writing. The first paper of the semester is usually ground out with great difficulty. As assignments increase so does facility. Having exercised the skills of writing, the students begin to find writing easier. This chain reaction is induced when students are given many opportunities to put their thoughts on paper. Though most teachers would grant children "the right to write," opportunity must accompany permission. A right that cannot be exercised is no right at all.

Many adults, including elementary- and secondary-school teachers, have faulty notions about the writing of children. Consider the following principles, derived from an evaluation of the written expression of children in grades one through six in the Grosse Pointe Public Schools:

1. Scores on standardized English tests do not measure or predict performance in actual written expression.
2. Children can and do learn to write in the primary grades.
3. There should be parallel development of oral and written expression.
4. Skills should be taught in relation to the actual language each child used, not by means of the nonlanguage that appears in some workbooks.[3]

These principles can provide further guidance about the functions of writing. Writing should provide the child with a chance to send up trial balloons. It should be a chance to venture beyond safe, correct but often unimaginative constructions. Invention should be rewarded. Only actual writing produces growth and provides a sample for evaluation. Writing is not underlining, circling, or matching words. It is frequently necessary for the teacher to listen to the young writer discuss his or her work. It is through dialogue about a piece that the child can grow and the teacher can appreciate not only what the child actually wrote but what he or she intended to say.

THE HARD REALITIES

In thinking about how to improve the writing of children, we must consider certain realities:

1. Writing is not easy.
2. Many adults do not like to write.
3. Many teachers do not like to write.

[3]Roger A. McCaig, "What Research and Evaluation Tell Us About Teaching Written Expression in the Elementary School," *The Language Arts Teacher in Action* (Kalamazoo, Mich.: Western Michigan University, 1977), p. 46.

4. The teaching of writing requires the reading of many, many papers.
5. The teaching of writing requires large blocks of class time.
6. Writing cannot be commanded.
7. Children do not write enough.
8. Many past practices in the teaching of writing have not worked.

These realities are painful, and they have brought the teaching of writing to a crossroads. Teachers can "right writing" only if they value the composing process. This means writing themselves, respecting the voice of each child, and nurturing any signs of its appearance. This means encouraging children to write at any and every opportunity.

DEVELOPMENTAL LEVELS IN WRITING

A developmental curriculum assumes that there are stages or steps in most children's learning. Very often if these developmental levels are ignored, the child's progress is impeded. The concept of readiness is basic to a developmental approach to teaching. Children faced with the task of learning to write have to be mature enough to begin the process. One educator has identified three factors that contribute to readiness for writing:

1. A basic oral vocabulary and an ability to use words in the major syntactic patterns
2. An understanding of the basic concepts that underlie the composing process: focus on a main idea, logical development, support and purpose
3. Competence in using the basic composing processes of searching, reflecting, selecting, organizing, writing, and revising[4]

These categories should not suggest that we cannot begin writing experiences with children who have not become fully competent in each area. They are guidelines for the teacher as he/she encourages children to write.

THE BEGINNING WRITER

Any child who has attained a degree of oral fluency can begin the writing process. Initially, writing is talk written down. At this stage, children express themselves beautifully, free from the restraints that boggle more mature minds. Here is what one six-year-old boy wrote:

> I saw clover.
> It was small white clover.

---

[4]Charles K. Stallard, "Writing Readiness: A Developmental View," *Language Arts* 54 (October 1977): 775–79.

It was wild,
So I picked it.
I did not know that the birds
Would miss it.[5]

Oral dictation is usually where writing begins for young children. It may come from an individual or be a cooperative effort. In the developmental process, individual writing usually follows dictation. It may begin as soon as the child can handle it, but should not be a signal to end oral dictation. When individual writing begins, neither quantity nor form should be stressed. Spelling and handwriting should also not be emphasized. Young writers have fragile souls, and they are easily discouraged. The teacher, in these early stages, should respond to all requests for assistance. The primary goal is for children to write and feel joy in their emerging linguistic power.

There are those who believe, and with good reason, that it is never too soon to begin the teaching of writing. A recent study of children who learned to write prior to formal instruction in kindergarten or grade one suggests that children who had writing role-models and who had a real reason to communicate (for example, with relatives and friends who had moved away) developed early writing skills.[6] This study also looked at learning to write in relation to learning to read and found that, for most of these early writers, interest in writing preceded interest in reading.

THE STAGES OF WRITING

We do not write to be understood; we write in order to understand.
—C. Day Lewis

Many authorities in the field emphasize the process aspect of writing. (See the work of Donald Graves, Janet Emig, James Squire, and Donald M. Murray.) From this perspective, writing is a composing process that has three stages. The length of time required for each stage will vary since writing is a highly personal affair.

The precomposing stage is the stage in which the writer gets his or her thoughts together. Children do it in different ways. Andy draws pictures; Elaine does dramatizations; Scott gathers information; others need to talk. The prewriting period is a time for brainstorming, a rehearsal for what is to come. Be patient! Before actual writing, children need time to find their own voices: time to daydream, look, listen, or ask questions.

The composing stage is when the actual writing occurs, the setting

[5]*Developing Children's Power of Self-Expression Through Writing* (Board of Education of the City of New York, 1953), p. 17.
[6]Mary Anne Hall, Sara A. Moritz, and Jodellano Statom, "Writing Before One—A Study of Early Writers," *Language Arts* 53 (May 1976): 582–85.

down of ideas on paper. At this time, the writer may be guided by the teacher if necessary. This assistance can mean answering questions, reinforcing a point of view, helping with mechanics, or clarifying vocabulary.

The rewriting stage is when writers proofread, edit, revise, recopy, and, in many cases, reexperience aspects of the precomposing stage. At this time, a writer asks, "What shall I leave out?" "What can I add?" "Am I saying what I want to say?" These stages will be discussed in detail later in this chapter.

Writing and Composing

Writing is not mechanics. The functional and very essential skills of grammar usage, punctuation, handwriting, and spelling are writing tools, not writing itself. The development of these skills is basic and should be taught in the context of the child's experience, as will be discussed in Chapter 14. However, as more than half a century of research indicates, teaching the mechanics of writing does not necessarily improve the skills of communication:

> Composing is not spelling. It is not grammar, not usage, not manuscript, not writing neat little snatches of perfectly formed sentences. It is neither writing with 'two-inch margins,' nor with perfect alignment . . . Composing is none of these things.[7]

This is not to suggest that language arts teachers should not devote time to the teaching of functional skills. Rather, the implication is that the two aspects of writing, composing and mechanics, should not be confused, especially in the classroom, where they have often been assumed to have a cause-and-effect relationship. Composing is putting ideas on paper. It involves the mechanical skills but confronts the writer with almost limitless options about choice of words, order, style, and originality. From here on, the word *writing* will be used to mean the combination of the two aspects.

The Precomposing Stage

Preparation for writing takes many forms. Kenny tells the class about his brother's college graduation; Margie draws a picture of "R2 D2"; Ann describes the fire she saw on the way to school. Neither child has yet put pen to paper but each is in the initial stages of the writing process.

Most teachers make an effort to select topics that will spur their students' interest. Sad to say, no topic, by itself, no matter how startling or

---

[7]James Squire, quoted in Donald H. Graves, "Language Arts Textbooks: A Writing Process and Evaluation," *Language Arts* 54 (October 1977): 819.

ingenious, is enough. Neither is the comment, "Write whatever you want." Children need time to become one with their subject matter, to mull over what they want to say, and to suit it to their skills and their audience. Too often, they may feel that they are working exclusively to meet the teacher's whim.

The typical ten-minute warm-up period is just about enough time to get a drink of water, sharpen pencils, and start to worry. It is hardly adequate for thinking through, for feeling, for personalizing. With so little preparation, most children find it impossible to produce writing that is creative or self-satisfying. Unless youngsters care about what they are writing, they will continue to moan and groan when the teacher says, "Today we are going to write." It may be helpful here to look at the approaches of two third-grade teachers as they guide the writing of their students.

It is Valentine's Day, and Janet Friedman's students enter the room armed with the usual paraphernalia—homemade lacy valentines, store-bought greeting cards, and boxes of candy. Everything will be shared with the teacher and favorite friends in the class. There is an air of expectancy and excitement as the children chatter and laugh. It's obviously a special day.

Trying to capitalize on what seems to be their natural motivation, Ms. Friedman suggests that the children write about Valentine's Day. After a brief discussion, the children begin to write and come up with the sort of clichés associated with greeting cards, billboards, and television commercials. Something has happened to the joyfulness that was in full evidence thirty minutes before. The balloon has been punctured. However, the teacher seems pleased; some products are recopied for the bulletin board, and the writing period ends.

Natalie Appel teaches across the hall from Janet, and her third-graders arrive with the same enthusiasm. Her approach is somewhat different. A good part of the morning is devoted to discussion and creative dramatic activities about Valentine's Day: its history, the good and bad feelings it generates, and the sharing of personal experiences. The teacher considers this time the precomposing period. The children are putting their thoughts together, trying on new ideas, and generally adding to their information about the holiday. Some youngsters are looking at books and pictures made available by the teacher. Others are planning further dramatics activities. A small group uses drawing as their preparation for writing. This is not unusual. The visual arts is the means by which many youngsters organize their perceptions of the world. One well-known study describes a seven-year-old who seesawed between drawing and writing, attending to one and then the other. Recording styles differ as children do; impressions are represented in different ways.[8]

---

[8]Donald H. Graves. "An Examination of the Writing Processes of Seven Year Old Children," *Research in the Teaching of English* 9 (Winter 1975): 227–41.

Ms. Appel notices that some children have begun to write; others are obviously still not ready. Each child has a distinctive style. "What should I write?" a few still ask who desire adult approval and are not yet ready to listen to their own drummer. These children are spoken to tenderly by the teacher. She thinks they are really asking, "Who should I be?" She responds with comments such as

> "What would you like to write?"
>
> "I certainly liked what you wrote last week."
>
> "It's hard for me to know what's right for you."
>
> "Don't worry! Whatever you feel is right."

The questions that children ask in such a situation often give evidence of their lack of confidence and their preoccupation with doing what will please.

Some children say, "I don't know what to write." "Are they verbalizing that they don't have enough thoughts and are not yet ready to write?" the teacher wonders. She decides to take a more active role. "How do you feel about Valentine's Day?" she asks. "Do you remember anything about Valentine's Day last year?" "Would you like to hear a poem that I wrote about the holiday?"

We have all experienced the phenomenon of not being able to express what we are thinking. What may be operating is the old language progression mentioned in the first chapter: one may understand something but be unable to say it, say it but be unable to read it, read it but be unable to write it.

The written work eventually produced by this class is of a higher quality and even greater in quantity than that produced by Ms. Friedman's group. Though the price exacted has been costly in terms of time, Ms. Appel can professionally defend the hourly expenditure because the children are growing in ability to conceptualize and use language. The children in her class are being allowed to discover for themselves how best to express their ideas. They are listening, speaking, and reading before they write. They are writing only when they are ready to do so. Their teacher is unwilling to run the risk of destroying the desire to write by demanding its appearance before it is ready to emerge.

The Composing Stage

When children are actively involved in putting their thoughts down on paper they are in the composing stage. The teacher, careful not to be intrusive, circulates among her students quietly answering and asking questions, making some brief comments of her own.

> *Encouraging feeling:* "I can just see that bird. You must feel strongly to have written so well about him."

Suggesting more detail: "Could you tell a little bit more about the way the house looked after the robbers left?"

Writing with an audience in mind: "That's a great story. Could you include some more information so that the reader will better understand why Danny could never go back to camp?"

Providing concrete suggestion: "Do you think that your ideas might flow more smoothly if you combined these two sentences?"

Encouraging more of the same: "I like the way that you are describing that beach at night."

Asking for more voice: "You really seem to understand what will happen if we continue to waste our natural resources. How could you show your feelings more strongly?"

Focusing on a broader view: "I can tell that you appreciated the mummies at the Tutankhamen Exhibit. Were there some other artifacts that also impressed you?"

Extending thinking: "Writing science fiction certainly seems like fun. Did you ever wonder why people are so fascinated by the possibility that other worlds exist?"

A word of caution: Suggestions from an authority figure can be taken as personal criticism. For some youngsters, such comments from a teacher would amount to an attack not only on their writing but on their whole being. It is understandable why many hesitate to reveal themselves. Whenever possible, the teacher should offer such suggestions in question form, always implying that the basic decisions on the matter belong to the writer.

The Rewriting Stage

> Read over your compositions, and when you meet a passage which you think is particularly fine, strike it out.
>
> —Samuel Johnson

Teachers should continually highlight the need for rewriting. As has been said by many, there is probably no such thing as writing—just rewriting. Too often, however, rewriting deteriorates into recopying, and children learn to play the game. They write less the first time! The following are one writing teacher's suggestions for helping children feel responsible for the act of rewriting:

1. Break the traditional classroom interaction; the student writes, the teacher points out the errors, the student corrects.
2. Give the child a choice as to which work in a folder should be rewritten.
3. Let the child make the ultimate decision about how the work is to be finished.
4. Have oral and/or written dialogues with the child in which time you give

your reactions and the child comments and asks questions. The writer, however, has the last word on what changes are to be made.

5. Do not mark up the whole paper. Aim at a few concrete changes in expression.

6. Give children the feeling that there are many ways to change a piece of writing. Change does not mean that they were wrong the first time.

7. Emphasize the content and the ideas over the mechanics.[9]

The timing of the rewriting stage is an important variable. Any rewriting must be done before the writer loses enthusiasm for the piece. This change in feeling may take weeks or only hours. The sensitive teacher will recognize the importance of entering before the door has closed.

During the rewriting stage, the child should be helped to consider once again who will read the work. The imagined audience should always be more than the teacher. In this context, the child will be encouraged to embrace other than authority figures and to consider factors beyond mere mechanics. Considerations like tone, vocabulary, and clarity will assume greater importance.

Editing and proofreading are skills that have an essential place in the rewriting stage. If the need to revise is understood at the beginning, the change is seen as positive growth rather than failure. Fewer young writers will ask, "Do I have to?"

HELPING CHILDREN TO WANT TO WRITE

Who doesn't like the sound of their own voice? What joy when we like what we have written. Dorothy Parker said it well, "I hate to write but I love having written." Children as well just have to taste the intoxicating nectar of their own voices to become hooked on writing. Consider Peter, a first grader, whose teacher on hearing the boy tell about a lighthouse he had visited while on vacation in New England, wrote down Peter's comments and read them back to him. The sound of his own words was heady and gratifying to the child. He wanted to hear more and asked if he could write the story again by himself.

Many teachers have noted that when children are excited and awakened about something, the desire to express is spontaneous. Yet, many children have become disenchanted with writing because it was presented as a mindless, impersonal exercise. This need not happen; most youngsters enter school afire with a sense of wonder about the world. Their spoken language is poetic; metaphoric expressions abound. Inanimate objects are given a life of their own. The fire needs only to be stoked by a sensitive teacher who believes that all children can write.

[9]Mimi Schwartz, "Rewriting or Recopying: What Are We Teaching?" *Language Arts* 54 (October 1977): 756–59.

ACTIVITIES FOR EXTENDING PERCEPTIONS
IN PREPARATION FOR WRITING

1. *Contemplating the fantastic*

Ask children to imagine that they live on a heretofore undiscovered planet. How do they spend their time? What do they eat? What are the predominant sights and smells? To whom do they speak?

2. *Listening to music*

Children listen to a musical tone poem such as "Till Eulenspiegel," which tells a story through music. Have them describe what they think is happening.

3. *Pretending to be somebody or something else*

After looking at several pictures of soldiers, children discuss what it would feel like to be one. What emotions might they experience?

4. *Looking at works of art*

Have children view several works by one artist, say Van Gogh. Tell them something about the artist's life. They can then make some judgments about the works of art. Help them to consider how the artist might have felt during the creation of these works.

5. *Discovering extraordinary relationships*

Have children discover connections between things in an inventive way: people and hurricanes, mirrors and numbers. Have them imagine that they are the horn in a car. Let them describe their experiences.

6. *Having an imaginary conversation with a well-known personality*

What would they say? How might the person respond? Are they behaving authentically?

7. *Reading stories and poems*

After reading a story, children can be helped to increase their identification with a well-defined character, by putting themselves in the character's situation. Would they have reacted the same way? Differently? Encourage them to act out a situation from the book.

8. *Combining the unusual*

Ask children to imagine inviting both animate and inanimate objects to their next party. Which ones would they choose? Why? How would they arrange communication among their guests?

9. *Inventing the unusual*

Children can devise "crazy" inventions: a machine that does their homework, a house that remembers, a car that has a mind of its own, a computer that prepares dinner. For some good ideas, see *1000 Inventions* by Alan Benjamin.

10. *Going ahead in time*

Children can consider what life may be like in 100, 500, or 1,000 years. Will people look, feel, or behave differently?

Implicit in the suggestions listed on page 325 is the belief that extending perceptions develops readiness for creative or practical writing. A child's personal spark may be felt not only in a poem but also in a thank-you note, a list of activities, a weather report, or a letter to a hospitalized classmate. Most important is the feeling that the writing is serving a purpose for oneself or others.

Receiving Writing

The phrase "receiving students' writing" is positive; it implies acceptance. The teacher who "receives" children's writing is furthering expression. Children will not write if they are afraid that their work will be ridiculed, demeaned, or rejected. In accepting a child's writing, you are accepting the child.

In what ways does receiving differ from evaluating? Evaluation by a teacher usually implies a rating, a decision made on quality with a grade appended. Receiving, at its best, is more positively oriented and, though evaluative, in some sense places minimal if any emphasis on the grade. Its major purpose is to encourage the child to write more and better.

Children should understand from the very beginning that they may write for themselves, for classmates, for the teacher, for parents, or for the community at large. For too long, students have been led to believe that they wrote only for the teacher and so a kind of external standard crept in. "What would she like me to say?" "What is easiest to write with correct spelling?" "Can I tell her what I really think?" When children appreciate that they are not writing exclusively for their teacher, a weight is lifted; as the audience expands a range of attitudes and standards are brought into focus. A classroom environment that encourages the sharing of writing among students places the teacher-child relationship in a different perspective. In this setting, children's opinions are sought and respected.

Evaluating Writing

Since we want to encourage young writers to critically read their own as well as others' writing, teachers should try to develop their criteria for writing in conjunction with the class. Along with informing the students, this collaboration will direct the teacher away from adult standards that are not applicable to children's writing. The Grosse Pointe Model for evaluating writing, referred to earlier, is designed to reflect and describe the actual writing behavior of children, not what adults believe it to be or think it ought to be.

Whatever standards teacher and students devise must allow for different forms of writing. An informative piece on the Mexican pyramids

---

DO'S AND DON'TS ON RECEIVING WRITING

DO	DON'T
1. Respond both orally and/or in writing to children's work.	1. Don't judge writing by what happens on individual papers. Writing is a process.
2. Let everyone in the class write and receive writing.	2. Try not to place a grade on writing.
3. Develop cooperative standards for evaluating writing with the children.	3. Don't always evaluate.
4. Frequently ask, "What made you write this?"	4. Don't use a red pencil. (One child described it as a bloody knife.)
5. Receive everything, but it is not necessary to react to everything. Respond in a way that encourages further writing.	5. Don't reject children's evaluations of writing.
6. Respond first as a reader, second as a teacher.	6. Don't command writing.
7. Encourage dialogues among students by means of established guidelines.	7. Don't comment too soon.
8. Encourage self-evaluation through dialogues, application of standards, and expressed appreciation for a unique perspective.	
9. Recognize that writing is personal property.	
10. Sometimes say, "You don't have to write anything."	

---

should be received differently from a haiku poem. An absence of paragraphs may work for a highly inventive dream sequence but not for a letter of complaint. What follows is a list of categories from which criteria may be developed:

1. *Content*
   What is the child saying or trying to say? Why did he or she write about a little bird? A baby brother? A bicycle? Does the work mean something special to the child?

2. *Organization*
   Is the composition or poem going someplace? If a story is being told, can the narrative structure be followed?

3. *Characterization*
   Are believable characters being developed? What do they look like? How do they feel? What are their reactions?

4. *Tone*
   Does the work have its own quality? Is it humorous? Angry? Sad? Detached?

5. *Voice*
   Has the writer expressed his or her own reactions? Is there a genuineness about the expression? Is there a consistent point of view?

6. *Sentence Length*
   Are both simple and compound sentences used?

7. *Vocabulary*
   Are the words used appropriate, varied, descriptive, imaginative?

8. *Spelling, Punctuation, Grammar*
   Are there repetitive errors? Are there patterns of expression that should be altered?

The best way of finding answers to the questions raised in the above categories is through conversations between writer and reader. Obviously, only two or three areas should be considered at one sitting. These dialogues may take place during any of the three stages of writing. These exchanges offer young writers the courage to be, evidence that what they write is read, and the impetus to stretch their thinking further.

Although mechanics may be mentioned in these conversations, they should not at any time be the primary focus. The teacher's initial responses should be to content rather than form.

THE COURAGE TO EDIT

It requires no courage to alter what someone else has written, but the courage to edit one's own work can come only from the feeling that it is a self-serving activity. The best editing of a student's writing results from evaluation done by the writer, the writer's peers, the teacher, or any combination of persons. But whoever is doing the editing must enter into the process with a healthy respect for the integrity of the work.

Editing may be approached from two aspects: (1) the remolding of ideas and (2) the correction of the mechanics of writing (punctuation, grammar, spelling, and so on). The correction of mechanics can be referred to as proofreading. It is certainly the least threatening aspect of editing and can be taught with relative efficiency. Dictionaries, grammars, language arts workbooks, and experienced people are the ready

QUESTIONS FOR THE WRITER-EDITOR

Of Prose

1. Did I say what I wanted to say?
2. Did I take too long to say it?
3. Was I convincing?
4. Could my vocabulary have been more expressive?
5. Do I repeat ideas or words too often?
6. Do my sentences vary enough? In length? In kind?

Of Poetry

1. Did I express honest feeling? Does my poem sound like me?
2. Am I beginning to move away from everyday words into poetic language?
3. Is my poem a unit of thought?
4. Do the words in my poem have a sense of movement? A nice flow?
5. If I used rhyming words, does the line sound as if I am rushing to rhyme?

resources. But the tools to assist a youngster in remolding his or her ideas are sometimes more elusive. The ability to edit one's own writing develops slowly, often impeded by reluctance and subjectivity. Sometimes, a series of questions placed on bulletin boards around the room can help. Language arts textbooks can also be helpful. *New Directions in English* is one series that prepares children to edit their own work by having them examine selections to determine whether the writing fulfilled its purposes. Questions are asked about the main idea, details, sequencing, and style.

Children devise rather inventive ways of editing their materials. They consult other students, use guidelines posted around the room, confer with parents and teachers, and generally enlist outside help if they genuinely care about the finished product. Granted, it is not always easy to get children to evaluate their writing. It happens only if there is trust. Thus it is more likely to occur when

1. Standards have been cooperatively developed.
2. The atmosphere in the classroom is an accepting one.
3. Direction and guidance in evaluating writing is available.
4. Writing is valued as a means of personal growth.
5. Written efforts are not rejected by the teacher.
6. Writing is not graded, only commented upon.
7. The reasons for evaluating writing are appreciated.

8. There is an opportunity to share writing with others.

9. Children have the chance to select their best writing.

PROOFREADING

Proofreading, an important aspect of evaluation, is one of the last stages of the editing process. Its focus is on form and mechanics. Some teachers provide proofreading instruction to students in small groups, with writing samples (not necessarily the children's work) as worksheets. But children also devise their own types of proofreading. Margie asks the best speller in the class to proofread her story. Cindy consults her best friend on punctuation. Eddie joins the group that is working with the teacher.

There have been classes in which the members of a rotating proofreading committee were available to read their classmates' work. First, the writer reread and corrected the material, then gave it to a friend for further suggestions and finally, if desired, asked for the advice of the proofreading committee.

Like other editing standards, proofreading criteria should be developed with the group. Obviously, grade level will determine the complexity and number of criteria, but some form of evaluation should begin as soon as children are ready to write. A second grader can look over his or her work to see whether each sentence begins with a capital letter. Third graders can add to their check list and consider paragraph and sentence construction. What is important is that children have an appropriate check list available. Here is an example:

Check List for the Proofreader

1. Have you capitalized the first word, the last word, and all the important words in the title?

2. Do all of your sentences give complete thoughts?

3. Does each paragraph tell about one topic?

4. Have you indented the first word of each paragraph?

5. Have you capitalized the first word of each sentence?

6. Have you used the correct punctuation mark at the end of each sentence?

7. Have you checked the spelling of each word?

8. Have you used *is, are, was,* and *were* correctly?

9. Have you left neat and even margins at the sides of your paper?

10. Is your writing easy to read?[10]

A natural motivation for editing and carefully proofreading the fin-

[10]Adapted from Walter T. Petty and Julie M. Jensen's *Developing Children's Language* (Boston: Allyn & Bacon, 1980), p. 401. Valuable information on proofreading may also be found in Dorothy Grant Hennings and Barbara M. Grant's *Content and Craft* (Englewood Cliffs, N.J.: Prentice-Hall, 1973).

ished product is the possibility of its display or public use. Classrooms, where writing is a way of life, should provide outlets for the finished product.

SHARING, DISPLAYING, AND PUBLISHING

Sharing a written work may bring a child into closer contact with his or her peer group, opening the gates to feelings of satisfaction, a sense of communion with others and even a sense of status. However, the decision to share the finished product should belong to the writer.

Teachers can encourage sharing by suggesting outlets for children's written work. But distinctions should be made between what is offered for oral sharing and what is presented for publication. Children can readily appreciate that a product to be displayed requires more careful editing because it serves as a model for others and is a final statement. Preparations for oral publication are usually less rigorous. Dividing a class into small groups for oral sharing has two distinct advantages: more children can participate, and the writer may feel less self-conscious during his or her presentation. Having children prepare an audiotape or television program of readings based on their writings is another means of sharing orally. Like a mask or puppet head, the synthetic medium may provide the sensitive child with a kind of anonymity. These productions may be shared with other classes, aired during assembly programs, or transmitted through the school media.

There are many opportunities for teachers to publish the work of their students. In this context, publishing means duplicating the child's work in any printed form: typing, rexographing, mimeographing, xeroxing, or commercial printing. Having a work printed in the class newsletter may mean as much to a child as having it published in a mass-market paperback. The audience the child desires most is his or her peer group.

Typing the children's edited work is a good beginning. Parents can be enlisted in this endeavor, and children can do some of their own typing. The finished product can then be displayed in a variety of attractive ways around the classroom and the school. Capitalize on the fact that children, like many adults, get pleasure from seeing their efforts in print.

In recent years collections of children's writing have grown in popularity, and some have even achieved commercial success. *The Me Nobody Knows: Children's Voices from the Ghetto*, one such collection, was even transformed into a theatrical success. Stephen A. Joseph, a teacher in Harlem, collated the poetic words of his students, recognizing their universal appeal. Arthur Jackson, a fifteen-year-old, wrote,

> I have felt lonely, forgotten or even
>   left out, set apart from the rest of
>   the world.
> I never wanted out. If anything I wanted in.

WAYS TO SHARE STUDENTS' WRITING

With the Class

1. Hang mobiles of written work.
2. String clotheslines of writing.
3. Prepare filmstrips and tape recordings of children reading their work.
4. Paste written products on fabric hangings.
5. Use bulletin boards and display cases.
6. Set up clipboards of writing collections on a particular topic.
7. Keep folders of students' writing.
8. Have students make individual or class books of their writing.

With the School

1. Distribute class newsletters.
2. Submit material to class/school magazines or yearbooks.
3. Give readings to other classes directly or over the public address system.
4. Prepare an Op-Ed weekly bulletin for posting.
5. Organize special assembly programs to present students' writing.
6. Prepare folders and bound books of writing for donation to the library or for circulation to other classes.

With the Larger Community

1. Encourage and send written work to local publications.
2. Submit work to magazines that publish children's writing, for example, "Child Life," "Cricket," and "Highlights for Children."
3. Arrange for students to read their writing at hospitals, nursing homes, and other schools.
4. Consider publishing a collection of students' work.

Nell Moore, age fourteen, wrote,

WHO LOOKS

Beneath the sidewalks
  to tunnels-
  merging
  separating-
  searching out the
  Earthy blackness;
Behind the neons

> proving
> camouflage
> for purple-veined faces;
> Past the faces
> hiding
> selves.[11]

Anthologies of children's writing have always been popular among teachers. *Miracles: Poems by Children of the English-Speaking World,* and *Journeys: Prose by Children of the English-Speaking World,* two books edited by Richard Lewis, are frequently used to inspire young students to write. The current wave of children's writing reflects the new realism in children's literature. There is a broader range of subjects; the approach is more direct, and greater literary license pervades.

A word of caution—publication should not be allowed to become the writer's only motivation. Frequent sharing should be a routine part of classroom life. Less than perfect pieces or those in various stages of development may be read. Satisfaction can be a private enterprise taking the form of a personal writing folder tucked deep into the recesses of a desk. For most children, the ultimate purpose of writing should be growth and individual discovery about who they are and how they think, not celebrity.

THE SPACE AND TIME TO WRITE

Glenn is sitting at his desk. Susan is lying on the floor. Cynthia sits propped up against the closet, and Danny leans on the window sill. They are all doing the same thing—writing. Mr. Gregory, the teacher, has no rules about where to write. There is a writing center in the room, but it cannot accommodate everyone. No matter where the writing is produced, the children know that it will be highly regarded by the teacher and that he will offer understanding responses. In his class, the need to write as a means of letting off steam is recognized. One child with problems has permission to write whenever he feels the desire. In all children, the desire to write increases as they sense that their communications are valued. The element of immediacy provided by the classroom audience is an important factor. A greater degree of maturity is required when students write for an invisible public. Try to encourage student-to-student communications in all of the above activities preparing the way for sharing with a larger group.

In its physical plan, Mr. Gregory's classroom is different from many traditional ones. As you enter the room, you may not be certain whether you are in a library, a crafts shop, or a museum. The setting is a pot-

[11]Stephen M. Joseph, ed., *The Me Nobody Knows: Children's Voices from the Ghetto* (New York: Avon, 1969) pp. 36 and 82.

pourri of school furniture and "homey" additions. The teacher has asked the children to post notices—and even this served as a meaningful writing activity—requesting old chairs, sofas, rugs, and bookcases. A number of contributions resulted.

The room is organized around centers of interest. The writing center is a well-equipped corner complete with dictionaries, alphabetical spelling lists, a thesaurus, reference books, and collections of poetry and prose. It contains a typewriter, tables, unusual objects, and a variety of writing instruments, including pens for calligraphy. Many materials other than the usual lined paper are available for the children to write on; these include adding machine tape, large newsprint, cardboard rollers, scraps of wallpaper, blank books, graph paper, and oak tag. Some surfaces like the sides of cartons, are huge; little bits of paper are suitable for intimate messages. Memorable quotes can be mounted on rollers around the Center. In one corner, there is a class mailbox with envelopes that can be sealed.

The other centers in the room (science, art, woodworking, and so on) foster writing as well. Sometimes they provide needed information; at other times, the catalyst for writing. The science center may be the place where Michael goes to check information about the migration of birds before he writes his report. In the art center, children are finding out what happens when they mix colors. They will record their observations and share them with the class. In the math center, three children have been learning the metric system by measuring their height and charting their growth. They are keeping careful records of the changes. For the past three months, a group of children have been observing a guinea pig in the science center and recording the vital statistics of her development. Their findings are reported to the class. Work in the centers—observing, describing, comparing, and recording—is basic to the writing program in this class.

Writing eats up time, and this voracious monster refuses to conform to schedules. Young students often require more time for getting their words down on paper than has been allotted. The teacher should allow work to continue at least until the essential thrust of what a youngster wishes to say has been completed. A variety of plans may be put into effect by teachers who want their students to write.

Edith Friedman, a fifth-grade teacher, schedules what she calls "Writing Days." The day is organized into flexible time segments during which children go through the precomposing, composing, and rewriting stages. Precomposing time may be spent independently in conference with the teacher or interacting with other children. It may involve talking into a tape recorder, typing out lists of ideas or brainstorming. The pacing of the various stages will vary with the child. At appropriate points, composing activities will be interrupted for physical activity, recess, lunch, and so on. During the actual writing time—different for each child—the teacher encourages the development of first and second drafts, often written without her assistance. Available as a walking speller or a grammarian, the teacher encourages the children to take the initiative in requesting help. There is adequate time during the Writing Day to rewrite, proofread, edit, and share. The children may be writing on a variety of creative or functional topics touching different aspects of the curriculum. Eric is doing his report on the relationship between rivers and the growth of cities. Arlene is busy writing up her research on her family's roots. Joseph is preparing an original story, and Linda is adding to her journal.

Ms. Friedman and her students appreciate the unhurried atmosphere of Writing Days. This expenditure of time is not a concern to this teacher. She feels that through the writing experience her students are translating curriculum into meaningful personal terms. In addition, they are developing fluency with language, learning to work independently, making judgments about the quality of written products, and augmenting a variety of cognitive and affective skills.

LET THE TEACHER WRITE TOO

In-service courses for teachers on writing usually focus on how to assist children to write more proficiently. It is assumed that the teacher is relatively comfortable with his or her writing skills. This is often a myth. Many educators have serious doubts and even anxieties about their abilities in this area. Probably very few people are satisfied with their level of writing; but in a communication-oriented profession like teaching, a writing deficiency is a distinct liability. Some teachers report experiencing a kind of literary "rigor mortis" when they are asked to write a letter, a report, or a detailed evaluation. In many cases, teachers themselves are the products of elementary and secondary schools that simply did not require much writing. The problem may have been compounded in college where the emphasis was on objective examinations that required brief completion answers, true-false responses, and multiple-choice selections. Many teachers may have had minimal opportunity to exercise their writing skills. As a result, they too avoid what has become a distasteful and arduous task—putting pen to paper.

Yet most teachers would like to write better and be more effective teachers of writing. More active participation in the writing process is the key. It is most important that the teacher struggle with the writer's dilemmas. "I can't begin; "I'm not saying what I want to"; "My work is uninteresting"; "I can't write on this topic." Without ongoing writing experiences, it is difficult for the teacher to appreciate the complexity, difficulty, and potential of the process as he or she guides the students. Would we expect a poor swimmer to teach lifesaving, an untrained mechanic to provide instruction in auto repair, or a tone-deaf person to give violin lessons?

What can you do to improve your writing skills? Now ask yourself the real question: "What am I willing to do?" "How much of an effort am I prepared to make?" The most important factor is personal motivation; next comes acceptance of the fact that writing improves with practice. Together, they are the pearl in your pocket. All you have to do is take it out and shine it up. No promises that you will write another *Rubaiyat* or be the next F. Scott Fitzgerald, but with motivation and practice you are guaranteed greater writing competence. Set realistic goals and keep clear communication at the top of the list. The writing process is not quite so mysterious as you may have been led to believe. For most of us mortals, it is more perspiration than inspiration, more practice than inherent ability, and more patience than talent. The ability to apply seat of pants to chair helps too!

Personal anxiety has a lot to do with how much and how well you write. In the book *Writing Without Teachers*, Peter Elbow looks at writing in a way that may relieve some of the tension that many people feel about the process. He suggests that you write a lot. Even the physical activity of writing will get your juices running and thoughts percolating. Since writing is talking to yourself, you need many stimuli to keep the ideas popping. An idea is like the little white cue ball on the pool table, it starts things going. There has to be a beginning. A giant redwood began with a seed. So it is with writing. Simply by writing you germinate ideas. Though you may choose to reject many of these thoughts, they in turn trigger others.

> The consequence is that you must start by writing the wrong meanings in the wrong words; but keep writing till you get the right meanings in the right words.[12]

In the same brief but very wise book, Elbow suggests giving up the conventional notion that writers clearly figure out what they want to say and *then* put it into language. In many ways, this notion sabotages efforts to write. How do you know what you want to say until you've said it? If you permit yourself the freedom to delay structure and allow the words to take over, the process will be far more efficient than it may seem. This is not to suggest that you should begin writing without any plan. However, excessive clarification and outlining may be accomplished at the expense of spontaneity and idea building. Furthermore, it is inefficient to be forced to conform to an organizational model that you developed before you knew what you wanted to say. "Think of writing then not as a way to transmit a message but as a way to grow and cook a message."[13]

If we could tack up a motto for teachers who want to improve their writing, it would simply say, "Keep On Writing." Write every day for at

---

[12]Peter Elbow, *Writing Without Teachers* (New York: Oxford University Press, 1973), p. 26.
[13]Elbow, *Writing Without Teachers, p. 15.*

WRITING CATALYSTS FOR TEACHERS

1. Write about a family experience from the past. Try to recall as many details about your thoughts and feelings at that time.

2. Look at a collection of photographs by an artist/photographer and write your reactions to several of the pictures. (The work of Diane Arbus, Henri Cartier-Bresson, or Margaret Bourke-White is very provocative.)

3. Before giving writing assignments to students do them yourself.

4. Describe the physical characteristics of a person whom you admire or despise.

5. Share your writing with a colleague. Ask for oral and written comments. Examine your own feelings about the tone and clarity of the comments. Were only value-laden words used? (I liked, I didn't like.) Were comments stated as polarities? (Good, bad.) Were comments helpful in that they suggested a direction? (You might want to further describe this character.) Were comments sometimes phrased as questions so that you could respond? (What did you mean by the phrase, "I do not deserve what I have"?)

6. Write a short poem about a deeply emotional experience.

7. Describe an embarrassing situation.

8. Respond in a letter or an essay to an editorial that you have recently read.

9. Start a journal or a diary. Write something in it every day, if only a few lines.

10. React to a literary work. Give your feelings about a character, a situation, or a mood.

11. Examine with a colleague a short but effective piece of writing. In what ways do the vocabulary, topic, sentences, organization, tone, and contrasts contribute to its strength?

12. Identify, discuss, and write metaphorical comparisons that heighten awareness of unlike things (cities and people, seeds and paintings, music and money).

13. Develop your sensory equipment by identifying with the feelings of an animal or plant. You may first have to increase your experience before you can empathize. (Smell some flowers, cuddle an animal, cook some vegetables.) Consider in how many other ways you can experience the flower, the animal, the vegetable. Write about your reactions.

14. Listen to a favorite musical selection that has no lyrics. Write about your feelings.

15. Consider that you may never have been asked to write on topics about which you really have something to say. Write and see how you really feel.

least ten minutes. Write what you ask the children to write. Writing is not a visual experience; it can not be learned by watching. Writing is not a spectator sport.[14] Pre-service and in-service courses that give actual writing practice can be very valuable, but they are not always available. Peter Elbow suggests teacherless writing classes where at least seven people commit themselves to a ten-week stretch of classes. If this option is not available, try some of the writing activities suggested in this chapter and the next two chapters. Remember that writing is a process and time is the tariff exacted. Be patient with yourself as you pass through the stages of precomposing, composing, and rewriting.

The Teachers and Writers Collaborative produces materials that might be helpful to you in the process of improving your own as well as your students' writing skills. TWC places professional writers in classrooms to work on a regular basis with teachers in order to encourage children to create their own literature. What groups like these are trying to do becomes apparent only if we as teachers ourselves experience the writing process.

Writing is a developmental process, one stage reinforcing the other. As you do your own writing, recognize the building block quality of each phase. Precomposing is thinking, editing is further thinking, and writing is the mortar for this interaction. What initially appears to be disorganization may not be that at all. Just keep writing. Write through your excuses no matter how often they raise their demonic heads. Don't get bogged down by one word or how to begin. Handle the discomfort, stay with the anxiety, and keep writing. Slowly, you will begin to pull yourself out. You may not like everything you write, but you will like the idea that while you are writing, you are growing.

Writing is an exercise in finding your own voice. If only for this reason, it is a personally important growing activity. We all have many forms of energy to release. Our intellectual capacities need nourishment and writing is good food. The sense of freedom that eventually accompanies a satisfying writing experience will have you clamoring for more of the same.

TEACHER COMPETENCES

The list of selected competences for teachers that follows may serve to summarize this chapter:

1. The teacher will be able to state and give examples of ways in which writing may be used as a growth process for adults and children
2. The teacher will be able to analyze his or her own writing assets and liabilities.

[14]See article by Doris Master, "Inservice Education–Not a Spectator Sport!" *Language Arts* 55 (May 1978): 597–601.

3. The teacher will carry out many of the writing exercises identified for the students.

4. The teacher will be able to plan writing activities that reflect the children's developmental levels.

5. The teacher will be able to assist children to develop writing readiness by planning activities that increase oral vocabulary and provide practice in syntactic patterning.

6. The teacher will be able to aid children's conceptual growth by highlighting activities in the identification and development of main ideas.

7. The teacher will provide practice in the basic processes relevant for composing: searching, reflecting, selecting, organizing, writing, and revising.

8. The teacher will give children the opportunity to dictate stories as long as this is necessary.

9. The teacher will be able to explain, recognize, and provide time for the three stages of the writing process.

10. The teacher will be able to utilize several means for extending children's perceptions as a preparation for writing.

11. The teacher will be able to devise many situations to facilitate the interpersonal sharing of written products of the teacher and the students.

12. The teacher will be able to develop standards for evaluating writing in conjunction with the students.

13. The teacher will be able to write evaluations that encourage further writing.

14. The teacher will be able to set the stage for continuing self-evaluation by the students.

15. The teacher will be able to find many means of sharing, displaying, and publishing children's written work.

16. The teacher will be able to provide the space, time, and atmosphere for encouraging writing.

17. The teacher will be able to respond to much of the written work done by the children.

18. The teacher will be able to determine whether writing is valued by the students.

19. The teacher will take opportunities to be a writer, too.

Afterview   Writing is a sharing process. The best writers expose their souls and share their authentic inner selves. "To thine own self be true," can be translated into a philosophy for teaching writing. It means providing time for children to prepare to write and to engage in the process of composing. It means supporting all forms of personal expression, not only writing activities. Writing is a process that gathers sustenance from and enriches each curriculum area. Teachers actively caught up in the writing process may be more likely to recognize its stages, its rewards, and its frustrations. Children must learn from their own experiences that writing improves with practice. Confidence in one's ability to write is the springboard to competence.

WHEN YOU WANT TO KNOW MORE

1. Speak with some children who say they hate to write. Find out why they feel this way. Can you identify any similarities in their negative reactions? Do they feel a sense of helplessness when confronted with blank paper? What can a teacher do to alleviate children's discomfort with the writing process?

2. Try to analyze your own attempts in getting writing started. Speak with some colleagues about their difficulties in beginning the process. Develop a list of "blocks" that stop writing from starting. Using your knowledge of these "blocks," how would you structure initial writing experiences for children?

3. Develop the practice of writing freely about anything for at least ten minutes a day. After one week, read over what you have written. What are you learning about yourself? What are you learning about your writing style? Repeat the practice for another week.

4. Look at some popular elementary language arts workbooks for children. Are many opportunities provided for children to do their own composing? Select the best examples of activities designed to assist the child in the composing process. Avoid activities that focus on the mechanics of expression.

5. Consult the section on sensory writing in James Moffet's *Student-Centered Language Arts and Reading*. What suggestions does Moffet offer for providing sensory stimulation as a source of writing material for children?

IN THE CLASSROOM

1. Carefully observe children as they write to see if they are developing their own ideas. Spend some private time with those children who seem to look to others for ideas. Help them to sink taps into their own experiences.

2. Plan a series of writing experiences in which the students are requested to write for each other. Have students rather than the teacher evaluate the writing. What changes do you notice in classroom atmosphere or student attitude?

3. When writing activities are developed, how much time is devoted to precomposing? Keep a chart for a two-week period to see whether more time is necessary. Poll the children for their opinions.

4. Recognizing the relationship between truthful writing and a positive self-concept, have a small group of children develop and execute writing topics designed to encourage positive feelings in the writer.

5. Consult Ken Macrorie's *Telling Writing*, particularly the section entitled Writing Freely. Use some of the ideas with your class to raise the level of "truth-telling," a prerequisite for effective writing.

SUGGESTED READINGS

Burnews, Alvina Treut; Jackson, Doris C.; and Saunders, Dorothy O. *They All Want to Write*. 3d ed. New York: Holt, Rinehart & Winston, 1964.

Clapp, Ouida H. *On Righting Writing*. Urbana Ill.: National Council of Teachers of English, 1975.

Cramer, Ronald L. *Children's Writing and Language Growth*. Columbus, Ohio: Merrill, 1978.

Evertts, Eldonna L., ed. *Explorations in Children's Writing*. Urbana, Ill.: National Council of Teachers of English, 1970.

Jackson, Jacqueline. *Turn Not Pale, Beloved Snail: A Book About Writing Among Other Things*. Boston: Little, Brown, 1974.

Macrorie, Ken. *telling writing*. 2d ed., rev. Rochelle Park, N.J.: Hayden, 1976.

Moffet, James, and Wagner, Betty Jane. *Student-Centered Language Arts and Reading, K-13: A Handbook for Teachers*. 2d ed. Boston: Houghton Mifflin, 1976.

Murphy, Richard. *Imaginary World: Notes on a New Curriculum*. New York: Teachers and Writers Collaborative, 1974.

West, William W., ed. *On Writing, By Writers*. Boston: Ginn, 1966.

Other Materials

Bernhardt, Bill. *Just Writing: Exercises to Improve Your Writing*. New York: Teachers and Writers Collaborative, 1977.

Gerbrandt, Gary L. *An Idea Book for Acting Out and Writing Language*. Urbana, Ill.: National Council of Teachers of English, 1974.

Norton, Donna E. *Language Arts Activities for Children*. Columbus, Ohio: Merrill, 1980. (See Chapter 5, "Writing Activities.")

CHAPTER 11

Creative Writing Is Basic

Preview Creative expression through language provides youngsters with a basic tool for leading effective, productive lives. Creative writing is life-enriching and essential. Since the nurturance of the feelingful side of children cannot be separated from the training of their cognitive faculties, this chapter will suggest cross-disciplinary activities that encourage a child to explore life with his or her whole being. The many faces of the creative encounter will be identified, along with preparatory strategies for heightening students' awareness of their own sensory abilities. Poetry will be discussed as a form of creative expression natural to children, and the ways in which a teacher of poetry can build on children's experiences with chants, rhymes, street games, and songs will be explored. A variety of poetic forms will be illustrated, along with guidelines for evaluating students' poetic appreciation and expression. Since a child's writing of prose often requires "wake up" and inspirational experiences similar to those commonly applied to the teaching of poetry, the chapter will suggest ways to catalyze creative prose writing using literature, the visual arts, and the world of fantasy. Finally, the evaluation of creative writing will be considered within a context that encourages children to continue to write more effectively and imaginatively.

"Creativity, the ability to explore and investigate, belongs to one of the Basic Drives, a drive without which man cannot exist."

—Viktor Lowenfeld

CREATIVE WRITING, linked as it is to the writer's innermost feelings, is basic to learning itself. And when there is a real reason to write, the skills associated with writing are likely to improve. Finding and expressing one's voice is a serious business, and it continues throughout life. To help children to discover and express this voice should be the primary objective of all creative writing programs. All humans have within themselves the need to express their own uniqueness. Unfortunately, somewhere in the process of coming of age (4? 14? 74?), many of us get the message that who we are should be repressed. Too often we put on masks, cloak our feelings, and attempt to close our creative vents. We never really succeed in this, however. The need to express our personhood either goes underground (setting the stage for neurosis) or emerges in a variety of expressions that exclaim, "This is me."

Creative activity does not necessarily require genius. Creativity can be part of an average person's daily life, as he or she arranges furniture, cooks meals, or writes lesson plans. Molding a pot, building a house, and writing a love letter can all be vehicles for creative expression. No one distills life in exactly the same way, for no one has lived in exactly the same space and time.

WHAT RESEARCH SAYS ABOUT CREATIVITY

All people can be creative.

Creative behavior thrives when nurtured and encouraged.

Creative functioning is fragile and atrophies when not used.

Levels of creative functioning vary.

Creativity requires an emotional set that is flexible and delays structure.

Creativity is nourished by independence.

THE CREATIVE ENCOUNTER

What is it? How do you know when you or your children are experiencing it? These are some of the questions that I asked teachers as I tried to understand the nature of the creative encounter. Their responses read like a description of the qualities that we associate with the creative person. What follows are teachers' anecdotal statements of children having a creative encounter:

1. *Seeing from a new perspective*
   "Annie who liked to draw had done many pictures of our school building. Her best and most creative view, however, was completed when she lay down on the grass outside the school. New details and perspective emerged, and the feeling expressed in the drawing was quite different from any she had done before."

2. *Communicating in a different medium*
   "After hearing the Cornish tale, 'Duffy and the Devil,' our class was so enthusiastic that they planned a pantomime for the other third grades. Because there would be no speaking, the children thought that background scenery and props were important to the audience's understanding of this delightful but not very well-known story. Participation took many forms: most of the children shared ideas, some painted pictures, some collected appropriate props, and a few did the actual construction of scenery. There were no exacting guidelines, but all the ideas seemed to mesh and the mood of the story was communicated."

3. *Uncovering new beauty in the ordinary*
   "Ellen brought a centipede to school. The children were very excited and many remained to observe it for a long time. Some children wrote simple but very feelingful one-line statements about the centipede. The directness and truthfulness of their responses gave them power."

4. *Seeing relationships*
   "The children were taking a nature walk when they heard frogs crossing the grass on their way to a nearby pond. Ted exclaimed, 'It's like an army going back to their camp.' This tickled the fancy of several children and when they got to the pond many began to search for other relationships: 'The weeds are the wood for their houses.' 'The reflection is their mirror.' 'The trees around the pond are protecting all the water animals.' Several children endowed the animals and plants with human capabilities."

5. *Combining the unusual*
   "Our class was making a model of Manhattan. Some children used blocks to construct buildings. Others however realized that the new buildings, because of their unconventional shapes, required the use of a greater variety of materials. The finished product used polyurethane foam, outdoor carpeting, Saran wrap, plasticene people, clay, string, linoleum, slabs of painted cardboard, wood, wire and stretch fabric. The materials taken out of their usual context not only presented a startling city, but suggested the possibility of still other materials which might further change the existing model."

6. *Searching for the personal meaning of things*
"After two months of intensive study of mainland China, I wondered if my fifth graders found any personal meaning in this relatively different culture. It soon became apparent that they found it in varied ways: 'I've gotten into Chinese cooking,' one girl responded. 'Our climate here is like a section of China, and I'm going to plant two kinds of Chinese vegetables.' 'I like doing calligraphy,' said Andrea, 'I can see why it took the Chinese artist so much time.' 'My parents took me to see the folk dancers from the Republic of China and I saw them dance some of the games and rituals that we learned about.' 'The Chinese fairy tales tell some of the same stories that my mother read to me, but just a little differently.' "

7. *Imagining and pretending*
"We had just finished a unit on the United States which emphasized the more dramatic events and personalities of the last twenty years. The children had done well on the paper-and-pencil evaluations, but I was even more delighted to discover that the unit had sparked their creativity. One group developed a docudrama about John F. Kennedy, speculating on the course history would have taken if the President had not been assassinated. In many ways, they were faithful to the essential facts of the era and the public personality of JFK. In some ways, their poetic license seemed even more exciting than the actual history. This reenactment spurred another group to develop their own version of Admiral Peary's successful North Pole venture."

DEVELOPING AWARENESS

The key to awareness lies in the development of our sensory equipment. Encourage children to carefully explore their surroundings, to note the natures of individual things. Firsthand experiences are a good place to begin. Encounters with literature, music, movement, and the visual arts should also be included. Anything that you can do to get children to stop, look, listen, and sense will awaken their awareness.

1. Ask students to do the following:
   a. Notice the beauty of the ordinary.
      Take a good look at a tree, a lemon, a cloud.
   b. Become conscious of the many variations in the most common objects. No two are alike! Compare two tomatoes, two daisies, two eight-year-old redheads.
   c. Recognize how the beauty of things is heightened when they are combined.
      Place an apple on a shiny green leaf, string together a row of shells, place an eggplant in front of a mirror.
   d. Take a close-up look at familiar things. Using a magnifying glass or microscope, look at a pea pod, a piece of driftwood, a feather.
2. Provide activities for children to make greater use of their senses. Utilizing task cards and the appropriate materials, one task card might read:

Task Card

Use your senses to respond to this flower.
a. Listen to it. Touch it. Smell it. Taste it. Talk to it.
b. How do you think it looks from above? Below? In profile?
c. How does it change when it's wet?
d. How is it made?
e. How much do you think it weighs?
In some way, share what you have discovered. Write, talk to some-one, or make a drawing.

3. Though immediate experiences are most desirable, children can also be asked to recall on-the-spot emotional moments of the past. Let your students "recollect in tranquility" an experience when they were afraid. Did they smell it? Hear it? Taste it? Touch it? See it?

4. The surrounding environment is an excellent starting point for your students to heighten awareness. Several years ago, the Museum of Contemporary Crafts in New York City attempted to help New Yorkers experience their environment more deeply. Using the city for sensual investigation, participants were asked to do some of the following as they roamed around the city:

    a. Speak to whatever creature-life you can discover.

    b. Find some water—splash. Listen to its music.

    c. Is there a wind about? Go with its movement for a bit.

    d. Record some dialogue overheard near you.

    e. Smile at three people and note their responses.

   After these experiences, participants were asked to share their reactions.[1] Any variation of the above would be valuable for developing sensitivity in children. The environment may be a subway, a corn field, a frozen lake, a deserted beach. Sharing may be oral, written or through any of the art media.

5. Brainstorm ideas about one thing. In response to the question "What are all the things that you can do with a piece of watermelon?" the children in one second grade responded with the following ideas:

   Cut the fruit, the rind, the seeds. Taste each part, smell each part. Close your eyes and touch each part.

   Squeeze the fruit and taste the juice.

   Place a piece of watermelon on a white paper, on a black paper.

   Dry the seeds and make a necklace.

   Compare the real slice of watermelon to a picture of one.

   Make a collage using the seeds of the watermelon.

   Weigh the watermelon.

   Write a poem about what it feels like to be a watermelon.

   Eat a piece of watermelon and a piece of pickle at the same time.

[1]Paul L. Montgomery, "Museum Theme: Stop, Look, Listen and Sense." *New York Times*, 24 April 1971, p. 31.

Developing awareness has to do with developing a feeling of emotional relatedness or empathy for others. Others include things and animals as well as people. Of course, empathy begins with giving *yourself* the permission to feel. For only after you yourself experience and accept the range of human emotions can you feel for others. Listed below are a number of empathic situations that many teachers have used for sparking creative writing. Think of some of your own as well.

1. You are a broken egg spreading slowly across a griddle. Describe your sensations and viewpoint.
2. You are a dollar bill in the hands of a beggar.
3. You are a black widow spider that has just captured a victim.
4. You are a cross-eyed jack-o'-lantern. How does Halloween look to you?
5. You are a record, a new hit tune. You have just been placed on a turntable and the needle is fast approaching.
6. You are a Cecropia moth, fully developed, ready to break through your cocoon.
7. You are a wave lapping at an abandoned lighthouse.
8. You are a sand castle, being gradually diminished by the incoming tide. How do you feel?
9. You are a bull who is sensitive to green, not red. How does this complicate your life?
10. You are the rope that has just squeezed the life out of a lynched man.
11. You are a new note on the musical scale and have just been sounded.
12. You are a mudpie being fashioned by a two-year-old. Describe your sensations.
13. You are the burned-out light on a Christmas tree.
14. You are the cork in a bottle of champagne that is about ready to let go.
15. You are a cow with a bone out of place in your nose. Whenever you want to "moo," it comes out as "boo." How do you feel?

HOW AWARE ARE YOU?

In your classroom, are feelings being offered by the students? Are they of interest to you?

Do you think that awareness, with its implications for freedom, lack of structure, and perceptual openness, can be taught?

Are you inclined to try new teaching approaches?

Are you questioning your own awareness?

The quest for heightened awareness should be pursued by both teachers and students.

In summary, we could say that creative expression is best nurtured by

1. Exposure to direct experiences with the real world
2. Access to vast amounts of raw material
3. A variety of stimuli
4. The development of the senses
5. Opportunities to experience and reexperience details
6. Contact with encouraging and creative people
7. Exposure to the creative and artistic endeavors of others

POETRY AND CHILDREN

> Inside every man there is a poet who died young.
>
> —Stefan Kanfer

Poetry is a form of written expression that uses language creatively. The poetic mode offers the writer a vehicle through which the imagination can flourish. Yet very few choose the poem as a means of self-expression. In fact, many adults reject poetry. They refuse to read it, let alone write it. Some adults maintain that any feeling they had for poetry was ruined by their experiences in school. Their comments are usually some version of the following:

"I had to memorize poems that I hated."

"There always had to be a 'right' meaning for a line of poetry, and rarely was it my meaning."

"I had teachers who read poetry as if it were a painful duty. They obviously didn't enjoy it."

"Poetry is supposed to have something to do with feeling. I never felt anything."

It is not that poetry has to make the reader feel good. It simply has to make the reader *feel*—sad, joyful, pensive, elated. As Emily Dickinson wrote, "If . . . it makes my whole body so cold no fire can warm me, I know that is poetry."

Somewhere in the process of schooling, the feeling aspects of poetry were sacrificed to an over-concern for memorization and meaning. Today, there has been improvement, but the prevailing attitude toward poetry is still indifference. Fortunately, however, some teachers manage to teach their students to enjoy the reading and writing of poetry. What is the secret? What methods can be used to make poetry an exciting and meaningful experience?

A good beginning is a teacher who likes poetry and children, and sees connections between the two. The language of children is creative and inventive as is the language of poetry. Poetry fills the days of many children: it is in the rhythm of their speech, the lilt of their walk, the cadence of their songs and nursery rhymes. The lore of childhood is filled with the special kind of poetry found in chants, street games, and finger plays. The repetitive quality, found so typically in poetry, is evident in children's speech and in the parodies children themselves compose. Typical of the popular repertoire is

> I'm Popeye the sailorman,
> I live in a garbage can,
> I eat all the worms
> And spit out the germs,
> I'm Popeye the sailorman, toot toot.[2]

Television commercials also offer children the opportunity to parody:

> Pepsi-Cola went to town,
> Coca-Cola shot him down,
> Dr. Pepper fixed him up,
> While drinking a bottle of Seven-Up.

In the scholarly work *One Potato, Two Potato: The Folklore of American Children*, Mary and Herbert Knapp devote a whole chapter to the kinds of rhymes that children develop as they learn to deal with the here and now. Very often, these rhymes express social hostility and take the form of parodies. "Parodic songs provide . . . an informal safety valve for the resentment of American school children.[3]

Jump-rope rhymes have been part of the life of children from frontier days. But, as the Knapps explain, it took the migration from rural farms to smooth city streets for children to put together the dozens of games and hundreds of rhymes that make up modern jump-rope lore. Many jump-rope rhymes reinforce skills learned in school; a recitation of the alphabet is involved in several of these verses, for example:

> Ice cream, ice cream, soda pop,
> Tell me, tell me, when to stop.
> A, B, C, . . .

There are more elaborate versions of the same verse, the rhymes being as varied as children's lives. There are rhymes about sibling rivalry

> Johnny over the ocean,
> Johnny over the sea,

---

[2]The jingles on this page and the following page are taken from Mary and Herbert Knapp's *One Potato, Two Potato: The Folklore of American Children* (New York: Norton, 1976), pp. 164, 165, 254, 113, and 126.

[3]Knapp, *One Potato, Two Potato*, p. 161.

Johnny broke a bottle and blamed it on me.
I told Ma, Ma told Pa,
Johnny got a whippin', ha-ha-ha.

and rhymes about popular fairy tales

Cinderella, dressed in yellow,
Went upstairs to kiss her fellow,
Made a mistake and kissed a snake,
Came downstairs with a bellyache.
How many doctors did it take?
One, two, three, . . .

So many qualities of the formal poem exist in these recreational rhymes that it is difficult to understand how children become indifferent to poetry in school. Eve Merriam writing in *What Can a Poem Do?* explains to children how natural it is for them to enjoy poetry:

A poem, in fact, is very much like you, and that is quite natural, since there is a rhythm in your own body: in your pulse, in your heart beat, in the way you breathe, laugh or cry; in the very way you speak.

Poetry's built-in music makes itself heard through the use of repetition. "This repetition," Merriam notes,

may serve to lull you to rest: "hushaby, hushaby, sleep, my baby, sleep." Or it can startle you awake: "clang, clang, clang went the cymbal; bang, bang, bang, went the drums."[4]

As you read some more about children's folklore, you will begin to recognize how natural the poetic mode is for children. Language play is a part of their lives when they enter school. Teachers can build on the home and street life of American children by using the poetry of their chants, rhymes, and songs.

In recent years, several established poets have turned their attention to the schools. Concerned about the state of the art, they have gone into the classrooms of America to demonstrate that poetry can be as relevant an art form as rock and roll. Poets in the Schools, an organization spearheaded by poets Kenneth Koch and Phillip Lopate, among others, has placed professional writers in classrooms and established workshops for teachers. The organization's publications, particularly *The Whole Word Catalogue*, are helpful resources for teachers interested in exposing their students to new ways of using language.

What is most significant about the work of this group is its general philosophy. Poetry is not seen as an esoteric art form reserved for the select few. It is within the potential and province of all of us to read and write in the poetic mode. We can all become one with a line of poetry—

[4]Eve Merriam, *What Can a Poem Do?* (New York: Atheneum, 1962), pp. 1 and 2.

not every line—but certain poems will certainly engage our feelings. With this philosophy, Kenneth Koch has had remarkable success presenting poetry to both the very young and the old.

In *Wishes, Lies, and Dreams*, Koch discusses teaching children how to write poetry. Much of his advice centers on what poetry does not have to be; it can be summarized as follows:

> Poetry does not have to rhyme.
>
> Poetry does not have to have meter.
>
> Poetry should not be presented as something that is difficult and inaccessible.
>
> Poetry should never be ridiculed.
>
> Specific poems should not be singled out as the "best." This assumes a poem that is the "worst."
>
> All the words in a poem do not have to be spelled correctly. (Spelling can be attended to later.)
>
> Punctuation and neatness are not the objectives in writing poetry.[5]

In describing what has worked with children in a ghetto school in New York City, Koch makes suggestions that can be summarized as follows:

> Begin every line of the poem with "I wish."
>
> Let each line contain a color, an animal, a silly word or a comic-strip character.
>
> Use a repetitive form. (Each line has a comparison or a sound.)
>
> Look for strange comparisons. One child, age four, said, "The sea is like a blue velvet coat . . ."
>
> Develop metaphor poems with older children. This variation of the comparison poem is more difficult but satisfying.
>
> Capitalize on the fact that children are changing physically. They like to write poems that have the pattern "I Used To/But Now."
>
> Recognize that the success of any approach depends upon the attitude of the teacher.[6]

Poems for Many Moods

Reading poetry aloud may serve to spark children's interest. Unfortunately, too much of the poetry that young children are exposed to in school tends to be cute rhymed lines written by adults especially for children. These often talk down to children and seem artificial in topic and

---

[5]Kenneth Koch, *Wishes, Lies, and Dreams: Teaching Children to Write Poetry* (New York: Vintage Press, Random House, 1970), pp. 8–30.

[6]Koch, *Wishes, Lies, and Dreams*, p. 9.

tone. Using the poetry of Blake, Herrick, Whitman, Donne, and many others, Koch asks children to identify a line that they liked. Never are they asked to explain the meaning of a specific line, for this implies that there is only one meaning. The emphasis is on personal appreciation of the poet's perspective. For example, Koch suggested that after reading "The Tyger" by William Blake, the teacher ask, "Did you ever question a beautiful and mysterious creature?" Similarly, a reading of Federico Garcia Lorca's "Sleepwalking Ballad" can generate a discussion of the poet's magical use of colors. The children were asked questions such as "Which word is greener?" "Which is brighter?" It was not possible for them to give an incorrect response.[7]

Children need assistance not only in developing ideas but in providing some structure for their thoughts. You may find it helpful to use particular poems as models of the ways in which poets go about doing their work. Be sure to use the work of children as well:

1. Poems that compare dissimilar objects:

TWINKLE, TWINKLE, LITTLE BAT

Twinkle, twinkle, little bat!
How I wonder what you're at?
Up above the world you fly,
Like a tea-tray in the sky.

—Lewis Carroll, *Alice in Wonderland*

OLD MAN

Old Man, once sturdy as a mountain
Now fragile as a twig,
It is many years and many storms till
A mountain is worn
But a twig can suddenly go snap.

—Jessica Siegal, age 13[8]

2. Poems that have surprise endings:

HOMEMADE BOAT

This boat that we just
built is just fine,
And don't try to tell
us it's not.

[7]Kenneth Koch, *Rose, Where Did You Get That Red? Teaching Great Poetry to Children* (New York: Random House, 1973).

[8]From *Miracles: Poems by Children of the English-Speaking World*, ed. Richard Lewis (New York: Bantam, 1977), p. 142.

The sides and the back
are divine—
It's the bottom I
guess we forgot. . . .
     —Shel Silverstein[9]

RICHARD CORY

Whenever Richard Cory went down town;
  People on the pavement looked at him:
He was a gentleman from sole to crown,
  Clean favord, and imperially slim.

And he was always quietly arrayed,
  And he was always human when he talked;
But still he fluttered pulses when he said,
  "Good-morning," and he glittered when he walked.

And he was rich—yes, richer than a king—
  And admirably schooled in every grace:
In fine, we thought that he was everything
  To make us wish that we were in his place.

So on we worked, and waited for the light,
  And went without the meat, and cursed the bread;
And Richard Cory, one calm summer night,
  Went home and put a bullet through his head.

                    —Edwin Arlington Robinson

3. Poems that ponder mysteries:

I NEVER SAW A MOOR

I never saw a moor,
I never saw the sea;
Yet I know how the heather looks,
And what a wave must be.

I never spoke with God,
Nor visited in Heaven;
Yet certain am I of the spot
As if the chart were given.

          —Emily Dickinson

I wonder
how God lives
in heaven
when the clouds

---

[9]Shel Silverstein, *Where the Sidewalk Ends* (New York: Harper & Row, 1974), p. 12.

seem to be collapsing
like broken birds.

—Jewell Lawton, age 8[10]

4. Poems that ask questions:

SKYSCRAPERS

Do skyscrapers ever grow tired
Of holding themselves up high?
Do they ever shiver on frosty nights
With their tops against the sky?
Do they feel lonely sometimes
Because they have grown so tall?
Do they ever wish they could lie right down
And never get up at all?

—Rachel Field[11]

A ROSE

Rose, why do you have petals and I don't
Why are you so small and eat with your feet?
Sometimes when I see you I bring you home to my house.
But why don't you take me to yours?
We are different, aren't we?

—April Parker, age 8

5. Poems that are full of sound:

THE NOISE OF WATER

All day I hear the noise of waters
    Making moan,
Sad as the sea bird is, when going
    Forth alone,
He hears the winds cry to the waters'
    Monotone.
The gray winds, the cold winds are blowing
    Where I go,
I hear the noise of many waters
    Far below.
All day, all night, I hear them flowing
    To and fro.

—James Joyce

6. Poems that make lists and are repetitive:

[10]From *Miracles,* ed. Richard Lewis, p. 163.
[11]Rachel Field, *Pointed People* (New York: Macmillan, 1930).

IT'S SPRING!

Snapdragon, snap,
Toadstool, turn,
Pussy willow, purr,
  Fireweed, burn,
Black-eyed Susan, wink,
  Sweet William, sing,
Forget-me-not, remember
It's Spring! Spring! Spring!
  Catnip, nip,
Dandelion, roar,
  Dogwood, bark,
Pitcher plant, pour,
  Bee blam, buzz,
Bluebell, ring,
Jack-in-the-pulpit
  Preach today,
It's Spring! Spring! Spring!

—Leland B. Jacobs[12]

SOUL

Soul is feeling
and love
soul is happiness
and soul is the way you feel
singing and dancing
soul makes me dance and sing
soul makes me feel like I'm floating in air
soul makes my heart cry and full of joy
soul really socks it to you
soul is beautiful
soul is power
the power you can feel socking it to you

—Inez[13]

7. Poems that focus on one thing:

GRASS

I saw the rolling leaves
Through the seed headed grass,
That were shivering away
Into the cracked branches,

[12]Leland B. Jacobs, *Just Around the Corner* (New York: Holt, Rinehart & Winston, 1964), p. 9.

[13]From *Can't you hear me talking to you?* by Caroline Mirthes and the Children of P.S. 15 (New York: Bantam, 1971), p. 94.

Where tall brown grass
Was looking greedily at me.

—Lorna (a young New Zealander)[14]

Focus on each of these conventional approaches used by poets. Before you ask children to write their own poetry using a particular approach, make sure that they really understand what to do.

Another form of structure for children's thoughts can be provided using the following suggestion:

> I would ask the children for ideas and simple lines of their own. When these came to them easily, and when a lot of hands were raised in the air to give me more and more of them, that is, when the children were obviously understanding the project and full of ideas, I would pass out paper and they would write.[15]

What Is Poetry?

Scholars and poets have provided us with many definitions of poetry. Carl Sandburg said that "Poetry is the synthesis of hyacinths and biscuits." Voltaire wrote, "Poetry is the music of the soul; and, above all, of great and feeling souls." But if, as Louis Untermeyer notes, "poetry is the most potent of human communications, it should also be the simplest and the most logical expression."[16] Let us attempt a list of poetry's attributes:

1. Poetry is an exotic art form; it is something special and different. The exotic aspect of a poem may be its perspective, its playfulness with words, or its symbols. T. S. Eliot's "The Hollow Men" may be so frequently quoted because it provides such a powerful symbolic picture.

> This is the way the world ends,
> Not with a bang but a whimper.

2. Poetry is economical; the words must be carefully selected. Brevity may add to its impact. The last two lines of Countee Cullen's "Yet Do I Marvel" have more meaning than whole books on the subject.

> Yet do I marvel at this curious thing:
> To make a poet black, and bid him sing.

3. Poetry appeals to our senses through images. Irene, a young girl in Oruarti, New Zealand, wrote:

---

[14]From Elwyn S. Richardson, *In the Early World* (New York: Pantheon, 1964), p. 123.

[15]Koch, *Rose, Where Did You Get That Red?*, p. 20.

[16]Louis Untermeyer, *A Treasury of Great Poems* (New York: Simon & Schuster, 1955), p. xviii.

The blue heron stands in the early world,
Looking like a freezing blue cloud in the morning.[17]

4. Poetry is musical. Its sound is as important as its meaning. We can read it, but it is more important that we listen to it. The following poem by David McCord is an exceptionally musical one; read it aloud to hear its sounds:

FATHER AND I IN THE WOODS

"Son,"
My father used to say,
"Don't run."

"Walk,"
My father used to say,
"Don't talk."

"Words,"
My father used to say,
"Scare birds."

So be:
It's sky and brook and bird
And tree.[18]

5. Poetry may or may not have rhythm and rhyme. Without either rhyme or rhythm this old Japanese Haiku captures a mood.

Above, the chorus,
listen! A single cricket
Shakes a golden bell.

—Kyoshi[19]

6. Poetry does not have to explain or do anything; poetry just has to be. It was Archibald MacLeish who said:

A poem should not mean
But be[20]

Here is a brief excerpt from "Epistle to Be Left in the Earth," by MacLeish. It is best left unexplained.

---

[17]From Richardson, *In the Early World.*

[18]David McCord, *Far and Few: Rhymes of the Never Was and Always Is,* illus. Henry B. Kane (Boston, Mass.: Little, Brown, 1952), p. vii.

[19]From *Birds, Frogs, and Moonlight,* trans. Sylvia Cassedy and Kunihiro Suetake, illus. Vo-Dinh (Garden City, N.J.: Doubleday, 1967), p. 9.

[20]Archibald MacLeish, "Ars Poetica," in *Streets in the Moon* (New York: Houghton Mifflin, 1926).

. . . It is colder now
                    there are many stars
                              we are drifting
North by the Great Bear
                    the leaves are falling
The water is stone in the scooped rocks
                              to southward
Red sun gray air
                  the crows are
Slow on their crooked wings
                        the jays have left us.

We cannot *tell* children what poetry is; its very nature eludes precise definition. But we can communicate a sense of poetry by reading poetry aloud and responding to students' own poetic attempts. Comments such as "That's a very unusual way of describing snow," or "How carefully you must have selected each word," or "Your poem makes me think of the sounds made by a big symphony orchestra," help youngsters focus on what is important in the art of poem-making. Slowly, they will even recognize the poetry in their everyday speech. Once students set down their thoughts in poetic forms, they will start to enjoy the poetry of others. Which comes first, reading poetry or writing it? That question is as difficult to decide as the chicken-or-the-egg controversy. The answer depends upon perspective, timing, and personal needs.

Is It Prose or Poetry?

One is not amazed,
At a first glance,
By a poem,
Which is as tight-closed
As a tiny bud.

Yet one is surprised
To see the poem
Gradually unfolding,
Revealing its rich inner self,
As one reads it
Again
And over again.

—Naoshi Koriyama[21]

An obvious distinction between prose and poetry is length. In the poem, each word has greater weight and the poet has less time to make

[21]From Stephen Dunning, Edward Lueders, Hugh Smith, *Reflections on a Gift of a Watermelon Pickle and Other Modern Verse* (New York: Lothrop, Lee & Shepard, 1967), p. 17.

a statement than the writer of prose. The shortened length does not guarantee that the poem will work more quickly. As suggested by Naoshi
Koriyama above, a poem has to unfold. Its essence has to be caught, and
this may require many rereadings, but brevity very often does increase
its power. Consider the last three lines of Robert Frost's well-known
poem "The Road Not Taken":

> Two roads diverged in a wood, and I—
> I took the road less traveled by
> And that has made all the difference.

Try writing in prose the content of these lines. You may find yourself
with several paragraphs, even several pages. Many meanings may be attributed to Frost's few words, but some of the poem's subtler implications would be lost in a wordy treatise.

The most noticeable difference between prose and poetry is that prose
is usually written from margin to margin, whereas poetry is not. Poetry
and prose thus look different on paper. Having shorter lines than ordinary prose writing contributes to poetry's rhythmic quality. The playfulness of the poem that follows owes much to the length of its lines and its
musical beat.

> Hurry, hurry, Mary dear,
> Fall is over, winter's here.
>
> Not a moment to be lost,
> In a moment we get frost!
>
> In an hour we get snow!
> Drifts like houses! Ten below!
>
> Pick the apples, dill the pickles,
> Chop down trees for wooden nickels.
> Dig the turnips, split the peas,
> Cook molasses, curdle cheese.
>
> —N. M. Bodecker[22]

Sometimes, children write poetry in prose form. They can be helped to
recognize that the shorter line will highlight the musical, imagistic, and
rhyming qualities of their work. The third grader who writes

> The saddest thing I ever saw was a little bird looking at another bird who
> was dead by the big glass door.

can be shown how to structure these thoughts so that the rhythm,
rhyme, and picture shine through:

> The saddest thing
> I ever saw
> Was a little bird

---

[22]N. M. Bodecker, *Hurry, Hurry, Mary Dear and Other Nonsense Poems* (New York: Atheneum, 1976), pp. 1–4.

Looking at another bird
Dead
By the big glass door.

Poetic Forms

"How can it be poetry? It doesn't rhyme," says an eight year old whose teacher has read the class a poem that does not rhyme. It takes a long time for children to overcome their years with nursery rhymes and allow that there are other poetic structures. A word of caution: the introduction of a new poetic form should not be a scientific examination. A microscopic inspection of poetry may kill the experimenter's interest. The first step in introducing a new poetic form is getting the children to fall in love with a particular poem—or at least to be smitten by it. Discussions of figures of speech, definitions, and historical background can all wait. When introducing a new poetic form, I find it best to read examples aloud to the class. Once children have the desire to imitate the form, they can learn the appropriate number of syllables and the length of the typical verse line.

Haiku   Haiku has been called the world's most overburdened poetic form—and probably for good reason. It does not require whole sentences and is an easy and satisfying form for children to write in. Haiku poems generally possess seventeen syllables—five in the first line, seven in the second, and five in the third. Adele Kenny, a poet and creative writing specialist, however, notes that the common belief that a haiku poem must have seventeen syllables is based on a mistranslation of the Japanese concept of syllable. More important than the correct number of syllables is the word picture that is presented. A teacher may thus be well-advised to ignore students' errors in counting syllables. The emphasis should be on feeling. Haiku poetry is most frequently about the small marvels of nature. The brevity of the form encourages the close-up look; nothing is too insignificant to dwell upon. Here are some haiku poems written by children and by some famous haiku poets:

A breeze stirs at dawn,
shaking a rain of trembling
dewdrops to the grass.
—Asayasu[23]

[23]The poems by Asayasu, Issa, and Basho are taken from *More Cricket Songs*, trans. Harry Behn (New York: Harcourt Brace Jovanovich, 1971), pp. 39, 23, and 8; the poem by Koson from *Birds, Frogs, and Moonlight*, trans. Sylvia Cassedy and Kunihiro Suetake, p. 47; and the poem by Ransetsu from *Haiku Harvest*, trans. Peter Beilenson and Harry Behn (Mount Vernon, N.Y.: Peter Pauper Press, 1962), p. 12.

Leaping flying-fish!
dancing for me and my boat
as I sail for home.
                    —Koson

Warbler, wipe your feet
neatly, if you please, but not
on the plum petals!
                    —Issa

Fields of wild daisies,
As far as the eye can see
God's own carpet.
                    —Barbara, age 10

Who breaks down the branch?
Hear the cracking plea for help
Nature's warning cry.
                    —Kenny, age 11

Haiku poetry is not always serious:

There goes my best hat
as down comes rain on my bald
pate, plop! plop! plop! Oh well . . .
                    —Basho

Haiku poetry may have a surprise ending:

In stony moonlight
Hills and fields on every side
White and bald as eggs . . .
                    —Ransetsu

After reading these and other haiku poems and before asking your class to do so, you may wish to write some of your own. Writing very short poems can be a lot of fun. Sometimes suggesting an opening line is a good way to begin: "The crickets are saying," "The hidden meadow," "Sun melted the snow," "What strange dreams I have."

One teacher planning to assign the writing of haiku poems took her class on a walk to a nearby field. Each student was asked to select one object—a blade of grass, a wild flower, a tree, a cloud—and look at it as long and closely as possible. Some children photographed what they saw from several vantage points. The haiku poems the students later wrote reflected the intensity with which they responded to their moments at the field.

If firsthand experience is not possible, you might want to use such filmstrips as *Haiku: The Mood of Earth* and *Haiku: The Hidden Glimmering*, by Ann Atwood. Atwood has also written two beautiful books on haiku, *My Own Rhythm: An Approach to Haiku* and *Fly With the Wind, Flow With the Water*.

Tanka   Once children have discovered the appeal of haiku, they may go on to tanka poetry. This form has thirty-one syllables arranged in five lines of five, seven, five, seven, and seven syllables. Of greater length than haiku poems, tanka poems allow greater detail; but their principal topic is also nature, particularly the seasons:

> When I went out
> In the Spring meadows
> To gather violets,
> I enjoyed myself
> So much that I stayed all night.
> —Akahito[24]

> On summer nights
> When I wonder, "Shall I go to bed?"
> At the single note sung
> By the cuckoo,
> Dawn suddenly breaks!
> —Tsurayuki

Cinquains   The cinquain form takes its name from the French word, "cinq." Using this five-line prescriptive form, the young writer is asked to describe in each line an action or a feeling in a limited number of words. A typical form for cinquain poetry:

Line 1: One word (title)

Line 2: Two words (describing title)

Line 3: Three words (an action)

Line 4: Four words (a feeling)

Line 5: One word (refer to title)

The cinquain form is satisfying for children and can serve as a temporary springboard into poetic expression. Since it can very easily deteriorate into a mechanical exercise, it should not be overused. The students' first cinquains are best done as a cooperative endeavor:

[24]The poems by Akahito and Tsurayuki are taken from *The Seasons of Time: Tanka Poetry of Ancient Japan*, ed. Virginia Olsen Baron, illus. Yasuhide Kobashi (New York: Dial, 1968), pp. 19 and 29.

Baby
Cuddly, smelly
Sitting on mommy
Sleepy, happy and unafraid
Me.
                    —Second-Grade Class

Eggs
Warm suns
Spurting out butter
So good to eat
Life.
                    —Fourth-Grade Class

Even adults enjoy playing with the cinquain. Here are two written by student teachers:

Teacher   Rock
Always perfect   Beautiful sounds
Seeing her mistakes   Shake my soul
Learning to be free   I tremble and feel
Growing.   Whole.

Try writing some of your own.

Concrete Poetry   Concrete poetry blends form and content as the poem takes on the shape of the subject matter. Sometimes called iconographic poetry, concrete poetry has grown in popularity during the past ten years. Modern poets have begun to use it with greater frequency. It has particular appeal for children because it is a visual as well as auditory medium. As a picture story, it can tap a child's creativity and assist in the expression of ideas (Figure 11-1). Two good books offering models of concrete poetry are Emmett Williams' *Anthology of Concrete Poetry* and Robert Froman's *Street Poems*.

11-1   Poem by John McEntyre reprinted from page 47 of *The Whole Word Catalogue I* by R. Brown et al., by permission of Teachers & Writers Collaborative, New York, N.Y. Copyright © 1972.

SOMETIMES IT'S HARD TO TELL IF YOU'RE LIVING IN A VERY MOUNTAINOUS REGION OR IF YOU JUST GOT A BAD HEART

11-2

After children have seen and heard such poetry, they might want to write their own. Ask your students to talk about and draw the shapes that they associate with a particular topic: bike riding, skiing, a part of the body, a musical scale, a tree. How can their words follow the shape that they have created? Figure 11-2 is an example of what a nine year old might invent.

11-3

The idea that words are not only symbolic receptacles for ideas but also physical objects can give rise to one-word poems. Ron Padgett of *The Teachers and Writers Collaborative* helped children create word pictures such as those shown in Figure 11-3.

Parallel Poems   These forms have been referred to in the discussion of the work of Kenneth Koch. Their primary advantage is that they get writing started. The structure is there, but it is open-ended enough to encourage imaginative responses. Like any of the other techniques, it is important that it not be abused. The Teachers and Writers Collaborative has developed many suggestions for using these forms. Here is a representative example:

I Wish:	Write a poem in which every line begins with "I wish . . ."
Colors:	Write a poem with a color in every line.
I Used to Be:	Write a poem that has the form "I used to be (a) _____ but now I'm (a) _____."
I Seem to Be:	Write a poem that has the form "I seem to be (a) _____ but I'm really (a) _____."
Lies:	Write a poem with a lie in every line.
I Remember:	Write a poem in which every line begins "I remember . . ."
Dreams of the Future:	Write a poem in which every line begins with "I am going to . . ."
Equivalent Poems:	"In the past they _____, but now we _____."[25]

Limericks.   The limerick has five lines, lines one, two, and five sharing one rhyme and lines three and four another. Similarly, lines one, two, and five have the same number of beats, as do three and four. The result is an a-a-b-b-a pattern. Edward Lear popularized the limerick over one hundred years ago, and the form has not yet lost its appeal (Figure 11-4). Books devoted exclusively to this humorous poetry are numerous. You might find *Laughable Limericks*, by Sara and John E. Brewton, and *Limericks by Lear* of particular interest.

Evaluating Poetry

The approach to poetry throughout this chapter suggests that children be exposed to "wake-up" experiences, experiences that will help them

[25] *The Whole Word Catalogue*, ed. Rosellen Brown et al. (New York: Teachers and Writers Collaborative, 1972), p. 105.

11-4

From *A Book of Nonsense,*
edited by Ernest Rhys.
Children's Illustrated Classics.
Elsevier-Dutton Publishing Co.,
Inc., New York, 1975. p. 39.

There was an Old Man of Coblenz,
The length of whose legs was immense;
    He went with one prance
    From Turkey to France,
That surprising Old Man of Coblenz.

discover and rediscover the wonders of their world. At this point, many of you are probably asking, "How do I know if I have succeeded?" What is crucial here, as in any evaluation procedure, is the yardstick that you use. If your concern is only the finished product and your examination focuses on literary styles and evidence of symbolic relationships, then many children in your class may be evaluated unfairly. The ability to manipulate symbols and develop a poetic style is often one of the final stages in children's intellectual growth. I vividly recall a conversation that I had with a fifth-grade girl during a writing period. Noticing her blank paper, I asked, "Can I help you to begin?" "Oh, I've begun," she said, looking me straight in the eye. "I just haven't put it down on paper yet." This youngster's comment places in bold relief the discussion in the previous chapter on the precomposing stage. We sometimes forget its importance and try to rush the process.

The world at large looks at the product. But the teacher must look at the developmental process as well. Sometimes this is very difficult to do. We become impatient. Here are some guidelines that you might want to consider in evaluating your students' success in appreciating and writing poetry:

1. The child has a heightened awareness and sensitivity to things and people.
2. The child is open to the poetic experience.
3. The child expresses in some way an appreciation of beauty in nature and in art.
4. The child gets enjoyment from poetry: its sound, its images, its rhythm.

5. The child wants to listen to, read, and/or write more poetry.

6. The child tries something new with poetry.

7. The child expresses genuine feelings.

8. The child is imaginative and reaches out to a world somewhat removed from immediate experience.

9. The child finds unusual comparisons and relationships in reality and art.

10. The child recognizes artistry in literary style.

DEVELOPING CREATIVE WRITING SKILLS

Writers are made not born. Young writers need help in developing their skills. A variety of suggestions have been offered for getting writing started. An important position has been accorded the use of literature, both prose and poetry, as an inspiration and model for the writing process. Stress has also been placed upon the need to offer the child many opportunities for oral expression. Of all the language arts, writing is the most cumulative; it builds on experiences in listening, speaking, and reading. Here are some additional activities that can set the stage for creative writing:

1. *Look differently at the same old things.*

Suggest that children distort, invent, rename, and compare things by taking them out of their usual context. This may be done verbally. If the ideas are popping, writing should follow naturally. You might get discussion started by asking students to

Compare a firefly and a spark plug.

Compare music and the color purple.

Compare circles and life.

Compare a grain of wood and a grain of sand.

Describe a mechanical giant clam. What does it look like? When would you use it? How much would it cost?.

Give yourself a new name.

Imagine that you are the traffic light on the corner.

The comparison of very different qualities has also been explored in such books as *Synectics* and *Making It Strange:*

Compare your feelings with a Gypsy Dollar Bill.

How are a giraffe and rubber band related?

What weather are you reminded of as you look at a popcorn machine?[26]

Some of the synectic exercises suggested in these books are bound to

---

[26]William J Gordon, *Synectics* (New York: Harper & Row, 1961); *Making It Strange*, prepared by Synectics, Inc. (New York: Harper & Row, 1968).

excite your students. Initially, such exercises may seem like hard work; however, this perception will change as your students develop a greater trust in their own powers of invention.

2. *Use books that heighten perceptual skills.*

Mary O'Neill's *Hailstones and Halibut Bones* teaches children to use all their senses in experiencing color. *The View from the Oak,* a book by Judith and Herbert Kohl, explores the ways in which animals experience space and encourages children to observe, look, and sense space and time from new perspectives. Using the haiku poetry of Issa, *Of This World: A Poet's Life in Poetry,* by Richard Lewis, prepares children to see the world through the poet's eyes. *A Tail Is a Tail,* by Katherine Mace, encourages the reader to empathize with animals that have tails. *Bubble Bubble,* a wordless book by Mercer Mayer, stimulates imaginative functioning by depicting the monsters a boy sees in the bubbles he blows.

3. *Use word association and a stream-of-consciousness technique.*

Start ideas flowing by presenting a line of poetry, a picture. Ask students to write down thoughts as soon as they pop into their heads. A thought may be an individual word. Stress that it doesn't have to make sense. Word association is like an X-ray of their thinking. And of course they can't make a mistake. The wilder, the more way-out, the better! Helen, a fourth grader, presented with the word *ghost,* added the words *scary, cave, dark, under, ocean,* and *waves.* Using these words, she wrote:

> I never knew a ghost had eyes,
> That scared me more than anything
> He took me to his cave
> Way down in the ocean deep
> And there I spent the rest of my days
> Keeping house under the waves.

A line of poetry—"Saddest of all things on the moon is the snail without a shell."[27]—started Janet on a repetitive poem:

> Saddest of all things is a head without a hair.
> Saddest of all things is a witch without a brew.
> Saddest of all things is a mushroom without a stem.
> Saddest of all things is a world without men.

And after viewing a picture of a snake, Barbara, age nine, wrote:

> "One day, long ago when I was five, I remember lying
> on the soft grass. I closed my eyes but I still saw
> everything. I felt the little bugs who came to kiss
> me, I tasted the smell of the grass. I was laughing
> when I opened my eyes. I wish that I could go back
> again to that hidden meadow."

[27]Ted Hughes, *Moon-Whales and Other Moon Poems* (New York: Viking, 1976), p. 34.

Films, musical encounters, and trips can also be used to stimulate simple word associations. The important thing is to help children extract the essence of a feeling. The poetic statement, whether in poetry or prose, distills a feeling or an idea into a few brief words and leaves the rest to the reader.

Using Figurative Language

The elementary-school child uses figurative language spontaneously in everyday talk. But most children are unaware that they are using metaphor when they refer to a witch as "a prune-face" or a little brother as "a hungry wolf." Knowing the figure of speech is unnecessary. What is important is that children recognize their power to create pictures in an unusual way.

Similes and Metaphors   Comparisons are a good place to begin. Children can appreciate that when someone uses the term *turkey* to describe another, the connotation is negative. The subject is being compared to a dumb bird.

Start children on the comparative process by having them consider clichés involving parts of the body: *body of knowledge, heart of the matter, head of the family, foot of the mountain, eye of the storm*. Next, suggest that the students devise their own comparisons, perhaps referring to less tangible aspects of the body, such as the walk, the voice, and the smile. A third-grade class wrote some very imaginative comparisons:

> My heartbeat is like the patter of raindrops.
> My arms when I am swimming are like bees' wings.
> My eye is a two-way mirror.
> My cry is like a wailing wind.

It matters little whether children recognize that similes use "like" or "as" and that metaphors compare unlike objects without using these words. The important thing is getting children to recognize that both similes and metaphors tie objects together creatively.

Bob Sample's *The Metaphoric Mind*, a fascinating text with vividly beautiful photographs, suggests how we can help children to develop metaphoric-mindedness. The ability to use metaphor does not depend upon age or chronological maturity. In fact, it may be easier for children to invent than to conform. Adults may place children into grooves which imprison both thought and imagination. In this context, Abraham Maslow once pointed out that one who has a hammer treats the whole world as if it were a nail. "Children, not caught in this bind, may take the same hammer and dig with it, weight down papers between which they press leaves, and/or use it to knock apples from a tree."[28] Encourage children to use their ability to invent and see things differently.

Personification   It is really fun to explore children's language for examples of personification. Soon after children develop some facility with the spoken word, they begin to give inanimate objects and animals human qualities. Egocentric beings that they are, all the world is judged from their own perspective. Thus, "the guinea pig wants to be kissed," "my teddy bear doesn't like you," or as one first grader dictated, "My house gets sad when I leave for school." Probably one of the most famous examples of personification is the following poem by Carl Sandburg:

FOG

The fog comes
on little cat feet.
It sits looking
over harbor and city
on silent haunches
And then moves on.

Here is how a nine-year-old Canadian boy describes the fog:

FOG

Fog is a puff of smoke
Blinding and thick
It's like a great god
Smoking a great pipe,
The eyes of the people show
    little tears
From the thickening smoke.[29]

Expanding Vocabulary   All the stylistic devices that have been mentioned encourage the use of descriptive words and phrases. Another technique that may be used is to ask children to rewrite bland and simple sentences so that they communicate effectively. Here is one beginning exercise:

"I have been in this lifeboat for two days. I am hungry, thirsty, and tired. I am wondering if I will be saved."

Help children to stockpile words that they can call upon in their writing. Start with the simple everyday words that they use and prepare charts with the class:

---

[28]Bob Samples, *The Metaphoric Mind: A Celebration of Creative Consciousness* (Reading, Mass.: Addison-Wesley, 1976), p. 84.
[29]From *Miracles*, ed. Richard Lewis, p. 122.

Word Choices

Descriptive Words:

happy	joyful, content, enchanted, cloudless
soft	flexible, limp, flimsy, downy, feathery
bad	evil, wicked, hateful, detestable, horrid, foul, venomous
beautiful	pretty, lovely, graceful, elegant, exquisite, comely, gorgeous

Action Words:

walk	march, step, stride, tramp, hike, trudge
do	work, perform, act, take in hand, shape, transact
leave	go away, depart, withdraw, take flight, evacuate
buy	purchase, shop, market, procure, invest

Using Literature as a Catalyst for Writing

Literature as motivation has been suggested in several places in this text. Here are some further ways to help students use the writing of others to spark their own work.

John Warren Stewig in *Read to Write: Using Children's Literature as a Springboard to Writing* cites numerous examples drawn from children's literature to spark writing. Starting with the premise that writing is a craft to be consciously learned, with specific skills to be acquired and practiced, he capitalizes on the child's natural interest in the story form.

"Pourquoi" stories which abound in children's literature provide a natural impetus for expression. Begin with Kipling's "Just So" stories and then acquaint children with a variety of folktales that give ethnic explanations of "why" the world is the way it is. A good place to begin is with Verna Aardema's *Why Mosquitoes Buzz in People's Ears*. Children will soon raise some of their own questions. The answers they write can be real or a potpourri of fact and fancy. Here are some "why" questions raised in one second-grade class:

Why does a cat have whiskers?

Why is there a face on the moon?

Why does the sun stay up in the sky?

Why do coconuts have milk?

How did the giraffe get spots?

How did the skunk get a smell?

How did the nightingale learn to sing?

How did the rainbow get its colors?

How did Abe Lincoln get to be so tall?

How did a cat get nine lives?

Legends and heroic tales are a rich source of writing experiences. The exaggerated characters in tall tales prompt children to develop their own creations. Every culture tells the story of its real and mythic heroes. Acquaint your students with characters and situations from different cultures and they will soon be creating their own. The tradition of myth-making is old, but the capacity to create new heroes and heroines is reborn in each generation. Here are some real and mythic heroes whom children will admire:

Paul Bunyan, John Henry, Pecos Bill, Kwasind, Davy Crockett (United States)

King Arthur, Robin Hood (England)

Rama (India)

Roland, Joan of Arc (France)

Odysseus (Greece)

Don't forget those who are legends in their own time. Children will have their own names to add to this list: John F. Kennedy, Martin Luther King, Jr., John Lennon, Elvis Presley.

The title of a book can in itself be a stimulus for creative writing. Some thought-provoking suggestions include:

Arthur Ransome, *The Fool of the World and the Flying Ship*. Farrar, Straus & Giroux, 1968.

Arlene Mosel, *The Funny Little Woman*. Dutton, 1972.

Susan Russo, *The Moon's the North Wind's Cookie*. Lothrop, Lee & Shepard, 1979.

Judy Blume, *Are You There God? It's Me, Margaret*. Dell, 1974.

Miriam Cohen, *Will I Have a Friend?* Macmillan, 1971.

Oscar Wilde, *The Selfish Giant*. McGraw-Hill, 1979.

Literature can be used as a model for writing. The elements of narrative can be identified through the comparison of two similar stories. After reading Bernard Waber's *Lovable Lyle* and Janice Udry's *Let's Be Enemies*, one third-grade teacher compared the two stories by introducing the following basic elements of narrative: plot, character, setting, and point of view.

Plot was examined through the identification of a problem or a conflict. Attention was given to the way in which the problem was resolved.

What was Lyle's problem?

What was the problem between James and John?

Character was discussed through the identification of specific behaviors of people and animals in the stories. The teacher asked,

"How do you know that Lyle was super-sensitive?"

"Did James and John behave like real boys do?"

Setting was identified through questions that related to place, and the appropriateness of that place for the story itself. *Point of View* came through when children considered the purpose of the author in writing the book.

Did he or she have a message?

What was it?

After comparing the two stories for the elements described above, the teacher asked the class to write their own stories about a misunderstanding. The story might or might not be about enemies. As the children discussed the elements of the story, some even using the new vocabulary, it was clear that the framework was helpful. For those children who were not yet ready to do their own work, the teacher continued this pattern of story analysis with different sets of stories. Other twosomes included Robert Larranga's *Sniffles* and Don Freeman's *Corduroy*, and Marjorie

11-5   From *The Blanket* by Francelia Butler in SHARING LITERATURE WITH CHILDREN, edited by Francelia Butler. Copyright © 1977 by Longman Inc. Reprinted by permission of Longman Inc., New York.

THE BLANKET
(French)
Retold by Francelia Butler

On a small farm in the South of France lived a man, his wife, and his son. With them lived his old father. This arrangement was not satisfactory to the wife. She was constantly complaining about the old man.

"When he eats, he slurps his soup," she said. "And he lets it drizzle down his beard. It makes me sick at my stomach and I cannot digest my food properly."

Her husband yielded to her demands and asked his father to eat his food in the adjoining room. But her complaints continued.

"Every time I look up from my plate," she said, "he is always staring out in my direction. I can't stand his eyes on me."

Finally, she made an ultimatum: "Either he goes or I do."

The son, sad about the affair, but having no choice but to lose either his wife or his father, chose to send his father away.

"I know it's winter, father," he said, "but my wife simply won't stand your presence here any longer. I must ask you to leave."

The father nodded. "Of course, son, I will go."

Remorseful at sending his father out in the middle of winter, the son asked his little boy to go to the barn and fetch the horseblanket.

"At least, father, the blanket will help to keep you warm."

The little boy left and was gone a long time. Finally, he returned, but he had only half the blanket. He had cut it jaggedly in two.

"What have you done that for?" the father demanded. "You have ruined a perfectly good blanket."

"Father," the little boy replied, "I was saving half of it for you and mother when you get old."

Sharmat's *Gladys Told Me to Meet Her Here* and Rosemary Wells' *Benjamin and Tulip.*

Francelia Butler in *Sharing Literature with Children* suggests exposing children to literature in thematic arrangements. Taking her suggestion and circles as the theme, I read the following stories to a fifth-grade class:

> —*Changes, Changes,* a picture book without words that ends the way it begins.
>
> —The French folktale "The Blanket," which is printed below.
>
> —*The Little House,* Virginia Lee Burton's classic story of a country house that is displaced by the city and then returned after many seasons to its country setting.
>
> —James Thurber's *The Last Flower,* a parable in pictures, begins with the words "World War III, as everybody knows, brought about the collapse of civilization." At many points during the book Thurber notes that "Nothing at all was left in the world except one man and one woman and one flower." The story ends with these very same words.

First I asked the children to tell some stories that begin and end in the same places. We then proceeded to discuss all of the important things in the world that move in circles—life cycles, seasons. Many children soon wrote their own circle stories and poems.

Using the World of Fantasy

Fantasy is attractive to most children and may serve as a springboard for creative writing. It enables the child if only temporarily to manipulate a world that often seems too fixed. When children write fantasy they can alter time and place; they can create supernatural beings, personify the inanimate and give human beings (particularly children) extraordinary qualities.

The success of fantasy is dependent upon the maintenance of a certain number of believable elements. Thus in a fantasy like Frank Baum's classic *The Wizard of Oz,* the characters, though magical, are true to their species: the tin man rusts, the scarecrow burns, the lion is strong.

Help children get their feet wet in writing fantasy using a singular perspective. Have your students imagine the following:

> *Being something unusual*
> Bjorn Borg's tennis racquet
> The eye of a hurricane
> The horse about to win the Kentucky Derby
> John Travolta's dancing shoes
> A computer
> A baby's rattle
> A skateboard

Being someplace unusual
On a space station
In a cage at the zoo
On top of Mount Everest
In the White House
On a pirate ship

Being an unusual person or animal
Popeye
Mohammed Ali
Ronald Reagan
Pippi Longstocking
A famous detective
A hostage
A newborn baby

As children become comfortable with using fantastic frameworks, encourage them to write their own collections of "what if" stories:

What if the sun didn't rise one morning?

What if all people looked alike?

What if cats had nine lives?

What if time stopped?

What if Peter Pan came to the schoolyard

What if all animals became extinct?

What if rabbits took over the world?

What if you turned into a dog?

If we encourage children to exercise their sense of fantasy when they are young, they may have a better perspective on reality later in life. In the opinion of psychologist Bruno Bettelheim

Many of the young people who today suddenly escape in drug-induced dreams, apprentice themselves to a guru, believe in astrology, practice "black magic," or in some other fashion escape from reality into daydreams were prematurely pressed to view reality as adults view it.[30]

EVALUATING CREATIVE WRITING

The previous chapter discussed most of the aspects to be considered in evaluating imaginative writing. A few further words may be helpful within the context of this chapter. The objective of evaluation as we know it is to get children to write more, to communicate better, and to find their own voices. Teachers looking at children's writing should ask:

[30]Bruno Bettelheim, "The Uses of Enchantment," *New Yorker*, 6 December 1975, p. 63.

Is the child using language more effectively and imaginatively as the term progresses? Does the written product communicate? Is a writing style emerging? Does the written response express individuality?

Does the writing continue? Is the child able to write longer works with sustained interest?

Does the child want to share the work?

Does the child understand why the mechanics of expression are important?

Does the child appear to get some satisfaction from the writing process? From sharing the finished product?

Afterview   To place the controversy about the correction of mechanics into perspective, teachers should distinguish between practical and creative writing. Certainly, for purposes of clarity, misspellings and grammatical and punctuation errors should be identified. But it is all a question of when and how. The context makes the difference. The next chapter will be concerned with mechanics, but we certainly don't want mechanically correct but dull writing from our students. A series of corrections or a low grade have negative effects on self-expression. Let's take it step by step. First, get the writing going; then teach the mechanics removed from the context of personal expression.

WHEN YOU WANT TO KNOW MORE

1. Give yourself some practice in metaphor-making. First, identify several song titles that use metaphors. Then, create several examples of metaphoric language around one theme: for example, the ocean, women, schools, fires.

2. Try to recall your experiences with poetry as a student in elementary school. What factors affected your present attitudes about the poetic mode? What are the implications for a teacher of language arts?

3. Read Rachel Carson's *The Sense of Wonder*, a book of photographs in which the author shares her young grandchild's awakening joy to the natural world. Try to identify aspects of your environment that stimulate your sense of wonder.

IN THE CLASSROOM

1. Ask several children to share their "folklore"—rhymes, street games, songs, chants. How might this poetry of childhood be used to motivate creative writing experiences in the classroom?

2. Ask children to imagine life in the future. Help them to be "futurologists" by focusing on specific aspects of daily life in the year 2000. What changes do they foresee? After a discussion, have them write on such topics as: future food, future transportation, future fun, future technology.

3. Have young children bring in the following types of pictures to stimulate storytelling and writing:

   a picture that tells a story
   a picture that gives a message
   a picture that you can smell
   a picture that shows a world made by people

4. Have students in the middle grades write creative responses to want ads in the local paper.

5. Ask students to write poems that do one of the following: have a surprise ending, compare unlike things, personify inanimate objects, ask questions. Compare results with samples in this chapter.

SUGGESTED READINGS

Arnstein, Flora J. *Children Write Poetry: A Creative Approach.* New York: Dover, 1967.

Esbensen, Barbara Juster. *A Celebration of Bees: Helping Children Write Poetry.* Minneapolis Minn.: Winston Press, 1975.

Frye, Northrop. *The Educated Imagination.* Bloomington, Ind.: Indiana University Press, 1964.

Gensler, Kenneth, and Nyhart, Nina. *The Poetry Connection: An Anthology of Contemporary Poems with Ideas to Stimulate Children's Writing.* New York: Teachers and Writers Collaborative, 1978.

Hennings, Dorothy G., and Grant, Barbara. *Control and Craft: Written Expression in the Elementary School.* Englewood Cliffs, N.J.: Prentice-Hall, 1973.

Lewis, Claudia. *A Big Bite of the World: Children's Creative Writing.* Englewood Cliffs, N.J.: Prentice-Hall, 1979.

Mearns, Hughes. *Creative Power: The Education of Youth in the Creative Arts.* New York: Dover, 1958.

Petty, Walter R., and Bowen, Mary. *Slithery Snakes and Other Aids to Children's Writing.* New York: Appleton-Century-Crofts, 1967.

Torrance, Paul E. and Myers, R. E., *Creative Learning and Teaching.* New York: Dodd, Mead, 1974.

Other Materials

Myers, R. E., and Torrance, E. P. *Invitations to Speaking and Writing Creatively.* Boston: Ginn, 1965.

Making It Strange. New York: Harper & Row, 1968.

Spencer, Zane A. *Flair: A Handbook of Creative Writing Techniques for the Elementary School Teacher.* Stevensville, Mich.: Educational Service, 1972.

Stewig, John Warren. *Read to Write: Using Children's Literature as a Springboard to Writing.* New York: Hawthorn Books, 1975.

PART IV

THE TEACHING
OF BASIC
WRITING SKILLS

CHAPTER 12

Teaching Practical Aspects of Writing

Preview In recent years, schools have placed the teaching of the practical aspects of writing in a new context. Research has shown that teaching the rules of grammar, punctuation, and capitalization is of dubious value unless the student understands the relevance of these conventions. When difficulties with mechanics become apparent in their written products, students should not be made to feel that the diagnosis of errors is the reason writing assignments are given. Where such a feeling exists, the desire to write diminishes.

The research of modern linguists has resulted in the identification of two new grammars in addition to the traditional grammar: structual grammar and transitional grammar. Each of the three types offers a different perspective and suggests varying practices. Each is represented in language arts textbooks used throughout the country. At present, it would be difficult to clearly identify what contribution each grammar can make to elementary-school teaching. Teachers would probably be wise to become familiar with all the grammars and extrapolate those aspects that suit the needs of their classes. In this chapter, activities will be suggested for all three types.

Sections on punctuation and capitalization will direct attention to the child's assessment of his or her own needs and will provide suggestions for activities that consider individual requirements. The perspective throughout the chapter will be that grammar, usage, punctuation, and capitalization are only tools to enhance the communication process. They are meaningless when taught alone.

LARGE NUMBERS of adults and children in our society seem to have gotten the message that self-fulfillment and instant gratification are synonymous. For these people, the old "iodine treatment," if it hurts it's good for you, may have been replaced by, "If it doesn't feel good right now, forget it." Both extremes can be destructive. One position ignores the special satisfactions that result from extended effort and persistence; the other denies that learning can be and is for many a joyful experience. Somehow teaching the practical aspects of writing has frequently been viewed as painful.

As teachers you will sometimes be asked for the "answers" to the country's educational problems; one of which is often phrased, "Why can't Johnny write?" The "back-to-basics" movement, when narrowly conceived, purports to have the answer with a return to uniform drills and exercises. Little consideration is given to how skill development is related to the total affective and cognitive functioning of the child. Clearly, the answer is not to constantly tell children, "Do as you feel." For then, we run the risk that there will be no awareness of the capacity for sustained effort. The result may be untapped abilities that would ultimately contribute to the child's sense of self-worth as well as to the society at large. Young people, if encouraged prematurely to follow the path of least resistance, will doubt whether they do in fact have the ability to persevere at all.

In our zealousness to respond to community pressure, it is important to recognize that a decreased emphasis has been placed on the teaching of skills in the last twenty years. The change in practices has reaped some rewards in terms of children's development. For many youngsters, the additional opportunities for free expression have resulted in a growing sense of self-worth. For others, greater freedom has meant greater motivation to do school activities. There are youngsters who now find school to be more personally meaningful because of the less structured, more innovative practices. We should not forget that many people who are the products of schools of the past and who were indeed drilled in the "basics" shun all writing activities. Educators and the public must question the criteria used to judge the results of education.

Part of the problem in teaching children the mechanics of writing is that the teaching is often made uninteresting. Teachers themselves may have a distaste for the elements of grammar and punctuation. Yet if, as John Dewey suggested, school life is properly a microcosm of life, then the appeal of activities in the classroom must be expected to vary—from dull to exciting, from mechanical to creative. One very effective teacher put it this way, "Everything that is taught in the classroom cannot be as riveting as when the science teacher demonstrates the eruption of the volcano." There will come a time when the students have to examine the minutest particles of lava, compile data following a rigid form, and write down their clearly stated conclusions legibly.

Take the children into your confidence and share with them this information about life in and out of classrooms. Indeed, certain aspects of the curriculum will be less exciting than others, but this does not mean that the ultimate rewards will not be as great. Gratification may just be delayed. The humdrum aspects of life are often a preparation for the more dynamic moments. Unfortunately, the notion that pervades our times is that life should be action packed and changing every six seconds.

Learning the skills of communication does not always fit this image. Writing, for example, requires perseverance and effort. Children have to be helped to appreciate that the learning is worth the struggle. Allow children to develop perseverance in small doses. Prepare shorter lessons. Carefully explain the long-term goals. Always point up the practical applications to the real world. Be lavish with your compliments. Attend to individual needs. Recognize and encourage any effort, no matter how minimal, on the part of the child who persists with a difficult task. The basic communication skills can be taught with techniques that are both imaginative and useful.

The two previous chapters have emphasized that learning to write is an integral part of a larger growth process. The mechanics of writing are best taught apart from this process, not while the child is writing independently. However, it is during the writing process that needs may be identified. The challenge for the teacher is to bridge this separation and help children to see that the learning of these skills is personally relevant to their own writing growth.

GRAMMAR AND USAGE

Grammar and usage are not the same, though the terms are often used interchangeably. A *grammar* is a system of general principles and particular rules for speaking and writing a language. It seeks to describe the forms, structure, and arrangement of words in the language. Sometimes the word *grammar* refers simply to any forms that people use in their speaking and writing. In this sense, it is merely descriptive of a pattern. *Usage* refers to the choice of words that has been established within a given grammatical structure. Usage is determined by such factors as geography, socioeconomic level, and the formality of the situation. Thus when a southerner asks, "Would you all like to come for dinner?" "you all" is a way of *using* the words in the language. It has nothing to do with the grammar of the language. Consider grammar as the basic structure of the language and usage as the differing details within that structure. All reptiles, for example, are cold-blooded, egg-laying, air-breathing animals with backbones who usually have a scaly covering. This is their "grammar." Their "usage" has tremendous variation dependent upon their geography, their habitat, their adaptive capabilities, and their size. Therefore, though we recognize the snake, the lizard, the turtle, and the crocodile as members of the same generic group, we can easily see how, despite a basic similarity, there are differences in size, color, and so on.

A frequently heard analogy compares grammar and usage to etiqette and manners.[1] Grammar, like etiquette, provides rules about what should be done. Usage, like manners, is the individual translation of these rules. Before you can describe someone's manners as "good" or "bad," you must have in mind particular rules of etiquette.

Strictly speaking, usage is not the construction or the order of the sentence but the choice of the word itself. "I is happy," is grammatical, but the choice of "is" instead of "am" is a question of usage and its appropriateness should be considered in the context of a specific situation. On the other hand, "Happy, I are" is not a strictly grammatical sentence because of the order of the words. In the English language, the meaning of a sentence is often determined by the order of the words. Thus, "the spider ate the fly" has a different connotation than "the fly ate the spider." Children understand the grammatical or ordinal aspects of the language at a very early age. Their difficulties more frequently occur with usage: "When critics cry for a return to the teaching of grammar . . . we can be certain that these representatives of the public really vant the classroom teacher to stress the teaching of 'correct usage.' "[2] We shall return to suggestions for teaching usage later on in this chapter.

TEACHING GRAMMAR: YES, NO, MAYBE

The study of grammar has its roots in ancient times. The Greeks thought it valuable in the teaching of poetry. The rules of English grammar are derived primarily from Latin, the language of the Romans. Throughout the Middle Ages grammar retained its place in the curriculum; and when elementary schools were first established in this country, the study of grammar was central. In fact, many adults may still refer to their early education as "grammar school." "Why then," they may ask, "has the teaching of grammar taken a back seat in the curriculum? Isn't it possible that more grammar instruction will right some of the wrongs that exist in contemporary education and help Johnny write better?" Our answer can only be that, for many, many years (at least since 1903), research studies have shown that the teaching of grammar does not improve speaking or writing. Learning about the structure of a language

[1] Robert C. Pooley, *Teaching English Grammer* (New York: Appleton-Century Crofts, 1957), p. 106.

[2] Iris M. Tiedt and Sidney W. Tiedt, *Contemporary English in the Elementary School* (Englewood Cliffs, N.J.: Prentice-Hall, 1967), p. 22.

does not help a child use the language more effectively. Is it defensible therefore to continue teaching traditional grammar simply because it has always been taught?

It is not that grammar is being discarded; it is being approached from different vantage points. Instruction is becoming more eclectic, selecting what is most appropriate for individual students and situations from each of the three kinds of grammars.

Three Grammars

Grammar has several different labels. The most widely used are *traditional, structural,* and *transformational* (generative). A debate has ensued for many years as to which type is most effective. The entire discipline is still in a state of transition, and translation into practice has not kept pace with theory. Most schools, if they teach grammar at all, use the "traditional" grammar with its established set of rules. The perspective of traditional grammarians is very different from that of those who belong to either the structural or the transformational school.

Traditional grammar is prescriptive; it specifies how the language *should* be spoken or written. It assumes a standard language that will be used the same way despite differences in geography or culture, a language that changes relatively little over the years. Structural grammar and transformational grammar, the work of modern linguists, are descriptive and scientifically analyze *how* the language is being used. Those engaged in their study work in the way anthropologists and archaeologists do; however, their raw material is language rather than artifacts. Though there is considerable doubt as to whether the theoretical study of grammar is valuable for elementary-school children, as teachers you should be familiar with the basic principles of the three major grammars used throughout the United States.

Traditional English grammar derives its rules primarily from Latin and Greek. It is concerned with

1. Kinds of sentences:
    Declarative
    Interrogative
    Imperative
    Exclamatory
2. How these sentences are made:
    With phrases
    With clauses
3. The classification of sentences:
    Simple
    Compound
    Complex
    Compound-complex

4. The eight parts of speech and their function in the sentence:

nouns	adjectives	prepositions	conjunctions
pronouns	adverbs		interjections
verbs			

Diagramming is a practice frequently used by those who teach traditional grammar. Many experts question its value, but some people claim that it has been a helpful device. Since some language arts texts for children still employ diagramming, teachers should be familiar with the technique:

The baseball player threw the ball to first base.

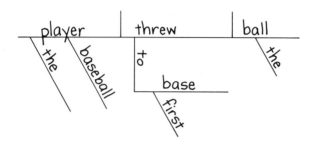

In the diagrammed sentence above; "player" is the subject, "threw" is the verb, "ball" is the direct object, and "the baseball" modifies "player." "The" modifies "ball," and "to first base" is a prepositional phrase modifying "threw." The focus is on the word and the sentence. There is no identification of the larger context—the paragraph. In addition, word order seems unimportant. The diagram does not indicate whether "to first base" is at the beginning or end of the sentence. Does "the baseball player" begin the sentence or come in the middle? There are those who say that "diagramming only develops better diagrammers." What has been your experience?

Traditional grammar is still taught in the schools. Language arts textbooks provide instruction in it, and much of the vocabulary has been retained. However, the structuralists and transformationalists are attempting to alter many aspects of the traditional approach.

Structural grammar derives its generalizations from an examination of the spoken language itself. Using the scientific method, linguists observe and analyze what does exist rather than what should exist. Problems arise in determining whether the number of samples is adequate for categorization, but the general approach has helped many to see language from a new perspective. Structural grammar was popularized through the work of Otto Jespersen, whose *Philosophy of Grammar* (1924) questioned the source of our grammatical standards. Also important to the growth of this grammatical approach was the work of Leonard Bloomfield, one of the first linguists to classify words according to their function or position in the sentence rather than their meaning. Previously, in the traditional grammar, a noun had been referred to only as a word that stands for a person, place, or thing. With structural grammar, a noun became identified by its position, form, and function, not its meaning. For example, in the sentence "The man's jacket," the word "man" is, in traditional terms, a noun; but it functions as an adjective.

From the work of the structural linguists, a new terminology has developed which can be helpful to the elementary-school teacher in evaluating textbooks, films, and programmed materials. Among the new terms are

> *phoneme:* the smallest basic unit of sound (Ma, Da, Ba).
>
> *grapheme:* a symbol used in writing: a letter of the alphabet, a punctuation mark, and so on (F, !).
>
> *morpheme:* a basic meaning-bearing unit of language. It might be a whole word or a part of a word (pre, dog).

For those of you who may wish to explore word and sentence analysis in greater detail, *The Structure of English,* by Charles Carpenter Fries, published in 1952, identifies its major principles. From the work of the structuralists have emerged concepts that can increase the elementary-school teacher's understanding of the relationship between children and language:

1. Language is systematic.
2. Language changes with time.
3. There are differences between spoken language and written language.
4. There are various levels of usage (standard, nonstandard).
5. Language is altered to meet the situation (kid talk, school talk, professional talk, and so on).

Transformational, or generative, grammar developed from the work of the structural linguists. Noam Chomsky became the recognized leader of the transformational grammar movement with the publication of his book, *Syntactic Structures* (1957). Though this grammar has certain applications for the elementary-school child, Chomsky himself cautions that premature teaching of it may prove disastrous. Transformational grammar emphasizes syntax—the way word relationships are indicated through word order.

Transformational grammarians are trying to find out how people develop the ability to create and understand an infinite number of different sentences, many of which they have never heard before. They are looking for universal structures that can be applied to any sentence and provide a key as to how sentences are made or generated.

Generative grammar is based on the assumption that once sentence generation is understood, any basic, or kernel, sentence can be expanded or generated in myriad ways. There are a variety of prescriptions for expanding these kernel sentences into transformed sentences. For example, the kernal sentence "The dog is a dalmatian" may be transformed in a variety of ways:

A dalmatian is a dog.

The dog is not a dalmatian.

Is the dog a dalmatian?

There is a dalmatian dog.

The kernel sentence may be transformed in still another way; it may be expanded. For example:

The dog with the red collar is a dalmatian.

The dog who lives next door is a dalmatian.

Their dog is a dalmatian; their cat is an angora.

One rationale given for teaching children to transform kernel sentences is that their writing may improve as they increase their experience with the patterns of language

Some language arts textbooks for children have attempted to develop what they call a "pluralistic" grammar, a grammar that makes use of the terminology and processes of all three major grammars. The familiar vocabulary—*nouns, pronouns,* and *verbs*—is used but children are also introduced to the language of the new grammar through references to *utterances, language patterns, structure words,* and *determiners.* Children also explore the concepts of form and function in the language.

Many teachers do not yet feel comfortable about teaching children the new grammar. Some believe that the vocabulary is unnecessarily intricate and complicated. Others question whether linguists are presently able to make more than a theoretical contribution to teaching. But for those challenged by the very real possibility that a child's command of language may be increased through these new systems, a number of references are available. A particularly good overview can be found in *Linguistics, English and the Language Arts,* by Carl Lefevre. You might also want to look at the translation for the classroom provided in *The Roberts English Series: A Linguistic Program.*

Whether you teach any of the three major grammars to your students is a decision that you will make based on your own background, your professional training, and the orientation of your school. Linguists are concerned with studying children's speech and reporting their findings. Teachers extrapolate the findings and translate them into activities that will help children to use language more effectively. There should be mutual respect between linguists and teachers. We must study each other's findings, appreciate the problems and potential of each other's work, and collaborate on appropriate adjustments.

Classroom Grammar Activities

Grammar in the classroom should not focus on formal study of the discipline. Research indicates that language ability does not improve with, in fact may be hampered by, this type of instruction. However, this fact does not preclude the teaching of grammar-related activities that evolve from an examination of children's needs. For some youngsters, this may even result in the discovery of grammatical principles that have personal meaning. Though such discovery is a desirable by-product, it is not the primary purpose of teaching grammar-related activities. What is most important is that children engage in language experiences that develop their ability to use and control the language.

Substitution   Children can be helped to recognize that the meaning of a sentence can be changed through a minor substitution. For example: "Andrew jumped" can be changed to: "Glenn jumped," "Scott jumped," "Kenny jumped"; "He jumped," "The boy jumped," "The child jumped"; or "The cow jumped," "The dog jumped," "The people jumped." The teacher can then introduce students to the changing of words other than nouns: for example, "ran" can be substituted for "jumped." Another kind of substitution can also be highlighted:

Tracy succeeded in the race
Tracy succumbed in the race.

The animal was funny.
The animal was furry.

Sylvester felt hopeless.
Sylvester felt helpless.

Sentence Expansion   To demonstrate the technique of sentence expansion, one teacher wrote this simple sentence on the chalkboard: Dreams end. The children then suggested ways in which this sentence might be expanded to paint a clearer picture. The fourth graders were already familiar with the terms *subject* and *predicate;* the new descriptive words were *adjectives, adverbs,* and so on:

Adding an adjective: Bad dreams end.
Adding an adverb: Bad dreams end *sadly.*
Adding an article: A bad dream ends sadly.
Adding a conjunction: A bad dream ends sadly *and* quickly.
Adding a phrase: A bad dream ends sadly and quickly most *of the time.*

Encourage students to suggest simple sentences for expansion. After some practice, they can work independently on their own sentence patterns.

Sentence expansion activities can evolve from the students' writing. Children can be helped to understand that more than one phrase may be used to expand their sentence. Glenn started with the sentence, "Fires burn." He then wrote, "Fires burn in the forest." "Could another phrase be added?" the teacher asked. Glenn responded with, "Fires burn in the forest at night." Encouraged further he continued, "Fires burn in the forest at night when there has been very little rain." After many such experiences, Glenn will realize that groups of words serve different functions in the sentence. The student need not be able to use the grammatical vocabulary (*clause, modifier, adjective,* and so on) in order to understand these functions. The grammatical rules may be arrived at inductively at a later time (Figure 12-1).

Sentence Combining   Since the early 1970s, linguistic texts have suggested sentence combining as a means of helping students create mature sentences out of simple sentences. And the results of some research,

12-1

Monsters scare.	Monsters scare people who believe in them.
Motorcycles race.	Motorcycles race in any kind of weather.
People yell.	People yell when they get excited.
Pigs eat.	Pigs eat anything.
Flowers smell.	Flowers smell even after you pick them.
Books tell.	Books tell many secrets.
Ships sail.	Ships sail to the most wonderful places.

though not conclusive, link sentence combining ability with reading proficiency.

Sentence combining is not grammar instruction; it is not an analysis of the structure of the language but a technique that provides practice in developing a variety of sentence patterns. Research by John Mellon and Frank O'Hare supports the thesis that when students are given the opportunity in an organized program to put sentences together, their ability to write more complex sentences is increased. A variety of programs and manuals are available.

Transformations are the myriad ways in which these kernels are combined and altered to produce more mature sentences. In the last section on sentence expansion, you saw how simple sentences were expanded through the addition of descriptive words. This is one aspect of sentence transformation. Another means of sentence transformation is the combining of sentences. The thoughts contained in the following four sentences

> The children pick the blackberries.
>
> The blackberries are sweet.
>
> The children bring the blackberries to mother.
>
> Mother makes blackberry pie.

can be combined in one sentence:

> The children pick the sweet blackberries and bring them to mother, who uses them to make pie.

As children become more skilled with sentence combining activities, they learn to use a variety of connecting words. Initially, they tend to string sentences together using "and" as one third grader did in this example:

> Someday I will be a movie star (1) and my house will be a castle (2) and my house will be on top of a big hill (3) and everyone will come for my autograph. (4)

The teacher can help such a student see how connectives and different sentence structures may be used to give writing variety. With assistance of this sort, the third grader was soon able to change her sentence to read

> When I am a famous movie star my house will be a castle on top of a hill where people will come for my autograph.

TEACHING USAGE

In today's classrooms, a teacher may be faced with children whose patterns of usage do not conform to those of standard English. Usage, as has been noted, refers to the *choice* of words in a particular situation. But the young child who selects a particular word for use is not in any real sense choosing. Usage depends upon geography and sociocultural factors over which the child often has little control. The most important factor in the child's word usage is the most immediate one, home environment. Since language usage is intimately tied to loved ones, heritage, neighborhood, and so on, an insensitive comment about word usage may be interpreted by the child as an attack on family and culture. "Whoever taught you to say ain't?" or "Everyone knows that there's no such word as vittles!" can effectively silence and intimidate almost any young child.

Teachers who have taught in more than one locality or who have even a minimal linguistic background quickly discard the notion of one "correct" way to express an idea. One language authority suggests that the following factors determine the language choices that children make:

1. Socio-economic-educational factors (Standard American English [SAE] to nonstandard English)
2. Situational factors (formal ceremony to slangy remarks to a friend)
3. Methodological factors (varying words for speech and writing purposes)
4. Historical factors (children's usage and adults' usage; Chaucer's usage and modern usage)
5. Occupational factors (jobs, hobbies, and specialized interest groups have their own phraseology and vocabulary)
6. Geographic factors (international, national, regional, and local dialects)[3]

Given the array of interlocking factors that affect children's language usage, what advice can be given to the teacher for guiding students? The best teaching seems to focus on helping children understand what usage is *appropriate* in a particular situation. Appropriateness will be discussed in a later section.

The English language has what seems an inexhaustible list of usage prescriptions. Which ones should the teacher emphasize? The answer depends on the needs of the class and the teacher's point of view. The research of Robert C. Pooley is quoted by many language arts specialists. Note the usage items that he suggests teachers emphasize:

Speech Forms Subject to Intensive Teaching in the Elementary School

Verb Forms	Pronoun Forms
ain't or *hain't*	my brother, *he* (and other double subjects)
I *don't* have *no*	*him* and *me* went. Mary
learn me a song	and *me* saw, etc.
leave me go	

[3]Jean Malmstrom, *Understanding Language: A Primer for the Language Arts Teacher* (New York: St. Martin's Press, 1977), p. 66.

have *ate*, have *went*, have *did*
 have *saw*, have *wrote*, etc.
he *begun*, he *seen*, he *run*, he
 drunk, he *come*, etc.
I *says*
he *brung*, he *clumb*
we, you, they *was*
was *broke* (for broken)
was *froze*
knowed, *growed*, etc.

hisself, *theirselves*, etc.
them books, *this here*
 book, *that there* book
it's *your'n*, *her'n*, *his'n*,
 our'n[4]

Pooley also recommends that we forget a number of specific items of usage that have been taught. Some of these are

1. Distinctions between *shall* and *will*
2. Any reference to the split infinitive
3. Elimination of *like* as a conjunction
4. Objection to the phrase "different than"
5. Objection to "He is one of those boys who is"
6. Objection to "the reason . . . is because . . ."
7. Objection to *myself* as a polite substitution for *I*
8. Insistence on the possessive case standing before a gerund[5]

In all teaching, the emphasis should be on diagnosis. Instructional programs are built on the strengths and weaknesses of individual students; and therefore require different techniques and approaches. Certainly, not all usage lessons have to be taught to every child. Some students may require continuing instruction on usage; others will need only a few sessions to correct their errors. Flexible grouping is the key.

In the early grades, standard usage of even the most basic kind can be taught only through example. The teacher serves as a model and invites children through example to adopt forms of usage that may differ from those they have learned outside the classroom. The meaningful context is the classroom setting in which there are opportunities for differing and appropriate usage.

Children in the primary grades enjoy using the tape recorder and listening to their own speech. Their level of usage awareness is often heightened when they hear their own words. The flow of appropriate language can also be encouraged through the reading of prose and poetry. Youngsters able to do so should be allowed to read to the class. Others can participate in choral speaking and a variety of creative dramatics activities.

Oral usage activities are valuable since problems in usage begin orally

[4]Robert C. Pooley, *The Teaching of English Usage* (Urbana, Ill.: National Council of Teachers of English, 1974), p. 183.
[5]Robert C. Pooley, "Dare Schools Set a Standard in English Usage?" *English Teachers Journal* 49 (March 1960): 180.

and then become problems in writing. Tape recordings (by students and others), role playing, creative dramatics, and readings from prose and poetry encourage listening and sensitivity to standard forms.

A certain amount of written drill is also helpful with older children:

1. Compare standard and nonstandard forms. Have children identify the standard form.

   > I have went to the movies.
   > I went to the movies
   >
   > I ate my lunch.
   > I have ate my lunch.

2. Provide repeated practice with standard forms but within a meaningful context. For example, children might discuss whether or not they like rock music. The teacher can say, "I like rock music. Do you? I know that Harry likes rock music." The students will orally use "like" and "likes" in questions and in positive and negative situations. Media can also be helpful at this stage. *The Language Master* repeats a prerecorded sentence and attunes the child's ear to standard usage by having the child repeat the sentence.

   Children can then proceed to written drills using the same usage patterns. Following an original drill on "like," students might be asked to select the correct verb form:

   > Phil (like, likes) rock music.
   > He (like, likes) rock music
   >
   > I do not (like, likes) rock music.
   > Do you (like, likes) rock music?

Many children's language arts textbooks offer practice in this type of exercise.

A most important factor that propels children to alter language is their recognition of its appropriateness. Role playing provides a good opportunity to highlight usage appropriateness. Situations like those that follow can be used to develop awareness of variations in oral usage:

1. You are not chosen for the all-city school chorus from your school. You believe that you are as qualified as several children who have been selected.
   a. Share your reaction with your best friend.
   b. Discuss the situation with the teacher in charge.
2. You are a candidate for president of the school council. Prepare a speech to be delivered to:
   a. The students in your grade.
   b. The younger children in the school.
   c. The teachers in the school.

Usage variation can also be recognized through written activities:

3. Your class needs money and materials for a carpentry center.
   a. Write a flyer that will be distributed to other students requesting their assistance.
   b. Prepare a letter to the Board of Education requesting economic aid.
4. You want to encourage support for the idea that the school should serve a more varied lunch menu.
   a. Present your ideas in written form to a small group of close friends.
   b. Write your reasons in a note to the manager of the cafeteria.

Because we are teachers, our feelings and attitudes are on display. It is through language, unspoken and spoken, that our students discover how we feel about them. Even our tone has an impact. If we believe, along with the National Council of Teachers of English, that children have a right to their own language, then we should communicate this to our students in many ways. They in turn will be more comfortable and fluent as they share with us. In time, some may even choose to emulate our language habits. The recognition that correct or incorrect usage is a matter of social context has important implications in the classroom. Teacher models who accept this position as well as students' rights to their own language will encourage children to operate on several levels of language usage. Appropriateness of language rather than an absolute standard will serve as the yardstick.

TEACHING PUNCTUATION

"Last year I visited a school in Ohio," Ms. Adams told her third-grade class, "where punctuation was not allowed. It wasn't allowed in the children's readers, texts or workbooks. I never saw a punctuation mark on a blackboard, a bulletin board or on a school notice. Children were not allowed to use punctuation even in their own writing. What do you think happened?" One wide-eyed student replied, "I bet it was great." "How could they understand what they were reading?" queried John. "Maybe they invented a whole new set of punctuation marks and you didn't recognize them," suggested Julie. "I bet it was a mess," volunteered Marshall. "Well," said Ms. Adams, "Those of you who thought that it was confusing and that something had to replace the usual symbols were right. We need punctuation to help us understand what the writer is saying."

Teachers can develop their students' interest in punctuation by highlighting the problems that would arise if they were forced to do without this convention permanently. Encourage children to consider why punctuation marks came about in the first place and how they serve as an aid to written expression. Unlike speaking, which relies on intonation, pauses, and body language, the written word must communicate without benefit of gesture or facial expression. Punctuation marks are the reader's markers or signposts. They send out messages that say stop, stress this, ask a question, and so on. Like music, language has its staccattos, legatos, accents, and pauses.

Like musical notations and the alphabet, punctuation marks have no intrinsic meaning. Students in the middle grades may be intrigued with the idea of developing their own punctuation symbols. Stress the importance of general agreement on the meaning of a particular symbol once it has been selected. The students in one fifth-grade class developed substitutes for most of the basic punctuation marks:

.	!	?	:	,	;	»	—	)
~	≈	∧	≈	c	c̃	xx	⊖	x

Using their alternatives, unravel the following:

Janet ran down the street ≈ Linda followed close at her

heels~ ×× Please come with me at once c ×× she told

Dr~ Grayson~ ×× It × s an emergency~ ××

Though punctuation is primarily a visual skill, speech may provide some clues about the punctuation that is being used. Voice intonation can point the way. Help children see this by repeating the same sentences on the chalkboard using the symbol that best expresses the voice variation. Many series of sentences such as the following can be developed by your students:

Susan is happy.   The tornado was frightening.
Susan is happy?   The tornado was frightening?
Susan is happy!   The tornado was frightening!

Punctuation Activities for the Primary Grades

1. When children begin to write, they need punctuation models. Prepare charts around the room that show terminal punctuation (stop signs). In the early grades, the period, question mark, and exclamation point are the essential symbols. Gradually, the comma may be introduced. At this stage, many youngsters are still struggling with the letter symbols. Charts that contain too many punctuation items compound their difficulty.

2. In preparing experience charts with the class, highlight the appropriate punctuation marks.

3. Read aloud from poetry and prose. Have students share their written work as well. Call attention to the voice intonation and its implications for punctuation.

4. Transcribe dictation from individuals or the class onto the chalkboard, noting the punctuation.

5. Use the tape recorder in a variety of ways. Distribute unpunctuated transcriptions and have students write in the correct punctuation marks as they listen to the tape recording.

6. Write several sentences on the chalkboard using no punctuation. For example:

> On April 28 our class is going on a trip to the Bronx Zoo bring your lunch and twenty five cents two pencils and a notebook have your permission slip signed by your parent return it tomorrow ask your mother and father if they would like to join us on the trip we will leave at 930

7. Have students prepare a scrapbook of artistic punctuation marks. This may be an individual, class, or group project. Punctuation signs may be animated. The drawings may be freely drawn or they may be pictures cut from magazines.

8. Children's books often present punctuation whimsically and can be of great assistance to the teacher. As early as the nineteenth century, writers for children reflected the need to present punctuation in an attractive way. In *Punctuation Personified*, a Mr. Stop shows the reader how to use punctuation marks. Young children can learn from and be entertained by such heavily illustrated books.

Punctuation Activities for the Intermediate Grades

Many of the activities suggested for primary grades may be adapted for intermediate or upper-grade children. Here are some further suggestions:

1. Read or have the children listen to a tape recorded paragraph. Using the intonations as clues for punctuation, have them transcribe the taped material. Discuss the variety of ways in which the paragraph may be punctuated.

2. Prepare worksheets to be used by individual children at their desks, in small skill groups, or by the entire class. A punctuation worksheet may serve both as a diagnostic tool and a corrective one. The worksheet below asks the student to explain why each period is used:

   1. The wardrobe was at the outer edge of the land of Narnia.
   2. J. T. is a great book.

3. The Electric Co. is a television program.
4. Buy Jimmy an ice cream cone.
5. Kenny said, "I enjoy my job . . . and the possibility of advancement."

3. Give students cartoons without captions. Have them write captions that are questions, statements, or exclamations.

4. Provide students with opportunities to proofread one another's work. Learning to recognize the punctuation errors of others helps students to recognize their own.

Learning Center Activities for Punctuation Practice

It is in a Learning Center that students may have intense exposure to materials that can help them learn to punctuate properly. Some of these materials might be:

1. *A Board Game:* The game is organized as a variation on "Parcheesi." The object is to be the first player to move a pawn from START to HOME. As players land on certain spaces, they are asked punctuation questions. They must answer correctly before they can advance. Children can construct the game themselves and the questions can be frequently changed.

2. *Folders:* The student selects a folder that contains six sentence cards with sentences in paragraphs. There are also a number of cards containing terminal punctuation (periods, exclamation points, question marks). The child attempts to match the sentence with the correct punctuation mark. Material is checked by the teacher (or by the child) using a key.

3. *Card Games:* In a matching card game similar to Casino, sentences are paired with correct punctuation. Using 3 × 5 index cards, write 26 sentences without terminal punctuation. On the other 26 cards, place terminal punctuation marks. Mix the two groups of cards. Each player should be dealt four cards; four cards are placed face up in the center. The players take turns matching punctuation and sentences, collecting the cards when they do so. The player to amass the greatest number of cards wins the game.

All of these punctuation activities will be more meaningful if the students can relate them to their own written expression. Individualizing the teaching of punctuation sometimes means giving up workbooks and drills and some teachers are reluctant to do this. A recent study by Lucy Calkins, however, does raise some important questions about existing practices in teaching punctuation. This researcher found that third-grade "writers" who had not had formal instruction in punctuation could define/explain an average of 8.66 kinds of punctuation. The children who had studied punctuation through classwork, drills, and test, but had rarely written, were able to define/explain only 3.85 kinds of punctuation.[6]

Once children recognize their own punctuation needs, a variety of appropriate activities should be made available to them. These may be teacher developed or textbook oriented. Most important is that we do not allow the busy work to get out of hand. When working in areas of basic skills such as punctuation, capitalization, spelling, and handwriting which need reinforcement exercises, it is important to frequently stop to consider whether your practice is related to your philosophy and the needs of the children:

Some General Principles

1. Each child does not have to be taught every punctuation skill. (Some are not ready, others know the skill.)

2. Children can discover punctuation rules inductively if they have many opportunities to deal with many writing samples.

3. Children should be diagnosed and grouped according to individual needs. Groups should change and be dissolved when necessary.

4. Teach only those punctuation items which the child's writing stage requires.

5. If emphasis on the elements of punctuation retards the writing flow, temporarily discontinue the focus or teach in isolation from creative, experimental writing sessions.

6. Punctuation is taught to assist the child in writing more effectively.

CAPITALIZATION

Capitalization, like punctuation, is an agreed-upon convention for the purpose of clearer communication. Children can appreciate that the incorrect use or omission of capital letters may serve to mislead the reader. Is Guy a name or just any male? Is China a country or a set of dishes? The capitalization rules noted below should be learned by all students in elementary school:

1. Capitalize the first word in any sentence or direct quotation.
    The boy told his friends, "Last night I caught a ball at the baseball game."

2. Capitalize the name of a person, country, city, state, mountain, river, or specific geographical area.

[6]Lucy McCormick Calkins, "When Children Want to Punctuate: Basic Skills Belong in Context—" *Language Arts* 57 (May 1980): 569.

Bobby Anderson took a trip through the western part of the United States. He enjoyed visiting the Grand Canyon, Death Valley, Old Faithful, and Disneyland.

3. Capitalize the name of a thing when it is a specific.
   The Sears Tower in Chicago is taller than either of the twin towers of the World Trade Center in New York City.

4. Capitalize proper adjectives.
   The German camera is frequently selected by professional American photographers.

5. Capitalize a person's title when it is used with the name or in place of the name.
   Commissioner Norton met Senator Kennedy at a conference of commissioners and senators concerned with urban problems.

6. Capitalize all the important words in a title as well as the first word.
   In 1975, *Arrow to the Sun* won the Caldecott Medal and *M. C. Higgins the Great* won the John Newbery Medal.

7. Capitalize initials, certain abbreviations and titles, and the pronoun "I."
   I met Dr. Hammer at a P.T.A. meeting.

8. Capitalize terms like mother, father, aunt, sister when they are used as names.
   Did you see Mother and Father? I saw your aunt in the garden.

9. Capitalize the days of the week, the months of the year, and specific holidays.
   Last year, Memorial Day was celebrated on a Monday, although May 30 was a Sunday.

10. Capitalize the name of a specific language, religious, racial, political, or governmental group.
    In our country, many religions are practiced (Catholicism, Judaism, Protestantism), many languages are spoken (English, Italian, Spanish), and a number of political groups express their viewpoints (the Democratic Party, the Republican Party, the Socialist Party).

In the primary grades, the emphasis on capitalization should be directly related to the child's experiences. Prepare or have youngsters develop identification cards showing their names, addresses, city, and state. Initially, it is not necessary to explain the reasons for the use of the capital letter. Allow the child to appreciate the visual form without making special reference to the principle. Young children will quickly recognize, for example, that the pronoun "I" looks incorrect when it is not capitalized. Other situations are more difficult. To help youngsters associate words in the capitalized and uncapitalized form, have them do matching exercises:

stop	You
mother	Television
you	Road
road	Stop
television	Mother

Rhymes

Some teachers enjoy developing their own rhymes to assist children in remembering capitalization rules. The one that follows is the author's. Such rhymes can be put on a chart since the visual aspect is primary:

CAPITAL LETTERS

Your friend's name as well as her street,
Must have a capital whenever they meet.
For Maine looks better
And so does Greta
When you use the capital letter.

A small letter is fine,
For a fruit on the vine
But a country or state
A capital must rate.
Or else, how would you know?
That you're in Ohio.

Be sure you don't write
To senator white
To reggie jackson
Or commissioner paxton.
Their answers will come slow
For they'll see you don't know
That capital letters are the way to go.

There is no month that looks like may,
And whoever saw this kind of friday,
Halloween demands a capital letter,
To keep the witches flying better.
Even the first letter of each line
In this poem begins with the capital sign.
So if it's something important—like you and me,
The capital letter just has to be!

Capitalization Books

Individual or class capitalization can be developed. Individual books allow each student to keep a record of his or her own capitalization problems, those that continue and those that have been corrected. A class book may serve as a reference list of all the capitalization items that have been covered.

A capitalization handbook that includes an explanation of each of the capitalization rules can be compiled by the teacher. Students should be encouraged to consult an appropriate section of the handbook before completing a work sheet keyed to that section. Here is a sample handbook entry:

Rule #2: The name of a *specific* person, animal, place, or thing is always capitalized.

	Nonspecific	Specific
person:	woman	Queen Elizabeth
animal:	dolphin	Flipper
place:	ballpark	Shea Stadium
thing:	home	White House

Designating specific grades for teaching capitalization rules would be arbitrary at best. A student's reading and writing levels should dictate the timing. Premature stress on the plethora of rules in language arts always risks students' enthusiasm for language. Wherever possible, the teacher should allow generalizations about capitalization to evolve from the students' experiences with language. As with punctuation, children must be convinced that there is a relationship between capitalization and communication.

TEACHER COMPETENCES

1. The teacher will be able to explain the difference between grammar and usage.
2. The teacher will be able to discuss the basic principles of the three popular grammars.
3. The teacher will be able to explain the meaning of basic linguistic terms: kernel sentences, utterances, transformations, and so on.
4. The teacher will be able to plan activities that use substitution, sentence expansion, and sentence combining.
5. The teacher will be able to plan activities that will assist children with usage appropriateness.
6. The teacher will be able to diagnose children's usage difficulties.
7. The teacher will be able to plan written activities that sensitize children to usage standards.
8. The teacher will be able to diagnose punctuation difficulties.
9. The teacher will be able to prepare individualized materials that will assist children with punctuation.
10. The teacher will demonstrate knowledge of the scope of the punctuation program for the elementary school.

11. The teacher will be able to develop learning center activities for punctuation and capitalization practice.

12. The teacher will demonstrate knowledge of the basic capitalization rules and their application at the elementary level.

Afterview   Throughout the country, schools are under pressure to go "back to basics." An initial reaction is to agree, for teachers as well as parents are anxious that students develop basic abilities. On further consideration, however, it becomes apparent that "back to basics" is a slogan carrying high emotional content but low specificity. What is meant by the slogan? It would appear that "back to basics" suggests a return to the "good old days" of rote memorization and the teaching of grammar. But the accumulated research of the last seventy-five years strongly suggests that the learning of grammar rules does not improve language fluency. Another interpretation of the slogan might be an increased emphasis on the mechanics of spelling, capitalization, punctuation, and so on. Important skills indeed! But are they as basic as the ability to think and express ideas coherently? Without this "basic," the tail is wagging the dog. For the mechanics exist only to correct, hone, polish, and generally bring a written product up to certain agreed-upon standards.

We must be cautious that basic skills are not separated from their contextual framework. Writing that is unrelated to composing is listless and lifeless. It is a return to our old mistakes. To assume that the basics of language development are the isolated skills and drills of yesteryear is to separate the wheat from the chaff and be left only with the latter.

WHEN YOU WANT TO KNOW MORE

1. Remember how you were taught grammar in elementary school. In what ways was it helpful? How does it compare with the teaching of grammar in today's elementary schools?

2. Kellogg W. Hunt in *Grammatical Structures Written at Three Grade Levels*, a Research Report for the National Council of the Teachers of English, sug-

gests looking at children's writing as a potential index of maturity. Read this report and analyze some samples of children's writing according to Hunt's guidelines.

3. Practice *sentence combining* with the sentences below, then ask a colleague or a student to do the same:

> The chef tossed a salad.
> The salad contained lettuce.
> The lettuce was fresh.
> The lettuce was picked from the garden.

Now transform these sentences through sentence expansion. Compare the different versions.

IN THE CLASSROOM

1. Ask several students to write a brief evaluation of a television program for each of the following: a friend, a parent, the television station. Help the children recognize the differences in their three written products and the reasons for the variations.

2. Consult the activity-centered workbook *Workjobs,* in which Mary Barratta Lorton suggests that teachers write down sentences dictated by children about their pictures. Ask the students to expand and transform such sentences.

3. Collect samples of the writing of a small group of students. Plan lessons in punctuation for each youngster based on needs evidenced in the written products.

4. If children in your class have difficulty writing complete sentences, plan a series of lessons in which you diagnose the origin of the difficulty and test ways to diminish it. Be sure to maximize student recognition of the need for speaking and writing in complete sentences.

5. Study each student's use of language and keep a record of the usage errors that each student makes in speaking or writing. How will you conduct your survey without making the students uncomfortable? Prepare a plan for individual and group instruction.

SUGGESTED READINGS

Anderson, Paul S. *Linguistics in the Elementary School Classroom*. New York: Macmillan, 1971.

Applegate, Mauree. *Easy in English*. New York: Harper & Row, 1963.

Chomsky, Noam. *Syntactic Structures*. The Hague: Mouton, 1957.

Fries, Charles Carpenter. *Linguistics, the Study of Language*. New York: Holt, Rinehart & Winston, 1964.

Hunt, Kellogg, and O'Donnell, Roy. *An Elementary School Curriculum to Develop Better Writing Skills*. Washington, D.C.: U.S. Department of Health, Education, and Welfare, Bureau of Research, 1970.

Lamb, Pose. *Linguistics in Proper Perspective*. Columbus, Ohio: Merrill, 1967.

Mellon, John C. *The Basic Sentence Types and Their Simple Transformations*. Culver, Ind.: Culver Military Academy, 1964.

Memering, Dean, and O'Hare, Frank. *The Writer's Work: Guide to Effective Composition*. Englewood Cliffs, N.J.: Prentice-Hall, 1980.

O'Hare, Frank. *Sentence-Combining: Improving Student Writing Without Formal Grammar Instruction*. Urbana, Ill.: National Council of Teachers of English, 1971.

Shaughnessy, Mina P. *Errors and Expectations: A Guide for the Teacher of Basic Writing*. New York: Oxford University Press, 1977.

Weaver, Constance. *Grammar for Teachers: Perspectives and Definitions*. Urbana, Ill.: National Council of Teachers of English, 1979.

Other Materials

Capitalization and Punctuation: Mastery in Language Mechanics. Woburn, Mass.: Curriculum Associates. (Workbooks and teacher's guide.)

Platts, Mary E.; Marguerite, S. Rose; and Shumaker, Esther. *SPICE: Suggested Activities to Motivate the Teaching of the Language Arts*. Stevensville, Mich.: Educational Service, 1960.

Strong, William. *Sentence Combining: A Composing Book*. New York: Random House, 1973.

The Write Channel. Bloomington, Ind.: Agency for Instructional Television, 1979. (Videocassettes and teacher's guides.)

CHAPTER 13

Handwriting and Spelling

Preview Accurate spelling and legible handwriting have no intrinsic value. They both exist to facilitate the composing process. Since most children enter school highly motivated to learn to write, teachers should provide daily classroom activities that keep alive the feeling that writing is a personally valuable skill.

The first section of this chapter will be devoted to the teaching of handwriting. The competences necessary to assist the teacher of manuscript and cursive writing will be identified and illustrated with specific teaching suggestions. The special problems of left-handed writers will be discussed along with strategies for their instruction and support.

The second half of the chapter will deal with the teaching of spelling. Selected learning principles and current research studies in spelling will be presented, and a classroom spelling program will be outlined. Some of the questions that will be raised include: How can spelling be individualized? Should spelling be taught as a separate subject? Can spelling serve as a springboard for developing interest in words? A sampling of spelling games will also be provided.

HANDWRITING

In a world that venerates computers, print-outs, and self-correcting type-writers, it is not surprising that interest in handwriting has shown a decline. Many people assume that legible handwriting is obsolete and that, like the button-hook and the Model T Ford, it has been replaced by more up-to-date contrivances. Obviously, this assumption is erroneous. Many situations still require a handwritten effort. Typewriters are usually impractical for note taking; and even when a typewriter is available, most of us prefer our love letters, notes of condolence, and other personal communications to be handwritten. In the real moments of our lives, we want to hear from a person not a thing.

The accelerating technology has produced much anxiety, and there is discernible resistance to an increasingly electronic existence. Many people have turned to the activities of a simpler past in an effort to ward off the dehumanizing effects of modern society. Rather than function as computerized clerks, they are taking up such arts as quilting, furniture making, and calligraphy. Calligraphy, a time-consuming highly decorative handwriting, is now a course offered in many adult education programs. Riding in on the coattails of the "Do It Yourself" movement, interest in handwriting is experiencing a new upswing.

However, the widespread development of handwriting skill is impeded because the process of composing, writing itself, is practiced less and less. Fewer people find the need or create the opportunity to write. The television set has commandeered our attention. When we do communicate, it is usually in the oral idiom. For many, spoken language aided by gestures and facial expressions, is richer, easier, and more accessible than writing.

If both handwriting and composing are practiced less, teachers are in a double bind. Mina Shaughnessy, in her study of the compositions of freshmen entering The City University of New York, found that poor handwriting affected composing. "It is not unusual," she wrote,

> to find among freshman essays a handwriting that belies the maturity of the student, reminding the reader instead of the labored cursive style of children. Often, but not always, the content that is carried in such writing is short and bare, reinforcing the impression of the reader that the writer is "slow" or intellectually immature. Yet the same student might be a spirited, cogent talker in class. His problem is that he has no access to his thoughts or personal style through the medium of writing and must appear, whenever he writes, as a child.[1]

The use of the typewriter and the telephone and the emphasis on oral communication have certainly decreased interest in handwriting. Yet it is a necessary skill. A price is often exacted for poor handwriting. Those

---

[1]Mina P. Shaughnessy, *Errors and Expectations, A Guide for the Teacher of Basic Writing* (New York, Oxford University Press, 1977), p. 15.

of us who write poorly are well aware of our liability. Like speech or dress, handwriting is a presentation of self; an indicator of ability and attitude. It makes a statement about the writer. There is even some research that indicates that poorly handwritten papers receive lower grades.

Getting Handwriting Started

Initially the child sees handwriting as a fun activity that brings with it the aura of being adult. Since most children enjoy the physical activity of putting markings on a blank paper, a teacher can motivate handwriting instruction by capitalizing on this artistic interest. Here are some general suggestions:

1. Provide many opportunities for children to use crayons, paint brushes, chalk, and markers of all kinds in order to develop their facility with this type of material.
2. Limit the amount of copying.
3. Provide models of good handwriting on charts around the room and on small cards that children can keep at their desks.
4. Offer positive praise while emphasizing some basic principles. "Janet, you must be proud of that letter. It's very straight." Or, "Richard, how you have improved. Almost every one of your *o's* is round."
5. Help children recognize that handwriting is a skill that improves with practice. Have them keep dated samples of their writing in a folder.
6. Develop handwriting experiences that are not isolated activities. As often as possible have children write for a purpose—as a means to an end. (Sending letters, making signs, preparing charts, doing name cards.)

Handwriting and Development

Anyone who has spent time in a primary classroom has observed this scenario in one form or another: Jeff sits huddled over his paper, covering his work with one hand, gripping the pencil with the other. He keeps squinting at the letters on a chart in the front of the room. As he tries to transcribe letters onto his paper, his body tenses. It's not that he's not trying; he just can't seem to do it. The explanation is not very complex. It is a matter of eye-and-hand coordination. Jeff may even be able to distinguish similar sizes and shapes, but he does not yet have the small muscle control required to recreate what he sees. He cannot make his hand do what his eyes tell him to do. In essence, we are making an unfair demand on this child by asking him to perform beyond his level of development. What about the other children in the class? Some have not yet reached this level of development and others have surpassed it.

Like all learning, handwriting proceeds in developmental stages. As the child gets ready for each new stage, there are signals. Watch for these signs, and you will be able to assist the child toward the next stage of development. Here are some questions to ask yourself as you observe children's writing:

1. Is the child able to make the seven basic strokes of manuscript writing?

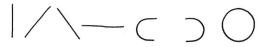

2. Is the child able to reproduce shapes?

3. Is the child able to reproduce forms and objects in his or her paintings? (See the illustrations on p. 413.)

4. Is the child able to recognize his or her own name, or individual letters in the name?

5. Does the child attempt to reproduce his or her name on paintings, name cards, and so on? Are these autographs increasingly more accurate?

The readiness program in handwriting has much in common with the art program. Initially, children work in large bold strokes, usually using finger paints and large paint brushes. Since small muscle control comes with practice and age, children need varying degrees of practice in order to develop manual dexterity. In addition, teachers should determine whether or not the children are able to visually discriminate various sizes and shapes. A painting or two done by the child may provide a clue: Can he or she draw "real things" and make accurate visual discriminations?

Build readiness for handwriting by providing opportunities to work with shapes. Ask children to compare things that have similar shapes: blocks and trucks, books and boxes, milk containers and toy trains. Have the children talk about and draw things that have more than one kind of shape (trucks, trains, planes, and other vehicles with wheels). A variety of activities should be offered that highlight the shapes of objects.

It is important for the teacher to be able to diagnose the cause of handwriting errors so that an appropriate instructional activity may be offered. Here are some typical errors made by young children:

Margaret, Age 5

Becky, Age 3

Margaret, Age 5

Sarah, Age 4

Margaret, Age 5

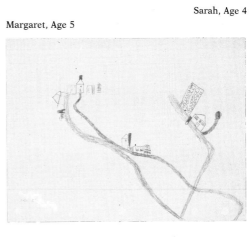

Abigail, Age 5

1. Ned is unable to form the *N* in his name.
   Instructional Activity:
   a. Provide practice with letters and shapes that have both vertical and slanted strokes.

   b. Have him trace geometric shapes with his fingers and then color.

  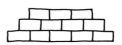

2. Thomas has a problem making his *o*'s round.
   Instructional Activity: Have him trace outlines with his fingers and then try to copy these shapes.

3. Sondra has difficulty writing even the simplest letters.
   Instructional Activity: Provide kinesthetic practice with three-dimensional objects, touching and molding them, and many opportunities to copy shapes that are similar to letters. There has been some discussion about whether tracing or copying is more effective in handwriting development. The recent research favors copying.[2]

The role of kinesthetic activities in handwriting development must be acknowledged. Make available to children as many letter shapes as possible in a variety of sizes, textures, and dimensions; these should be letters they can pick up, trace, copy, and stamp onto paperlike potato prints. Use sandpaper letters so that children can feel the shape of the letters. Experiences with clay, play dough, wet sand, cray-pas, colored chalks, and pipe cleaners serve to develop hand-to-eye coordination and small muscle acuity. Cutting out shapes, fitting puzzles together, and looking at different shapes also serves to heighten the children's readiness. Working at the chalkboard will also aid both large and small muscle development without undue strain. Many of the mathematics materials, used for counting, can contribute to kinesthetic growth.

[2]Eunice N. Askov and Kasper N. Greff, "Handwriting: Copying Versus Tracing as the most Effective Type of Practice," *Journal of Educational Research* 69 (1975): 96-98.

To fully appreciate the child's level of handwriting development, the whole concept of use of space must be considered. From the area of movement, we know that children may be helped to achieve higher levels of space perception in a gradual sequence. Handwriting facility has much to do with how children view the spaces around them. How do they insinuate their bodies and its extensions (paint brushes, baseball bats, and the like) into those spaces? Carefully observe how your students use the spaces around them:

1. When they occupy space do they stay relatively confined? Or do they move out?
2. Do they focus on details in a small area and use broad movements in a large space?
3. Do their paintings make full use of the surface, or are they confined to small sections of the paper?
4. When they write, are they more comfortable with lined or unlined paper? Try the old experiment and ask them to make three cats on a fence.
   Do they look like this?

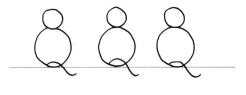

Or this?

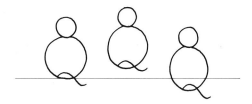

How a child uses space provides clues to the child's developmental level. A number of variables stressed in research on developmental factors in handwriting are outlined on p. 416. They can be an aid in diagnosing where children are on the handwriting continuum.

Motivation

Children are motivated to write when they see the need to do so. Muscular coordination, comfortable physical conditions, and the personal recognition that handwriting activities are functional will provide most students with the desire to write. Help children see that handwriting is not an end in itself. Just as the learning of phonics is a tool for acquiring

DEVELOPMENTAL FACTORS IN HANDWRITING

Question

Discussion and Meaning for Writing

1. How do children change in their use of thumb and forefinger together?

1. A poor grip reduces control. At first it is difficult for children to use this position unless they have already used it in composing with other materials.

2. How does the continuousness of a child's writing change?

2. At first children must stop and start due to the unfamiliarity of the movements as well as what they are composing. The observer is interested in finding out if motor issues are contributing to erratic movements as opposed to spelling and idea formulation.

3. How do the position of the elbow and the stability of the body axis change?

3. The reduction of elbow motion increases the efficiency of thumb and forefinger, and speed and ease of writing. At first there is great elbow motion, along with motion of the entire body. Until this other motion can be reduced, children will have difficulty with the small motor demands of writing.

4. How does the position of the writing surface change in relation to the child's midline?

4. At first children face the paper straight on, not knowing how to accommodate to the left or right of the midline. Gradually children understand the space (the paper) they are dealing with in relation to their own body activity.

5. How does the child's distribution of strength change?

5. The child has to suppress large muscles in order for small muscles to gain control. Pressure on the point of the writing instrument as well as body position gives this information. Observe the change in light and heavy lines on the child's paper.

6. How does the child's use of writing space change?

6. (This has been discussed but a few more details are offered to aid observation.) On a sheet of unlined paper a child will first chain letters at most any angle. The control of large muscles also makes it difficult to use space with precision. Also, the meaning of language, word concepts, sentence units, etc., lead to different kinds of spaces between words. At first we note that children run words and sentences together. As language meaning increases the spaces begin to appear. Audience sense also contributes to this development.

Reprinted from "Preconditions for the Development of Writing in the Child," by J. Ajuriaguerra and M. Auzias, in *Foundations of Language Development*, vol. 2, ed. Eric and Elizabeth Lenneberg (New York: Academic Press, 1975).

reading facility and developing skill in kicking a ball is a prelude to many happy hours in sport, the development of a legible handwriting is a device for sharing ideas with others.

Begin by teaching handwriting in relation to the total school program. Daily classroom activities offer a variety of opportunities:

Send notes to a friend, the teacher, a classmate who is ill.

Prepare signs and charts for the room.

Keep scores in a game.

Tabulate class election results.

Make weather charts.

Write the plan for the day.

Place suggestions in written form in a Suggestion Box.

Prepare posters.

Write labels for books and other interesting items in the room (plants, science equipment and so on).

Since handwriting is inextricably related to the composing process, many of the suggestions offered in the chapters on the practical and creative aspects of writing can be applied to the teaching of handwriting. Try letter writing to pen pals, editors of local newspapers, famous personalities, authors, and illustrators. Provide opportunities to write invitations, notices, diaries, articles, reports, and original stories and poems. Utilize class projects as sources for multifaceted writing experiences. One fourth-grade class, planning an international luncheon, wrote down a variety of questions, leaving room for writing in the answers:

What materials will we need? _____

Where shall we get them? _____

How much will it cost? _____

Who will participate? _____

What labels and signs are necessary? _____

Such purposeful activities can help youngsters recognize handwriting for what it is: a way to bridge the gap between a raging desire to communicate and a modest ability to do so. It is a giant step in a child's life when his or her hand fashions the letters and then the words that tie him or her to the adult world.

An Environment for Writing

It has been pointed out in previous chapters that if the classroom is organized around varied experiences, the need to write will arise consistently. An environment conducive to writing

—is physically comfortable (proper lighting, comfortable seats and desks, writing models that can be easily seen)

—offers opportunities to use a variety of materials (paint brushes, chalk, markers, crayons, pencils, pens)

—provides emotional security in the form of encouragement, individualized objectives, and adequate time

—offers opportunities for ideas to be conveyed in writing rather than speaking (printing names on possessions, writing captions for bulletin boards, advertising a class project to the rest of the school)

As in all learning situations, attitudes and expectations about handwriting may be transmitted nonverbally. Does the teacher make provisions for children who are too immature for writing experiences by giving them special opportunities and assistance? Does the atmosphere encourage the more able writers to assist the less able? Does the teacher make certain that children who are less successful writers still have a place in the projects being developed? Do seating arrangements change frequently without undue emphasis on varying degrees of ability?

Since handwriting is physically demanding, it is best developed in a relaxed atmosphere. A study by Carter and Synolds, "Effects of Relaxation Training Upon Handwriting Quality," provides some direction in this area.[3] Using brain-injured children, the researchers hypothesized that these youngsters were trying too hard to write effectively. Through an audio-taped relaxation program they found that not only did handwriting improve in the experimental group over the control group but that there was a transfer effect to nonverbal experimental learning situations.

Teaching Manuscript Writing

Manuscript writing, or printing, is usually the first form of handwriting taught to children. An important consideration is its simplicity; printed letters are easier to form than those of cursive writing, or script. Furthermore, since manuscript writing is evident in books, newspapers, and signs in the outside world, children enter school most familiar with this form of lettering.

Competences for the Teacher of Manuscript Writing:

1. *The teacher demonstrates an ability to diagnose at least three different stages of writing growth.*
    a. Prewriting stage—Child does not form letters, may not see difference between letters, cannot copy own name.
    b. Model stage—Child copies own name and other words accurately.
    c. Memory stage—Child is able to write own name and other words without looking at model.

[3]John L. Carter and Donald Synolds, "Effects of Relaxation Training Upon Handwriting Quality," *Journal of Learning Disabilities* 7 (April 1974) 53-55.

2. *The teacher is able to demonstrate for the children proper positioning for the body, the paper, and the pencil when writing.*
   a. Child sits back comfortably in the seat. Both feet are on the floor, elbows on the edge of the desk.
   b. Paper is placed straight on the desk.
   c. The pencil is held lightly with the thumb and second finger resting the pencil on the middle finger.

3. *The teacher is able to demonstrate knowledge of basic techniques and principles for teaching manuscript writing.*
   a. Models and copies are always provided for children's use (Figure 13-4).
   b. All letters and numbers are made with straight lines and circles.

   load

   c. All straight letters begin from the top.

13-4

Model Manuscript Letters

    d.   All circle letters begin at the 2 o'clock position.

    e.   Move from left to right in writing letters.

    f.   Space circular letters close together. _boom_

    g.   Space straight letters farther apart. _till_

    h.   Space words one finger apart when using ruled paper.

    i.   Write on the line.

    j.   Capital and tall letters are initially made two spaces high, small letters one space.

    k.   Group letters and numbers with similar structure for instruction (Figure 13-5).

13-5   Grouping Model Letters

Reprinted by permission of the Board of Education of the City of New York from *Handbook for Language Arts, Pre-K, Kindergarten, Grades One and Two*, 1965–66 Series, No. 8, pp. 164–65. New York City, 1965–66.

4. *The teacher is able to assist children by identifying individual errors.*
   a.   Shapes of letters: letters are not properly formed.

   The boy ran to his mother.

   b.   Spacing: letters and words are too close or too far apart.

   Today isa   sunnyday.

   c.   Size: letters are not consistent and proportionate.

   I have a Pet gerbil.

   d.   Alignment: letters do not sit on the line.

   We are learning to write.

5. *The teacher recognizes that variations in letter forms exist and permits their use while stressing legibility and consistency.*
   Manuals from different parts of the country and various school systems provide different forms. Figure 13-6 shows the major variations. Legibility and consistency are the primary criteria. Individuality in style is not an error.

6. *The teacher is able to develop handwriting activities that grow from relevant needs in the classroom.*
   The content of what children write is different in each class. The interests, abilities, and activities in each class vary in the many ways that the children do. In Mr. Sobel's first grade, the children are setting up a store. Learning mathematics was the catalyst, but a great deal of writing is necessary when listing necessary equipment, making labels, stating responsibilities, keeping records, and assigning students to "watch the store."

7. *The teacher utilizes a variety of materials to develop handwriting skills.*
   a.   Handwriting workbooks
   b.   Samples of manuscript writing from children's trade books
   c.   Charts and models of manuscript letters
   d.   Transparencies of manuscript writing used in the overhead projector
   e.   Class folders with dated writing samples from each child
   f.   Chalkboard, newsprint, lined and unlined papers of varying widths

13-6

**Typical Variations
in Letters and Numbers**

Reprinted by permission of the Board
of Education of the City of New York
from *Practices and Problems in
Handwriting*, 1947, No. 9, p. 34. New
York City, 1947.

8. *The teacher is able to plan and carry out activities that focus on self-evaluation.*
   a.   Set up realistic, short-term individualized objectives using a contractual-type arrangement.
   b.   Help individual children diagnose their handwriting weaknesses by comparing their work to manuscript models. Focus on one error at a time.
   c.   Make appropriate selected worksheets available so that children can have practice in correcting handwriting errors. (Some teachers keep file boxes with these worksheets that the children use as necessary.)
   d.   Encourage children to keep records of their practice with worksheets (Figure 13-7).
   e.   Provide practice in copying and writing from dictation (allowing the use of models as necessary). Evaluate work with child.
   f.   Correlate handwriting with spelling, placing the emphasis on spelling.
   g.   Encourage children to share handwriting growth with parents.

13-7   **Student's Penmanship Worksheet**

```
Name: Janet Ricardo

I did a worksheet today.

      Skill                    Date

   Lines              October 20, 1981

  Spacing             November 10, 1981

  Capitals            December 3, 1981
```

Teaching Cursive Writing

The transition from manuscript writing to cursive writing usually occurs at the end of the second grade or at the beginning of the third. Here are some of the factors that determine a child's readiness to make this transition:

> Ability to write all manuscript letters with ease without using a model
>
> Ability to read cursive writing
>
> An expressed desire to write in cursive

The teacher can improve children's facility in reading cursive writing simply by using it in the classroom: on the chalkboard, in personal notes, on name cards for each child, on all new charts and labels.

Competences for the Teacher of Cursive Writing:

1. *The teacher is able to demonstrate major differences between cursive and manuscript writing.*

Manuscript	*Cursive*
Letters made separately	Letters are joined
Straight lines and circles	Letters use upstrokes, ovals, connecting strokes
Vertical writing	Writing slanted from right to left
Small letters and capitals similar	Small letters and capitals may differ

13-8

Model Cursive Letters

Reprinted by permission of the Board of Education of the City of New York from *Teaching Handwriting*, 1960–61 Series, No. 3, p. 14. New York City, 1960–61.

2. *The teacher is able to utilize procedures that prepare children to make the transition from manuscript to cursive writing.*

   a. Practice the transition with lower-case simple letters.

Print the word. (Hold the paper straight.)	Connect the letters.	Slant and alter the letters. (Slant the paper.)
at	at	at
hop	hop	hop
duck	duck	duck

acdghijlm
acdghijlm
acdghijlm

nopqtuvwxy
nopqtuvwxy
nopqtuvwxy

befrksz
befrksz

a clown doll
a clown doll
a clown doll

13-9

Comparing Manuscript Letters to Cursive Letters

Reprinted by permission of the Board of Education of the City of New York from *Practices and Problems in Handwriting*, 1947, No. 9, p. 50. New York City, 1947.

b. After using simple words that do not undergo radical changes in the transition, children can write their own names and then proceed to sentences. Be sure that children work with sentences that are meaningful to them. They should begin the use of cursive writing on a small scale: the first sentence in a composition, a title for a report, task cards, comments when proofreading someone else's work.

c. Help the children focus attention on the major differences between specific manuscript letters and their cursive counterparts. Keep models of both on display (Figure 13-9). Point out capitals that differ significantly from their lowercase letters

A D F G I J Q S T Z

and lowercase letters that change when they are joined to other letters.

b e f k r s z

3. *The teacher is able to provide instruction in cursive writing*
   a. The writing surface is slanted to the right for right-handed writers, to the left for left-handed writers (Figure 13-11).
   b. Most letters in a word are joined, except some capital letters.

D F O P Q T V W X

   (This encourages the child not to lift the writing instrument from the paper until the word is completed.)
   c. A uniform slant should be maintained. Children can check the slant by making their own dotted parallel lines.

slant your letters

   d. Pause at the base line before ending a letter to determine whether it is the last one of the word.
   e. Adapt end strokes of letters to suit the desired spacing.

last

   f. After the word has been completed, *t*'s are crossed and *i*'s are dotted.
   g. Cursive letters that differ from manuscript letters.

b f r s z e m n

   h. Letters with similar structure are grouped for purposes of teaching.

l b f   v x   H K

See Figure 13-10.

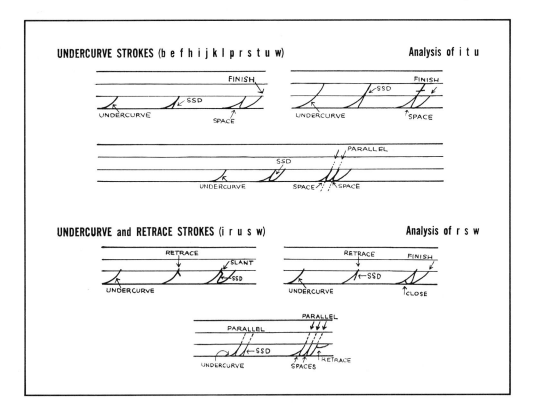

13-10   Cursive Letter Analysis

Reprinted by permission of the Board of Education of the City of New York from *Teaching Handwriting*, 1960–61 Series, No. 3, p. 18. New York City, 1960–61.

4. *The teacher refers to basic cursive writing factors when providing instruction and evaluating the children's work.*

   a. Size—"I'm glad to see that all your *a*'s, *o*'s, and *i*'s are the same height." (All letters of the same case should be the same height.)

   b. Slant—"Your writing is very clear because all the letters slant toward the right." (All letters should slant toward the right and be parallel to each other.)

   c. Shape—"That *f* is just right. It looks just like the model on the chart." (Each letter should be similar to the model.)

   d. Spacing—"It's easy to read your writing because the spacing is the same between letters and words." (Similar space should be kept between letters and words.)

   e. Alignment—"Most of your words are on the line. The paper is very legible." (All letters and words are on the line.)

5. *The teacher provides activities that will increase writing speed without sacrificing legibility.*
   a. Children take timed tests.
   b. Timed practice with the same selection once a week. Children can keep a record of their progress.

6. *The teacher is able to organize procedures for students' evaluation of handwriting.*
   a. Children appraise writing done at the chalkboard, focusing on one aspect at a time. (Are letter lines too thin, or too thick? Are they too high?)
   b. A speed test is given, and a small committee examines the papers for legibility.
   c. An anonymous paper is projected before the students and examined for its use of space. The teacher accepts corrections of the errors in spacing only.
   d. Students evaluate their own handwriting growth by comparing dated samples from their writing folders with one of the various commercial lettering charts.
   e. Students are encouraged to set standards for legible writing that focus on the following factors: arrangement, form of letters, size, spacing, alignment, neatness. Their standards are transcribed onto a class chart and/or a personal check list.

The Left-Handed Writer

We live in a right-handed world, and for some people being a "lefty" can be uncomfortable. Language provides us with some clues as to how the world has viewed left-handedness. The word "sinister" with its connotations of evil is derived from the Latin *sinistre,* meaning left. Similarly, *gauche,* the French word for *left,* has come to mean awkward, out of place, or wrong. The average class may have three or four left-handed children (about 12 percent of the population has this inherited trait), and it is the teacher's responsibility to make the left-handed students feel comfortable. It might be helpful to identify some "southpaws" who became famous athletes—Babe Ruth, Sandy Koufax, Bruce Jenner, Mark Spitz, for example—as well as other well-known "leftys"—Harry Truman, Gerald Ford, Judy Garland, Alexander the Great, Charlemagne, Leonardo Da Vinci. Read some poems about left-handers to your class. Eve Merriam has two charming ones: "A Ballad for Left-handers" and "A Left-handed Poem."

Until relatively recently, the left-handed child had not received the appropriate assistance and support from right-handed teachers. Some years ago, it was even considered desirable to change a child's handedness. Several studies now indicate that such changing may have a nega-

tive effect on the child's speech and produce reversals in the writing itself. What the left-handed child needs most is instruction and support to
be what he or she was born to be. Here are some suggestions:

1. Let hand dominance be determined by the child. When there seems to be
   a question, observe how the child uses his or her hands in other activities
   (eating, dressing, throwing a ball, painting, putting books on a shelf, and
   so on). Another clue is legibility of writing. With which hand are letters
   most legible? The pressure "to be like everyone else" should be minimized.

2. Seat left-handed children together when giving new instruction or practice sessions in writing.

3. Provide considerable practice at a chalkboard with ruled lines.

4. Show the left-handed child another way of slanting the paper when writing. It is usually more comfortable and efficient for the left-handed writer
   to tilt the paper down closer toward the body. Observe what position
   helps the child achieve greater legibility (Figure 13-11).

5. Provide encouragement and support.

13-11   Hand and Paper Placement

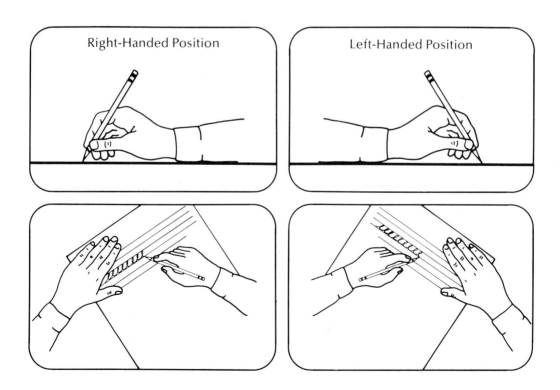

SUGGESTED HANDWRITING ACTIVITIES: YOUNG CHILDREN

1. *Picture dictionaries and alphabet books.*

2. *A graffiti wall.* Set aside one portion of a wall and cover it with paper. Encourage each child to print his or her name and write a message to the class. The graffiti wall can be ever-changing if the children place riddles, comments, and messages on the wall using thumbtacks.

3. *Different forms of print.* Children write their names using all lower-case letters, all capitals, or varying forms of print. Have models available.

4. *Message books.* Have a special time for messages to be written.

5. *Class address and phone file.* Using a lined master have the children write the necessary information. Duplicate copy for each student.

6. *An illustrated book about themselves.* Duplicated pages can be distributed or children can do all their own work. Use one page for each statement.
   My name is _____. I look like this:
   I weigh _____. I am _____ feet, _____ inches tall.
   Here is my hand (trace it).
   My house is at _____. Here is a picture of my house:
   The members of my family are _____ .
   My favorite foods are _____. I don't like
   _____.

7. *Autograph books.* Children can make a book and collect autographs from their classmates, friends, and family. Community helpers can also be asked for their signatures:
   Mail deliverer's autograph _____
   Police officer's autograph _____
   Baker's autograph _____
   Salesperson's autograph _____
   Dentist's autograph _____
   Nurse's autograph _____

8. *Hidden letters.* Help children recognize and then draw situations where letters are hidden pictures.

9. *Concrete words and letters.* Give children practice at depicting words and letters concretely.

10. *Creative alphabet books.* Share a variety of alphabet books that provide imaginative depictions of letters. Sonia Delauney portrays each letter of the alphabet as a basic form in her stunning book *Alphabets*. Photographs are the medium used in Matthiesen's well-loved *ABC An Alphabet Book*. Brian Wildsmith's *ABC Book* is most attractive to young children. The artistic depiction of the letter form itself and a single illustration for each letter provide a simple but beautiful introduction to letter shapes.

SUGGESTED HANDWRITING ACTIVITIES: OLDER CHILDREN

1. *Recording data.*

2. *Preparation of materials for duplication.* Children can prepare masters and duplicate notices, announcements, play scripts, coral poems, and so on.

3. *Unusual surfaces.* Encourage children to practice their handwriting and send communications on wallpaper samples, adding-machine tape, paper towel rollers, cardboard boxes, and so on.

4. *Captioning.* Give children a number of cartoons minus the caption. Have them attach their own captions.

5. *Print styles.* Bring in samples of the many varieties of print styles. Let children try their hand at them. Have them cut out samples of print from advertisements and analyze the design of each.

6. *Historical documents.* Share with children copies of famous documents (U.S. Constitution, Declaration of Human Rights, Declaration of Independence, Emancipation Proclamation) and have them notice the cursive type of print used.

7. *Writing tools.* Have children experiment with a variety of writing tools: felt markers, ballpoints, charcoal pencils, calligraphy pens, stylus pens. Use these instruments on a special wall set aside for this purpose.

8. *Facts about writing.* Have children consult resources such as *The Guinness Book of World Records* and share some lesser-known but interesting facts about writing (for example, that "The Lord's Prayer" was written twenty-five times on a piece of paper half the size of a postage stamp).

9. *Write original books.*

10. Use Oscar Ogg's classic, *The 26 Letters,* as an historical introduction to written English.

11. *Practice sentences that use all twenty-six letters.* Children can try to make up their own sentences. The old standby is "The quick brown fox jumped over the lazy dog."

12. *Learn about the history of writing.*

SPELLING, A TOOL FOR ACCURACY

For many people, poor spelling is a problem that persists into adulthood. Like dieters searching for a painless diet, poor spellers seek out an easy way to solve their spelling problems. A recent trip to a large New York bookstore revealed no less than fifteen self-help books on spelling; among them were *Correct Spelling Made Easy, Spelling Your Way to Success,* and

How to Be a Better Speller. The major remediation technique suggested was the application of spelling rules. The poor speller was also advised to use a dictionary, keep lists of misspelled words, listen carefully, and analyze words for their structural components.

If anything, such books confirm that there is no easy road to spelling success. No "master plan" fits everyone's spelling problems. Spelling proficiency is an individual matter. To return to the diet analogy, perhaps the trick is not to get fat in the first place. If we are to save future adults the search for a spelling remediation plan, the ability and desire to spell accurately should be developed as soon as children are ready to write the language.

Spelling and the Language Arts

Spelling should be introduced as a functional tool in the language arts program. Correct spelling has no intrinsic value. Like legible handwriting, it exists only to facilitate the composing process. The child who has developed spelling power has a larger reservoir of words to call upon and can write more quickly and with greater authority.

Since all the language arts are interrelated, facility in one contributes to growth in another. The child who hears and pronounces a word accurately has a better chance of spelling it correctly. Efforts to develop listening and speaking skills reinforce spelling abilities. Reading and spelling are also mutually dependent. Power in one area nourishes the other. It is in the area of writing, however, that children become most aware of the importance of spelling. Their spelling assets and liabilities are most apparent in the process of composing.

Some Learning Principles Applied to Spelling

Fortunately, research in learning has provided educators with certain touchstones with which to guide our practice in the classroom. What do we know about children's learning and how can it be applied to teaching of spelling?[4]

(1) *Children learn most effectively when they are ready to learn.*
Readiness for spelling evolves sequentially in relation to the other language arts. Rich experiences in oral and spoken language develop the child's word sense. Activities in reading as well set the stage for beginning spelling. It is inefficient, maybe destructive, to provide spelling in-

---

[4]The learning principles that follow have been adapted from "Using What We Know in Teaching," Letter to Supervisors, Series 12, No. 8, April 1959, The University of the State of New York, The State Education Department, Albany, New York.

struction for a child who has not yet mastered the words in an early reader or its equivalent. To separate spelling from the order in which language is acquired (listening—speaking—reading—writing), before any skills have developed, is to ignore the principles of development and maturation.

(2) *Children learn most effectively what is related to their purposes and interests.*

A child's interests and concerns provide the reason for learning to spell accurately. Many studies suggest that spelling failure is often linked to a lack of motivation. Though all spelling activities may not be of impelling interest, many can be. Observe how carefully Mark is listing the names of his baseball heroes and their batting averages for the class newspaper. Cindy and John, preparing a spelling game for a group, are carefully checking each word. Mildly competitive conditions can be used to encourage students. "How many words can this table find using the word 'post'?"

(3) *Children learn through repetition when what is learned is functional for them.*

Practice is essential for spelling growth but it must be meaningful to the child. Not everyone makes the same kind of spelling errors. Beyond a certain point, everyone does not even need to learn the spelling of the same words.

Laurie is interested in dinosaurs. She has a functional reason for learning to spell "pterodactyl," "triceratops," and "brontosaurus" accurately. Kevin is building a home for the gerbils and is making a list of supplies for the custodian. If he wants the correct materials, it's important that he spell accurately. He is very involved checking the spelling of "lumber," "wrench," and a number of other words so that his list will not be misinterpreted. When children pursue their own interests, there are repeated meaningful opportunities to use the words. Repetition, for its own sake, however, has little to do with learning.

(4) *Children learn most efficiently when they can see relationships between what they are learning and what they already know.*

Good teaching goes from the known to the unknown. In the case of spelling, "known" may have several interpretations.

   a. What is known may be words in the children's listening, speaking, or reading vocabulary.

   b. What is known may be the recall of past experiences.

   c. What is known may be the application of a previously applied generalization to a new situation.

   d. What is known may be other rhyming words. "If I can spell old, I can also spell bold."

   e. What is known may be a frequent error. "In some words, I always reverse the letters."

(5) *Children learn at different rates, and the same child learns at different rates at different times.*

In learning spelling, children move at different rates from one step in the sequence to another. They also require varying amounts of time to gain mastery of specific words. For some children, this may mean more time to write, for others the opportunity to dictate their thoughts and see them written down.

From Noah Webster to Programmed Spellers

Despite a ponderous title and a portrait of the author that scared children, *The First Part of a Grammatical Institute of the English Language* (1783), a spelling book by Noah Webster, became a best seller. Twenty-four million copies were sold, and a spelling craze began:

> Previously spelling had been little taught, but now it absorbed a large share of the student interest and enthusiasm, and the pupil who could "spell down the whole school" ranked second only to him who surpassed the rest in arithmetic.[5]

The "Old Blue-back" speller as it came to be called became many students' main textbook. The paper was coarse and the print often illegible. More importantly, the explanations were far too complicated and formidable for the young mind. There were long columns of words frequently interspersed with readings meant to teach children to read and "to know their duty":

> A good child will not lie, swear, nor steal. He will be good at home, and ask to read his book; when he gets up he will wash his hands and face clean; he will comb his hair and make haste to school; he will not play by the way as bad boys do.[6]

Webster's speller also contained a series of eight short fables that appealed somewhat more to children (Figure 13-12). Despite its many flaws, including overt sexual stereotyping, the "Old Blue-back" stands unrivaled among American textbooks with respect to circulation and length of life.

Other spelling books competed with Webster's text, conveying information about punctuation and reading as well. Some were more attractive than others, like Parson's *Analytical Spelling Book*, which was published in Portland, Maine, in 1836 (Figure 13-12).

The nineteenth-century spellers served as spelling guides, primers, language books, programmed texts, sources of general information, and moral tracts. The trend in spelling books had changed somewhat by the

---

[5]Clifton Johnson, *Old-Time Schools and School-Books* (New York, Macmillan, 1904), p. 172
[6]Johnson, *Old-Time Schools*, p. 177.

Noah Webster and his Spelling-book   179

you? said the old Man, then I will fetch you down; so he pulled up some tufts of Grass and threw at him; but this only made the Youngster laugh, to think the old Man should pretend to beat him down from the tree with grass only.

FABLE I.—*Of the* BOY *that ſtole* APPLES.
From a Webster's speller dated 1789.

Well, well, said the old Man, if neither words nor grass will do, I must try what virtue there is in Stones: so the old Man pelted him heartily with stones, which soon made the young Chap hasten down from the tree and beg the old Man's pardon.

MORAL

If good words and gentle means will not reclaim the wicked, they must be dealt with in a more severe manner.

The book ends with "A Moral Catechism" of about a dozen pages. The topics considered are "Of Humility, Of Mercy, Of Revenge, Of Industry," etc., and include such questions and answers as:—

Other Spellers   225

Boys must learn to spell, read, and write,
And try to learn with all their might;
Then they will be wise, good, and great,
And, in due time, may serve the state.

No. 5.

 Ram and Dam.

Has the dam a lamb? | cram   cramp
What is a dam? | dram   damp
What is a lamb? | ham   camp
Ann can catch the | sham   scamp
lamb by the ham. | slam   lambs

No. 6.

 **Nag and Bags.**

A nag and some bags. | snag   hag
Jack holds the nag. | bag   shag
It is a black nag. | brag   Jack
See the rags on Jack's | rag   tack
back. | rag-ged   tact
| cags   act

A Page.
From Parsons's *Analytical Spelling Book*, 1836.

Parsons's *Analytical Spelling Book*, Portland, Maine, 1836, was decidedly more attractive in its makeup

13-12 **Excerpts from Webster's and Parson's Spellers**

Reprinted from *Old-Time Schools and School Books* by Clifton Johnson, New York, Macmillan, 1904, pp. 179 and 225.

1930s and 40s. At this time, spellers were primarily lists of words with a brief word-study exercise attached to each lesson. Observing today's proliferation of spelling texts and workbooks, we once again see the spelling book assuming many responsibilities. Many of these books are comprehensive language arts programs. The question to be asked is, "Are these hundreds of exercises valuable for the teaching of spelling?" The early "spellers" too had a certain usefulness; so do these spelling programs. They provide drill in handwriting, synonyms, word origins, phonics, structural analysis, and a host of other skills. But some experts maintain that such books are confusing to the learner. They question how we are building spelling power when we give a child a workbook page on consonant blends. But in overall approach, these materials seem little different from those old-time spellers that attempted to instruct the child on all aspects of life while peripherally developing spelling consciousness.

Current Research in Spelling

Current research in spelling suggests that we question some long-established practices. Old standbys like focusing on the "hard spot," learning words through syllabication, and writing words several times are simply not working. Furthermore, increasing the time spent on spelling is not the solution either. Read the findings noted below. Consider their implications for the methods and materials to be used in the teaching of spelling.

(1) The correct spelling of a word cannot be guaranteed unless the specific word itself is examined. Learning generalizations when exceptions are so numerous does not assure correct spelling. There seems to be no escape from the direct teaching of the large number of common words which do not conform to any phonetic or orthographic rule.[7] Lillie Davis found that the silent *e* rule is applicable 63 percent of the time with words frequently used by young children. On the other hand, the *ay* rule where *y* is silent, giving *a* its long sound as in "display" has 83 percent applicability but the frequency with which these words are used may not warrant learning the generalization.[8]

(2) Children learn to spell more accurately when they are in a program that uses only a meaningful word list and the pretest-study-retest method and does not utilize any spelling book, workbook, or programmed materials.

Robert Hillerich reports on several studies that compared children who used some of the major spelling programs with those who followed the simpler, researched approach to spelling. The latter group spelled better after spending only three-fifths as much time on spelling.[9] Thomas Horn also reported that the corrected test appeared to be the most important single factor contributing to achievement in spelling.[10] Similarly Leo A. Cohen found that the language arts exercises in most "spelling" books did not contribute to spelling proficiency.[11]

---

[7]Ernest Horn "Phonetics and Spelling," *Elementary School Journal* 57 (1957): 432.

[8]Lillie Smith Davis, "The Applicability of Phonic Generalizations to Selected Spelling Programs," *Elementary English* (May 1972): 706–12.

[9]Robert L. Hillerich, "Let's Teach Spelling—Not Phonetic Misspelling," *Language Arts* 54 (March, 1977): 302.

[10]Thomas D. Horn, "The Effect of the Correct Test on Learning to Spell," *Elementary School Journal* 47 (1917): 235.

[11]Leo A. Cohen, "Evaluating Structural Analysis Methods Used in Spelling Books," (Ph.D. dissertation, Boston University, 1969).

(3) Methods of teaching spelling have involved primarily five approaches: Study of the whole word, the "hard spot," the individual letters of each word, using a list, using words in context. The research of Hazel Smith indicates that the most effective approach to use with a class is the whole-word method with the words presented in context.[12] This study reinforced the findings from previous studies. As far back as 1929, Ernest Horn found that marking "hard spots" in words had dubious value for spelling growth.[13] However, research today indicates that using the word in context is a distinct aid to spelling ability.[14]

(4) Questions have always been raised as to whether spelling instruction should occur incidentally in the classroom evolving naturally from language arts activities or whether it should be approached systematically. The research seems to indicate that both approaches should operate with children receiving some systematic instruction in spelling. James A. Fitzgerald suggests that the "systematic teaching of spelling should begin where incidental learning leaves off."[15] Robert L. Hillerich suggests that no more than one hour a week need be spent on systematic instruction.[16]

(5) Misspelling has different causes; therefore a variety of methods and approaches have to be tried and adapted to meet individual needs. Mina Shaughnessy found four main causes of misspelling: the spelling system itself, differences between spoken and spelled English, ignorance of the rules that do work, and the inexperienced eye.[17] Obviously, the ways of helping students who misspell for these different reasons must vary. Before remediating errors, the teacher *with the child* must diagnose and classify the errors. The section on Remediation provides some suggestions.

Research has raised serious questions about the value of spelling books and published spelling programs. Though spelling books may be used as valuable language arts resources, highlighting for both students and teachers the fact that spelling development is keyed into all aspects of language growth, most popular spelling programs fragment the learning of spelling. The assumption is made that directed practice in a wide variety of word-study exercises will improve spelling proficiency. Current research strongly suggests that this is not so. A *potpourri* of language exercises may even serve to confuse the learner. The attitude that, "It can't hurt," must be carefully analyzed.

[12]Hazel A. Smith, "Teaching Spelling," *British Journal of Educational Psychology* 45 (1975): 68–72.

[13]Ernest Horn, "The Influence of Past Experience Upon Spelling," *Journal of Educational Research* 19 (1929): 283–88.

[14]Cohen, "Evaluating Structural Analysis Methods."

[15]James A. Fitzgerald, *The Teaching of Spelling* (Milwaukee: Bruce Publishing, 1951), p. 25.

[16]Hillerich, "Let's Teach Spelling," p. 302.

[17]Shaugnessy, *Errors and Expectations*, p. 175.

The learning of spelling should be placed squarely in the lap of writing activities, rather than compartmentalized. Growth in spelling is linked most closely to the desire and opportunity to write. Many and varied writing experiences with opportunities to use words in context should be the cornerstone of today's spelling programs. Spelling programs should be used selectively with attention to applicability of material and individual needs. There are too many tangles in the teaching of spelling. We must face the reality that the teacher, not a book, must make judgments on what should be taught and the method to be used.

A Sample Spelling Program

It is not difficult to develop a sound spelling program with the student at the center if you keep in mind what we know about how children learn and how they learn to spell. The components of an effective spelling program are (1) a basic word list, (2) a pretest, (3) a study plan, (4) procedures for instruction, (5) a retest, (6) records of progress, (7) review tests, and (8) diagnostic, evaluative, and remedial efforts.

A Basic Word List   Word lists are usually keyed to grades, each list attempting to offer the words most frequently needed and used by children at a particular grade level. The words in published word lists should be based on research into the words that children use in their writing. Whether your source is a commercial publisher, local school district, city, or state, you can ascertain how the basic list was developed from the manuals.

The teacher should evaluate any spelling list before applying it. Is the list complete? Does it include words necessary for children from a specific geographic area or ethnic background? Should some words be added because of particular community, school, or classroom activities?

Basic word lists may be expanded to meet the individual writing needs of children. However, it is important not to overburden the student with an excessively long list. If writing more seems to mean getting a longer list of words to be studied, students may take the course of least resistance and write less.

The Pretest   Using the words from personalized standardized lists, the teacher gives a pretest to help the child determine his or her spelling deficiencies. The teacher dictates the words (the children have not seen the words previously) and then displays the correct spellings using the chalkboard, transparencies, or large charts. The students should immediately check their words, writing the correct spelling next to any errors. The teacher checks that the misspelled words have been rewritten correctly, and the papers are placed in folders as a record of spelling progress.

STUDENT'S SPELLING SCHEDULE FOR THE WEEK

Monday
1. Give your partner a pretest. Say the word. Use it in a sentence. Say the word again.
2. Mark his or her test. Circle the errors.
3. Now your partner will give you a pretest. He or she marks your test.
4. Both of you must correct your own mistakes (five times each on the test page).

Monday night and Tuesday in school
1. Do unit work or a special assignment using your words.
2. Correct last week's final test (ten times each mistake).

Wednesday
1. You check your partner's unit work. Use the answer book.
2. Circle any mistakes and show your partner what he or she did wrong.
3. Your partner checks your unit work.

Thursday
1. Play spelling games with your partner.
2. Look at the spelling games list for ideas.
3. Try different games each week.

Thursday night
1. Study your words.
2. Take a practice test at home.

Friday
1. Partners give each other final tests.
2. Tell your partner which words to underline.
3. Use your spelling notebook for this test.
4. Give your spelling notebook to the teacher to be marked.
5. Give the book to the teacher to be marked.

Ideally, spelling pretests should be different for each child. However, the teacher may be unable to manage the logistics. Second best is grouping the children according to levels of difficulty. Those children who with some regularity have no spelling errors on pretests should proceed to the next level of difficulty.

The number of words given on a specific pretest is a matter of professional judgement. Traditionally, elementary-school teachers have used from 10 to 25 words in the lower- and middle-class grades and 25 or more in the upper grades. The ability of the children to concentrate, the difficulty of the words, and their own motivation will influence your judgment as to the number of words.

The Study Plan   The word-study plan noted below has been applied, with variation, over the years. It is most effective when children receive assistance and encouragement in its use.

1. Look. Pronounce. Recall the meaning. Spell orally.
2. Close your eyes. Try to see the word.
3. Check now to see if you were correct.
4. Cover the word and write the word from memory. Compare. If correct do this as many times as necessary to *fix* the word in your mind.
5. If incorrect go back to step 1 and repeat.

This study plan and its many variations provide the child with the opportunity to use aural, visual, and kinesthetic clues for learning a word.

Procedures for Instruction   Instruction in spelling has three basic components: word usage exercises, use of reference materials, and writing activities. The word usage exercises employed should provide students with opportunities to use their spelling words in a meaningful context. Students and teachers can develop sentences and paragraphs that reinforce the meanings of words used in writing and other curriculum areas. Selected pages from spelling books may be used to point out the need to use the right word. The teacher may choose to adapt the typical word usage exercise shown in Figure 13-13. He or she may also choose to highlight the misunderstandings and often humorous results when words are misspelled because of typographical or writing errors.

Many reference materials should be available and appropriate. Students should be taught to use alphabetized lists of words at their level of difficulty to check their spelling. For developing spelling ability, these "spelling dictionaries" are superior to the conventional dictionary, particularly for the poor speller who is unable to find words even in a junior dictionary. "How can I find the word if I can't spell it?" is a common cry. Consider the difficulty involved in trying to find the spelling of a word like *believe,* even for the child who knows the beginning sounds. Does the word have two *e*'s after the *b*? What follows the *1*? Two *e*'s? *ie*? *ei*? It's a formidable problem for some youngsters. In addition to the spelling lists published by many school systems, some of the commercial dictionaries are very attractive. Pictures are plentiful and context is emphasized. They can be particularly helpful when the word is a concept (like *first*) rather than a specific object. Another recent and helpful lexicon for the upper grades is *The Spellex*™, which contains over three thousand words listed alphabetically.[18] Its format is simple, and it provides a rapid spelling check. Children who labor over spelling labor over their writing.

---

[18]George Moore, Richard Talbot, and G. Willard Woodruff, *The Spellex*™ *Word Finder* (Newton, Mass.: Curriculum Associates, 1976).

13-13

Word Usage Exercise

Reproduced by permission of the publisher, from the *World of Spelling—Level 4—Heath Spelling Program* by Owen Thomas, Irene Dryick, Alan Luther. © 1978, D. C. Heath and Company.

preheat	remove	uncover
prepaid	replace	unkind
preschool	return	unload
pretest	review	unlock
rebuild	rewrite	untie
recall	unbutton	unwrap

D. Clyde D. Coder has been practicing his new code, using five of the lesson words. This is the "next-letter" code. To solve the code, write the letter *before* the one that Clyde used.

QSFQBJE   VODPWFS   VOMPBE
PREPAID   UNCOVER   UNLOAD

SFCVJME   VOCVUUPO
REBUILD   UNBUTTON

E. Al Most is writing a story, but again he has trouble finding the right words. Can you *replace* his meanings with some of Frieda's Wall Words?

It was almost Christmas, and Santa's Candy Elf was gathering candy for the boys and girls. He (went back) __returned__ to the elf candy factory. He (opened the lock on) __unlocked__ the door, (took the lid from) __uncovered__ the candy jar, (took out) __removed__ the candies he had left behind, and (put back) __replaced__ the lid of the jar. The elf started to leave when he heard a noise and (remembered) __recalled__ that he had left the door open. When he got home, he (opened the buttons of) __unbuttoned__ his coat. He took the candy from his pocket, bit into one piece, and said to himself, "Oh, no. I forgot to (take the wrapper off) __unwrap__ it. Now Santa will know I ate some of it!"

16

Try to utilize the suggestions in the writing chapters to promote interest. Encourage children to do their best with a spelling word and not get "stuck" on one word. They should write down as much of the word as they know and continue with their ideas.

The Retest   Rather than wait for everyone in a particular group to complete their word study, the teacher might give retests whenever children indicate their readiness. With this degree of individualization, it is far more efficient for the children to test each other (using some variation of the partner system). Children can keep records of their scores and correct the misspelled words. The teacher can check to see whether or not the children have accurately corrected errors and identify those children who still need further work. Some teachers set a benchmark of 90 percent accuracy before a particular group of words is considered learned.

After both the pretest and the retest, children should be given time to proofread their papers, dot i's, and cross t's, and correct letters that might be confused.

Records of Progress   Two principles guide the record-keeping procedure in spelling:

1. Children spell more accurately when they are motivated to do so.
2. Positive reinforcement (evidence of progress) produces greater learning than negative reinforcement (evidence of failure).

With these principles in mind, the teacher should have the students keep records of their own progress. Figure 13-14 shows a fourth-grade child's record from her notebook. The results can also be charted on graphs (Figure 13-15).

Another form of record keeping involves children developing a personal dictionary or card file of words that they use in their writing or have misspelled with frequency. We should help children learn to read and spell those words that have the greatest attraction for them.

Teachers should keep a record of students' spelling progress; a card file usually works best (Figure 13-16). The teacher may list words that children misspell and try to analyze them with the students for common or

13-14   **Student's Spelling Log**

My Spelling Record

Name: Danny Perrin

Pretest Date	Words to Study	Retest Date	Number of Correct Words	Words to Study
9/25	broadcast, gloves, glasses, hitting	9/29	18	broadcast, hitting
10/2	nylon, stomach, handkerchief	10/6	19	stomach
10/9	journey	10/15	19	journey

13-15
Student's
Spelling Graph

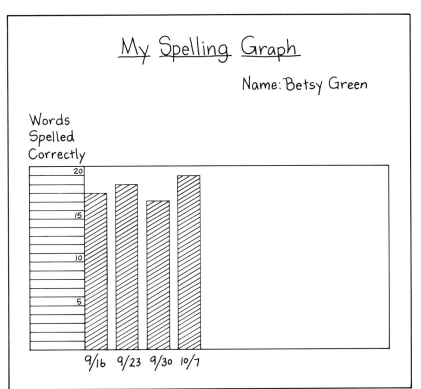

13-16   Teacher's Record of Student's Spelling

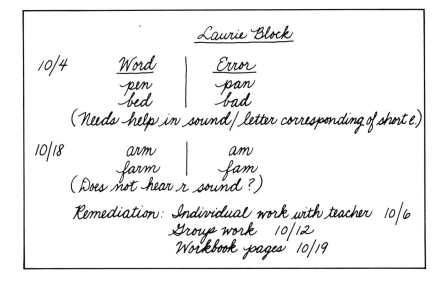

repetitive errors. If the error is common to a few children, a group lesson may be given. Otherwise, individual practice is given with worksheets. The teacher should always stress meanings of words whether working individually or in groups.

Children can gain insight into their spelling through an examination of their own writing in the presence of the teacher. Obviously, a paper covered with correctons can have a negative effect on the child's desire to write. It takes the propitious moment for the teacher to identify with the child any misspellings. However, since this may sometimes take a prohibitive amount of time, at the very least the teacher should keep a record of each child's spelling errors. Observing a pattern in a child's misspellings is the beginning of a remediation procedure.

Review Tests   At the end of the spelling unit or after a period of a few weeks, teachers or student partners should give review tests. Such tests serve as diagnostic and evaluative tools for both the student and the teacher. Since they are more comprehensive than the weekly tests, patterns in a child's misspelling are more likely to emerge. If the teacher wants to stress the contextual framework, review tests may take the form of dictated sentences rather than lists of words.

For those children who evidence a large number of errors in review tests, teachers might ask the following questions:

1. Is the spelling level too difficult?
2. Has the child's mode of learning (visual, oral-aural, kinesthetic) been taken into consideration?
3. Are there indications of other difficulties in language activities?
4. Is the child ready for the general level of academic work in the classroom?

Diagnostic, Evaluative, and Remediation Efforts   Diagnosis and remediation have a cause-and-effect relationship. We are blowing in the wind when we attempt to help students correct misspellings if we and they are ignorant of their causes. Furthermore, for the student it seems like an impossible task. The only answer seems to be memorization. "How can I possibly memorize all those words?" Johnny thinks.

Finding the cause of the error, not placing a mark on a paper, is one of the main reasons for evaluation. In essence, we evaluate to guide our hand, to point a finger at the pattern of error, not at the child. Studies suggest that helping students see the patterns of their spelling errors has a twofold effect: students do not feel overwhelmed by a seemingly endless number of words that can be learned only through memorization, and they are provided with a means of increasing their spelling ability.[19]

Research has not yet clearly identified the great variety of spelling problems. However, there are some questions that children and their teachers can ask as they closely observe spelling errors:

[19]Shaugnessy, Errors and Expectations, p. 305.

1. Are the errors the result of mistakes in handwriting?

2. Are the errors the result of phonetic irregularities in the language? (*ghost, toast, nation*)

3. Are the errors the result of mispronunciation? (*git* for *get, pitcher* for *picture*)

4. Are the errors the result of a confusion of words that sound alike but are spelled differently and have different meanings (homophones)? (*two, to, too—blue, blew—know, no*)

5. Are the errors the result of visual inattention and poor memory?

6. Are the errors caused by contextual confusion? (The wind lifted the kit [kite] high in the sky.)

One way of answering these questions is by keeping a list of the misspelled words: both the error and the correct spelling. Through careful examination, repetitive errors and their origins will become apparent. Here is one fifth grader's list:

Date	*The Word*	*What I Wrote*
10/7	little	liddle
	library	libary
10/14	just	jist
	goes	gose
10/21	playing	playin

The errors in Josh's case are obviously related to pronunciation difficulties. It is important to develop the student's awareness of the relationship and then provide assistance with pronunciation.

A Word about Spelling Generalizations

There are at least ten spelling rules or generalizations commonly taught in the elementary grades. One of the problems with teaching spelling rules is the large number of exceptions. However, if you feel that it is a helpful procedure for a particular group of students in your class consider the following:

1. Select only those rules that have few exceptions and can be applied to a large number of words.

2. Do not assign the rule for memorization.

3. Help students derive the rule inductively based on their experiences with words. Provide numerous examples and then ask, "What do these words have in common?"

Research has shown that bright children, capable of internalizing generalization, may make a large number of spelling errors because they are incorrectly applying these generalizations. Spelling ability and intelligence are not necessarily positively correlated.

SOME BASIC SPELLING RULES
(But there are always exceptions.)

Plurals

Plurals of most nouns are formed by adding *s* to the singular, for example, tigers, girls.

Nouns ending in *s, x, sh,* and *ch* form the plural frequently by adding *es,* for example, churches, foxes, classes, dishes.

Plurals of a few nouns change form, for example, children, mice, feet.

Silent e

A word that ends in silent *e* keeps the *e* before a suffix beginning with a consonant, for example, hopeful, statement, surely.

A word that ends in silent *e* drops the *e* before a suffix beginning with a vowel, for example, mining, adorable.

Possessives

The possessive of a singular noun is formed by adding an apostrophe and *s,* for example, Scott's, baby's, mother's.

The possessive of a plural noun ending in *s* is formed by just adding an apostrophe, for example, students', players', cats'.

Double Consonants

A one-syllable word that ends in one consonant following one short vowel usually doubles the final consonant before a suffix beginning with a vowel, for example, betting, hottest.

A word of more than one syllable that ends in one consonant following one short vowel usually doubles the final consonant before a suffix beginning with a vowel, provided the accent is on the last syllable, for example, forgetting, permitted.

Changing y *to* i

A word ending in *y* and following a consonant frequently changes the *y* to *i,* for example, tries.

A noun ending in *y* preceded by a consonant forms the plural by changing *y* to *i,* for example, babies, cities.

Spelling Games

For many decades the ultimate spelling game in America was the spelling bee. In some areas, it became not only a classroom tool but a common spectator sport involving local and regional contests. Spelling bees did little to develop spelling proficiency, however. The weak spellers never progressed vary far in the competition and probably developed an extra distaste for spelling because their inadequacy publicly was displayed.

Many games have mistakenly been termed spelling games. Most are really games that develop general language skills. The games mentioned below specifically emphasize usage or accurate spelling. Again, individualization and grouping are important considerations: all children should not play all games. Encourage your most proficient spellers to adapt commercial games and to invent their own.

The Scrabble Pattern Forming words across or down in crossword fashion using letters taken from a common pot. Each letter usually has a point value (X = 10, A = 1). A specified time limit (use an egg timer or stopwatch) may be imposed. For younger children, the rules may be simplified; for example, do not require that letters interlock in crossword fashion.

The Jotto Pattern The object of this game is to guess the opponent's word through the use of an eliminating alphabet. It is through discovery of the letters and their placement in the word that the secret word is guessed. The fewer guesses necessary, the higher the score.

Hangman Pattern One player selects a word and challenges the other players to guess it. Dashes are written to represent each of the letters in the word (_ _ _ _ _ _ _); sometimes, the first letter is supplied. Each time the player guesses one of the missing letters, it is inserted. Incorrect guesses are steps toward the completion of a hanged human figure. A total of nine errors on the part of any player results in a finished drawing and "hanging."

Guess-My-Word Pattern Players are challenged (by the person who is "it") to guess a word and spell it correctly. Clues that are given have a wide variation and give the game its many forms.

"This word starts with *p* and ends with *r*. It's in the room."

"I am thinking of a place in our country."

"I am thinking of two words that start with *ten* and are six letters each."

Ghost Pattern In a specified way, each player gives a letter in an attempt to build a word. The object is to avoid having the word end on your turn. Each time it does the player receives a letter of the word Ghost. The first person to accumulate all the letters loses.

Puzzles Thousands of puzzle books and games purporting to teach spelling have come onto the market. How can the teacher intelligently select the most valuable materials for building spelling skills? Since many children learn to spell by seeing a visual picture, puzzles that stress the whole word can be an aid to increasing proficiency. Many of these puzzles go under the generic name "Word Search." Children are asked to look at a puzzle that may just seem like a lot of letters. Under close examination, they find words that go up, down, across, back and diagonally. Sometimes the words have a single theme—for example, the circus. In the easier puzzles, the players are directed to search for specific words. Most children enjoy word-search puzzles, and the puzzles may contribute to spelling growth by increasing visual skills.

EVALUATION OF HANDWRITING AND SPELLING

Specific evaluation suggestions have been provided throughout the chapter. However, the teacher of handwriting and spelling should also consider the following questions in a general evaluation of the instructional program in these areas:

1. Have I identified individual needs with the children?
2. Am I able to state my objectives in performance terms?
3. Do I provide enabling activities that facilitate the process of learning the specifics?
4. Am I able to distinguish between spelling errors and mistakes in usage (*blue* for *blew*) or handwriting (*pot* for *pat*).
5. Am I able to assist the child's evaluation of his or her performance by using my professional judgment and written measures?
6. Am I able to articulate and justify my instructional procedures?

Afterview   Legible handwriting and accurate spelling are necessary survival skills. They are most easily acquired when learners recognize that their written communication is enhanced by proficiency in these areas. The view that handwriting and spelling are valuable tools will increase motivation. When handwriting can keep pace with the flow of ideas in the composing process, both handwriting and expressive writing improve.

Spelling is a functional tool learned best in the context of children's daily concerns and encounters. With understanding of the relationships between spelling and the other language arts, both children and teachers can develop spelling programs that increase spelling power along with language fluency. Current research raises some important questions about the use of spelling workbooks and language arts texts. But as in the teaching of reading, no one method of teaching spelling is suitable for all children. Misspelling has different causes and therefore the ways of helping students must vary.

WHEN YOU WANT TO KNOW MORE

1. Identify all the possibilities for teaching handwriting as a relevant skill in a particular social studies unit.

2. Try to analyze your learning style for spelling. How do you master an unfamiliar word? Is your pattern always the same? Learn the spelling of several new words. What techniques did you employ? What are the implications for the teaching of spelling to children?

3. Examine a few "spelling" workbooks. Identify those pages that teach subjects other than spelling skills (word study, phonics, syllabication, and so on). Do these activities increase spelling proficiency? What questions should be asked about the amount of time spent by children working with these books?

4. Prepare a card file of games that can be used to develop spelling competence.

5. Find out what established practices in the teaching of spelling are being questioned in your school district. How has the change manifested itself?

IN THE CLASSROOM

1. Discuss the problems of being a "lefty" with the left-handers in your class. Plan a project in which students prepare a manual with useful information on coping with "lefty" problems. A good source of information is The Left Hand People, 9 Rice's Lane, Dept. NYB, Westport, Ct. 06880.

2. To alert children to the role of print in our lives have them bring in and analyze pictures that show the various places where print appears: for example, billboards, advertisements, newspapers, television, book titles, road signs, subway signs, and so on.

3. Using Joanne Berstein's *Fiddle with a Riddle* as a guide, have children develop and share their own spelling riddles.

4. Research has shown that visualization is of considerable assistance in learning to spell. Plan three lessons that focus on the visual aspect of spelling.

5. Establish an individualized spelling program for your class. Plan a schedule for a week. What record-keeping systems will you establish for the children and yourself?

SUGGESTED READINGS

Burnes, Paul C. *Improving Handwriting Instruction in Elementary Schools,* 2d ed. Minneapolis, Minn.: Burgess Publishing, 1968.

Freeman, Frank N. *Guiding Growth in Handwriting.* Columbus, Ohio: Zaner-Bloser, 1965.

Frith, Uta, ed. *Cognitive Processes in Spelling.* New York: Academic Press, 1980.

Hanna, P. R.; Hodges, R. E.; Hanna, J. S. *Spelling: Structure and Strategies.* Boston: Houghton Mifflin, 1971.

Horn, Thomas D., ed. *Research on Handwriting and Spelling.* Urbana, Ill.: National Council of Teachers of English, 1966.

The February 1980 issue of *Language Arts* (vol. 57, no. 2) presents as its theme "The Child as Linguist." A number of articles relate to topics in this chapter.

Other Materials

Barham, Margaret. *Dictionary Skills Books A–C.* Englewood Cliffs, N.J.: Scholastic Book Services, 1976.

Discovering Spelling Patterns. New York: McGraw-Hill Films. (Filmstrips.)

Moore, George; Talbot, Richard; and Woodruff, G. Willard. *Spellex™ Word Finder.* Newton, Mass.: Curriculum Associates, 1976. (An alphabetical listing of words to assist students in checking spelling accuracy.)

CHAPTER **14**

Words and Forms of Written Expression

Preview   This chapter alerts the teacher to the many ways in which imaginative work with words can increase a student's conceptual and linguistic competence. A center for the dissemination of language (a learning center devoted to language explorations) will be described, and suggestions for its establishment will be provided. The use of words will be discussed chiefly in terms of five intentions: to amuse, to confuse, to grow on, to group, and to name. Sample task cards will be suggested throughout, along with games and worksheets. Sections on sexism and racism will be included to highlight the linguistic implications of these practices. A discussion of creative groupings will describe ways to foster creative thinking and language expression. And practice will be provided in developing the categories as well as in naming the attributes.

   The final sections of this chapter will discuss the procedures necessary for organizing written expression when writing letters, outlines, autobiographies, journals, and completing various forms. Throughout, the emphasis will be on accuracy—and individuality—in the communication of ideas as a tool for practical purposes. Further activities are suggested using the newspaper as an aid in teaching writing skills for several different purposes.

451

"One of the most important uses of language in all culture is the performance of magic. . . . Wherever language exists, it is used in the attempt to constrain, or appease, or flatter, or beseech the spirit world."

—Richard Mitchell

WORDS

It is never too soon to stimulate children's interest in words. Start in kindergarten. The classroom offers the teacher many opportunities to play with words: tell a joke, share a pun, highlight amusing malapropisms and typographical errors, develop acronyms, use foreign words, quote confusing headlines. Encourage your students to become word hunters. Have them embark on a safari to collect rhymes without reason, riddles, puzzles, unusual names, mixed metaphors, obsolete words, and colorful phrases. Suggest that they listen for unusual expressions as carefully as they would listen for sounds if they were alone in the jungle.

As a teacher, you should also keep up with the patois of your students, the language of commercials, and the patter of the politicos. Watch for newly hatched expressions, and listen for what George Q. Lewis calls "boners" and "bloopers"—amusing short mistakes and king-sized boners.

Your students will soon realize that words can amuse and confuse, inform and deform, entertain and ascertain. Let word play become nearly an obsession in your class. Wordmania is a desirable social disease, one that enables students to apply their creative energy toward a desirable goal.

The Language Dissemination Center

A comfortable, inviting area reserved for language learning can become a part of the child's daily life in the classroom (Figure 14-1). Based on the assumption that teachers cannot always give direct instruction, a language dissemination center provides the opportunity for individualized instruction. Through challenging self-teaching materials, students can be encouraged to consider how words and phrases clarify or obscure, and to discover the many ways in which people interact with language. How we consume it, interfere with it, change it, and pollute it! In the center for the dissemination of language, students can discover how "we use words" and "words use us." Although students may suggest tools and activities for the center, it should be the teacher who initially equips and organizes it. Try to keep the center current by changing, revising, and rearranging the materials in it periodically. Discard whatever is outdated or fails to attract. Each Monday morning, you or a group of students might display a new headline that is a good example of doublespeak, a cartoon about language pollution, or the latest book for children on genealogy. Keep a box of "fake word gems" outside the center and encourage students to rummage in it. (Be sure to invite students to share the responsibility for updating materials and to search for language innovations.)

It is important to awaken children to the vast treasures of language and to help them understand the many ways in which words can be used.

14-1   **Language Dissemination Center**

From *Running a Muck* by John Caldwell.
© 1978 by John Caldwell. Used by
permission of Writer's Digest Books.

Using Words to Amuse

Homonyms and Homographs   Homonyms, or homophones (the linguistic term), are words that sound alike but are spelled differently and carry different meanings. Homographs are words that are spelled the same but have different meanings. They may also have different pronunciations, as in *read* or *lead*. Since illustrations can help to lessen the confusion of these sound-alikes, you may want to prepare charts of homonyms and homographs and ask your students to illustrate them (Figure 14-3). Children can then illustrate or dramatize the meanings of the combined homonyms listed below. Suggest the use of a dictionary for unfamiliar words.

a bare bear	a scented cent	a sweet suite
a new gnu	a knight at night	a dear deer
a hoarse horse	a nose that knows	a plain plane
a tired tire	a hairy hare	a fair fare

Children will also enjoy reading about homonyms in two delightful new books: C. Imbior Kudma's *Two-Way Words* and Cynthia Basil's *How Ships Play Cards.*

14-3

Homonym Chart

Puns   Puns are almost always playful. They involve the humorous use of words or parts of words to extract different meanings. Punning may involve changes in pronunciation, spelling, or meaning:

> Pronunciation: I would like to see you. *Lettuce* get together.
>
> Spelling: Come to our house for a *cellar* bration.
>
> Meaning: The writer said, "My pen has *made me a prisoner."*

Try the following activities:

1. Have your students draw their own illustrations for puns, or provide the illustrations and let them guess the puns. Good words for this purpose include *sweetheart, bulldozer,* and *doubleheader.*

2. Have students devise puns as definitions of such colorful words as *kidnap, cowboy, grownup, pullman, dandelion.*

3. Make a collection of puns in advertisements from newspapers and magazines:
   "A touch of class" (ad for fine glassware)
   "Rolling Stones" (ad for jewelry)
   "Christmas Stuffing" (ad for things to put in a Christmas stocking)

Wags to Witches, by Victoria Gomez, is a book that all young punsters will appreciate.

Riddles   Riddles have enticed children for a long time. In many cases, the riddle relies on the pun: "Why is a railroad track like a happy family?" "Because it has close ties" will be the correct guess of many young children. A variety of riddle books are available. Among the best for very young children are those by Bennett Cerf and Joanne Bernstein's, *Fiddle With a Riddle*. Older elementary-school students will enjoy the brain-teasing riddles in *Professor Egghead's Best Riddles*, by Rose Wyler. Encourage children to make up their own riddles about books, films, television programs, or any subject (noses and feet are favorites), and challenge a partner or group to guess the answer. *Tyrannosaurus Wrecks*, by Noelle Sterne, is a new book of dinosaur riddles that was selected in 1979 as a Children's Choice Book. Also share with your students *high on a hill*, a book of Chinese riddles by Ed Young. These humorous riddles are printed in Chinese as well as English. Provide class time to

1. Share riddles
2. Do a page of riddles and check them with an answer key
3. Make personal collections of riddles and bind them together
4. Hang riddle books on a clothesline strung across the room

Media Mistakes   Each morning thousands of humorists and word enthusiasts eagerly attack the daily paper in search of typographical errors and misconceptions. Many send their findings to other publications, which are often glad to publish them. We enjoy reading them, possibly because we can so easily identify with the human imperfections they suggest. Here is a television listing from a newspaper in Rutland, Vermont:

"Guest: singer: Isaac Bashevis."

The *New Yorker* magazine reprinted the error and asked, "Is he a lyric tenor?" The matter is particularly funny since Isaac Bashevis Singer is the well-known recipient of the 1978 Nobel Prize for literature and the author of several fine books for children.

1. Encourage children to search for media mistakes and even plan their own.
2. Keep collections of media mistakes available. *The Dictionary of Bloopers and Boners*, by George Q. Lewis, has many that can be enjoyed by school children (for example, "Wanted: Woman to sew buttons on third floor," and "Dentist, part or pull time").[1]

[1]George Q. Lewis, *The Dictionary of Bloopers and Boners* (New York: Scholastic Book Services, 1973).

In the center, provide category cards leaving room for the children to illustrate popular media mistakes.

Rhymes without Reason   Rhymes with no intent to express deep feelings can provide children with many humorous and creative moments. Even when it cannot be called poetry, the rhyming of short phrases can help build word power. Here is an example of a task card to develop this playfulness with words:

> **Task Card—Rhyming Words**
>
> List and draw a picture of bugs that can be described by two rhyming words. Here are some suggestions:
>
> 1. a shy fly
> 2. a wee flea
> 3. an Ida spider
> 4. a poached roach
>
> Now try scary things:
>
> 1. gory story
> 2. rich witch
> 3. host ghost
> 4. fool ghoul
> 5. level devil

Using Words to Confuse

When words are overused, meaning may be obscured. Sometimes, the purposes of the speaker are well-served by this impreciseness. In many situations, however, the lack of clarity serves to confuse the listener. Children should become aware of how "words use us" and "we use words" to confuse as well as clarify meaning.

Euphemisms   For a variety of reasons, we sometimes choose to use a word or phrase that is less precise than others at our command. Janet, in order to spare the feelings of an overweight friend describes her as a "hearty eater." A campaign manager who wants his candidate to be impressive writes about her career as a "stateswoman" rather than a "politician." Andrea's parents, uncomfortable with the reality of death, tell their daughter that grandma has "passed on." "Does that mean," Andrea wonders, "that grandma will pass this way again?"

Help your students recognize such everyday substitutions for more direct expressions. In many cases, euphemisms may be a psychological necessity.[2] They offer that little bit of time needed to come to grips with the truth. Uncertain teenagers have "blemishes" rather than "pimples,"

[2]"Telling It Like It Isn't," *Time*, 19 September 1969, p. 27.

and airlines have "containers for motion discomfort" rather than "vomit bags." The need for a euphemism is influenced by cultural attitudes, personal perspective, and the immediate circumstance. Words considered unpleasant in one era or situation are not necessarily unpleasant in the next. As the world, the situation, and the audience change, so do our euphemisms.

The following are examples of task cards that can be used to teach children to recognize euphemisms:

Task Card 1
1. Write the *real* meaning of the underlined phrases below:
    a.   John *passed away.*
    b.   Mary *lost* her husband John.
2. Write a letter to Mary offering your condolences. Try not to be euphemistic.

Task Card 2
1. What is the *real* meaning of the following sentences?
    a.   Grandpa is *on in years.*
    b.   Grandpa is *a senior citizen.*
2. Describe grandpa. Try not to be euphemistic.

Task Card 3
Rename the places listed below, without creating new euphemisms:
Powder Room
Rest Room
Detention Center
Relocation Center
Lounge
Comfort Station

Task Card 4
What do the following people do?
Realtor
Mortician
Superintendent
Landscape architect
Custodial engineer
Intelligence agent
Security officer

Task Card 5—Do You Know:
Which is bigger?
The large size or the economy size
Colossal olives or jumbo olives
Which costs less?
A cheap coat or an underpriced coat
What is the difference?
Between a tavern and a saloon
Between an odor and a smell
Between bad breath and halitosis
Between being fired and being discharged

Colloquial Expressions   Colloquial expressions are another way to confuse our language. When I overhear conversations on our college campus, I am often surprised to discover that I do not always understand what is being communicated. Is it the proverbial "generation gap," or is it that the speakers are not even communicating with each other? For example: Is a "meaningful relationship" the same thing to all college freshmen? Does the term mean today what it meant five years ago? Language, like food, can lose its vitality when it is not fresh. What is the real meaning of *truly centered, with it, turkey?*

Always asking people to give precise definitions of their favorite figures of speech is probably impractical. But some teachers have found that asking children to provide examples of everyday phrases (pictorial or written) has a twofold value: (1) It helps students focus on the many meanings of words, and (2) it gives the teacher greater insight into the cultural expressions of students. To increase sensitivity to colloquial expressions, have a small group of students prepare illustrated collections of popular everyday phrases and place them in large manila envelopes. Other students may then react to their classmates' interpretations. Some popular expressions that might be explored are *let it all hang out, right on, do your own thing, getting it all together,* and *grossed out.*

As teachers, we too might well examine some of our favorite phrases and jargon. Do we really communicate with each other when we speak of "alternative classrooms," "multidisciplinary approaches," and "developmental lags"? The new editors of *The English Journal,* a publication of the National Council of Teachers of English, have declared war on educational jargon. Kenneth Donelson and Alleen Pace Nilsen consider the following terms buzz words and hope not to see them used in articles submitted to their journal: *actualize, coping strategies, dialoguing, educational media specialists, languaging, prioritize, terminal student.*

Doublespeak

> Investigation of Human Ecology—the name given by the Central Intelligence Agency to a secretly funded organization in the 1950s and 1960s for experiments in sensory deprivation and other aspects of human behavior control
> —Runner-up for the 1977 Doublespeak Award given by the National Council of Teachers of English

Each year the National Council of Teachers of English presents its Doublespeak Award to a public statement that is a prime example of pseudo-communication, a statement that conceals rather than reveals meaning. In a world that uses doublespeak to persuade, manipulate, and seduce people of all ages, usually for commercial purposes, language arts teachers have a special responsibility to heighten students' awareness of the possible misuses of public language. Young children are particularly vulnerable, for they have very limited resources with which to critically evaluate the language in their lives. Long before they enter school, children are cajoled by television and radio commercials to behave in a way that is in the interest of the sponsor. Even news broadcasts may deceive, and the language of commentators may be confusing. In 1979, the Doublespeak Award went to the nuclear power industry for jargon and euphemisms "used about the Three Mile Island accident." An explosion was an "energetic disassembly"; a fire, "rapid oxidation"; and a reactor accident was described as a "normal aberration." That television is seldom operated in the public interest is not usually recognized by children. Many youngsters, even some of school age, cannot always clearly distinguish the commercial from the program. Teachers have an obligation to help children learn to recognize the techniques of persuasion.

Here are some activities for this purpose:

1. Have your students bring in advertisements from magazines and newspapers and ask them to analyze the persuasive qualities of the language and pictures. What things are compared? A diamond and happiness? A cigarette and fun? What sort of language is used? Are the words interesting? Are they "loaded" words, such as *motherhood, America, freedom?* Are any of the words used meaningless? Is the statement fact, or opinion? What mood does the picture impart through color and setting? These ads and some of the evaluative comments can be compiled in a class book. The collection can serve as a review of advertising techniques.

2. Listen to radio commercials with your class. Have the students write down "catchy" sentences and then answer such questions as: Is the commercial truthful? Is it believable? What strong emotion-filled words—*love, success,* and so on—have been used to influence you? Has language been humorously manipulated to make you "like" the product?: "Our fish is good. No bones about it."

3. Discuss specific television commercials. Have your students write down the exact words and then analyze the statements for doublespeak qualities.

4. Give a class Doublespeak Award. The students can submit entries (original or from the media) for a period of, say, two months. The class can then vote for the most outstanding entry, giving reasons for their choice.

Sexist Language   Many sections of this text and numerous research studies have underscored the impact of sexism on language and thinking. Often presenting a stereotypic, outdated, or unreal picture, sexist language is particularly confusing to the young consumer of language. See *Sexism and Language,* by Alleen Pace Nilsen et al., for a useful analysis of sexist language in and out of the classroom. Here are some worksheets on sexist language that can be available in the center:

Worksheet 1—Job Titles
Objective: To encourage awareness of equal job opportunities.
Revise the job titles in Column A so that they apply to either sex.

Column A	Column B
chairman	(chairperson)
fireman	(firefighter)
newsman	(journalist, news reporter)
policeman	(officer)
salesman	(salesperson)

Worksheet 2—Who Will Do It?
Objective: To encourage awareness of the arbitrariness of certain roles.
For each household activity below, identify the sex that usually performs the job and explain why its assignment to a member of that sex is appropriate or inappropriate.

Washing the dishes.
Fixing a leaky faucet.
Making lunch for the family
Writing a thank-you note for a wedding present.
Taking out the garbage.
Going to the supermarket.
Getting the cat out of a tree.

Worksheet 3—How Else Can You Say It?
Objective: To recognize that certain terms have no female counterpart.
Replace each of the terms below with one that includes both men and women. If necessary, coin a new word.

mankind
gentleman's agreement
forefathers
fellowship
kingdom
bachelor's degree

Worksheet 4—Equal Time
Objective: To recognize the ways in which language may treat males more favorably than females.
Rephrase each sentence below so that it slights neither men nor women:
1. Writer's wife becomes mayor.
2. Stop complaining about the homework. You sound like a bunch of old women.
3. It's just an old wives' tale.
4. He is a man's man.
5. All men are created equal.

Worksheet 5—A New Dictionary
Objective: To appreciate that language is always changing.
Alone or with a classmate prepare a dictionary that defines some new terms. Some words to include might be women's liberation, feminist, Ms., chauvinist, and chairperson. Poll the class for some other new terms. A good reference is the *Non-Sexist Language Guidelines*, developed by Alma Graham for the American Heritage Publishing Company.

Worksheet 6—Changing the Clichés

Objective: To focus on the ways in which daily language perpetuates sterotypes.

In the clichés below reverse the male or female noun or pronoun. What difference does it make? Can you identify other clichés?

> He is a family man.
> May the best man win.
> No man is an island.
> A woman's place is in the home.
> We are all descended from the family of man.
> Woman's work is never done.

Racist Language   As a teacher you should assume a responsibility for alerting students to linguistic racism. You should be willing and able to discuss (1) racial discrimination as a reflection of society, and (2) the ways in which words and phrases are used to reflect a point of view. As linguist S. I. Hayakawa has pointed out, "when racial discrimination is done away with, offensive words will either disappear or else lose their present connotations."[3] Certainly, racist expressions were originally a result not the cause of racism; however, their use may contribute to its perpetuation. In developing class activities that help children identify racist language, the teacher must be highly sensitive to the special identifications of every child in the class.

Using Words to Grow On

Words can grow and words can shrink. Little words can overpower big ones. (James Joyce thought *yes* was the most potent word in the English language, *cuspidor* the most beautiful.) Words can be cut in two and like the worm can go on to live a new life. Some words are like the lizard; they grow a new part when the original one is severed. Words are truly magic yo-yos capable of limitless possibilities. Here are some activities that will show your students that language will never stop growing and changing.

Tosspots   The term *tosspots* has been coined to describe a compound word that combines a noun and a verb—for example, *scarecrow*.[4] Why not set up an actual tosspot in the part of the classroom that serves as the language center? Throw into it definitions of words that are linguistic tosspots. Have the students guess the appropriate compound. Expand

---

[3]S. I. Hayakawa, "Words with Built-in Judgments," in *Language Awareness*, 2d ed., ed. Paul Escholz, Alfred Rosa, and Virginia Clark, (New York: St. Martin's Press, 1978), p. 211.

[4]Andrew E. Norman, "Tosspots and Wraprascals," *Verbatim: The Language Quarterly* 5, no. 1 (May 1978): 1–3.

the definition of *tosspot* to include double nouns (Figure 14-4). Other toss-pots include:

eyeball	flycatcher	handyman
buttermilk	circuitbreaker	upsidedown
birdhouse	dumbwaiters	brainwash
fishhook	playboy	egghead

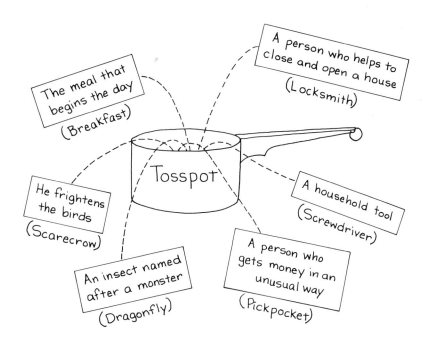

14-4   **Tosspots**

James Thurber, the humorist, was a tosspot master. Here are some of his inventions:

kissgranny (man who seeks out older women)

grabcheck (big spender)

hidebottle (secret drinker)

Your students may want to invent tosspots of their own. Here are some created by fourth graders:

fishburger (seafood sandwich)

bangcan (drum)

misskisser (mouth)

doublebubbler (great gum chewer)

tailwagger (happy dog)

New Words   Edward de Bono, an authority on creative thinking, notes that the "usable" meanings of words are always changing. Political, social, and scientific events cause us to slough off, alter, or invent words. You may want to keep a classroom notebook that has been divided into such categories as ecological words, space words, jogging words, computer words. (Leave room for other categories to be added.) Invite your students to find words for each category. This can become an ongoing activity to be attempted whenever a child is in the language center. The following lists were compiled by a third-grade class:

Space Words	*Computer Words*
life-support systems	programming
space stations	input
blast off	processing
meltdown	memory bank
countdown	hardware
launch pad	software
astronaut	module
lunar module	data banks
booster	positive feedback
cosmonaut	terminal
go	

Environmental Words	*Television Words*
pollution	wrapup
biodegradable	talk show
pesticide	Betamax
anti-pollutant	media
air quality	dissolve
recycle	soap
passive energy	teleprompter
	rabbit ears

Fractured or Extended Words   Another form of new word reflects the increased tempo of our lives. In a hurry, we cut some words down to at least half their original size. Have your students seek out and keep lists of such words:

phone (telephone)	disco (discothèque)
lib (liberation)	sub (submarine)
gym (gymnasium)	plane (airplane)
bus (omnibus)	cab (cabriolet)
soph (sophomore)	pants (pantaloons)

Words, like fashions, have their vogue. Nothing seems quite so out of date as a word that has had its day. However, words like an old dress can still have some life when they receive a new twist. Some words have been adapted to the times through the addition of prefixes and suffixes.

One fifth-grade teacher concerned about keeping her students verbally up-to-date equipped them with a "survival kit" of prefixes and suffixes. The students were asked to apply each prefix or suffix to different base words and come up with as many meaningful compounds as possible; they could even mint some of their own. Here are some of the results:

mini-poll	teach-in	super-mom
mini-course	love-in	super-burger
mini-committee	sit-in	super-car
mini-system	plug-in	super-star

Back to Roots   When children recognize that a knowledge of word roots will increase their language power, they begin to enjoy word-building activities. Given a root, your students can be challenged to see how many leaves they can discover (Figure 14-5). Other root words that may serve as word builders include *world, cover, ship, close, apple, count.*

Conduct a root marathon. Specify a root and see how many related words your students can list in five minutes. Be flexible and encourage idioms and word combinations. Remember your purpose is to build excitement about words. A good choice for idiomatic expressions is the word *sit.* Children will usually think of *sit on the fence, sit out, sitting pretty, sit tight, sit it out.* The humor of such idiomatic expressions can be appreciated when we ask children to draw a picture that shows exactly what the words say. Usually, little thought is given to their literal translations.

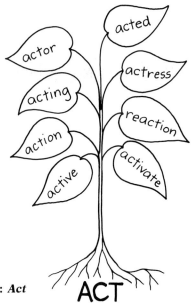

14-5   **Root Word:** *Act*

Using Words to Group

The ability to see relationships is closely related to language development. In the larger sense, it has to do with thinking itself. Some children
never have to be taught that a zebra, a lion, and a moose are all in the
category we refer to as "animals." Others, however, have to be helped to
group objects or ideas into usable, verbal categories. In helping children
discover how things are classified, start simply. Have them group pictures into categories such as things that move, animal words, measuring
words, and holiday words. Abstractions—sick words, open words, and
sunny words—should come last. As children grow in their understanding
of the grouping process, they will begin to discover new relationships
among seemingly unrelated objects.

When teaching linguistic grouping to very young children, you might
fill a box with brand labels of cereals, names of television programs, and
beverages that have distinctive typography. Ask the students to place
each of these in the appropriate section of a "grouping box." Many young
children will have a surprisingly good sight vocabulary of such words.
The typical "nonreading" first grader will be able to recognize the names
of several favorite foods and drinks (Figure 14-6).

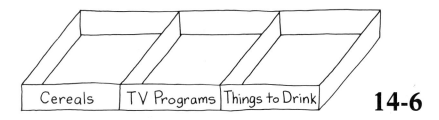

Cereals   TV Programs   Things to Drink   **14-6**

Or you might ask slightly more mature students to label pictures of
miscellaneous items—train, wagon, doll, milk, eggs, bread, football,
chess board, jump rope. After the pictures are labeled, have the students
create groupings for them. Many classifications are acceptable as long as
the concept of common features is recognized. Thus milk, eggs, and
bread may be classified as *food*, or *things we eat for breakfast, items
found in the supermarket,* or *objects that are white.* One first-grade class
made drawings and categorized items throughout the term. They began
with items such as *things that run, things that fly,* and later considered
items such as *things that change, things that help people,* and so on.

A teacher of the middle grades might encourage the development of
personal lists of categorized words to be used for future writing. The
members of one fourth-grade class created booklets of word groupings.
The headings of some of the pages in these booklets were

Cooking Words	Power Words	Mean Words
Scary Words	"No" Words	"Smelly" Words
Royal Words	Sad Words	"CB" Words
Candy Words	Moving Words	Music Words

As they develop word classifications, students expand their vocabularies and begin to recognize that one word can have multiple meanings—and thus can be classified in various ways. Sports words often have very different meanings in other contexts. Have your students draw pictures that show different meanings of such words as *dive, tackle, ball, strike, curve, stroke, goal, ace,* and *love*.

Older students can develop cross-cultural classifications. Some of these word classifications might include:

> *Places to live:* log cabin, apartment house, houseboat, wigwam, igloo, castle, farmhouse, split-level house, mobile home, camper
> *Breads:* flatbread, matzoh, pita, croissants, tortillas, oat cakes, cornpone
> *Games:* bocce, badminton, cricket, jai alai, pelota, mah-jongg, rugby, backgammon

Creative Groupings   A variety of techniques may be used to foster the development of creative thinking within specified categories. The category may be a problem, (What should we include in the class newspaper?), a topic (Rock music), or a concept (Change). Brainstorming is one popular means mentioned in other chapters for stimulating creativity within a specified framework. Some suggest attribute analysis as another means of encouraging flexibility within a creative framework.[5] Students can be encouraged to list the attributes of such entities as: families, democracies, music, death, work, and highways.

Many school activities require students to organize their efforts into usable categories. Whether doing a report, preparing a class party, or starting a club, your students will benefit from knowing how to develop an organizational framework. Early training in the process of structuring words and concepts can be very useful.

Idioms   Grouping idioms on the basis of some common word is another approach to classifying terms. Children seem to particularly enjoy idioms that include references to parts of the body. Have task cards in the language center that direct students to list and illustrate such body-related idioms as the following:

Back	*Ear*	*Eye*
get one's back up	lend an ear	eyeball to eyeball
you scratch my back . . .	turn a deaf ear	pull the wool over
turn one's back on	all ears	one's eyes
		see eye to eye

[5]Morris I. Stein, *Stimulating Creativity,* Vol. 2 (New York: Academic Press, 1975), p. 243.

Face	*Heart*	*Nose*
keep a straight face	eat one's heart out	lead by the nose
face the music	learn by heart	look down one's nose
show one's face	take heart	thumb one's nose

Foot	*Finger*	*Head*
put one's best foot forward	point a finger at	lose one's head
put one's foot down	lay a finger on	make head or tail of
put one's foot in it	wind around one's finger	turn one's head

Animals are another common element in idiomatic expressions. Encourage your students to collect expressions that refer to animals and to illustrate them:

Dogs	*Wolves*	*Birds*
go to the dogs	keep the wolf from the door	eat like a bird
let sleeping dogs lie	wolf down	as the crow flies
all bark and no bite	cry wolf	bird in the hand

Food-related idioms also abound in our language, and not infrequently people are told to "eat their words." After providing some starters like "spill the beans" and "take the cake," suggest that your students make up their own idioms involving food.

Using Words to Name

One relatively unexplored way to interest children in language is to help them realize that many words are borrowed from names. People have given their names to places, clothes, machines, foods, animals, and parts of the body.[6]

Listed below are several activities that can be used in the language center or with groups of children to help heighten awareness of "what's in a name?" The discovery may involve a lesson in history or geography or just plain fun. Your students develop "name collections" in folders, books, or index files.

1. Analyze names important in your life:—Why did your parents select your name? What does it mean?—What does the name of your street mean? Where do you think it got its name?—Does your last name tell something about your family?—Do the first names of the members of your family tell something about them?

---

[6]Two important books for children on this subject are *Place Words* (New York: McKay, Washburn, 1969) and *People Words* (New York: McKay, Washburn, 1966), both by Bill Severn.

2. Using the Yellow Pages of the telephone book, find listings of people whose last names are particularly appropriate for the jobs they do: a jeweler named Silver, Goldsmith, Sterling, or Diamond; a locksmith named Keyes, Locke, or Bolt; a dentist named Dr. Paine or Dr. Gumm.

3. Using the white pages of the telephone book select names at random and then come up with an occupation that might have inspired the name:

   Ellen Crystal (glass blower)
   Arthur Carpenter (builder)
   Bertha Banks (teller)
   Hilda Goodfriend (guidance counselor)
   Dan Frankfurt (butcher)
   William Postal (mail carrier)
   Burt Seaman (sailor)

   An amusing collection of names can be found in *Remarkable Names of Real People,* by Ephraim Tutt.

4. People's names often become the names of things. What people are associated with the terms below, and why do we use their names?

braille	ceasarean
ferris wheel	zeppelin
bowie knife	teddy bear
dunce	sandwich
watt	pasteurization

5. Write a birth announcement that tells why the name was chosen. Here is one example based on the meaning of a common first name:

   Amy and Arthur Jones
   announce the birth of
   Phillip
   who will love horses.

6. Look at a map of the United States. Find names of places that end in one of the following:

   bridge (Stockbridge)
   hill (Stonehill)
   port (Davenport)
   brook (Stony Brook)
   wood (Brentwood)

   Does the name provide a clue about the characteristics of the location?

7. Find places on the map that are named after famous people: Washingtonville, Jefferson City, Stanleyville, Halifax, Victoria, Columbus.

8. Prepare a street map and then name the roads, streets, and avenues descriptively. Add features to the map that show why each name was chosen (Figure 14-7).

9. Many athletic teams adopt the names of birds and animals. List as many of these teams as you can and suggest why you think the name was chosen.

Philadelphia Eagles	St. Louis Cardinals
Miami Dolphins	Chicago Bears
Detroit Lions	Atlanta Falcons
Seattle Seahawks	Toronto Bluejays

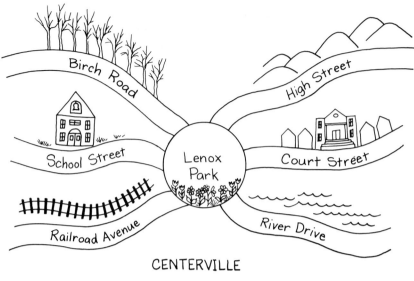

CENTERVILLE

14-7   **Picture-Name Map**

10. List some of the strange names of towns and villages in the United States. See if you can figure out how they got their names.[7]

Midnight, Miss.	Santa Claus, Ind.
Wounded Knee, S.D.	Chili, Wisc.
Steamboat, Nev.	Zigzag, Ore.
Pie Town, N.M.	Bird in Hand, Pa.
Burnt Corn, Ala.	Hungry Horse, Mont.
Two Egg, Fla.	

11. Automobile manufacturers often try to suggest the power and speed of their products by naming them after wildlife. Prepare a list of car models that were named after animals, birds, or fish.

Young children who are interested in the origin of common words will enjoy *What's That You Said?*, by Ann E. Weiss, a beginning reading book on etymology.

FORMS OF WRITTEN EXPRESSION

Though many forms of written expression usually follow a structure, they may be taught creatively. A business letter of complaint may reflect individuality as much as a short story does. Practical writing has its in-

---

[7]The correct explanations can be found in Myron Quimby's *Scratch, Ankle, U.S.A.* (Cranbury, N.J.: A. S. Barnes, 1968), and in George R. Stewart's *America Place-Names* (New York: Oxford University Press, 1970). However, I would encourage children to devise their own explanations.

ventive side, just as creative writing has its functional aspects. In teaching specific forms, the teacher is providing students with basic guidelines and in that sense is encouraging imitation. However, the guidelines are not the reason for the use of the form. The major objective of the letter, the article, or the outline is the efficient and effective communication of personal ideas. Looked at from this perspective, even the most structured forms offer built-in opportunities to express individuality. Students are more likely to become enthusiastic about learning and using basic written patterns if they feel that these forms have legitimate purposes and room for self-expression. The form itself should not be viewed as an end but rather as an effort toward effective communication.

Writing Letters

In Mr. Bergdorf's third grade, letter writing activities begin with note writing. Early in the term, there is a daily fifteen-minute note writing period. During this time, the students write notes to classmates, friends outside the class, Mr. Bergdorf, other school personnel, relatives, and so on. The emphasis is on delivery. The communications are delivered either personally or through the mail. A classroom mailbox has been constructed out of a carton.

Guidelines are established with the help of the class, and the students are encouraged to reread their notes before they are posted. Among the questions they have agreed to ask as they proofread are: "Will it be understood?" and "Is it legible?"

Friendly Letters   Early on, your students should be helped to recognize that personal letters serve a purpose. Letter writing should not be considered an activity designed only to build spelling and punctuation skills, though the improvement of these skills may certainly be a desirable by-product. From an examination of actual letters, we see that children have a need to write different kinds of friendly letters:

Personal Reaction Letters

1. To relatives and friends who live far away bringing them up-to-date on the latest events
2. To a favorite celebrity telling a little about themselves and asking some questions
3. To pen pals telling about themselves and asking some of their own questions[8]
4. Congratulating a friend who has just won a contest

[8]The names of American or foreign pen pals can be obtained from the American Friends Service Committee, 160 North Fifteenth Street, Philadelphia, Pa., or from the American Red Cross, Youth Services, Eighteenth and E Street, N.W., Washington, D.C.

5. To authors or illustrators discussing their books

6. To a class or school publication reporting an event

7. To the editor of a local newspaper expressing a point of view (very often these letters get published)

8. To a classmate who is in the hospital

9. To a classmate who has suffered the death of a loved one

10. To the teacher to express concern about something going on in the class

Letters of Request

"Would you visit our class?" "Do you have any materials on one-day canoe trips?" "Very often, requests are best stated in a letter," says Ruth Blank, a fourth-grade teacher in Lake Placid. Here are some real requests children might make in letters:

1. Asking a person in the community to come to class and discuss a skill or hobby

2. Asking parents and other family members to attend a school function

3. Asking authors or illustrators to come to class to discuss their books

4. Asking school administrators for materials

5. Asking a museum, factory, library, and so on, for permission to visit

6. Asking an expert for an answer to a puzzling question

Letters of Thanks

1. To friends or relatives for presents

2. To visitors who have shared their experiences with the class

3. To other children or classes in the school for some presentation

4. To school administrators who have made available additional equipment

Fantasy Letters

1. From Dorothy thanking the Witch of the East for the ruby slippers

2. From Cinderella thanking her godmother for the beautiful clothes

3. From the Mad Hatter inviting Alice to attend a tea party

4. From the Wright Brothers inviting their mother to watch the flight of their new machine

5. From Elvis Presley thanking his mother for buying him a guitar

6. From the President of the United States inviting you to attend a White House affair

Try to use a visual approach when teaching the form to be followed in friendly letters. On a chart or transparency, block out the correct form and punctuation as shown in Figure 14-8. Guidelines should also be given for addressing the envelope. Models showing proper form, capitalization, and punctuation should be colorful and clear and available for several types of envelopes.

14-8

**Sample
Friendly Letter**

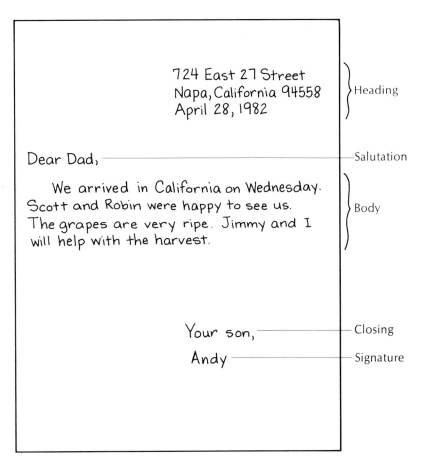

724 East 27 Street
Napa, California 94558
April 28, 1982

} Heading

Dear Dad,————————————————Salutation

　　We arrived in California on Wednesday.
Scott and Robin were happy to see us.
The grapes are very ripe. Jimmy and I
will help with the harvest.

} Body

　　　　　Your son,————————Closing

　　　　　　Andy————————Signature

In addition to creating sample letters and envelopes, you may want to keep available for your students:

　Books of published letters by children

　Collections of friendly letters by one person

　Letters to newspaper editors and columnists

　How-to books on letter writing, for example, Stan Tusan's *Girls and Boys Write-a-Letter Book*

Students will learn to use correct letter form only if they are motivated to write. The selection of relevant topics and the delivery of the letter are major factors in helping children see that letters are a wonderful way to make and keep friends.

Business Letters   Business letters are more demanding than personal letters. Very frequently, the recipient of a business letter has had no other contact with the writer. Thus the letter may have an important role as a presentation of self. After showing students facsimiles of poorly written business letters, the teacher might ask "Do you think that the writer got the information he requested after sending such a confusing note?" or "Is it possible that the director of the aquarium decided not to respond to this letter because it was so sloppy?"

The business letter requires greater concentration on form than the personal letter does—and sometimes greater clarity in the presentation of ideas. As in teaching the friendly letter, the teacher should have the form of the business letter and envelope available on charts and/or transparencies. The students should be made aware that the business letter contains all the parts found in the friendly letter plus the name and address of the person and/or company to whom the letter is being written (Figure 14-9).

Motivation is as important in writing business letters as it is in writing the friendly letter. In a child's experience, the writing of a business letter may be required in order to:

14-9

Sample Business Letter

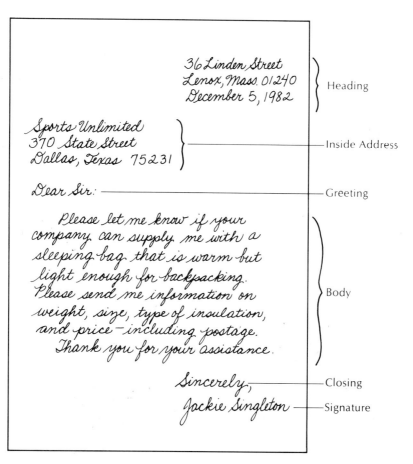

36 Linden Street
Lenox, Mass. 01240
December 5, 1982 } Heading

Sports Unlimited
370 State Street
Dallas, Texas 75231 } —— Inside Address

Dear Sir: —— Greeting

    Please let me know if your company can supply me with a sleeping bag that is warm but light enough for backpacking. Please send me information on weight, size, type of insulation, and price—including postage. Thank you for your assistance. } Body

        Sincerely, —— Closing
        Jackie Singleton —— Signature

1. Order materials from a catalog
2. Ask for brochures and free materials from a business or public service organization
3. Order premiums advertised on packages, in television commercials, and so on
4. Complain about a defective purchase or unsafe business practice
5. Express a point of view about a television program or commercial
6. Volunteer services to a museum, zoo, community center, or hospital
7. Voice an opinion to an elected official
8. Criticize a publication's style or content

Several questions relevant to other aspects of written expression should be considered in teaching letter writing. Should the child recopy a letter? Should an "uncorrected" letter be mailed? Suitable answers may come from the students themselves if they understand that letter writing is a courtesy and that written communications should be legible and easily understood. The students must learn to consider who is receiving the letter: a friend? a relative? a teacher? a stranger? a foreign-language speaker? Just as we adopt levels of language for different speaking situations so we establish flexible levels for content and form for different letter writing situations. Help your students recognize that certain letters almost always require a second draft. Others do not.

The questions below can be displayed on a chart so that students may refer to them as they proofread their letters:

1. Is the letter clear? Does it say what I want it to say?
2. How does it look? Does it look as if I cared?
3. Do I feel comfortable about sending it?
4. Shall I ask a classmate or the teacher to read it?
5. Does it serve its purpose?

You may want to have your students design and reproduce their own personalized stationery and envelopes. They can also design greeting cards, thank-you notes, and the like.

A final word. Most letters are meant to be mailed. Each student should have a package of envelopes, postcards, a few stamps, and even some unlined stationery. Have a mailbox in the classroom. Once your students overcome their fears of letter writing, you may need a bigger mailbox.

Filling Out Forms

A bulletin board bearing copies of a variety of forms can be a valuable classroom fixture. As early as second grade, students are asked to complete forms. They encounter order forms for books, applications for library cards, and permission slips for trips. Children should be encour-

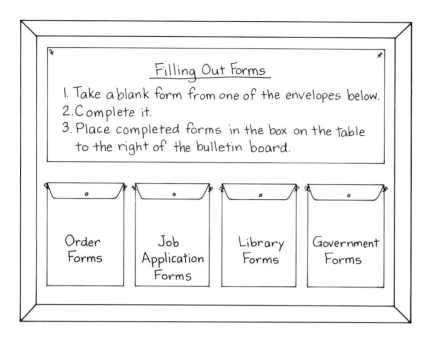

aged to practice filling out both these forms and those that they will confront in later years. The bulletin board can be changed periodically to anticipate the forms that the students will soon have to complete (Figure 14-10).

Knowing how to fill out coupons is another survival skill in American society. Give your students practice by asking them to bring coupons to class and complete them. Guidelines for this practice can be posted on a chart:

1. Read the instructions on the coupon carefully.
2. Provide all necessary information.
3. Print clearly.
4. Be sure that your envelope includes the coupon and any other necessary materials before you seal it.
5. Be sure to address the envelope correctly and to write your name and return address clearly on the envelope.
6. When sending money, tape it to a piece of paper.

Outlining

Even before they are halfway through elementary school, students may discover that good schoolwork requires a knowledge of outlining. In a world in which hardly an hour goes by without new opinions and data being added to our information reservoirs, the ability to structure information is essential. Outlining is the student's principal means of structuring a large body of verbal material.

When attempting to teach outlining, start simply with a subject that is known and of interest to the group. The initial outlines need not be very detailed. Your objective is to develop a way of thinking. One second-grade class created the following outline in one of its first attempts:

Favorite Television Programs

1. Family Programs
    Brady Bunch
    Sanford and Son
    Happy Days

2. Nature Programs
    Those Amazing Animals
    Wild Kingdom
    Camp Wildnerness

3. Science Fiction Programs
    Battle Star Gallactica
    Star Trek
    The Incredible Hulk

4. Cartoons
    Tom and Jerry
    Superfriends
    Popeye

In the intermediate grades, outlining skills become more important. The process of outlining may serve to organize ideas for a composition, prepare the foundation for an oral report, or guide the organization of a party. The correct use of Roman and Arabic numerals and the alphabet should not be the main focus, but it should be discussed and illustrated on a chart. Children need considerable practice in preparing outlines, but not all the outlines created have to be used. They may serve only to develop the ability to organize. What is most important, as in all learning, is that the students see the value of outlining. How will it help them? Is it just another procedure? When should they use it?

It is good pedagogy to prepare an outline with your students that is based on a shared class experience. After one fourth-grade class watched the animated television version of C. S. Lewis' *The Lion, the Witch and the Wardrobe,* the teacher helped the students prepare an outline using this form:

The Lion, the Witch and the Wardrobe by C. S. Lewis

I. Main Characters
   (List them.)
   A.
   B.
   C.
   D.
   E.
   F.

II. Plot
   (List important incidents.)
   A.
   B.
   C.
   D.

III. Place
   (List the settings in which the story took place.)
   A.
   B.
   C.
   D.

IV. Ideas
   (List the author's major points of view.)
   A.

   B.

   C.

Somewhat later students can be asked to learn the basic rules for labeling the items in an outline:

1. Roman numerals (I, II, II, . . .) are used for main topics.

2. Capital letters (A, B, C, . . .) are used for subtopics.

3. Arabic numbers (1, 2, 3, . . .) are used for details.

and to apply them in completing more detailed outlines:

Write the Title

   I. (Write a main topic.) _____
      A. (Write a subtopic.) _____
         1. (Write a detail about the subtopic.)
            _____
         2. (Write another detail about the subtopic.)
            _____

  II. (Write another main topic.) _____
      A. (Write a subtopic.) _____
         1. (Write a detail about the subtopic.)
            _____
         2. (Write another detail about the subtopic.)
            _____

 III. (Write another main topic.) _____
      A. (Write a subtopic.) _____
         1. (Write a detail about the subtopic.)
            _____
         2. (Write another detail about the subtopic.)
            _____

Recognizing that there is something arbitrary about the content of an outline is part of the process. Students should understand that an outline about outer space may include information on space stations, equipment, and forms of life, or information on particular astronauts, scientific attitudes, and the pros and cons of space programs. Making appropriate topic choices is an important aspect of the learning experience.

Outlines are valuable for both oral reports and written ones. Suggest that your students use them for informal presentations as well as for those that are more detailed. Encourage outlining when your students are planning an international lunch or writing a report on "zoos of the future." Here is an outline developed on a creative topic by a group of ten-year-olds:

Who Am I?

    I. A Doer
      A. I ride a bicycle.
      B. I play games.
      C. I arrange things.

    II. A "Goer"
      A. I go on long trips.
      B. I go to visit my friends.
      C. I go to the movies.

    III. A Learner
      A. I learn about the world.
      B. I learn science.
      C. I learn about me.

    IV. A Dreamer
      A. I dream that I will be famous.
      B. I dream that I will go to the moon.
      C. I dream that I will save the world.

Here is a slightly different outline, from a sixth grader. The approach is chronological, but the emphasis is still on self-understanding:

Growing Up

    I. In Elementary School
      A. I want to be president of my class.
      B. I want to be first clarinetist in the band.
      C. I want to get good marks.

    II. In High School
      A. I want to have fun.
      B. I want to play on the football team.
      C. I want to get good marks.

    III. After High School
      A. I want to go to college like my brother.
      B. I want to live in a faraway place and come home for Thanksgiving.
      C. I want to drive a car.

    IV. As an Adult
      A. I want to have an interesting job.
      B. I want to have children.
      C. I want to travel around the world many times.

Writing Autobiographies and Journals

Journals, or diaries, are usually "on the spot" reactions. Autobiographies are usually backward glances. As practice in creating an autobiography, your students might list a few important events from their lives in random order. Can they remember how they felt during each incident? Here are some first statements from a sixth grader:

Year	What Happened	How It Felt
1976	My mother had twins. Our house became very busy.	I was proud.
1974	I went to Italy and saw my grandmother for the first time.	I was a little embarrassed.
1978	Our dog Duffy died. My father cried.	I was very unhappy and so was our whole family.

Statements of this sort may later be placed in chronological order and expanded. What is important is that the children increase their appreciation of their personal histories. If a child is anxious for further details about a particular event, encourage the questioning of family members.

Questions that encourage children to think about writing autobiographically can be placed on charts around the classroom:

1. What important events happened in your life?
2. Can you remember when you first learned to walk?
3. Can you recall a frightening experience?
4. What was school like on your first day?
5. Why do you have special memories of a particular birthday?

Many teachers who have had success in using the autobiographical form have their students prepare a time line of important events in their lives since birth. This time line can be used as a skeletal framework in developing the autobiography (Figure 14-11).

14-11

Personal Time Line

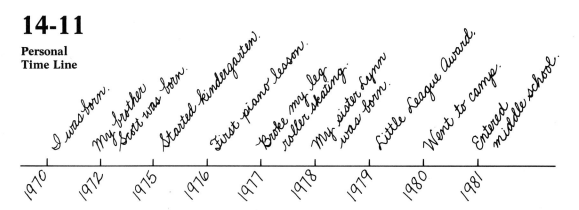

It is difficult to assign autobiographical writing. Like most expressions of self, it must evolve from the child's desire to tell his or her story. Help your students recognize that most writing has autobiographical elements.

The autobiography is not a favorite form among younger children. However, it is a valuable tool in building self-awareness as well as in learning to develop an organizational framework. Encourage primary children to complete fill-in questions about themselves. *My Book About Me*, by Dr. Seuss and Roy McKie, has some helpful suggestions. It asks young readers to draw their feet, write about their favorite foods, describe their houses, and write about their "longests" (walks, bike rides, plane trips, fish catches).

The journal may be a more personal form of writing than the autobiography. The keeper of a journal does not necessarily have to share its contents. In addition, the "dailiness" of journal writing builds writing fluency: we learn to write only by writing. Encourage your students to keep a folder (which can later be bound) or a special book in which they may frequently record their experiences and reactions.

14-12

Student's Journal

My Journal

January 12, 1982

Today we began to gather information on mummy cases. I found out that _____

_____

_____

_____

January 21, 1982

Today we visited the Metropolitan Museum of Art's exhibition on ancient Egypt. There were many photographs and artifacts. The mummy cases ____

_____

_____

January 22, 1982

Today we began to build our own mummy case _____

_____

_____

Educators who feel that the development of self-concept is as important as growth in cognitive skills note that children can focus on their feelings through a journal. Sidney B. Simon, a pioneer in the Values Clarification Movement, suggests that children keep journals that are lists of statements beginning with "I learned that I . . . ."

A journal, of course, is not necessarily a personal revelation. Some journals are project oriented. Their focus may be setting up a terrarium, making a film, or building a mummy case (Figure 14-12). Encourage children to look at the forms followed by several journal writers before they begin their own records.

Writing Dialogue

Some children have a good ear for dialogue. They know how the Fonz speaks, what Winnie the Pooh's expressions are, and just what a scared child would say. Though they do not usually know the correct written form, many first and second graders are anxious to write down lines of dialogue. Encourage them to do so with as few restrictions as possible. Many children start off very excited about writing direct speech but soon revert to indirect speech because the form for dialogue becomes too burdensome. The teaching of correct form can be postponed until students are fluent and comfortable with writing the spoken language.

For fun and learning, have your students supply dialogue for characters in comic strips. Blank out the dialogue in several popular comic strips and let the students replace it with their own. You may be surprised at the accuracy with which students reproduce the words of "The Incredible Hulk" or "Captain Marvel." Much controversy surrounds the use of comics in the classroom, but if used selectively, comics can be a valuable aid in helping children focus on the various ways we speak with one another. Other activities for teaching dialogue include having students write captions for cartoons and having them write dialogue between characters who would be unlikely to meet, for example, R2D2 and Superman, Moby Dick and King Kong, Mighty Mouse and the Cowardly Lion.

The correct form for writing dialogue need not be explained until after the child has begun to write direct quotations. Some children will observe how dialogue is written in books and then inductively arrive at the rules. Among children in the upper grades (and younger ones who are ready), the following questions may be addressed:

1. What is dialogue? How do you know when you are reading it?
2. Is it important to know how to write dialogue?
3. How is dialogue punctuated?
4. How is dialogue paragraphed?

Using the Newspaper to Teach Written Expression

One of the most useful tools in teaching the organization of writing is the newspaper. Teachers can use newspaper articles to help students recognize several different purposes of writing. Subscribing to a newspaper written specifically for children can increase the usefulness of this approach. The following are some activities involving newspapers that will help in the building of writing skills.

Writing Headlines   You can give students the opportunity to focus on main ideas by giving them a copy of a newspaper with the headlines deleted and asking them to create new ones. As a reverse procedure, provide headlines and have your students write appropriate articles for them. Here are two interesting headlines from a recent copy of the *New York Times:* "A 'Monster' Sighted in Chesapeake Bay"; "U.S. Trying to Breed an Ideal Bee."

Recognizing Writing Styles   To help students recognize that individual writing styles vary, ask them to write on an issue in the style of

    The "Dear Abby" column
    The editorial page
    The front page

Writing a News Article   To help students write objectively, ask them to write a journalist's eyewitness account of a real event. Have the students proofread each other's work to ensure that the writer's feelings are not apparent. Some topics might be

    An accident on my block
    A fight in school
    My brother's wedding
    The District Dance Festival

Writing an Obituary   To provide an understanding of how writers may purposely leave out certain details, have your students write an obituary in which only good qualities are noted. The obituary may be about: a fictional character (Captain Hook), something that has been used up (a squeezed-out lemon), or a real person who has died (a deceased President of the United States).

Report on a Folktale Event   To help students recognize the effect of reporting style have them record a well-known literary event in a brief article. Such headlines as these might be needed:

"Cinder Girl Becomes Princess"

"Wolf Murdered by Pig"

"Panic Created by Henny Penny"

"Emperor Naked in Streets"

"Seven Dwarfs Share Housekeeper"

Parody a Newspaper   During a *New York Times* strike, the editors of the *National Lampoon* published a bogus newspaper named "Not the New York Times." They parodied every aspect of the newspaper's coverage. Headlines proclaimed, "Marathon Runners Blamed by City for Bridge Destruction." Weather was forecast as "mostly present today, still there tomorrow." Strange recipes were attributed to literary and political figures. Advertisements reflected cheaper airplane fares because of a "new just-short-of-the-runway policy." Ask your students to parody a newspaper. Offer the following suggestions:

Write about a real sports event but give it an unusual ending.

Prepare an ad that pokes fun at a well-known product.

Write about a new but ridiculous article of clothing.

Change the details in writing about a world event.

Write want ads for impossible jobs.

> **Afterview**   Using language accurately is not antithetical to using it creatively. Children who are enthusiastic about words tend to make discriminating vocabulary choices; they use words that authentically communicate a personal orientation. It is essential that teachers help their students develop an academic foundation in which the creative use of language is valued. Imagination can play an important role in almost any communication, and the ability to recognize categories, classifications, and concept hooks is essential to skilled language production. Precise language need not be routine or mechanical. Learning to use words creatively is a critical process.

WHEN YOU WANT TO KNOW MORE

1. Collect examples of "doublespeak" from newspapers and television. What generalizations can you make about the words that are used? How can "doublespeak" activities be adapted to the classroom?

2. Five approaches to classifying words are suggested in this chapter. Suggest other approaches and devise appropriate activities for applying them in school.

3. How sexist is your dictionary? Examine four unabridged dictionaries published within the last fifteen years. How is sexism defined in each? What can you conclude about definitions in dictionaries?

4. Write two one-paragraph versions of "Little Red Riding Hood." Use euphemistic language in the first version and educational jargon in the second. What words contribute most to obscuring meaning?

5. Making up puns and riddles is a highly creative exercise. Before asking children to write some, try developing your own. Focus on the following subjects: famous names, animals, eating, people, politics.

IN THE CLASSROOM

1. Keeping the materials in a learning center up-to-date is sometimes a problem. Organize a system for changing, revising, and rearranging the available information periodically. How can students help you meet this responsibility?

2. Develop and use some language awareness activities that help your students identify racist language.

3. Capitalize on children's interest in *Star Trek* and organize a "Trekkie" Day. Plan a variety of experiences using the vocabulary of science fiction.

4. Encourage children to do research on the origin of words and to keep notebooks on their derivations. Use Bill Severn's *Place Words* and *People Words* as references.

5. Develop a series of letter-writing sessions with your class in which children have "real" reasons for writing. Investigate the possibility of "pen pals."

SUGGESTED READINGS

Cheyney, Arnold B. *Teaching Reading Skills Through the Newspaper*. Newark, Del.: International Reading Association, 1971.

Dale, Edgar. *The Word Game: Improving Communications*. Bloomington, Ind.: The Phi Delta Kappa Educational Foundation, 1975.

Deighton, Lee C. *Vocabulary Development in the Classroom*. New York: Teachers College Press, Columbia University, 1969.

Dillard, J. L. *Black English: Its History and Usage in the United States*. New York: Random House, 1972.

Evans, Bergen. *Comfortable Words*. New York: Random House, 1962.

Farb, Peter. *Word Play: What Happens When People Talk*. New York: Alfred A. Knopf, 1974.

Kean, John M., and Personke, Carl. *The Language Arts: Teaching and Learning in the Elementary School*. New York: St. Martin's Press, 1976.

Lakoff, Robin. *Language and Woman's Place*. New York: Harper & Row, 1975.

Littell, Joseph Fletcher. *How Words Change Our Lives*. Evanston, Ill.: McDougal, Littell, 1971.

Lodwig, Richard, and Barrett, Eugene. *Words, Words, Words: Vocabularies and Dictionaries*. New York: Hayden, 1973.

Miller, Casey, and Swift, Kate. *Words and Women*. Garden City, N.Y.: Doubleday, 1977.

Nilsen, Alleen Pace, et al., *Sexism and Language*. Urbana, Ill.: National Council of Teachers of English, 1977.

Perez, Samuel A. "Teaching the Art of Writing Personal Letters." *Language Arts* 54 (1977): 795–97.

Pilon, A. Barbara. *Teaching Language Arts Creatively in the Elementary Grades*. New York: Wiley, 1978.

Van Allen, Roach. *Language Experiences in Communication*. Boston: Houghton Mifflin, 1976.

Verbatim: The Language Quarterly. Essex, Conn. (Contains articles, book reviews, commentary, correspondence, and short items pertaining to all aspects of language.)

Other Materials

All About Letters. Urbana, Ill.: National Council of Teachers of English 1981. (Poster.)

Copyrights and Acknowledgments

Index